FROM
SEED
TO
BLOOM

FROM SEED TO BLOOM

How to Grow Over 500 Annuals, Perennials & Herbs

EILEEN POWELL

Plant Illustrations by Mallory Lake

except as noted

STOREY
BOOKS
Schoolhouse Road
Pownal, Vermont 05261

> The mission of Storey Communications is to serve our customers by publishing practical information that encourages personal independence in harmony with the environment.

Edited by Deborah Balmuth

Cover and text design by Cindy McFarland

Cover illustration © R. Brickman, 1994

Illustrations in "Introduction" by Judy Eliason, except pages 13, 18 (lower left and lower right) by Alison Kolesar, page 18 (upper right) by Brigita Fuhrmann, and page 19 by Elayne Sears

Text production by Therese G. Lenz

Indexed by Northwind Editorial Services

Copyright © 1995 Eileen Powell

The information in this book is true and complete to the best of our knowledge. All recommendations are made without guarantee on the part of the author or Storey Books. The author and publisher disclaim any liability in connection with the use of this information. For additional information, please contact Storey Books, Schoolhouse Road, Pownal, Vermont 05261.

Storey Books are available for special premium and promotional uses and for customized editions. For further information, please call Storey's Custom Publishing Department at 1-800-793-9396.

Printed in the United States by Vicks Lithograph and Printing

10 9 8 7 6

Library of Congress Cataloging-in-Publication Data

Powell, Eileen, 1953–
    From seed to bloom : how to grow over 500 annuals, perennials & herbs / Eileen Powell.
        p.   cm.

    Includes index.
    ISBN 0-88266-259-7 (pb)
        1. Annuals (Plants) 2. Perennials. 3. Herbs. 4. Flower gardening. 5. Herb gardening. I. Title.
    SB422.P69   1995
    635.9—dc20   94-35380
                    CIP

CONTENTS

Acknowledgments

Sincere thanks are owed to the following people for their help in the production
of this book:
Lisa Crowning who generously shared her time and knowledge
to help unravel the reproductive mysteries of some
of the more obscure plants;
the infinitely patient and talented staff of Storey Communications,
in particular Gwen Steege and Deborah Balmuth,
whose enthusiasm and creative insight are responsible
for turning my duckling into a swan;
and special thanks to Daphne Hay for constructive criticism
and input in the early stages, and for support and encouragement
over the long haul.

INTRODUCTION TO SEED STARTING

THERE ARE MANY GOOD REASONS for starting your own plants from seed. Most gardeners are first prompted to venture down this road by that great motivator: **necessity.** How often have you spotted in a magazine or gardening book a *Campanula* in the precise shade of blue that will transform your summer garden to utter perfection, only to discover that the variety you want is simply not available locally, nor is anything remotely resembling it? Unusual, exotic, or marginally hardy plants that you are not able to find at your local nurseries may be obtainable in the form of seed.

Another major reason many gardeners turn to growing from seed is economic. The **cost** of mature plants that are finicky and difficult to grow from seed is often prohibitive. Buying these plants in seed form can make them affordable and will certainly provide a challenge. Also, if you are planning a mass planting of any sort — petunias, impatiens, marigolds — starting the plants from seed will lower the cost considerably.

A final factor, related to the last point, is plant **health.** When planting a mass display, it's tempting to buy the greatest number of plants for the least outlay, which often results in the purchase of plants of infe-

rior quality. Sadly, these plants are unlikely to give you the magnificent display you would get from plants that have had a healthy start.

Should I Start my Seeds Indoors or Outdoors?

Whether it makes more sense for you to tend seedlings indoors or outdoors will depend on the quantities of plants you wish to grow and the amount of suitable space you have in your home, compared with the feasibility of devoting space in your garden to seed beds. Tending seedlings grown outdoors in one bed that has been prepared specifically for this purpose is easier than hunting down individual containers scattered about your house. Starting seeds indoors rather than outdoors has the primary advantage of providing you with hardy plants that can be moved outdoors as soon as the weather permits, giving you extra weeks of color in early spring.

You probably will have a significantly higher success rate with plants that are started in the safety of your home. Initially, the germination rate is markedly higher indoors, and of those seeds that do sprout outdoors, some are likely to be lost to extreme weather (torrential rain, unseasonably high or low temperatures) or wildlife (rambunctious dogs are particular culprits). It's also surprisingly easy to mistake your very young seedlings for weeds and remove them diligently or, conversely, to exercise so much caution that your seedlings are overwhelmed by weeds before you can confidently distinguish one from the other.

These reasons are sufficient in themselves, but for me the most compelling reason for filling my living room with trays of pungent black earth every winter is the almost mystical pleasure this process brings at every stage. Why would I miss out on the miracle of the birth of a seedling by letting it happen in my garden when I can watch the entire miraculous show right in my living room?

Having made such a good case for starting seeds indoors, why would you even consider starting them outdoors?

In a few cases, seedlings kick up such a fuss at being transplanted that it is simply more prudent to start them outdoors. Annual poppies are a classic example of the reluctant emigrant: Even approaching the task with the skill and care of a surgeon, these delicate creatures will respond by wilting and subsequently expiring before your eyes once they are lifted from the soil.

If you don't have sufficient space in your house for numerous seed trays, starting seeds outdoors will still provide abundant blooms at considerably less cost than buying mature plants, although you will naturally have to wait rather longer for them to flower.

If you have decided to embark on the adventure of starting your garden indoors, give consideration to two variables in your life: time and space.

Filling a few flats with growing medium, popping in the seeds and standing back to watch your garden grow is not inordinately time-consuming and can be fun and rewarding. But the time required to care for even the most obliging seedlings multiplies as the number of seedlings increases, and some varieties will require particularly close attention and precise care.

If you can accommodate one or two fussy varieties, but feel an entire crop of prima donnas is more than you want to take on, consider limiting the *quantity* of plants you start from seed, or perhaps be very discriminating in your *choice* of plants. If you don't have

the time or inclination to coax difficult seeds to life or coddle delicate young seedlings, you may prefer to grow the easier plants on your list from seed and purchase the difficult ones from a nursery. Seeds that require high maintenance are listed as "difficult" in the "Germinating, Requirements" section under the individual plant entries in this book.

Seeds

Seeds that are capable of germinating are termed "viable." Some seeds are only viable for a very short time and should be planted as soon as obtained, but most will retain a high degree of viability over long periods if kept chilled. You can keep a sealed container in the refrigerator for seeds that were not used this year — or even several years before. Older seed should be sown rather more liberally as the germination rate is likely to be considerably less.

Purchasing Seed: Purchasing high-quality (which often means more expensive) seed is essential. Although the difference will not be apparent to the eye, seeds sold by a reputable seedsdealer have been nurtured and handled in a way that is conducive to success at your end and will produce healthier plants. Do not be tempted by "bargain" seeds.

Armchair gardening can provide pleasures equal to outdoor gardening for fanatics unable to get their hands into the soil in the winter; it can also be a helpful process in garden planning. For me, winter begins officially with the arrival of the first glossy garden catalogue, and I lose no time in beginning the long and pleasurable process of studying every entry. I urge you to gather together all your catalogues, sink into a comfortable chair (preferably with a view of the garden), and with bold felt-tip pen in hand, wantonly circle any plant that takes your fancy. At the end of this reckless exercise sanity must prevail, but this process of visualizing everything the heart desires is a useful one, as it will lead to a more distinct image of your dream garden. Your fantasies can be analyzed to good purpose and will help to make your vision a reality.

Study the plants you've chosen, to determine your

overall preferences. Is your fantasy garden composed of delicate pastels? Vibrant primaries? Succulents? Large, dramatic plants or alpine miniatures? Will you need to provide a site for vines, water plants, shade-lovers?

Having analyzed your list, it is then possible to return to your catalogues with a more level head, sitting at your desk now with feet firmly planted on the ground, to determine which of your fantasies can become a reality. Some plants will be rejected because of their obvious unsuitability to your geographic location (with all the will in the world, you will never grow flourishing larkspur in Florida or show-stopping freesia in Maine). You may want to prune other plants from your list because your garden does not provide an appropriate habitat (abandon any ideas of growing roses if your garden is permanently cloaked in heavy shade), or because the plant would appear out of place visually in your existing garden (it's simply not possible to fit a giant cactus gracefully into a cottage garden). Some plants may be crossed off the list because the effort required to grow them from seed is out of proportion to the pleasure they provide as mature plants (I finally gave up growing *Eustoma* from seed for this reason), but there should be room in every garden for a few experimental plants that you crave despite the unfavorable odds that they will flourish.

Having compiled a list of those plants you plan to grow from seed, fill in order forms without delay and send them on their way. The temptation will be great to dash to your local nursery with list in hand, intending to return with all of those precious seed packets and begin planting immediately. Try to resist the urge as this route most often leads to disaster. Many of the seeds on which your heart is set won't be available in the variety or color you have chosen and around which your grand scheme revolves. It takes a lot of character not to break down at this point and purchase a substitute, but if you weaken now the result will be a diluted version of your dream garden, often accompanied by diminished enthusiasm.

Collecting Seed: Before investing the time — and, indeed, the emotion — involved in the propagation of seeds you've painstakingly collected yourself, it is worth doing a little research to determine whether your efforts will pay off. Whereas most of the plants mentioned in this book can be propagated by seed (some more readily than others), not all will develop into clones of their parents, and, in some cases, the result may be quite surprising. This element of surprise can be intriguing — or disappointing. (See page 4 for a more detailed discussion of how to predict a plant's appearance.) Purchasing hybrid seeds from a reputable seed dealer is the only way to ensure that you'll end up with the plant you expected.

In other words, collecting seeds by hand can be entertaining and, if you're careful and lucky, rewarding, but you cannot rely upon it as a dependable source for many plants.

If you decide to take a chance with the propagation of seed that you've collected, I would suggest embarking on this venture in a spirit of experimentation, starting the plants in an out-of-the-way corner of the garden, possibly with the vegetables or in a cutting bed. Successful plants can then be transplanted to your main beds and less attractive ones committed to the compost heap. If any particularly successful plants result, remember to propagate these either by division or cuttings to obtain a true clone.

Collecting seeds at the correct time can be a little tricky as the seed must be completely ripe, but not yet released by the plant. As with purchased seeds, those you collect yourself should be stored in a closed container in a cool place until sowing time.

A Word of Warning on Wildflower Seed

Many wildflowers are not available through nurseries or seed catalogues and may seem like obvious targets for seed collection. But before collecting wildflower seed contact your local native plant society or Audubon Society to determine whether the plant is endangered. Removing endangered plants from the wild is prohibited, and even the collection of seed may be restricted.

Starting Seeds Indoors

Finding a suitable space to give over to flats of seedlings for several months can be a problem, but with a little creative thinking and possibly some rearranging

A QUICK LESSON IN NOMENCLATURE

What's the Difference Between a Variety, a Cultivar, and a Hybrid, and Do I Really Need to Know?

Predicting a plant's appearance depends on understanding the difference between a species, a variety, a cultivar, and a hybrid. Although the subject is a little more complicated than the following implies, these simple definitions will be adequate for determining whether specific plants are likely to grow true from seed. Of course, this information will be useful only if you have some means of determining the full name of the plant in question, such as a carefully labeled perennial in your neighbor's garden.

Species: For our purposes, "species" can be defined as the equivalent of a person's first name; i.e., the name that distinguishes him from his brothers, sisters, and cousins. In the case of plants, though, the names appear in the reverse order: rather than being called John Jones, a plant is known as Jones John. In the plant name *Viola cornuta*, *Viola* is the "family" name (Jones) and *cornuta* the "first" name (John). A straight species can be propagated from collected seed with certainty that the resulting plants will bear a close resemblance to their parents.

Genera	Species
Viola	*cornuta*

Form or Variety: A *naturally occurring* variation from the straight species is a form or variety. Often a variety will have a different flower color from the straight species. Incidentally, the word "variety" is frequently (and incorrectly) used interchangeably with the terms "species," "cultivar," and "hybrid." Forms and varieties *probably* will come true from seed.

Genera	Species	Variety
Gentiana	*septemfida*	var. *lagodechiana*

OR

Genera	Species	
Gentiana	*septemfida*	*lagodechiana*

Genera	Species	Form
Dicentra	*spectabilis*	f. *alba*

OR

Genera	Species	
Dicentra	*spectabilis*	*alba*

Cultivar: When plants *of the same species* are bred to produce a distinct variation that has specific desirable characteristics (e.g., bloom size or color), the resulting plant is called a cultivar. In other words, a cultivar is a variety (as defined previously) that has been engineered by humans. The name of the cultivar appears in single quotes after the name of the species. Although the outcome is not guaranteed, there is a good chance that a cultivar will come true (or nearly true) from seed. However, if you have your heart set on an exact duplicate of the parent, you should use an asexual method of reproduction (see pages 17-19).

Genera	Species	Cultivar
Helichrysum	*monstrosum*	'Dwarf Hot Bikini'

Hybrid: A man-made cross *between different species or different genera* — this is how a hybrid differs from a cultivar, which is bred from only one species. The hybrid condition is denoted by an × either before or in the middle of the plant's name. Hybrids will *not* come true from seed.

Genera	Hybrid	Species
Pelargonium	×	*domesticum*

OR

Hybrid	Genera	Species
×	*Heucherella*	*domesticum*

of furniture, it's very possible. Seedlings can be grown in a sunny window, but the sturdiest plants are grown under artificial lights (see page 10). When considering potential locations for flats, remember that there are few things more irresistible to a cat than a tray of soil in an out-of-the way corner! Children have also been known to harvest unattended crops prematurely and with less care than we might use ourselves.

Where space is limited, an inexpensive shelving unit — one that can be assembled and dismantled easily and fitted with fluorescent lights — might provide sufficient space for all your flats. When not in use, the entire operation can be stored in an attic, garage, or under a bed.

A two-tiered trolley (such as an old-fashioned drinks trolley) can be loaded with flats, which are then conveniently mobile. The trolley can be moved out of the sun during the hottest part of the day, then wheeled back when the sun has moved. A fluorescent light will be necessary for the plants on the lower tier.

Any free space on *any* shelf should not be overlooked: bookcases, kitchen cabinets, bedroom closets, laundry room counters, workshop tables. Don't forget the space on top of cabinets. If there is insufficient natural light, be creative about hanging fluorescent lights.

Temporary shelving can be made from planks resting on stacked bricks. (You may already have experience with this form of construction from your first apartment!) The shelves can be located on top of a desk or table in a south-facing window.

If you end up with seed trays scattered about the house, don't forget where they are!

Before you begin your seed-starting adventures, there is some essential equipment you need to assemble.

Containers

Suitable containers come in all shapes and sizes. The only absolute requirements are that the vessels be scrupulously clean and afford proper drainage. The two main styles of container in which seeds can be planted are seed trays and individual seed containers.

Seed trays, which are also known as "flats," allow seedlings to grow communally, sharing growing medium and eventually mingling roots. Acceptable alternatives to the store-bought plastic trays include:

❊ Shallow wooden boxes with slats spaced at least ⅛ inch apart to allow for proper drainage.

❊ Clay flower pots. Soak new clay pots in water for several days. A layer of broken pottery or small pebbles placed in the bottom of the pot will permit free drainage and prevent the growing medium from leaking out through large drainage holes.

❊ A plastic one-gallon milk jug, cut off two inches from the bottom. Punch drainage holes from the inside of the jug.

❊ Large plastic buckets can be cut to form trays, with drainage holes added. Local delicatessens may be a good source for these.

❊ A cardboard milk carton with the top stapled shut and one long panel removed, thereby forming an oblong trough. Punch drainage holes in the bottom.

Individual seed containers provide each seed with its own small ball of soil. The container may be single, such as an old yogurt tub, or multiple, such as an egg carton. Your options include:

❊ Plastic "market packs," either newly purchased or recycled. Used ones may be available from a cooperative local garden center, but must be thoroughly cleaned before using.

❊ Manufactured peat pots.

❊ Two-inch plastic or clay flower pots.

❊ Yogurt or similar containers with drainage holes punched in the bottom.

❊ Egg cartons, either styrofoam or cardboard. Punch

several holes in the bottom of each compartment and use the lid as a drainage tray underneath the container.

✽ Individual pots can be made easily from newspaper or paper bags. Cut a nine-inch square using three layers of paper. With a pencil, divide the square into thirds one way and then the other, creating a tic-tac-toe grid. Cut from the outer edge to the center square once at each corner, fold flaps up and secure with a staple or tape. This creates an individual three-inch pot. Pots made from paper can be planted directly in the ground, and so are useful for seedlings that prefer not to have their roots disturbed.

✽ A less elaborate cylindrical pot can be fashioned from paper. Cut a length of paper the desired height of the pot by about eight inches long. Attach the ends with glue or tape to form a cylinder, and you have a bottomless container. Stand cylinders upright, side by side, in a tray that has sides high enough to provide support, then fill with growing medium and sow.

✽ Cylindrical pots can also be made out of the cardboard tubes from paper towels, wrapping paper, or toilet rolls, cut two to three inches tall.

✽ There are now many innovative products that are easier and usually neater to use than the traditional alternatives. For instance, you can buy individual pellets that expand when moistened or styrofoam cell packs that contain a dry compressed growing medium. Most of these items are rather expensive, but are certainly amusing to try, and you might want to include a new one with your seed order.

In a number of ways seed trays have advantages over individual pots: They are less expensive, take up less space, and are quicker if you are doing mass plantings of one variety. But if you are growing plants that resent root disturbance, individual pots are the best choice. When it's time to transplant seedlings grown in pots, the plant is lifted out of its pot with the root ball intact and almost no root disturbance takes place. If peat pots or other porous or degradable containers have been used, the plant goes in the ground pot and all.

Growing Mediums

As with many things in life, the preparation of a growing medium for your seeds can be as simple or as complicated as you choose to make it. At the simplest end, you need do no more than choose a bag of ready-mixed growing medium from the hardware store and proceed to sow. At the opposite extreme, you may bring into use all your knowledge of alchemy, sorcery, or even chemistry to concoct your own surefire super-soil. From my experience, the simpler method produces successful results in almost every case.

Seedlings are often started in a soil-less, nutrient-free medium, as an overabundance of nutrients is actually detrimental to plants in the very early stages of life. Seeds started in such a medium will require either frequent feeding in later life, or transplanting to a container with a nutrient-rich, soil-based medium. Seeds started in individual containers should be planted in a soil-based mixture that will sustain the plant throughout its life indoors. A good commercial potting soil mixed with a lighter substance (such as vermiculite) will do for this purpose. These seedlings can then remain in the same container until they are ready to be transplanted outdoors.

Homemade growing mediums: The essential qualities of a growing medium are that it will drain freely, is disease-free, and is not too high in nutrients. Some acceptable home-mixed growing mediums are:

✽ A combination of one-half vermiculite or perlite and one-half sphagnum peat (measure by volume, not weight). Frequent feeding will be required by seedlings that are grown on in this medium (i.e., seedlings that will not be transplanted to a larger container at the two-leaf stage).

✽ Equal quantities of good garden soil (if your own soil is less than perfect, purchase a bag of pasteurized potting soil), clean, coarse builders' sand, and peat moss. Garden soil first should be sterilized by spreading in a shallow pan and baking at 275°F for at least 30 minutes. (WARNING: The aroma of cooking soil is *bad.*) Purchased soil will not need to be sterilized. If you have any doubts as to whether your medium will drain well, add a layer of coarse sand at the bottom of the container. Less frequent feeding will be required using this soil-based mix.

With the addition of nutrients (one teaspoon ground limestone per quart plus one teaspoon bonemeal), either of the above mediums will provide a suitable environment for your seedlings throughout their indoor life. Regular feeding with a liquid fertilizer still will be necessary after three true leaves have appeared (see "Care of Young Seedlings," page 11).

Plants that may require a specialized soil mixture include succulents, orchids, and wildflowers, among others.

Preparing Seeds

Most seeds can be sown straight from the packet, but occasionally the seed casings are so tough that they require to chipping and/or soaking before planting in order to hasten germination. If chipping or soaking is necessary, this is noted in the "Germinating, Requirements" section of the individual plant.

Chipping is the process of removing a small sliver from the end of a seed, using a sharp knife.

Soaking seeds in warm water, usually for 24 hours, helps to soften seed cases, thereby facilitating speedy germination.

Sowing Seeds

The preparation of seed trays for sowing is a most satisfying task, in many ways akin to baking: First you assemble the ingredients, then you measure and mix, and finally you pour the batter — or growing medium — into the prepared containers. With some determination, this need not be a messy job should you prefer to leave the grimier aspects of gardening out-of-doors.

Step 1: Prepare Containers

To avoid the possibility of exposing seedlings unnecessarily to disease, clean all containers thoroughly with a solution of nine parts water to one part household bleach before filling with growing medium. Diligently scrub containers that have held plants in the past, as disease can cling determinedly to even small particles of soil left in a container.

Water must be able to drain freely from the bottom of your containers or the soil will become waterlogged, drowning roots and fostering fungal diseases. Drainage holes can be burned through plastic with a lighted cigarette, or punched through more flammable materials with a pencil point, ice pick, or tapestry needle.

Line clean containers with a layer of newspaper cut to fit neatly into the bottom. This will prevent the growing medium from disappearing through drainage holes.

Step 2: Prepare Growing Medium

Dry soil-less growing media are almost impossible to moisten through normal watering, but must be dampened thoroughly *before* seeds can be sown. Half-fill a plastic bag with the medium and add water at the rate of about one part water to four parts soil. Mix well by squeezing the bag gently until the water is evenly incorporated. The medium should be damp but not wet.

Step 3: Fill Containers

If the seedlings you are starting in flats will be transplanted shortly to more spacious quarters, they may be started in a nutrient-free growing medium. If you prefer to keep seedlings in the same flat until they are moved outdoors, use a soil-based medium (e.g., potting soil) which will provide nutrients to the seedlings throughout their indoor life.

Individual containers should be filled with a richer, soil-based medium. You may also want to add a layer of sand or other porous material to the bottoms of these containers to ensure perfect drainage. Fill the containers, distributing the soil evenly. Tamp the soil lightly and top up, keeping the final soil level about ½ inch below the rim of large pots, ¼ inch below small or shallow containers. Market packs can be filled with a spoon and tapped lightly on a flat surface to settle the soil.

Filling container and tamping the soil.

Sowing seeds.

Step 4: Sow Your Seeds

Possible confusion at sprouting time can be eliminated by sowing only one variety of seed per container. However, if only a few plants of each variety will be grown, sow in one container those that have similar requirements for germination and that will germinate at roughly the same time.

Step 5: Label Containers

As you sow, label each container with the variety of seed, date planted, and the range of dates when you might expect germination. Also mark the germination dates on a calendar; if you are growing a great variety of plants, this will make your life considerably easier.

Step 6: Water

Growing medium that has been premoistened should not require additional watering at this point. But if watering is required, stand each container in a tray of water to dampen the medium to the point where it is moist but not wet. Do not allow containers to stand in water once the soil surface is moistened. If a fungicide is to be used in order to deter damping-off (see page 9), now is the time to use it.

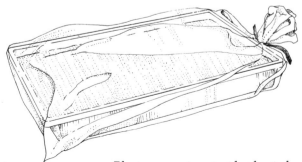

Placing container inside plastic bag.

SOWING DEPTH

As a general rule of thumb, seeds should be covered to three times their diameter.

Very small seeds can be mixed with a little fine sand to facilitate even distribution on the soil surface.

Small to medium seeds can be sprinkled directly from the packet onto the soil, or you can shake the seeds from the packet onto your palm and sow individually. If the seeds require covering, scatter a fine layer of growing medium over them.

Large seeds can be sown individually in rows in a tray or sown one per small pot.

Very large seeds (e.g., beans) should be sown in individual pots.

Seedlings that do not transplant well should be started in biodegradable pots that can be planted directly into the ground (e.g., peat pots). If transplanting is particularly stressful to a plant, this will be noted in the individual plant listings.

Step 7: Cover Containers

Cover containers with a piece of glass or plastic wrap, or place each inside a plastic bag and secure in a manner that will keep air out but will also allow easy opening to check on the germination progress. The plastic bags that newspapers arrive in on rainy days are ideal, but any clear plastic bag will do. Those seeds that do not require light should be covered with an opaque material such as newspaper, cardboard, or aluminum foil in addition to the glass or plastic covering.

Care Before Germination

Containers of seeds requiring darkness to germinate may be draped with an opaque cover, or simply placed in a closet or any dark and safe place that can be kept at a suitable temperature. Those requiring light should be placed in a bright location that does not receive *direct* sunlight. A temperature of 65°–70°F will suit most seeds, and all will perform best if the temperature is constant. A moderate amount of bottom heat will speed germination considerably but is not necessary.

Light and temperature requirements of individual seeds are specified in the plant entries.

Watering: If the growing medium has been moistened sufficiently before sowing, additional watering probably will not be necessary until the seeds have germinated. But do check the containers regularly for signs of dryness — once a seed or seedling has been allowed to dry out completely, it can never be resuscitated. To moisten, place the entire container in a tray of water, allowing it to drain when the soil surface appears damp, or mist the soil gently from above. Do not allow containers to sit in water for longer than it takes to moisten the soil surface.

A more modern and efficient method of watering seedlings is through capillary matting. Capillary matting is a highly absorbent, relatively inexpensive fabric that, in effect, does your watering for you. Stretch the fabric out, either soaking thoroughly or immersing one end in a reservoir of water. Press seed trays or individual pots firmly down onto the matting, and *voila!* The soil will absorb as much water as it needs — but not more — and so you avoid either overwatering or underwatering. If it is not convenient to place a reservoir near the matting, simply water the fabric from time to time, ensuring that it never becomes dry.

If algae appears on the mat, remove it at once and soak for a half hour in water and laundry detergent. Rinse repeatedly until the water runs clear and replace your trays.

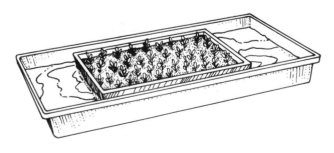

Moistening soil by standing container in a tray of water.

DEALING WITH DAMPING-OFF

How to Avoid It

✼ Sterilize all seed containers and any instruments used in the process of sowing (see page 7).

✼ Use only sterile growing media, such as vermiculite or sterilized soil (see page 6).

✼ Sow seeds thinly to allow healthy air circulation between seedlings. Promptly thin overcrowded containers.

✼ Thoroughly moisten the growing medium in your seed trays with chestnut compound before sowing. Chestnut compound is a gentle fungicide made of two parts copper sulfate to eleven parts ammonium carbonate (by weight). Dilute the mixture at the rate of ½ ounce to one gallon water.

✼ Water seed trays from below. When growing plants that are particularly susceptible to damping-off, keep soil on the dry side.

✼ Damping-off can be stimulated by the presence of nitrogen. Always allow seedlings to develop three true leaves before using any fertilizer.

What to Do if You Detect It

✼ If even one of your seedlings exhibits signs of damping-off, remove it and, for caution's sake, its immediate neighbors, from the container at once.

✼ If the soil appears to be too moist, take immediate action by moving the containers away from other plants in order to increase air circulation and placing an absorbent material on the soil surface. Crushed charcoal is most successful, but in desperation I've even used blotting paper.

✼ Return the containers to their normal location and resume cautious watering (only from below) once the soil has dried out sufficiently.

Care After Germination

When the first signs of life become evident in the form of a few green crooks nosing their way out of the soil, the process of removing the container's covering can begin. A very gradual exposure is what is desired here. Remove opaque coverings completely, then lift just a corner of the plastic or glass covering, allowing only a small amount of air to reach the seedlings. If plastic coverings are used, holes can be punched in the material to allow controlled amounts of air into this miniature greenhouse. Gradually increase the opening or punch additional holes every few hours until the covering is fully removed. The entire process should take about one day. The reason for this extremely slow process is that, if air is allowed to enter too suddenly, damping-off may result.

Damping-Off: If you find your seedlings lying prone on the soil with the leaves green but the base of the stems blackened and shriveled, they have probably fallen victim to damping-off. Damping-off is a sickening fungal disease that can wipe out every seedling in a flat in less than a day. Damping-off can strike at any stage in a young plant's development and is usually due to excess moisture combined with a lack of ventilation. You need experience damping-off only once to be instilled with a lifelong dread of this disease, and extreme caution is a small price to pay to avoid a visit from this grim reaper.

Light and Temperature: Once seeds have germinated, they prefer a temperature kept constantly around 60°F; sturdier plants will be produced at this moderate temperature. Sufficient light is also essential for strong, healthy development of seedlings. Once seedlings have sprouted, the containers should be placed in a bright location, but not in strong sunlight. Although a south-facing window will do, it is not ideal. Plants that have been grown in even a sunny window may become spindly due to receiving too much heat in relation to light. Also, without added insulation, the nighttime temperature next to your windows may drop too drastically for the plants' liking.

If your windows fail to provide ideal light and temperature or adequate space to contain your embryonic plantation, fluorescent lights can provide an excellent

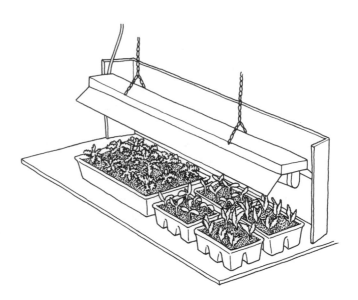

Hang fluorescent lights as close to seedlings as possible.

alternative. Cool-white forty-watt fluorescent bulbs will be sufficient for starting seeds that will eventually be planted outdoors. Grow lights, which are considerably more expensive, are only necessary if plants are intended to flower and fruit indoors.

Seedlings should be placed very close to fluorescent lights — three to four inches away — and lights should be left on for about fifteen hours a day. Plants grown under fluorescent lights will require more frequent watering and feeding than those grown in natural light.

Seedlings growing in natural light should be moved gradually into more direct sunlight as they mature and strengthen, but they should always be protected from direct midday sun.

Water: Check the soil frequently for signs of dryness. When the soil surface appears dry, stand containers in tepid water, allowing the trays to drain once the surface is moist. Or the soil can be moistened by misting well. On an unusually hot spring day, the soil may need moistening more than once a day, but particular care should be taken not to overwater. Always water plants in the morning rather than in the evening.

Food: Before true leaves appear on your seedlings, the plants will put out *cotyledon*, usually one pair. These are similar in appearance to true leaves, but contain sufficient nutrients to nourish the seed and sustain the young seedling for a short time. *You* will be responsible for providing the seedling with additional nutrients as soon as the plant has developed three true leaves.

Seedlings that are growing in a rich medium (i.e., soil-based) should be fed with a liquid fertilizer applied at one-half the rate recommended by the manufacturer. Apply this weak solution twice a week for the first three weeks, then use a full-strength fertilizer about every ten days.

Seedlings that have been started in a nutrient-free medium normally will be transplanted before fertilizing becomes necessary (see "Care of Young Seedlings," below). If for any reason transplanting is delayed beyond the appearance of the first three true leaves (and sometimes the real world does interfere even with gardening), feed these seedlings with a half-strength solution twice a week until they are transplanted.

Feed only *after* watering.

Care of Young Seedlings

Seedlings should be given more space as soon as the first pair of true leaves has developed; delaying even until the seedling has two pairs of leaves is unwise as the stem will be considerably longer and more prone to breakage or damage by this stage. Seedlings that have been left to grow too long before thinning or transplanting will become spindly, weak, and more susceptible to disease.

Seedlings can be either thinned or transplanted to individual pots (the process referred to as "pricking out") so that each plant will have satisfactory air circulation and sufficient space for strong and healthy development.

Thinning: Seedlings grown from very fine seeds that have been scattered on the surface of a flat probably will need thinning before they are large enough to be handled easily. Pulling up unwanted plants by the roots is the butcher's way of performing this operation and will result in disturbance of neighboring plants and possible root damage. The safest way to thin is by carefully snipping off unwanted plants at soil level, thereby leaving all roots undisturbed. Thin to one plant every 1½ to 2 inches.

Pricking Out: Pricking out is a wonderfully delicate operation similar in many ways to fine needlework in that it requires nimble fingers, careful attention, and patience. The work should be performed at a table where you have plenty of space and at a time when you will not be hurried.

Prepare containers as for sowing (see page 7), using a container that will hold a sufficient quantity of soil for the mature seedling. Generally, a plant grown from a large seed, such as a morning glory, will require far more space than a tiny seed, such as a lobelia. Line containers with a layer of newspaper neatly cut to fit the container. A thin layer of a porous material (e.g., sand or perlite) may be added here to promote free drainage. Fill the containers — either flats or individual pots — with a nutrient-rich growing medium to ½ inch below the rim. Tamp the soil, top up, then tamp again.

Prick out seedlings by gently loosening a small clump of seedlings from the tray using a knife, fork or small stick. Employing a pencil as a dibble, make one small planting hole for each seedling. If you are transplanting to flats, the holes should be spaced about 1½ to 2 inches apart; if you're transplanting to individual containers, use a separate container for each seedling. Carefully separate individual seedlings from the clump and plant one per hole, positioning the plant to sit at the same level in the soil as before transplanting. Tamp lightly around each seedling with the pencil. Seedlings that have been started in small individual containers should be moved to larger containers with as much of the root ball in tact as possible.

Moisten the soil by placing the containers in a shallow dish of tepid water and allowing this to be absorbed slowly, or thoroughly moisten the soil using a mister. Label the containers with the plant variety and the date when they can be safely planted out.

Pricking out seedlings.

Transplanting into divided flat.

Do not place seedlings in direct sunlight or under fluorescent light for about 24 hours after transplanting. If the plants still show signs of stress after one day, check that the soil is moist. Water from below or mist the soil if necessary, and do not place containers in direct light until the seedlings have perked up. Stressed seedlings will not grow vigorously.

To water, misting the soil may be the safest method in the early days, especially when dealing with tiny seedlings. In warm, sunny locations, the soil may require moistening twice a day, and smaller containers will require more frequent watering than large ones. Once plants are sturdier, they can be watered very carefully from above or by standing containers in water that will be absorbed from below. At this stage, the soil probably will require moistening no more than once or twice a week, but do continue to check the soil daily, and water mornings rather than evenings.

Feed plants only after watering. For the first three weeks after transplanting seedlings, apply a half-strength fertilizer twice a week. After this, a full-strength fertilizer can be applied every ten to fourteen days. Feed plants only *after* watering. I like to make a note on the calendar to remind myself when to fertilize.

Preparing Seedlings for Life in the Garden

Most annuals and perennials can be planted outdoors safely after the last expected frost date, and many perennials will not object to being planted out a week or two earlier. But some plants are best kept inside until the soil is thoroughly warm, and early planting will only stunt their growth. Check each plant's preference as listed in the individual plant entry in the following chapter before planting out.

Hardening Off: Plants that have been grown from seed indoors will need to be "hardened off" before planting in the garden. This is the process of exposing young plants to the harsher, more extreme outdoor environment *gradually*. The hardening-off process is necessary to reduce transplant shock and will result in plants that adapt more readily and resume growing more quickly once they have been planted in the garden. Seedlings will require hardening off whether they are planted out in the spring or the autumn.

About two weeks before seedlings are to be transplanted, cease feeding and diminish watering slightly. At this time, plants that are growing in flats may be divided by cutting through the soil with a knife, leaving each plant with its own square root ball; leave these divided plants in their flats until they are planted out.

Begin acclimating plants to the outdoors on a mild, windless day approximately one week before they are due to be transplanted. Place plants, in their containers, in a sheltered spot outdoors where they will receive only filtered light. In the shade of a large tree, against a north-facing wall, or on a shady porch is ideal. Leave the containers outside for about half a day before returning them to their usual spot indoors. Each day for a week leave the seedlings outside for a progressively longer period and in a progressively more exposed location. By week's end, they will be outside all day and all night in conditions similar to those they will experience in their final home.

Starting Seeds Outdoors

Ideally, seeds started outdoors should be sown in a specially designated seed bed. The seed bed allows you to keep an eye on each plant without having to search for it, and the plants will be immeasurably easier to tend. From my experience, it actually requires less time to tend seedlings in a seed bed and later transplant them than it does to care for seedlings that were started *in situ.*

Most home gardeners in America do not use seed beds, but for those who wish to, I will briefly describe their preparation.

Location of Seed Beds

Seed beds are best sited in an out-of-the-way corner that is not a focal point from the house. Near a vegetable bed or garden shed would be the perfect spot, assuming it would receive plenty of light. Locating beds against a fence or wall provides shelter from drying winds, but be sure that young plants will not be shaded excessively.

Soil Preparation

Ideally, seed beds, like flower beds, should be prepared in the autumn for spring sowing.

❖ Follow the procedure on page 15 for preparing either new or existing beds. Nitrogen should not be added at this stage as it will only foster weak seedlings.

❖ Make a smooth fine-textured soil surface. After breaking down clods as far as possible with a spade, rake over the soil surface repeatedly with a short-tined rake to minimize bumps and crevices in which seeds can be lost.

❖ Water the bed thoroughly, allowing the soil to drain for at least 24 hours before sowing begins.

Raised Beds

Although a seed bed can be prepared at grade level, the best results will be obtained from a raised bed. A seed bed need be nothing more than an area of about 3 feet by 6 feet, edged with timbers and filled with a good, rich loam. Amend the soil annually as you would for beds at grade level.

Starting Seeds In Situ

If a plant is particularly sensitive to root disturbance, sowing *in situ* is the likeliest way to success.

Gazing at your flower beds in March, you may see vast stretches of inviting, accessible, bare earth. In fact, the flower beds probably don't look all that different from a large seed bed. And it may seem like unnecessary work to start plants in a seed bed only to move them to the flower beds later, when you could just as easily sow the seed in the exact location where the plant ultimately will be grown. But remember that in another month, much of this empty space will be crowded with young plants and become more like a jungle by the day. In such a situation, tiny seedlings are easily lost, squashed, shaded, and overlooked.

Many seeds will not germinate in cold soil and early sowing will accomplish nothing more than unnecessarily exposing the seeds to adverse elements; seeds sown too early actually may rot before they have a chance to sprout.

SOWING SEEDS OUTDOORS

Fine seeds: Mixing fine seeds with sand will make even distribution over the soil surface easier. Press the seeds lightly into the soil using a board or the back of a spade or trowel. Seeds that require light for germination can be left as is; cover those that require darkness with a porous material, such as sand, perlite, or peat moss, through which the young seedlings can push themselves with ease.

Large seeds: Scratching a shallow furrow with a stick is preferable to making individual planting holes; in a large bed, it's all too easy to lose track of where you have planted individual seeds. Fill in the trenches with a porous material, such as vermiculite.

Mark off areas of different plants with string or twigs and label with a plant marker or popsicle stick to avoid later confusion. Water beds very carefully as it is all too easy to wash your seeds away entirely or cause them to collect into a small clump where they will quickly become overcrowded and difficult to handle. I prefer to use a hand mister initially, graduating to a *very* fine hose spray after seeds have sprouted.

Care of Young Seedlings

Seeds started outdoors will be easier to care for if they are all located in the same bed, making it possible to feed and water them as a group. Plants still will need to be thinned or transplanted when the first pair of true leaves appear, following the same procedures as for seedlings started indoors (see page 3), and fertilizing will be necessary. Feed with a half-strength liquid solution twice a week for the first three weeks, then increase to a full-strength solution every ten to fourteen days.

Tender young seedlings may require shade from drying winds or unseasonably hot sun. A board propped up at either end makes an effective sun-shade, or you may use newspaper or plastic or wire mesh suspended over plants and anchored with twigs or skewers.

When seedlings are young and delicate, water in the morning rather than evening to allow leaves to dry in the sun, thus minimizing the risk of fungal diseases. Water very carefully with a gentle spray.

Plants started outdoors naturally will not require the hardening-off process and can be transplanted to their permanent site at the same stage you would transplant seedlings started indoors.

Preparing the Garden and Planting

If you make one resolution this year, it should be to begin soil preparation in the autumn rather than waiting until the spring, when so many other jobs are demanding your immediate attention. An added benefit of digging over the soil in autumn is that the process exposes many pests that would otherwise overwinter underground, emerging in the spring to feast on your tender young seedlings.

Test Your Soil

The first step to preparing beds should begin weeks before your spade hits the soil. This step, which is so often neglected by beginners and experienced gardeners alike, is to have the soil professionally tested. A soil test is necessary to determine. The relative alkalinity/acidity of the soil, what is known as the *pH level*. Soil pH levels vary naturally in different geographic

---

Decoding the Mysterious pH Numbers

THE NUMBERS	WHAT THE NUMBERS MEAN
5.0–6.0	This soil is definitely acid
6.0–7.0	This soil is only somewhat acid
7.0	Neutral soil
7.0–8.0	Somewhat alkaline (also called "limy") soil
8.0–9.0	This soil is decidedly alkaline

---

locations and can also be affected by external conditions, such as proximity to building materials, which are often extremely alkaline, or pine trees, whose fallen needles can make the soil very acid. On a scale of 0 to 14, a pH level of 6.0 to 7.5 usually will be satisfactory.

Many plants will perform happily in a wide range of pH levels, and you need only ensure that your soil measures within this broad range. Others are very particular, and the soil may need to be amended drastically if you are to have any success.

A note here about plant choice: If your pH level is naturally unappealing to a chosen plant, it makes more sense to select a different plant for that location rather than to continually fight the soil's natural inclinations.

A soil test will also tell you the nutrient content of the soil. Beds in which annuals and perennials are planted year after year will inevitably become depleted of nutrients, and the soil will need to be enriched annually. A soil test will determine which nutrients are missing from the soil and the precise quantities of supplements required to restore the soil to good health.

Soil testing kits can be bought at garden centers and hardware stores, and I assume some people have success using these. But from my experience they are expensive and unsatisfactory, leaving me feeling no wiser after all the rigamrole of filling test tubes and comparing colors than I was at the outset. Commercial testers do exist, but they can be expensive.

In most areas, the simplest and most efficient method of having soil tested is through the local Cooperative Extension Service. A quick phone call to your Extension agent will provide you with details on how to proceed with the operation, as well as the cost. There may be a charge for the testing service in your state (usually minimal), or it may be performed free of charge. If there's a charge, do not let that put you off. There is almost no better way to spend your gardening dollars than to have a professional soil test.

To be sure of getting a sample that reflects accurately the soil throughout your bed, take several samples from large beds, mixing the soil well. If you are preparing more than one bed, have at least one sample tested from each bed.

Amending Soil

Amending your soil to suit the plants you are growing is a vital step. Like a baby, a young plant needs specific nutrients and a physical environment that will support healthy development. If you provide these from the very beginning, you will be rewarded with healthier plants that are less susceptible to stress and disease, as well as bigger, more abundant blooms.

Organic vs. inorganic supplements: To carry the analogy a bit farther, the difference between feeding your garden with organic vs. inorganic supplements is comparable to nourishing a human body with a healthy and balanced diet vs. relying on vitamin pills. Obviously the former method is preferable, but there are times when the latter is appropriate; for instance, to provide more rapid treatment in an emergency. Similarly, there is a place in the garden for inorganic fertilizers, but I try to limit their use to emergency treatment for a plant that may not recover without immediate first aid.

Preparing Beds

If the soil was not prepared in the autumn, try to do so a week or so before transplanting begins, adding those supplements recommended in your soil analysis.

Beds that were dug over and amended in the autumn with organic supplements and soil conditioners will require only a light digging and leveling in the spring before planting can begin. This should be done about one week before planting out begins, but again, proceed with caution and dig only when the soil is suf-

ficiently drained that cultivation will not harm the natural soil structure.

The best way to determine whether your soil is ready for digging is to roll up your sleeves, plunge in your hands, and collect a fistful of soil. Form the soil into a ball, then drop it from waist height onto the ground. Does it land with a thud and spread out rather than crumbling? If the answer is yes, the soil is still too wet to work and digging now would cause compaction, reducing the soil's capacity to hold air and drain freely. If the ball of soil breaks fairly easily when it hits the ground, this is the sign that you can begin soil preparation. Very dry soil should be watered and left for twenty-four hours before you start to dig.

New Beds: If seedlings are to be planted in a new bed or in large sections of an existing bed, the entire area can be prepared at once.

In large beds, spread an inch of manure, compost, peat moss, or other organic matter over the entire planting area. To this add soil amendments as recommended in your soil analysis, and dig over the soil to a depth of six to eight inches, mixing well to ensure even distribution of all additives.

When working in large beds, take care not to compact the soil you've so carefully prepared by walking through it. A wide board placed on the soil will distribute your weight more evenly and cause little damage, or a more permanent solutions can be provided with stepping stones positioned throughout the bed. With thoughtful choice of material and careful placement, these stepping stones can add visually to your winter garden and provide interesting features around which to group your plantings.

Using a fine spray, water the beds thoroughly twenty-four hours before transplanting begins.

Existing Beds for Transplants: Start by deeply watering all areas to be planted about twenty-four hours before transplanting begins. If seedlings will be scattered throughout existing beds, prepare the soil in each small area separately. Sprinkle over the soil a handful of organic matter and individual amendments (e.g., bonemeal, blood meal, wood ash) or a commercial complete fertilizer (organic, please), following the directions on the package, and lightly dig over the soil using a trowel.

Transplanting

The perfect time for planting out your seedlings is on a mild, overcast day. If the perfect day does not coincide with the need to transplant, do at least avoid planting during the hottest part of the day, leaving the job until late afternoon.

Water newly planted seedlings with a gentle sprinkler immediately. Try not to drench the leaves if you are watering late in the day.

From Flats: Water plants an hour or two before transplanting. Tap flats gently on the ground to loosen soil and, with a trowel, carefully loosen one plant from the flat — the soil already should have been cut into blocks containing one plant each (see page 11). Dig a hole in the bed large enough to hold one plant. Keeping as much soil around the root ball as possible, place the plant in the hole at the same level at which it grew in the flat, gently firming the soil around it. Continue

transplanting, spacing the seedlings at the distances recommended in the individual plant listings.

From Individual Containers: Loosen the soil from the edges of the pot by tapping lightly on the ground or gently rolling flexible containers between your palms. Carefully ease the plant and root ball from the container and plant as described above.

From Biodegradable Containers: These seedlings can be planted in the ground container and all. Cut off any edges that protrude above the soil level before planting as they can act as a wick, drawing water away from the plant. Slit the sides in two or three places to allow roots to grow through more easily. Plant in the ground, keeping the soil levels even.

Protecting New Transplants

Newly transplanted seedlings are more susceptible than mature plants to environmental stress and attack from garden pests. They require special attention for the first few weeks after transplanting.

Stress: Plants, like people, will display visible signs of stress when they are deprived of physical essentials (such as water) or subjected to sudden changes (such as transplanting). New transplants are particularly susceptible to stress and should be checked frequently for signs of wilting or distress, especially for the first few days. If plants look pale or begin to droop as the sun rises in the sky, check that the soil is moist. If desiccation is not the problem, heat may be causing the stress. Protect despondent seedlings with a sun shade fashioned from newspaper or, better yet, fine plastic or wire mesh through which filtered light can penetrate, held in place with skewers, sod pins, or sturdy twigs. Be sure to allow healthy air circulation. Remove this cover gradually, allowing more direct sunlight to reach the plants over several days.

Foiling Cutworms and Slugs: Young plants are irresistible to many garden pests, most notably cutworms and slugs, which can decapitate an entire bed of new transplants overnight.

A good defense against these loathsome creatures is a paper collar encircling each plant. These can be

Transplanting Seedlings to the Garden

Step 1: Remove plant from flat.

Step 2: Dig a hole large enough for one plant.

Step 3: Place plant level with ground.

made from paper cups, cardboard rolls, milk cartons, or lightweight card (such as a file card).

To fashion a collar from a paper cup, remove the bottom, slit down one side, and carefully encircle the seedling, overlapping the ends to create an unbroken barrier. Push the cup gently into the soil deeply enough to keep it anchored. Cardboard rolls can be slit down the side, cut into two-inch sections, and set in position with ends overlapping. Flexible card can be wrapped easily around plant stems and pushed into the ground to anchor. Secure the ends with tape, if necessary. As the cutworm does its damage by encircling the plant's stem, the space between stem and collar should be less than one inch. Collars can be removed once plants are well established as the older, tougher stems are not appealing to cutworms.

A cutworm collar.

Don't get too relaxed at this point, though, as the slugs have only temporarily returned to the moist underside of your decorative rocks, waiting to emerge one night and devour your *Hostas.*

Keeping Plants Cool, Moist, and Weed-Free: Mulching beds will ultimately save you time and energy, and will make your plants healthier and happier by keeping the soil cool, moist, and weed-free. Apply a two-inch layer of shredded hardwood, leaf mold, compost, cocoa shells — or any organic mulch that you prefer — when young plants are sufficiently tall and strong that they won't be overwhelmed by the mulch. Newly planted perennials — whether propagated by seed, division, or cuttings, whether homegrown or store-bought — will benefit from a second application of mulch after an initial hard freeze to help them through their first winter.

Enjoy Your Garden!

Finally all of your little protégés are in the ground, bravely pushing their roots deep into the rich and welcoming soil that you've so carefully provided for them, their heads reaching skyward before bursting into glo-rious bloom. Pat yourself on the back and take every opportunity to admire your garden. But don't forget that the work doesn't stop here. Apart from watering and weeding, plants may need pinching, staking, deadheading, and frequent inspection for signs of pests and diseases. Be something of a vigilante in your garden.

To make your life a little easier, draw up a calendar of gardening jobs you will need to perform throughout the year, based on the specific needs of the plants you are growing (this information is provided in the plant care section in the individual listings). This way you'll be reminded to pinch back the salvia before it's lying flat across the candytuft, to feed the petunias, or *not* to feed the nasturtiums. Filling in the calendar will be a time consuming job initially, but after years of proving to myself over and over that I really won't remember to pinch back the mums or stake the young asters unless it's written down in front of me, I don't begrudge the time spent on this task each spring. In the end, you're doing your plants a favor by making sure they'll get the attention they need at the time they need it, and they will repay you with robust growth and profuse blooms.

Asexual Propagation

Growing new plants from seed is usually quite easy and inexpensive, but is not always appropriate, and so it is necessary to use asexual methods of reproduction at times. Why can't all plants be propagated by seed? Some plants are simply very difficult to grow from seed; the seed may be viable for only a short time or the germination time too long or the seedlings too delicate. Another important reason for using vegetative methods of propagation is that many plants do not grow true from seed (i.e., they will not bear all of the characteristics of the parent plant). Artificially bred hybrids, for instance, will not grow true from seed.

The most common methods of asexual propagation are described below. Some plants are agreeably open to several methods, others are less obliging; perennials having a long taproot, for instance, are rarely divided successfully. Each plant's propagation preferences are listed in the individual entries, as well as the frequency with which plants may be (or should be) renewed, where appropriate.

Cuttings

Leaf: Remove individual leaves (still attached to their stems) from the parent plant and insert them in a growing medium (occasionally this can be water) until roots have grown. In some cases, the leaf may be laid on the soil surface and slits made across the veins of the leaf, from which new plants will grow.

Root: Cut long pieces of root from the parent plant; this can be done with a spade below the soil surface, without uprooting the parent. These long pieces are then cut into one-inch to two-inch sections. Thick roots can be planted standing upright, either in individual pots or directly in the garden; thin roots should be laid on the soil surface and covered shallowly with earth.

Stem: Using a very sharp knife, cut the tip of a side-shoot (i.e., not the plant's main stem) containing at least three leaf joints. Remove the leaves from the bottommost leaf joint and insert the cutting in a growing medium, burying the bottom leaf joint. Roots will grow from the buried portion.

Division

Roots: This is the simplest and most common form of perennial propagation. Plants are dug, roots and all, and substantial clumps carefully teased out using the hands, or divided with two garden forks inserted back to back, or cut through with a sharp instrument, depending on the size and fragility of the plant. These new clumps are then replanted.

Dividing roots.

Some perennials die back in the center as they become older; if this has happened, the deteriorating part of the plant should be discarded and only the vigorous outer clumps replanted.

Tubers: A tuber is a thick, fleshy root found on some perennials. Tubers are divided either by carefully untangling them from each other or by cutting them apart. Each piece that is to be replanted must contain at least one growth bud (also called an "eye"), as well as a piece of the old stem. Tubers are usually replanted with the eye an inch or two below the surface.

Layering

While still attached to the parent plant, a portion of one stem is either pinned down to touch the soil surface or is actually buried. Before long, roots will develop where the stem is in contact with the soil; the stem can then be cut from the parent.

Layering a plant stem by securing it with rocks.

Offset

A miniature version of the parent plant which can be detached and cultivated to create a new plant is called an offset. Bulblets and cormels are offsets, as are rosettes and runners.

Detaching an offset to create a new plant.

Runners

Many ground-cover plants grow long, flexible stems that reach out along the ground, usually sprouting tiny roots at intervals. When detached from the parent and planted with the roots held firmly in the soil, these runners will quickly develop into strong plants.

Propagating Bulbs and Corms

Most bulbs can be divided every year or two if a rapid increase of stock is desired; on the other hand, many can be left almost indefinitely without the need of division.

Bulbs and corms are usually propagated by the separation of small, newly developed bulbs from the parent plant. The following terms are commonly used to describe these young bulbs and corms.

Bulbil: A bulbil is avery small bulbs that is, uniquely, produced *above ground*. Bulbils usually form at the base of a leaf, one bulbil per leaf, all the way up the stem. These can be detached, planted, and grown on to flower, usually in two or three years. Bulbils are most often found on lilies.

Bulblet: A small bulb that forms from the base of the parent bulb is a bulblet. This develops fairly quickly until it is large enough to sustain itself. Bulblets are relatively large and easily detached from the parent bulb. Normally they will bloom one or two years after division.

Corm: A corm actually lives for only one season, but during that season it grows replacements in the form of one large new corm, plus several tiny cormels. Discard the old corm and plant the new one, which will flower the following year.

Cormel: Many corms produce a crop of miniature corms, known as cormels, which grow along the base of the old corm. Detach these and grow in a nursery bed for several years until they are of flowering size.

Scale: Some bulbs are made up of large "scales," which can be detached and planted, usually flowering one or two years after planting.

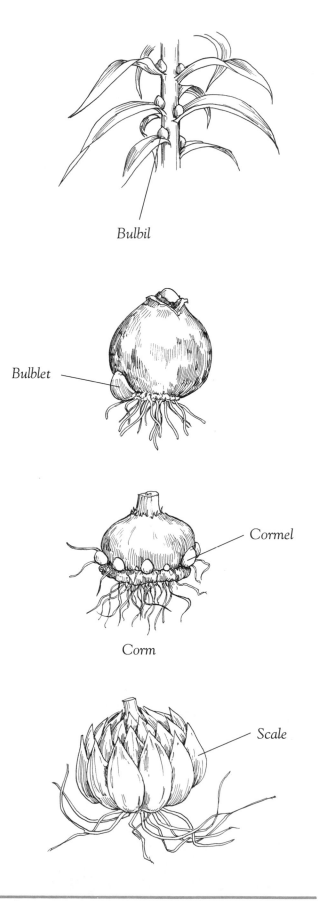

Bulbil

Bulblet

Cormel

Corm

Scale

GENERAL DESCRIPTION OF PLANT TYPES

TYPE	SEED/BULB	PLANT
Half-hardy annual (HHA)*	These plants require a longer growing period than hardy annuals, and are usually started indoors 4–8 weeks before planting out. In zones 8–10, the growing season may be long enough to start some half-hardy annuals outdoors.	Plant seedlings out after the last frost in spring. These annuals will survive cold weather, but not frost. Discard plants after blooming or at the end of the growing season.
Hardy annual (HA)*	Sow seeds outdoors in early spring when a light frost is still possible. For an earlier start, sow seeds indoors 4–8 weeks before planting out. In zones 8–10, seeds can be started outdoors in late autumn; a few hardy annuals can even be sown at this time farther north.	Hardy annuals will withstand several degrees of frost, but not a hard freeze. Seedlings that were started indoors are usually transplanted to the garden around the last frost date, but established plants can be set out earlier. Discard plants after blooming. In zones 8–10, seedlings can be planted out in autumn; mulch applied afer the first light frost in autumn may bring young seedlings through the winter in the North.
Warm-season annual	The seeds of annuals designated in individual plant entries as preferring warm weather generally will not germinate in cold soil. Sow seeds outdoors 2–3 weeks after the last spring frost, or start indoors 4–8 weeks before transplanting to the garden.	Warm season annuals should not be planted out until the air and soil are becoming warm, 2–3 weeks after the last spring frost. It may be hard to wait, but nothing will be gained by planting earlier, and damage can be done that will actually retard a plant's development.
Cool-season annual	The seeds of cool-season annuals can usually be sown outdoors in early spring when the soil is cool and a light frost is still possible; in zones 9–10, seeds can be sown in early autumn. Or start seeds indoors to give plants an early start, 4–8 weeks before transplanting seedlings to the garden.	Transplant seedlings or set out purchased plants after the last spring frost.
Hardy biennial (HB)	Sow seeds outdoors between early spring (*before* the last frost) and summer, or in autumn.	Biennials are normally started in a nursery bed in the spring, then moved to their flowering position in autumn. The reason for this is that biennials do not flower until their second year, and so contribute litle to a flower bed in their first year. Seeds that are started in autumn can be sown where they will flower. In the first year, the ground should be mulched after the first frost in autumn. Discard plants after blooming in their second year, allowing for seed disbursal if self-seeding is desired.

---

* As well as being categorized as hardy or half-hardy, annuals are sometimes described as "warm season" or "cool season" plants.

GENERAL DESCRIPTION OF PLANT TYPES

(continued)

TYPE	SEED/BULB	PLANT
Half-hardy perennial (HHP)	It is more difficult to generalize about the half-hardy perennials than any other group; the degree of frost tolerance ranges from minimal to *almost* frost hardy. To be safe, then, let us say that the majority of half-hardy perennials can be sown or planted outdoors around the last frost date. To get an earlier start, sow seeds indoors 6–10 weeks before planting out.	Although some half-hardy seedlings can be set out *before* the last frost date, others prefer quite warm temperatures, so here again it is difficult to make generalizations. Waiting until there is no chance of frost before planting seedlings outdoors may be unnecessarily cautious but will at least guarantee safety. In the autumn, plants should be mulched before a hard frost or, where winters are very cold, plants should be dug and overwintered indoors.
Hardy perennial (HP)	Seeds may be sown directly outdoors wherever these plants can be grown; you may prefer to start fussy or difficult seeds indoors 6–10 weeks before transplanting to the garden.	Most hardy perennials can be transplanted to the garden either before the last spring frost or in early autumn. Where summers are very hot, set plants out a week or two before the last frost; where winters are harsh, wait until the last frost date. Hardy perennials need little winter protection, but a mulch applied after the ground has frozen will prevent heaving.
Half-hardy bulb (HHBb)	In most climates, half-hardy bulbs (which are usually summer-blooming) should be planted in the spring, dug up in the autumn, and stored indoors over winter. In the South, they can be left in the ground all year. Where hardiness is marginal, plant bulbs in a warm, sheltered position (e.g., near the house) and mulch before the ground freezes.	Where hardiness is marginal, plant bulbs in a warm, sheltered position (e.g., near the house) and mulch in autumn before the ground freezes.
Hardy bulb (HBb)	Hardy bulbs are usually planted in the autumn and left in the ground all year. Mulch in winter after the ground freezes to prevent heaving. As these bulbs *require* a cold period, they should be lifted after blooming where summers are hot and either discarded or stored in a cool place (e.g., in a refrigerator or cool garage) over the summer.	Mulch in winter after the ground freezes to prevent heaving.

A PLANT -BY- PLANT GUIDE TO GROWING FROM SEED

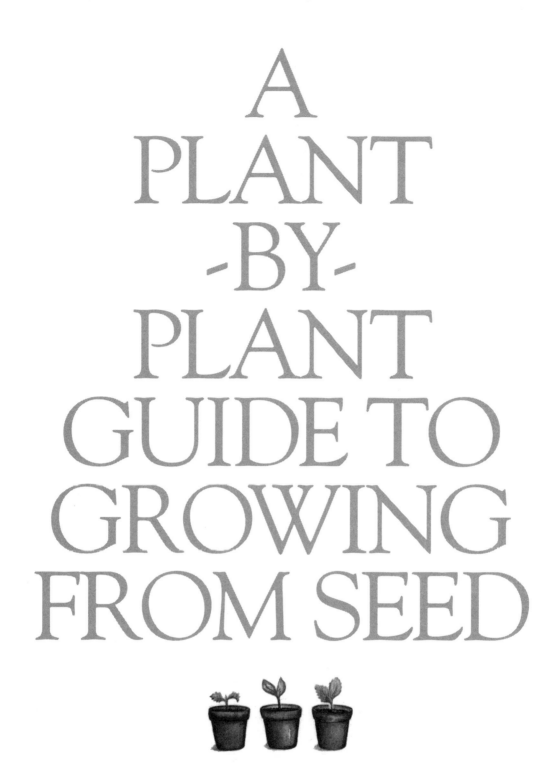

Abronia

Sand verbena, Wild lantana

Type HHP treated as HHA
Zone Prefers the long, cool growing season of the Pacific Coast
Flowering Season June to July

Genus of low-growing or prostrate plants up to 10" tall native to western North America. Clusters of tubular, fragrant flowers are yellow, white, or red. Use in the border or rock garden.

Sowing
Indoors 6–8 weeks before planting out, in peat pots.
Outdoors Autumn, only in zones 9–10.
Depth ¼".

Germinating
Time 15–20 days.
Requirements Remove husk before planting. 55°–65°F.

Planting Seedlings Outdoors
Time After last frost.
Spacing 12"–15".
Light Full sun.
Soil Prefers light, sandy soil; tolerates quite dry situations.

Caring for Plants
Do not disturb established plants.

Propagating
Self-seeds in mild climates.

Acaena

New Zealand bur

Type HP
Zone 6–8
Flowering Season July to frost

Evergreen, mat-forming perennials and subshrubs native to South America, Australia, and New Zealand. Flowers are inconspicuous, but leaves and brightly colored burs make this vigorous little plant useful as a ground cover or in the rock garden.

Sowing
Indoors At least 12 weeks before planting out.
Outdoors Spring or autumn.
Depth ¼".

Germinating
Time 30–100 days.
Requirements Very difficult. 50°–60°F.

Planting Seedlings Outdoors
Time After last spring frost or in early autumn.
Spacing 3"–5".
Light Full sun to part shade.
Soil Sandy or gritty. Will not tolerate standing water.

Caring for Plants
Difficult. Do not water from above. Provide winter mulch north of Philadelphia.

Propagating
Divide in early spring or take cuttings.

Acaena microphylla

A-Annual P-Perennial B-Biennial HHA-Half-hardy annual HA-Hardy annual HB-Hardy biennial HHP-Half-hardy perennial HP-Hardy perennial HHBb-Half-hardy bulb HBb-Hardy bulb

25

Acantholimon

Prickly thrift

> **TYPE** HP
> **ZONE** 7–9. Must have dry winters and summers.
> **FLOWERING SEASON** July to August

Fine-textured, cushiony perennials bearing abundant star-shaped flowers and needle-like leaves. Usually evergreen, these little plants are native to desert regions and are most at home in rock gardens or tucked into the crevices of walls.

GERMINATING

REQUIREMENTS Growing from seed not recommended; seed is hard to obtain and germination is unreliable.

PLANTING SEEDLINGS OUTDOORS

TIME Set out purchased plants after last spring frost or in early autumn.
SPACING 3"–5".
LIGHT Full sun.
SOIL Alkaline; sandy or gritty. Ideal for dry-stone walls.

CARING FOR PLANTS

Plants are slow to establish and almost impossible to move. Mulch with straw in winter.

PROPAGATING

Difficult. Take cuttings in early spring or late summer and overwinter in a cold frame.

Acantholimon glumaceum

Acanthus

Bear's breeches

> **TYPE** HP
> **ZONE** 6–10: A. *balcanicus*, A. *spinosus*; 8–10: A. *dioscoridis*, A. *mollis*. Does not tolerate high heat and humidity.
> **FLOWERING SEASON** Late spring through summer

Large, rather stiff perennials of 1'–4' used in the border for dramatic effect. Flowers, usually in shades of purple, appear in bottle brushes above deeply cut, spiky leaves. This Mediterranean native may be evergreen or deciduous.

SOWING

INDOORS Late winter to early spring, in peat pots.
OUTDOORS Early spring, when soil is still cool.
DEPTH ¼".

GERMINATING

TIME 21–25 days.
REQUIREMENTS Easy. 50°–60°F.

PLANTING SEEDLINGS OUTDOORS

TIME After last spring frost or in early autumn.
SPACING 36"–48".
LIGHT Full sun to part shade. Flowers best in sun, but needs some shade where the afternoon sun is very hot.
SOIL Deep, rich, well-drained, with a pH level of 6.0–7.0. Highly drought tolerant, but will not survive in wet sites.

CARING FOR PLANTS

Easy. Water regularly during growing season, but allow plants to become somewhat dry after flowering. Do not disturb roots. In the South, cut plants back hard after flowering. In northern climates, mulch with salt hay in winter. Cut stems back to ground level in spring.

PROPAGATING

Take root cuttings or divide in autumn.

Acanthus mollis (Latifolius group)

A-Annual P-Perennial B-Biennial **HHA**-Half-hardy annual **HA**-Hardy annual **HB**-Hardy biennial **HHP**-Half-hardy perennial **HP**-Hardy perennial **HHBb**-Half-hardy bulb **HBb**-Hardy bulb

Achillea

Sneezewort, Yarrow

Type HP
Zone 3–8: *A. ptarmica*,
A. millefolium; 3–10: *A. clypeolata*, *A. filipendulina*,
A. tomentosa, *A. x wilczekii;*
5–9: *A. chrysocoma*,
A. clavennae, *A. taygetea;*
6–9: *A. erbarotta spp. rupestris;*
7–10: *A. ageratifolia*,
A. x kellereri
Flowering Season Late spring to early autumn

Easy and useful perennials, 6"–48" tall, grown in meadows or to lend a carefree or naturalistic look to the border; small species are attractive in rock gardens. Leaves are usually soft and feathery, with tiny flowers borne in dense clusters on flat heads; beguiling shades of pink have now been added to the ubiquitous yellow.

Sowing

Indoors 8–10 weeks before planting out.
Outdoors Early spring or early autumn.
Depth Surface.

Germinating

Time 10–100 days.
Requirements Easy. Light and 60°–65°F.

Planting Seedlings Outdoors

Time Early spring, when soil is cool and a light frost is still likely, or early autumn.
Spacing 12"–24".
Light Full sun.
Soil Will grow in poor, dry soil, but performs best in a good loam with a pH level of 5.5–7.0.

Caring for Plants

Easy. Divide every 3–4 years to maintain vigor. Very tall or floppy species may need support. Cut plants to ground level in autumn. To dry for indoor displays, cut flowers at their peak and hang upside-down in a dry, shady place.

Propagating

Divide after flowering in spring, in autumn south of zone 6; take basal cuttings in spring.

Achillea filipendulina

Acidanthera

Abyssinian sword lily

Type HHBb
Zone A: 3–8 (with a heavy mulch, bulbs may survive in the ground in zones 7 and 8); P: 9–10
Flowering Season Late summer to autumn

Lovely summer-blooming corms native to Africa. Leaves are scant and sword-shaped; flowers are wonderfully fragrant, with long, sharply pointed, pure white flowers, blotched a deep chocolate in the center. Plant in masses as flowering is unreliable.

Sowing

Indoors Spring.
Outdoors Seed: after last frost, in zone 10 only. Bulb: late spring.
Depth Seed: just cover. Bulb: 3"–5".

Germinating

Time 30–90 days.
Requirements 50°–55°F. As seeds germinate, transplant to 5" pots, leave in shaded outdoor location for the summer, bringing indoors for the winter. After 1–2 years of this treatment, allow bulbs to rest over the winter without water, then plant out the following spring.

Planting Seedlings Outdoors

Time After last frost.
Spacing 6"–12".
Light Sun.
Soil Average, well-drained.

Caring for Plants

Water regularly during growing season, applying liquid fertilizer every 3–4 weeks. Watch for slugs and aphids. Where winters are cold, dig up corms 6–8 weeks before last frost and store in a cool, frost-free place. Replant in spring.

Propagating

Divide corms in late spring.

A-Annual P-Perennial B-Biennial HHA-Half-hardy annual HA-Hardy annual HB-Hardy biennial HHP-Half-hardy perennial HP-Hardy perennial HHBb-Half-hardy bulb HBb-Hardy bulb

Aconitum

Aconite, Monk's-hood, Wolfsbane

TYPE HP
ZONE 3–8: *A. carmichaelii,*
A. columbianum, A. napellus,
A. volubile, A. lycoctonum spp.
vulparia; 5–8: *A. anthora,*
A. x cammarum, A. henryi; 6–8:
A. uncinatum. Does not tolerate
high heat and humidity.
FLOWERING SEASON Late summer to
early autumn

Much neglected, curiously old-fashioned
perennials with mysterious, hooded, purple
or white flowers borne majestically on stems
of up to 8'; its impressive size limits this
somewhat fussy plant's usefulness to the
back of the border.

SOWING

INDOORS Start seeds outdoors.
OUTDOORS Autumn.
DEPTH Surface.

GERMINATING

TIME 5–270 days.
REQUIREMENTS Sow seeds in flats and sink
these into the ground against a north-
facing wall, covering with glass. Moisten
soil as necessary. Bring flats indoors in
spring. Transplant seedlings to individual
pots after 8 weeks and to the garden in
autumn.

PLANTING SEEDLINGS OUTDOORS

TIME Autumn.
SPACING Small species: 8"–10". Tall species: 24"–36".
LIGHT Prefers part shade, but withstands
full sun if soil is kept moist. In the South,
provide shade from hot midday sun.
SOIL Cool, moist, humus-rich, with a pH
level of 5.0–6.0. Add well-rotted manure
at planting time.

CARING FOR PLANTS

Mulch and water frequently in summer.
Stake tall species in windy sites and cut back
to ground level in autumn. Divide carefully
every 3–4 years.

Aconitum napellus

PROPAGATING

Divide carefully in spring (or in autumn
south of zone 6).

Acroclinium

See *Helipterum*

Actinidia

Arguta, Bower actinidia, Bower arguta, Chinese gooseberry, Kiwi vine, Kolomikta vine, Silver vine, Tara vine, Yang-tao

TYPE HP
ZONE 4–8: *A. arguta, A. kolomikta, A. polygama;* 7–9: *A.
chinensis.* Fruiting and general
performance will be most
successful in warmer climates.
FLOWERING SEASON Late summer

Mainly deciduous, woody climbers native
to China and Japan. The most popular species, *Actinidia kolomikta,* has striking and
unusual foliage: young leaves emerge with
a purple hue, then change to a variegation
of pink and white. Vines grow to 12' on a
wall or fence.

SOWING

INDOORS October to November.
OUTDOORS Early spring, when soil is cool
and a light frost is still possible, or late
autumn.
DEPTH ⅛".

GERMINATING

TIME 60–90 days.
REQUIREMENTS Easy. 50°F.

PLANTING SEEDLINGS OUTDOORS

TIME Spring or autumn.
SPACING Plant vines singly, or 2' apart if
fruiting is desired.
LIGHT Sun or shade. Variegated leaves will
have better color in full sun.
SOIL Well-drained, fertile, humus-rich, and
moist.

CARING FOR PLANTS

Except for *A. polygama,* one plant of either
sex is required for pollination and fruiting;
to ensure pollination, grow 3–4 plants in
one group. Prune in early spring, cutting
back as necessary and thinning out stems
to retain neat appearance. Water plants well
during dry periods and provide a trellis for
support. Plants flower on 2-year-old wood.

PROPAGATING

Take cuttings in summer.

A-Annual P-Perennial B-Biennial HHA-Half-hardy annual HA-Hardy annual HB-Hardy biennial HHP-Half-hardy perennial HP-Hardy perennial HHBb-Half-hardy bulb HBb-Hardy bulb

28

Adenophora

Ladybells

Type HP
Zone 3–9
Flowering Season Summer

Summer-flowering perennials bearing a strong resemblance to *Campanulas*. 18"–4' plants bear pale blue, bell-shaped flowers and are most often used in the border.

SOWING

Indoors 8–10 weeks before planting out, in peat pots.
Outdoors Early spring, when soil is cool and a light frost is still possible, or early autumn.
Depth Surface.

GERMINATING

Time 30–90 days.
Requirements Easy. 50°–55°F.

PLANTING SEEDLINGS OUTDOORS

Time Early spring, when soil is cool and a light frost is still possible, or early autumn.
Spacing 12"–24".
Light Full sun or part shade.
Soil Moist, rich, well-drained loam.

CARING FOR PLANTS

Water and deadhead regularly. Do not transplant.

PROPAGATING

Take cuttings in spring.

Adlumia

Allegheny vine, Climbing fumitory, Mountain fringe

Type HB
Zone 5–9. Favors the climate of New England and will not thrive in extreme heat and drought.
Flowering Season June through August

Dainty climber that looks very much like a white-flowered bleeding heart. This charming plant reaches 15' and is native to the woods of the eastern United States; it is most at home in a naturalistic garden.

SOWING

Indoors 6–8 weeks before planting out, in peat pots.
Outdoors After last frost.
Depth ¼".

GERMINATING

Time 14–42 days.
Requirements Easy. 55°–65°F.

PLANTING SEEDLINGS OUTDOORS

Time Early summer.
Spacing Grow vines singly.
Light Part to full shade.
Soil Cool, moist, sandy, humus-rich, and not too acid.

CARING FOR PLANTS

Easy. Requires a trellis for support and protection from wind. Mulch with organic matter to keep soil cool and moist; water regularly during dry spells. Vines grow very slowly their first year, but will take off in their second.

PROPAGATING

May self-seed once established.

A-Annual P-Perennial B-Biennial HHA-Half-hardy annual HA-Hardy annual HB-Hardy biennial HHP-Half-hardy perennial HP-Hardy perennial HHBb-Half-hardy bulb HBb-Hardy bulb

Adonis

Pheasant's eye, Red Morocco

TYPE HA or HP
ZONE A: 3–9; P: 3–9. Will only grow well in cool climates with a nighttime temperature below 65°F.
FLOWERING SEASON A: summer; P: early spring

Low-growing, clump-forming annuals and perennials bearing buttercuplike flowers of yellow or white; perennials are useful for their very early flowering. Plants are most effective when situated along a path, in the rock garden, or massed among early bulbs.

SOWING

INDOORS Start seeds outdoors.
OUTDOORS A: after last frost. P: spring or autumn.
DEPTH Just cover.

GERMINATING

TIME A: 14 days. P: 30–120 days.
REQUIREMENTS 60°–65°F. Annuals are easy to grow from seed; perennials require rather more care.

PLANTING SEEDLINGS OUTDOORS

TIME A: after last frost. P: autumn or very early spring, when soil is still cool and a light frost is still possible.
SPACING Small species: 5"–8". Larger species: 12".
LIGHT Sun or part shade.
SOIL Prefers moist, sandy soil with a pH of 6.0–8.0, but will tolerate dry.

CARING FOR PLANTS

Cultivation variously described as easy and difficult. Apply fertilizer to perennials immediately after flowering. Plants will disappear in midsummer; mark their locations to avoid disturbing the roots. Apply a thick winter mulch in zones 3–5. Perennials propagated by division produce more blooms than those grown from seed.

PROPAGATING

Annuals self-seed freely. Very carefully divide perennials after flowering in spring, although plants prefer not to be disturbed.

Aegopodium

Bishop's weed, Goutweed

TYPE HP
ZONE 3–9
FLOWERING SEASON June

Easy-care, low-growing, rhizomatous perennials inclined to become weedy, as the common names imply. Most bear clean, attractive, if unexceptional, foliage and are useful as ground covers. White flowers, which are held on tall stalks high above the foliage, are considered by some a liability.

GERMINATING

REQUIREMENTS Not grown from seed.

PLANTING SEEDLINGS OUTDOORS

TIME Set out purchased plants in spring or autumn.
SPACING 6"–8" for ground cover or edging, otherwise 10"–12".
LIGHT Prefers part shade, but will tolerate full sun.
SOIL Ordinary; withstands wet, dry, or poor soil.

CARING FOR PLANTS

Very easy, thriving almost anywhere. Once established, plants may be difficult to eradicate. If colonies show signs of taking over your garden, remove flowers to prevent self-seeding or mow to the ground periodically. When growing variegated species, pull up any plants that revert to green.

PROPAGATING

Divide in spring north of zone 7, or in autumn in the South; self-seeds.

Aegopodium podagraria

Aethionema

Stone cress

> **Type** Short-lived HP, usually grown as A or B
> **Zone** 5–9. Moderately tolerant of high heat, but not humidity (except A. x *warleyense*, which thrives in both).
> **Flowering Season** Early spring to early summer

Short-lived perennials and subshrubs native to the Mediterranean region. Plants are evergreen or semi-evergreen and bear clusters of tiny pink, white, or lilac flowers in profusion. Use in the crevices of stone walls or in rock gardens; tall species may be useful at the front of the border.

Sowing

Indoors 10–12 weeks before planting out. Start A. *arabicum* outdoors only.
Outdoors After last frost.
Depth Just cover.

Germinating

Time 30–90 days.
Requirements 60°–65°F.

Planting Seedlings Outdoors

Time Spring or autumn.
Spacing 4"–7".
Light Full sun.
Soil Well-drained, sandy. Add 1 teaspoon lime to each planting hole.

Caring for Plants

Water regularly and feed occasionally. Trim lightly after flowering. Plants are short-lived and may die out after 1–2 years, but will survive longer in a dry, sunny position.

Propagating

Divide or take softwood cuttings after flowering; self-seeds.

Aethionema grandiflorum

Agapanthus

African lily, Blue African lily, Lily-of-the-Nile

> **Type** HHP
> **Zone** P: 9–10; A. x *'Headbourne Hybrids'* may be hardy to zone 6 if a heavy winter mulch is provided. May be grown as an annual north of zone 9.
> **Flowering Season** Summer

Sophisticated, refined, and irresistible plants. Clumps of funnel-shaped blue or white flowers are held on strong 2'–4' stalks; gently arching leaves are thick and straplike. Pots of these elegant plants are essential on any sunny patio.

Sowing

Indoors Any time.
Outdoors Spring.
Depth Seed: just cover. Roots: 2"–4".

Germinating

Time 20–90 days.
Requirements Rarely grown from seed; 60°–70°F.

Agapanthus campanulatus

Planting Seedlings Outdoors

Time After last frost.
Spacing 18"–24".
Light Full sun to light shade.
Soil Moist, well-drained.

Caring for Plants

Easy. Plants grown from seed will bloom in 3–4 years. Fertilize every 2 weeks during the growing season and water frequently. Deadhead regularly. Blooms most profusely when roots are somewhat crowded. North of zone 9, dig plants in autumn and store in sand in a cool, frost-free location, replanting in spring.

Propagating

Every 4–5 years divide evergreen forms in spring or autumn, deciduous in autumn. Soak roots in water for several hours to ease division.

Agastache

(synonymous with *Brittonastrum*)

Hyssop

TYPE HP
ZONE 4–9: *A. nepetoides*;
  6–9: *A. cana, A. foeniculum,*
  A. urticifolia; 8–10:
  A. mexicana. Prefers cool
  temperatures.
FLOWERING SEASON Summer

Summer-blooming plants of 2'–6' bearing spikes of purple, blue, or green flowers above anise-scented leaves. The coarse texture of these perennials makes them most useful in a wildflower garden. Most species are native to North America and Mexico.

SOWING

INDOORS 6–8 weeks before planting out.
OUTDOORS Autumn.
DEPTH Just cover.

GERMINATING

TIME 30–90 days.
REQUIREMENTS 55°F.

PLANTING SEEDLINGS OUTDOORS

TIME After last frost.
SPACING 12".
LIGHT Sun or very light shade.
SOIL Well-drained, fairly rich.

CARING FOR PLANTS

Plants grown from seed will bloom in 2 years. Feed annually in spring and renew every year or two to maintain vigor. Transplant only before plants bloom.

PROPAGATING

Divide in spring in zones 4–6, early autumn in the South. Take cuttings in late summer. Self-seeds.

Ageratum

Flossflower

TYPE HHA
ZONE Prefers warm summers
FLOWERING SEASON June to frost

Attractive annuals and biennials with downy flowers of pink, white, or palest blue to deepest violet. Plants may form compact mounds suitable for edging, or stand erect up to 24". All are useful in the border; tall species are also at home in naturalized gardens.

SOWING

INDOORS 6–8 weeks before planting out.
OUTDOORS After last frost, when soil is quite warm. Where winters are mild, seed again in late summer for autumn bloom.
DEPTH Surface.

GERMINATING

TIME 5–14 days.
REQUIREMENTS Light and 70°–75°F.

PLANTING SEEDLINGS OUTDOORS

TIME After last frost.
SPACING Dwarf species: 6". Medium species: 6"–10". Tall species: 12".
LIGHT Full sun, with light shade where summers are hot.
SOIL Very adaptable. Prefers a pH level of 5.0–6.0.

CARING FOR PLANTS

Easy. Deadhead regularly, feed monthly, and water during hot, dry weather. Pinch out tall species to encourage a bushy habit.

PROPAGATING

Some species self-seed to the point of being invasive.

A-Annual P-Perennial B-Biennial HHA-Half-hardy annual HA-Hardy annual HB-Hardy biennial HHP-Half-hardy perennial HP-Hardy perennial HHBb-Half-hardy bulb HBb-Hardy bulb

32

Agrostemma

Corn-cockle

TYPE **HA**
ZONE **Prefers cool temperatures**
FLOWERING SEASON **Summer**

Dainty, easy annuals, 2'–3' tall, covered in tiny, deep pink, trumpet-shaped blooms. At home in cottage gardens and borders.

SOWING

INDOORS 6–8 weeks before planting out.
OUTDOORS Early spring, when soil is cool and a light frost is still possible, or early autumn where winters are mild.
DEPTH ⅛".

GERMINATING

TIME 14–21 days.
REQUIREMENTS 55°–65°F.

PLANTING SEEDLINGS OUTDOORS

TIME After last frost.
SPACING 9"–12".
LIGHT Sun.
SOIL Tolerates most soils, but a rich, well-drained loam will give the best results.

CARING FOR PLANTS

Easy. Deadhead regularly to prolong flowering and prevent self-seeding. Water during dry spells. Support with stakes or twiggy branches pushed into the ground.

PROPAGATING

Self-seeds freely.

Agrostis

Cloud grass

TYPE **Short-lived HP grown as HA**
ZONE **Prefers warm temperatures**
FLOWERING SEASON **June to July**

Annual grass, 18" tall, with flat green leaves and bearing a haze of fragile flowers that give the plant its common name, Cloud grass.

SOWING

INDOORS 4–6 weeks before planting out.
OUTDOORS Early spring, when soil is cool and a light frost is still possible, or late autumn.
DEPTH Surface.

GERMINATING

TIME 21–25 days.
REQUIREMENTS 50°–55°F.

PLANTING SEEDLINGS OUTDOORS

TIME After last frost.
SPACING 6"–8".
LIGHT Sun or light shade. (*Agrostis* is one of the few grasses that will tolerate shade.)
SOIL Very adaptable, but prefers good drainage.

CARING FOR PLANTS

Easy. Feed regularly and do not allow soil to dry out. Pick all flowers to prevent self-seeding. To dry for flower arrangements, cut stems just before blooming and hang upside-down in a dark place.

PROPAGATING

Seed only.

A-Annual P-Perennial B-Biennial HHA-Half-hardy annual HA-Hardy annual HB-Hardy biennial HHP-Half-hardy perennial HP-Hardy perennial HHBb-Half-hardy bulb HBb-Hardy bulb

Ajuga

Bugleweed

> TYPE HP
> ZONE 3–10. *A. genevensis* and *A. reptans* do not like hot, humid locations.
> FLOWERING SEASON Late spring to midsummer

Vigorous, mat-forming plants, usually perennial and evergreen, useful both for their attractive foliage of deep green, bronze-purple, or variegated pink and cream, and for the impressive forest of upright blue or purple flowering stems borne in spring. This European native may be used as a ground cover or in a small shady planting.

SOWING

INDOORS Start seeds outdoors only.
OUTDOORS Early spring, when soil is cool and light frost is still possible.
DEPTH Just cover.

GERMINATING

TIME 21–28 days.
REQUIREMENTS 50°–55°F.

PLANTING SEEDLINGS OUTDOORS

TIME Set out purchased plants in spring or autumn.
SPACING 6"–12", depending on how quickly you wish to cover the ground.
LIGHT Sun or shade.
SOIL Thrives in quite dry soil with a pH level of 5.5–7.0. Must have very good drainage to prevent root rot. Tolerates poor soil.

CARING FOR PLANTS

Easy, although careful attention produces a more handsome ground cover. Feed once in spring and water regularly. Diligently weed new ground-cover plantings, deadhead after flowering, and remove fallen leaves from beds in autumn to obtain the look you see in garden books. Do not plant near grass as *Ajuga* will quickly and ineradicably make itself at home in lawns.

PROPAGATING

Root stolons in spring or autumn.

Ajuga reptans

Alcea

See **Althaea**

Alchemilla

Lady's mantle

> TYPE HP
> ZONE 3–8. Does not like excessive heat and humidity.
> FLOWERING SEASON Summer

Large genus of low-growing perennials useful for their attractive and unusual, crimped, pale green foliage and spray of green or pale yellow flowers. Good edging plants, ground covers, or rock garden inhabitants; incomparable as a foil for plants of strongly contrasting color.

SOWING

INDOORS 6–8 weeks before last frost.
OUTDOORS Early spring, when soil is still cool, or late autumn.
DEPTH ⅛".

GERMINATING

TIME 21–30 days.
REQUIREMENTS 60°–70°F.

PLANTING SEEDLINGS OUTDOORS

TIME Spring or autumn.
SPACING Small species: 12". Large species: 12"–18".
LIGHT Full sun or part shade. Prefers shade where sun is very hot.
SOIL Moist, well-drained. Enrich with humus in hot, dry climates.

CARING FOR PLANTS

Easy. Deadhead to prevent self-seeding. Top-dress with compost in autumn. Harvest flowers at their peak and hang upside-down in a dark room to dry for winter arrangements.

Alchemilla mollis

PROPAGATING

Divide in early spring in zones 3–6, early autumn in the South. Also self-seeds.

A-Annual P-Perennial B-Biennial HHA-Half-hardy annual HA-Hardy annual HB-Hardy biennial HHP-Half-hardy perennial HP-Hardy perennial HHBb-Half-hardy bulb HBb-Hardy bulb

34

Allium

Golden garlic, Lily leek, Wild onion

> **Type** HBb
> **Zone** 3–8: *A. aflatunense;*
>   3–9: *A. moly, A. oreophilum;*
>   4–9: *A. cernuum,*
>   *A. christophii, A. giganteum;*
>   5–8: *A. neapolitanum*
> **Flowering Season** Spring or
>   summer, depending on species

Large genus of spring- and summer-flowering bulbs ranging in height from 6"–5'. Best known for their dramatic balls of blue, purple, or pink flowers above stiff, upright stems, although many other forms exist. Uses are as varied as forms.

SOWING

Indoors Any time.
Outdoors Seed: spring or autumn. Bulb: autumn.
Depth Seed: surface. Small bulb: 3"–5". Large bulb: 6"–8". Rule of thumb: cover bulb with twice its diameter of soil.

GERMINATING

Time 14–365 days.
Requirements Difficult. Place seeds in a plastic bag together with moist growing medium and refrigerate for 30 days. Provide light and 55°–65°F thereafter. Grow in flats for 1 year, then pot up singly and sink pots in the ground outdoors in spring. Move to the garden in autumn.

Allium tuberosum

CHARLES JOSLIN

PLANTING SEEDLINGS OUTDOORS

Time Autumn. Set out purchased chive plants in spring; where summers are very hot, plant in late summer or autumn for winter harvest.
Spacing Small species: 3"–4". Medium species: 4"–6". Large species: 12". Chives: 5"–6".
Light Full sun to light shade.
Soil Very well-drained, not too rich. Chives prefer soil amended with plenty of manure or compost and a pH level of 6.0–7.0.

CARING FOR PLANTS

Easy. Bulbs grown from seed will flower in 2–4 years. Feed once in spring and remove faded blooms after flowering to prevent prolific self-seeding. *A. giganteum* may need staking. Chives will be edible in 1 year when grown from seed. Feed with 5–10–5 and divide every 2–3 years to maintain vigorous plants. May be potted up and brought indoors for winter use.

PROPAGATING

Divide spring-flowering bulbs in late summer, summer-flowering bulbs in spring. Many species will self-seed and become invasive.

Alonsoa

Mask flower

> **Type** HHP usually treated as
>   HHA
> **Zone** A: 1–8; P: 9–10. Prefers
>   the climate of the Pacific
>   Northwest and will not flower
>   well in hot, humid weather.
>   Requires night temperatures
>   below 65°F.
> **Flowering Season** Early summer
>   through first frost

Branching, upright plants creating a rather untidy tangle of stems, leaves, and flowers. Blossoms are flat with wavy or reflexed petals and prominent yellow stamens; petals are pink, white, or red. 12"–36" tall. Grown in the border or cutting bed.

SOWING

Indoors 6–8 weeks before planting out.
Outdoors After last frost.
Depth Just cover.

GERMINATING

Time 14–21 days.
Requirements 60°F.

PLANTING SEEDLINGS OUTDOORS

Time After last frost.
Spacing 10"–12".
Light Full sun.
Soil Light, well-drained, fertile.

CARING FOR PLANTS

Pinch back seedlings when 2"–3" tall to promote bushiness. Staking may be necessary on windy sites. Much loved by aphids.

PROPAGATING

Take cuttings.

A-Annual **P**-Perennial **B**-Biennial **HHA**-Half-hardy annual **HA**-Hardy annual **HB**-Hardy biennial **HHP**-Half-hardy perennial **HP**-Hardy perennial **HHBb**-Half-hardy bulb **HBb**-Hardy bulb

35

Alstroemeria

Lily of Peru, Lily-of-the-Incas, Peruvian lily

> TYPE HHP
> ZONE 7–10. Prefers cool, damp winters and sunny, warm summers.
> FLOWERING SEASON Mainly summer, though some species bloom in spring or autumn

Perennials prized for their extraordinarily lovely trumpet-shaped flower borne on tall, erect stems. These South American natives should be given their own bed due to their invasive tendencies; exquisite cut flowers.

SOWING

INDOORS 8–10 weeks before planting out, in peat pots.
OUTDOORS Early spring, when soil is still cool, or early autumn.
DEPTH Seed: just cover. Roots: 6"–8".

GERMINATING

TIME 15–365 days.
REQUIREMENTS Difficult. Soak seeds in warm water for 12 hours before sowing. Provide 65°–70°F thereafter.

PLANTING SEEDLINGS OUTDOORS

TIME After last frost.
SPACING 15"–18".
LIGHT Full sun; sun or part shade where summers are very hot.
SOIL Well-drained, humus-rich. Cultivate to a depth of 15" to avoid root rot, to which *Alstroemeria* is highly susceptible.

CARING FOR PLANTS

Most species require 1 annual feeding in late winter, although A. *aurantiaca* prefers light monthly feeds. Plants disappear altogether after blooming; mark locations to avoid unintentional root damage. Mulch in early winter and do not disturb roots. Staking may be necessary. Once established, A. *ligtu* develops deep, invasive roots and can be difficult to eradicate.

Alstroemeria pelegrina

PROPAGATING

Very carefully divide in autumn. Successful division is difficult.

Althaea

Hollyhock

> TYPE HA or HP, often treated as B
> ZONE 2–9. Likes warm temperatures, but not excessive heat and humidity.
> FLOWERING SEASON Summer to early autumn

Charming upright plants evoking old-fashioned cottage gardens and Impressionist paintings. New species are often double-flowered and confined to a modest 2'–3', while old-timers tower over the border at 5'–6'. Available in almost every color.

SOWING

INDOORS 6–8 weeks before planting out, in peat pots.
OUTDOORS A or P: after last frost; 1 week before last frost in warmer climates. B: July.
DEPTH Surface.

GERMINATING

TIME 10–14 days.
REQUIREMENTS Easy. Light and 60°–70°F.

PLANTING SEEDLINGS OUTDOORS

TIME A or P: after last frost. B: early autumn.
SPACING 18"–36".
LIGHT Full sun or light shade.
SOIL Rich, moist, well-drained, with a pH level of 6.0–7.5. Will tolerate dry soil.

CARING FOR PLANTS

Easy. Unrestricted air circulation is essential. Stake tall species and feed and water regularly during growing season. Cutting back stalks immediately after flowering may produce a second blooming. Mulch well in autumn. Do not move mature plants. May be troubled by powdery mildew, rust, leaf spot, Japanese beetles, or slugs.

PROPAGATING

Will self-seed, but resulting flowers may differ in color from the parent's.

A-Annual P-Perennial B-Biennial HHA-Half-hardy annual HA-Hardy annual HB-Hardy biennial HHP-Half-hardy perennial HP-Hardy perennial HHBb-Half-hardy bulb HBb-Hardy bulb

36

Alyssum (Annual)

(synonymous with *Lobularia maritima*)

Sweet alyssum

> TYPE HA
> ZONE 1–10. Prefers cool spring
>   temperatures.
> FLOWERING SEASON Late spring
>   through early autumn

Compact, reliable edging plants just 3"–4" high form a river of white, pink, or purple color when in bloom. Perform well in pots and hanging baskets as well as borders.

SOWING

INDOORS 4–6 weeks before planting out.
OUTDOORS 2–3 weeks before last frost date.
DEPTH Surface.

GERMINATING

TIME 5–14 days.
REQUIREMENTS Light and 55°–75°F.

PLANTING SEEDLINGS OUTDOORS

TIME After last frost.
SPACING 6"–8".
LIGHT Full sun or very light shade.
SOIL Ordinary, well-drained, with a pH level of 6.0–7.5.

CARING FOR PLANTS

Easy. Water during very dry spells and avoid overfertilizing as this produces lush foliage at the expense of blooms. Shear plants after first flowering to encourage a stronger second bloom.

PROPAGATING

Self-seeds.

Alyssum (Perennial)

(synonymous with *Aurinia saxatilis*)

Basket-of-gold, Gold-dust, Madwort

> TYPE HP
> ZONE 3–8: *A. montanum,*
>   *A. saxatile* (syn. with *Aurinia saxatilis*), *A. serpyllifolium;*
>   3–9: *A. alpestre;* 4–9: *A. idaeum, A. moellendorfianum;*
>   6–9: *A. wulfenianum;* 7–10:
>   *A. spinosum*
> FLOWERING SEASON Spring or
>   summer, depending on species

Shrubby, low-growing perennials, sometimes evergreen. Grown for their yellow flowers and used in rock gardens or as an edging; stunning when seen in full bloom cascading over a stone wall.

SOWING

INDOORS 8–10 weeks before planting out.
OUTDOORS Early spring or early autumn.
DEPTH Surface.

GERMINATING

TIME 5 days.
REQUIREMENTS Cool temperatures and light.

PLANTING SEEDLINGS OUTDOORS

TIME Early spring, when soil is cool and a light frost is still possible, or early autumn.
SPACING 12".
LIGHT Full sun.
SOIL Tolerant of many soils, but must have perfect drainage; very rich soil produces weak, leggy plants. Prefers a pH level of 5.5–7.5.

Alyssum saxatile

CARING FOR PLANTS

Easy. Water only during droughts. After flowering, cut back stems by one-third.

PROPAGATING

Take cuttings in summer.

A-Annual P-Perennial B-Biennial HHA-Half-hardy annual HA-Hardy annual HB-Hardy biennial HHP-Half-hardy perennial HP-Hardy perennial HHBb-Half-hardy bulb HBb-Hardy bulb

Amaranthus

**Amaranth, Flaming fountain,
Fountain plant, Joseph's coat,
Love-lies-bleeding, Molten fire,
Prince's feather, Summer poinsettia,
Tampala, Tassel flower**

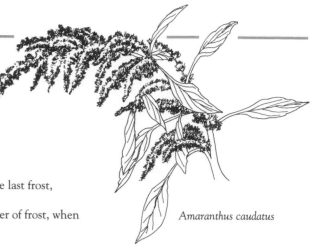

Amaranthus caudatus

TYPE HHA
ZONE 3–10. Does best in warm
   temperatures.
FLOWERING SEASON Summer
   through early autumn

Bushy, 3'–4' tall annuals grown for their
extraordinary — some might say alarming
— tassels of deep red or green flowers;
some species have erect flowering stems
or interesting yellow and red foliage. Use
in containers or as an accent in the border.

SOWING

INDOORS 6–8 weeks before last frost,
   in peat pots.
OUTDOORS After all danger of frost, when
   soil is warm.
DEPTH Just cover.

GERMINATING

TIME 10–15 days.
REQUIREMENTS Easy. 70°–75°F.

PLANTING SEEDLINGS OUTDOORS

TIME After last frost.
SPACING Small species: 9"–12". Tall species: 18".
LIGHT Full sun to half shade.
SOIL Tolerant of most soils; prefers a pH
   level of 6.0–7.0. Rich soil produces larger
   but less brightly colored leaves.

CARING FOR PLANTS

Easy. Water frequently and feed occasionally during the summer.

PROPAGATING

Seed only.

Amaryllis

Belladonna lily, Naked ladies

TYPE HHBb
ZONE 5–10; 8–10: *A. belladonna*.
   Prefers hot, dry summers.
FLOWERING SEASON Late summer
   to autumn

Autumn-flowering bulbs bearing large,
trumpet-shaped flowers on sturdy 18" stalks.
These South African natives are difficult to
incorporate successfully in the border, but
are attractive in pots or might make an interesting display massed on their own.

SOWING

INDOORS Late winter, in individual pots.
OUTDOORS Seed: after last frost. Bulb: late
   summer.
DEPTH Seed: just cover. Bulb: Zones 5–6:
   10", ideally against a south-facing wall;
   Zones 7–8: 6"–8"; Zones 9–10: just cover.

GERMINATING

TIME 21–120 days.
REQUIREMENTS 65°–75°F.

PLANTING SEEDLINGS OUTDOORS

TIME Late spring to early summer.
SPACING 9"–12".
LIGHT Full sun.
SOIL Average or rich, moist, and well-
   drained.

CARING FOR PLANTS

Plants grown from seeds may take up to 8
years to flower. As soon as flowers open,
pinch off anthers to prolong blooming.
Move with care, retaining a large root ball,
and do not divide frequently as plants may
not flower for several years after division or
moving. Provide a thick winter mulch.
Bulbs may be lifted after flowering and
stored indoors where winters are severe.
Bulbs planted against a south-facing wall
may survive cold winters.

PROPAGATING

Divide bulbs after blooming.

A-Annual P-Perennial B-Biennial HHA-Half-hardy annual HA-Hardy annual HB-Hardy biennial HHP-Half-hardy perennial HP-Hardy perennial HHBb-Half-hardy bulb HBb-Hardy bulb

38

Ammi

Bishop's weed, Queen Anne's lace, White lace flower

> TYPE HHA
> ZONE Prefers cool weather
> FLOWERING SEASON Late spring to
>   early summer

Naturalistic annuals bearing stiff, upright stems topped by 6"-wide flower heads smothered in tiny white blooms. At home in a wildflower garden or informal planting; useful for cut flower arrangements.

SOWING

INDOORS 6–8 weeks before last frost.
OUTDOORS Early spring, when soil is cool and a light frost is still possible, or late autumn.
DEPTH Just cover.

GERMINATING

TIME 7–25 days.
REQUIREMENTS 55°–65°F.

PLANTING SEEDLINGS OUTDOORS

TIME After last frost.
SPACING 12".
LIGHT Full sun to light shade.
SOIL Prefers soil that is fertile and quite moist.

CARING FOR PLANTS

Water regularly until plants are established, then only during dry spells.

PROPAGATING

Seed only.

Ammobium

Winged everlasting

> TYPE HHA or A treated as B
> ZONE 2–10
> FLOWERING SEASON Summer

Somewhat coarse everlasting annuals with showy white flowers on upright, 2'–3' tall plants. Use in the border or cutting bed.

SOWING

INDOORS 6–8 weeks before planting out.
OUTDOORS Early spring or early autumn.
DEPTH Just cover.

GERMINATING

TIME 10–15 days.
REQUIREMENTS 60°F.

PLANTING SEEDLINGS OUTDOORS

TIME Spring, when night temperatures will stay above 50°F.
SPACING 10"–15".
LIGHT Full sun.
SOIL Grows well in average, well-drained soil; will tolerate quite dry soil.

CARING FOR PLANTS

Easy. Water only during dry periods.

PROPAGATING

Self-seeds.

A-Annual P-Perennial B-Biennial HHA-Half-hardy annual HA-Hardy annual HB-Hardy biennial HHP-Half-hardy perennial HP-Hardy perennial HHBb-Half-hardy bulb HBb-Hardy bulb

Amsonia

Blue star

TYPE HP
ZONE 4–8: *A. tabernaemontana*;
   6–8: *A. ciliata*
FLOWERING SEASON Summer

Neat, attractive, clump-forming perennials, 2'–3' tall, bearing dainty, blue, star-shaped flowers atop long, supple stems. Use these North American natives in naturalistic or woodland settings, or in shady informal beds.

SOWING

INDOORS 8–10 weeks before planting out, in peat pots.
OUTDOORS Midspring or autumn.
DEPTH Just cover.

GERMINATING

TIME 28–42 days.
REQUIREMENTS 55°–60°F.

Amsonia tabernaemontana

PLANTING SEEDLINGS OUTDOORS

TIME Late spring.
SPACING 18"–36".
LIGHT Light shade; full sun only where soil is moist.
SOIL Cool, moist.

CARING FOR PLANTS

Easy. Prune lightly to maintain neat appearance. Water occasionally during dry spells. Feed in early autumn. Divide periodically to keep plants healthy and blooming, but otherwise avoid root disturbance.

PROPAGATING

Divide in early spring, early autumn in zones 7–8. Take cuttings in summer. May self-seed.

Anacyclus

Mount Atlas daisy

TYPE HP
ZONE 6–9. Does not like excessively hot and humid summers, nor very wet winters.
FLOWERING SEASON Spring to midsummer

Prostrate alpine perennials (which actually come from North Africa) with white — or, less frequently, yellow — daisylike flowers and dense grey foliage. Grow in rock gardens or in the cracks of stone walls.

SOWING

INDOORS Pre-chilled seeds 8 weeks before planting out.
OUTDOORS Autumn.
DEPTH Just cover.

GERMINATING

TIME Usually 30–60 days, but may take up to 3 years.
REQUIREMENTS Easy. Place seeds in a plastic bag together with moist growing medium and refrigerate for 48 hours. Provide light and 55°–60°F thereafter.

PLANTING SEEDLINGS OUTDOORS

TIME After last spring frost or early autumn.
SPACING 12"–18".
LIGHT Sun.
SOIL Dry, rather gritty. Hates lime.

CARING FOR PLANTS

Easy. Where summers are very hot, cut plants back hard after blooming. Surround with stone chips to ensure good drainage and protect from winter wetness.

PROPAGATING

Take cuttings in summer, or divide in spring.

A-Annual P-Perennial B-Biennial HHA-Half-hardy annual HA-Hardy annual HB-Hardy biennial HHP-Half-hardy perennial HP-Hardy perennial HHBb-Half-hardy bulb HBb-Hardy bulb

Anagallis

Pimpernel, Poor man's weatherglass, Shepherd's clock

> TYPE **HHA, or HHP treated as HHA**
> ZONE **A: 2–10; P: 5–7: A. *tenella*; 8–10: A. *monellii***
> FLOWERING SEASON **Early summer to early autumn**

Low-growing, bushy plants smothered in small, star-shaped blooms, usually of deep blue or red, that smell distinctly of honey. Use at the front of the border or in rock gardens.

SOWING

INDOORS Not recommended due to difficulty in transplanting. If attempted, sow seeds in peat pots 6 weeks before planting out.
OUTDOORS After last frost.
DEPTH ⅛".

GERMINATING

TIME 30–42 days.
REQUIREMENTS 50°–65°F.

PLANTING SEEDLINGS OUTDOORS

TIME After last frost.
SPACING 5"–9".
LIGHT Full sun.
SOIL Tolerates most soils.

CARING FOR PLANTS

Easy. Mulch after planting. Do not move.

PROPAGATING

Annuals self-seed. Divide perennials in autumn, in spring in zones 5 and 6, or take cuttings.

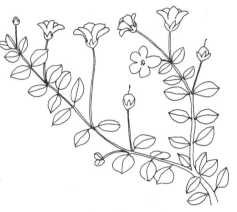

Anagallis arvensis

Anaphalis

Pearly everlasting

> TYPE **HP**
> ZONE **3–9; 3–8: A. *margaritacea*, A. *triplinervis*; 6–8: A. *cinnamomea***
> FLOWERING SEASON **Summer**

Upright perennials with small white everlasting flowers used in dried arrangements. Flowers are borne in clusters above 8"–36" stems. Leaves are lance-shaped, silver, and slightly woolly. Grow in cutting beds or borders.

SOWING

INDOORS 6–8 weeks before planting out.
OUTDOORS Early spring, when soil is cool and a light frost is possible, or late autumn.
DEPTH Just cover.

GERMINATING

TIME 10–60 days.
REQUIREMENTS 55°–65°F.

Anaphalis yedoensis

PLANTING SEEDLINGS OUTDOORS

TIME After last frost.
SPACING 9"–12".
LIGHT Full sun or light shade.
SOIL Prefers good drainage. With the exception of A. *triplinervis*, these plants are very drought-tolerant.

CARING FOR PLANTS

Easy. Cut back after flowering to encourage a second bloom. Provide winter mulch in northern zones.

PROPAGATING

Divide in spring in the North, in autumn south of zone 6. Take cuttings in spring.

A-Annual P-Perennial B-Biennial HHA-Half-hardy annual HA-Hardy annual HB-Hardy biennial HHP-Half-hardy perennial HP-Hardy perennial HHBb-Half-hardy bulb HBb-Hardy bulb

Anchusa

Alkanet, Bugloss, Cape forget-me-not, Summer forget-me-not

> Type HA or HP
> Zone A: 1–10; P: prefers cool weather. 3–8: *A. azurea*; 5–7: *A. caespitosa*.
> Flowering Season Midsummer to late summer

A diverse genus of plants that may be upright or mat-forming, evergreen or deciduous; most are grown for their small, intensely blue, usually tubular flowers. Tall species belong at the back of the border; small species are suitable for rock gardens or beside stepping stones.

Sowing

Indoors 6–8 weeks before planting out.
Outdoors A: early spring, when soil is cool and a light frost is still possible, or late autumn. P: after last frost. In the South, seeds may be started in early spring or late autumn.
Depth Just cover.

Germinating

Time 7–30 days.
Requirements 70°F.

Planting Seedlings Outdoors

Time After last frost.
Spacing Small species: 10"–12". Large species: 18"–30".
Light A: full sun. P: full sun to light shade.
Soil Moist, with a pH level of 6.0–7.5.

Caring for Plants

Easy. Keep well watered. Feed once in spring and again during the growing season. Plants may require staking. Cut back stems by one-half after flowering to stimulate a second bloom. Cut back to ground level in autumn Transplant with care.

Propagating

Annuals self-seed and may become a nuisance. Divide or take root cuttings of perennials in spring.

Anchusa azurea

Androsace

Rock jasmine

> Type HP often grown as HA
> Zone 3–8. 4–6: *A. lanuginosa*; 5–7: *A. carnea, A. primuloides*; 4–7: *A. sempervivoides*. Plants do not like extreme heat or drought.
> Flowering Season Spring, summer, or autumn, depending on species

Very low-growing (2"–6"), short-lived plants, often evergreen, bearing small, pointed, needlelike or woolly leaves and small, cup-shaped or flat, pink, white, or red flowers. These mountain natives are happiest in rock gardens.

Sowing

Indoors Any time.
Outdoors Early spring, when a light frost may still occur, or autumn.
Depth Surface.

Androsace lanuginosa

Germinating

Time 30–365 days.
Requirements Difficult. *Indoors:* Place seeds and moistened growing medium in a plastic bag and refrigerate for 2 weeks. Provide light and 50°–55°F thereafter. *Outdoors:* Prepare ground well, press seed lightly into the soil, then cover with a glass jar pushed firmly into the ground.

Planting Seedlings Outdoors

Time Early spring or autumn.
Spacing 6".
Light Full sun, but appreciates some afternoon shade where summers are very hot.
Soil Gritty or sandy. Add stone chips to improve drainage, if necessary. Prefers a slightly limy soil.

Caring for Plants

Can be difficult. Water during dry spells, taking care to keep water off of rosettes. Plants may require protection from heavy rains. Apply a light mulch of stone chips in winter.

Propagating

Detach rosettes from the parent plant in summer. Pot up and grow indoors, planting out rooted rosettes the following spring.

A-Annual P-Perennial B-Biennial HHA-Half-hardy annual HA-Hardy annual HB-Hardy biennial HHP-Half-hardy perennial HP-Hardy perennial HHBb-Half-hardy bulb HBb-Hardy bulb

42

Anemone

Japanese anemone, Pasque flower, Snowdrop windflower, Windflower

> TYPE HBb or HP
> ZONE 3–9: *A. canadensis,*
> *A. sylvestris;* 4–9: *A. × lesseri,*
> *A. nemorosa, A. tomentosa;* 5–9:
> *A. magellanica, A. narcissiflora;*
> 5–10: *A. apennina, A. blanda,*
> *A. caroliniana, A. hupehensis,*
> *A. × hybrida, A. ranunculoides;*
> 6–10: *A. baldensis, A. deltoidea,*
> *A. × fulgens, A. polyanthes,*
> *A. pulsatilla* [synonymous with
> *Pulsatilla vulgaris*] (will not
> tolerate high heat and humidity);
> 7–10: *A. coronaria* (will not
> tolerate high heat and humidity),
> *A. pavonina, A. vitifolia*
> FLOWERING SEASON **Any time**
> **from early spring through late**
> **autumn, depending on species**

Large, hugely diverse group of perennials ranging from 6"–4' tall and bearing blossoms of every color, bar yellow, at any time from spring through autumn. Most species are more effective when planted in large clumps, either in the border or woodland garden.

SOWING

INDOORS See "Germinating, Requirements."
OUTDOORS Seed: See "Germinating, Requirements." Corm: Most can be planted in midautumn, but tender species should be planted in spring in cold Northern areas.
DEPTH Seed: just cover. Corm: 3"–5", with the fuzzy side facing upwards.

GERMINATING

TIME 15–180 days.
REQUIREMENTS *Autumn sowing:* Sow seeds in market packs, sink in the ground against a north-facing wall, and cover with glass. Moisten soil occasionally, if necessary. Bring indoors in spring to 60°–70°F. *Spring sowing:* Sow seed in moistened medium, secure in a plastic bag, and refrigerate for 2–3 weeks. Sink containers in the ground in a shady location and cover with glass. Transplant seedlings as they appear.

PLANTING SEEDLINGS OUTDOORS

TIME Early spring, when soil is cool and a light frost is possible, or early autumn.
SPACING Small species: 5"–8". Large species: 12"–15".

Anemone japonica

LIGHT Most species prefer part shade but will tolerate full sun with plenty of moisture.
SOIL Average, with humus or well-rotted manure added and a pH level of 6.0–7.5. *A. coronaria* must have cool, moist, well-drained soil.

CARING FOR PLANTS

Easy. Water regularly, mulch in summer to keep soil cool, and leave roots undisturbed. Provide mulch where winters are severe, or lift plants after foliage dies and store in a cool, frost-free place, replanting in spring.

PROPAGATING

Take root cuttings in spring or summer; divide in spring.

Anemonella

Rue-anemone

> TYPE HP
> ZONE 4–7
> FLOWERING SEASON **Spring to**
> **early summer**

Charming, low-growing (4"), woodland perennials grown for their delicately tinted, pink or white, cup-shaped flowers and fine, fern-like foliage. Best suited to a naturalistic setting or rock garden.

SOWING

OUTDOORS Tuber: late summer to early autumn.
DEPTH Tuber: 1".

GERMINATING

REQUIREMENTS Plants are most easily propagated by division.

PLANTING SEEDLINGS OUTDOORS

SPACING 5"–7".
LIGHT Part shade.
SOIL Rich, well-drained, woodland, with plenty of organic matter added; prefers a pH level of 5.0–7.0.

CARING FOR PLANTS

Keep soil moist while plants are in bloom. Shelter plants from winds. Mulch well in autumn. Do not disturb roots except when dividing, which should be done infrequently (no more than once every 3–5 years).

PROPAGATING

Divide tubers in very early spring, or after foliage has died back in autumn.

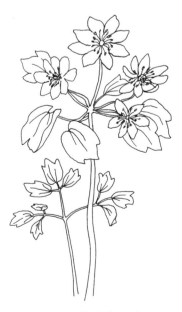

Anemonella thalictroides

A-Annual P-Perennial B-Biennial HHA-Half-hardy annual HA-Hardy annual HB-Hardy biennial HHP-Half-hardy perennial HP-Hardy perennial HHBb-Half-hardy bulb HBb-Hardy bulb

43

Anethum

(synonymous with *Peucedanum*)

Dill

> TYPE HA
> ZONE 3–10
> FLOWERING SEASON June through
> October, with successive
> sowings

2'–3' herb bearing feathery blue-green leaves and flat clusters of minute yellow flowers. Because the habit is somewhat ungainly plants are best left in the herb garden.

SOWING

INDOORS 6–8 weeks before planting out.
OUTDOORS Sow seeds every 2 weeks for continuous blooms. In zones 3–8, sow from early spring through midsummer; in zones 9–10, from late summer through midwinter.
DEPTH Surface.

GERMINATING

TIME 21–25 days.
REQUIREMENTS Start seeds in vermiculite at 60°–75°F.

PLANTING SEEDLINGS OUTDOORS

TIME As soon as seedlings develop true leaves and are large enough to handle.
SPACING 10"–12".
LIGHT Full sun.
SOIL Rich, well-drained, with a pH level of 5.5–6.5. Add compost or manure at planting time.

CARING FOR PLANTS

Feed in early spring with 5–10–5. To keep plants growing vigorously all summer, water abundantly, especially during hot, dry spells. Shelter from strong winds and do not plant near fennel as these two herbs will cross-fertilize freely with unpredictable results. Before first frost, harvest leaves and freeze, either whole or chopped. Dill can be potted up and grown indoors; give 5 hours of sunlight a day.

PROPAGATING

Self-seeds.

Anoda

> TYPE HHP usually grown as
> HHA
> ZONE A: prefers cool climates.
> P: 9–10
> FLOWERING SEASON Summer
> through first frost

Upright plants similar in appearance to *Geraniums*, with leaves that may be lobed or entire, and pretty, veined, cup-shaped flowers, usually solitary, in blue, yellow, purple, or white; 12"–30" tall. Attractive in combination with many other plants in the border.

SOWING

INDOORS 6–8 weeks before planting out.
OUTDOORS After last frost.
DEPTH ¼".

GERMINATING

TIME 14–21 days.
REQUIREMENTS 55°–60°F.

PLANTING SEEDLINGS OUTDOORS

TIME After last frost.
SPACING 12".
LIGHT Sun, with light afternoon shade where summers are hot.
SOIL Ordinary, well-drained.

CARING FOR PLANTS

Easy. Deadhead regularly and water only during very dry spells. Plants may require staking. Flowering is considerably inhibited by wet summer weather. A heavy autumn mulch may bring plants through the winter north of zone 9.

PROPAGATING

Seed only.

Anomatheca

See *Lapeirousia*

Anredera

See *Boussingaultia*

A-Annual P-Perennial B-Biennial HHA-Half-hardy annual HA-Hardy annual HB-Hardy biennial HHP-Half-hardy perennial HP-Hardy perennial HHBb-Half-hardy bulb HBb-Hardy bulb

Antennaria

Cat's-ears, Ladies-tobacco, Pussy-toes

> **TYPE** HP
> **ZONE** 3–8
> **FLOWERING SEASON** Spring through early summer

Mat-forming, evergreen or semi-evergreen perennials native to North and South America; used in rock gardens, around paving stones, or as ground cover. Leaves are small and woolly, sometimes grey-green; tubular flowers, usually borne in clusters, may be white, pink, or red; plants are usually under 6".

SOWING

INDOORS Late winter to early spring.
OUTDOORS Early spring, when soil is cool and a light frost is still possible, or autumn.
DEPTH Just cover.

GERMINATING

TIME 30–60 days.
REQUIREMENTS 55°–60°F.

PLANTING SEEDLINGS OUTDOORS

TIME Autumn or spring.
SPACING 12".
LIGHT Full sun.
SOIL Poor, somewhat dry.

CARING FOR PLANTS

Easy. Use judiciously as plants may become invasive. Deadhead regularly.

PROPAGATING

Divide in late summer or autumn; take cuttings in summer.

Anthemis

Chamomile, Dog fennel, Golden marguerite

> **TYPE** HP
> **ZONE** 4–9. All species object to high heat and humidity; **A. marschalliana is most tolerant of high temperatures.**
> **FLOWERING SEASON** Summer to autumn

Genus of upright or mounding perennials, 6"–36" tall, with white or yellow, daisylike flowers; foliage may be green or silvery, is sometimes scented and sometimes evergreen. Use in borders, rock gardens, or drystone walls.

SOWING

INDOORS 8–10 weeks before planting out.
OUTDOORS Early spring or early autumn. *A. nobilis* should be started indoors only.
DEPTH Surface.

GERMINATING

TIME 8–14 days.
REQUIREMENTS Light and 70°F.

PLANTING SEEDLINGS OUTDOORS

TIME Early spring, when soil is cool and a light frost is still possible, or early autumn.
SPACING Small species: 6". Large species: 12"–24".
LIGHT Prefers full sun, but will tolerate part shade.
SOIL Average to poor, well-drained, and slightly limy. Very tolerant of dry soil.

CARING FOR PLANTS

Easy. Susceptible to mildew and should be sited in an open location where air can circulate freely. Plants may require staking where heavy rain and wind are frequent. Divide every 3–4 years if plants show signs of deteriorating.

PROPAGATING

Divide in spring, or take cuttings in autumn. Some species will self-seed.

Anthemis tinctoria

A-Annual P-Perennial B-Biennial HHA-Half-hardy annual HA-Hardy annual HB-Hardy biennial HHP-Half-hardy perennial HP-Hardy perennial HHBb-Half-hardy bulb HBb-Hardy bulb

45

Anthericum

St. Bernard's lily, Spider plant

> TYPE HP
> ZONE 3–9. Does not like hot, dry
>   weather.
> FLOWERING SEASON Spring

Airy, upright perennials bearing grassy
leaves and racemes of delicate, white, trumpet-shaped flowers on 18"–36" stems. For
borders and naturalistic gardens.

SOWING

INDOORS 8–10 weeks before planting out.
OUTDOORS Early spring, when soil is cool
  and a light frost is still possible, or early
  autumn.
DEPTH ⅛".

GERMINATING

TIME 30–90 days.
REQUIREMENTS Soak seeds in warm water
  for 12 hours; provide 50°F thereafter.

PLANTING SEEDLINGS OUTDOORS

TIME Spring or autumn.
SPACING 6"–8".
LIGHT Part shade.
SOIL Moist, with plenty of organic matter
  added.

CARING FOR PLANTS

Easy. Plants grown from seed will bloom in
2–3 years. Feed in spring, water regularly
in summer, and mulch to keep soil cool and
moist. Where summers are hot, cut plants
back hard after blooming.

PROPAGATING

Divide in autumn; in zones 7 and 8, divide
after flowering in spring.

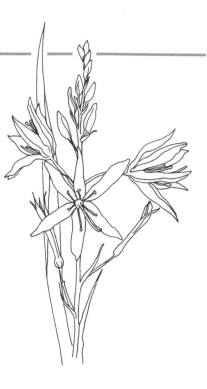

Anthericum liliago

Anthriscus

**Beaked parsley, Chervil,
French parsley**

> TYPE HA
> ZONE 3–10. Does not perform
>   well in high heat and humidity.
> FLOWERING SEASON May to June

Upright herb with flat, green, indented
leaves similar to parsley; flat clusters of tiny
white flowers appear atop sturdy 18" stems.
Suitable only for the herb garden.

SOWING

INDOORS 6–8 weeks before planting out, in
  peat pots.
OUTDOORS Every 3–4 weeks from early
  spring through late autumn. Where summers are very hot, sow from late summer
  through autumn only.
DEPTH Surface.

GERMINATING

TIME 14 days.
REQUIREMENTS Light and 50°–60°F.

PLANTING SEEDLINGS OUTDOORS

TIME After last frost.
SPACING 9"–12".
LIGHT Part shade.
SOIL Light, moist, with a pH level of 6.0–7.0.

CARING FOR PLANTS

Water regularly during dry spells. Where
summers are very hot, cut plants back hard
midseason. Mulch lightly in autumn to protect seeds. Leaves are tastiest early in the
season. Harvest for cooking *before* flowers
open, freezing any that are not used immediately. Carefully dig and pot up plants to
grow indoors over winter, giving 4–5 hours
of sunlight and a cool location. Chervil does
not transplant well.

PROPAGATING

Self-seeds.

A-Annual P-Perennial B-Biennial HHA-Half-hardy annual HA-Hardy annual HB-Hardy biennial HHP-Half-hardy perennial HP-Hardy perennial HHBb-Half-hardy bulb HBb-Hardy bulb

46

Anthyllis

Jupiter's beard, Kidney vetch, Lady's finger

> TYPE HP
> ZONE 3–8
> FLOWERING SEASON Late spring

Very low, spreading perennials with unusual, erect, fernlike leaves and covered with masses of attractively contrasting, pink or red, cloverlike flowers. Use in rock gardens, wall plantings, between pavers, or edging a well-drained border.

SOWING

INDOORS Late winter to early summer. A. *tetraphylla* is best started *in situ*.
OUTDOORS Autumn.
DEPTH ⅛".

GERMINATING

TIME 30–60 days.
REQUIREMENTS Difficult. Soak seeds in warm water overnight; sow seeds and leave undisturbed at 50°F.

PLANTING SEEDLINGS OUTDOORS

TIME Spring or autumn.
SPACING 12"–24".
LIGHT Full sun to part shade.
SOIL Poor, dry, with good drainage and a pH level of 5.0–6.0.

CARING FOR PLANTS

Easy once established, but this may take some time.

PROPAGATING

Take cuttings in summer.

Anthyllis vulneraria

Antirrhinum

Snapdragon

> TYPE HHP usually treated as HHA
> ZONE A: 1–10; P: 8–10. *Antirrhinums* must have a cool spring, and will not flourish where temperatures are high for long periods.
> FLOWERING SEASON Late spring through late autumn

Actually a subshrub though usually grown as an annual, these obliging plants are the backbone of many public gardens, providing months of color ranging from pale pastels to vibrant reds and oranges. Dwarf plants of 6" may be rather floppy; taller 2' species are sturdier. Natives of southern Europe.

SOWING

INDOORS 8–10 weeks before planting out.
OUTDOORS Not recommended, except in cold frames, where seeds may be sown in late summer to early autumn.
DEPTH Surface.

Antirrhinum majus

GERMINATING

TIME 10–21 days.
REQUIREMENTS Light and 55°F. Sow in vermiculite to avoid damping-off and water only from below.

PLANTING SEEDLINGS OUTDOORS

TIME After last frost in the North; autumn in zones 8–10.
SPACING Dwarf species: 6". Tall species: 12".
LIGHT Full sun or very light shade.
SOIL Tolerant of all but very heavy soils; prefers a rich, neutral soil.

CARING FOR PLANTS

Easy. Pinch back young plants after 4–6 leaves have appeared to encourage a bushy habit. Feed lightly twice before first flowers appear. Stake tall species when young, removing stakes when plants fill out. Deadhead often. If blooms become scarce, cut plants back drastically, feed and water generously. Susceptible to fungal diseases — be sure to buy resistant plants or seeds.

PROPAGATING

Seed only.

A-Annual P-Perennial B-Biennial HHA-Half-hardy annual HA-Hardy annual HB-Hardy biennial HHP-Half-hardy perennial HP-Hardy perennial HHBb-Half-hardy bulb HBb-Hardy bulb

Aquilegia

Columbine

TYPE HP
ZONE 3–9
FLOWERING SEASON Midspring to
early summer

Lovely European natives with dainty, intricate flowers, often of more than one color, held high on thin stalks above delicate, toothed leaves; 4"–36" tall. Grow in any shaded location where their subtle beauty will not be overlooked; essential to any woodland planting.

SOWING

INDOORS See "Germinating, Requirements."
OUTDOORS See "Germinating, Requirements."
DEPTH Surface.

GERMINATING

TIME 30–90 days.
REQUIREMENTS *Spring sowing:* Sow seeds in flats of moistened medium, place flats in plastic bags, and refrigerate. After 2–3 weeks, remove and sink flats in the ground in a shady location, covering with glass. Transplant seedlings as they appear. *Summer sowing:* Sow seeds in flats, sink flats in the ground against a north-facing wall, and cover with glass. Moisten soil occasionally, if necessary. Leave outdoors from summer to spring. Bring indoors in spring to a light location at 65°–75°F.

PLANTING SEEDLINGS OUTDOORS

TIME After last frost.
SPACING Small species: 6"–12". Large species: 15"–20".
LIGHT Part shade is usually prefered, but *Aquilegias* will tolerate full sun where summers are very mild.
SOIL Humus-rich, moist but well-drained, with a pH level of 5.5–7.0.

CARING FOR PLANTS

Aquilegia seedlings are very delicate; keep out of strong sunlight and water gently and often. Deadhead regularly to encourage continuous blooming and prolong the plant's life. Tall species may require support. If leaf miner is present, remove affected

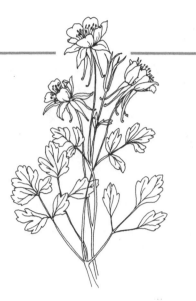

Aquilegia chrysantha

leaves immediately. Short-lived — replant every 3–4 years. Provide winter mulch in northern zones.

PROPAGATING

Often self-seeds. Different species grown close together may result in hybridized offspring, which may be fun — or annoying. You can divide plants in spring, although this does not produce strong specimens.

Arabis

Rockcress, Wall cress

TYPE HP
ZONE 3–7: A. *alpina;* 3–9: A.
procurrens; 4–9: A. x *arendsii,*
A. *caucasica;* 6–8: A.
aubretoides, A. *blepharophylla;*
6–10: A. *ferdinandi-coburgi.*
Hot, humid summers may cause
plants to rot.
FLOWERING SEASON Early spring

Diminutive, dainty, mat-forming perennials useful in rock gardens, wall plantings, or edging. Clusters of very small, scented white flowers are borne above evergreen leaves in early spring.

SOWING

INDOORS 6–8 weeks before planting out, in peat pots.
OUTDOORS Early spring, when soil is cool and a light frost is still possible, or late autumn.
DEPTH Surface.

GERMINATING

TIME 14–25 days.
REQUIREMENTS Light and 70°F.

PLANTING SEEDLINGS OUTDOORS

TIME After last spring frost, or early autumn.
SPACING Small species: 5"–9". Tall species: 12".
LIGHT Most species require full sun, but some will take light shade.
SOIL Average, well-drained, with a pH level of 5.5–7.0; tolerant of poor soil.

Arabis albida

CARING FOR PLANTS

Easy. Cut plants back after blooming to maintain a neat habit and limit self-seeding. Do not disturb roots.

PROPAGATING

Divide in spring in zones 3–6, or in autumn south of zone 6. Take stem cuttings in late summer. Self-seeds freely.

A-Annual P-Perennial B-Biennial HHA-Half-hardy annual HA-Hardy annual HB-Hardy biennial HHP-Half-hardy perennial HP-Hardy perennial HHBb-Half-hardy bulb HBb-Hardy bulb

Arctostaphylos

Bearberry, Bear's grape, Hog cranberry, Kinnikinick, Manzanita, Mealberry, Mountain box, Sandberry

> TYPE HP
> ZONE 3–7
> FLOWERING SEASON June

Prostrate shrub grown for its neat, dark evergreen foliage, abundance of small pink or white flowers, and cheerful, bright red fruit. Use as a ground cover for small spaces, or in combination with large-leaved plants such as *Hostas*. Native to Europe and Asia as well as North America.

SOWING

INDOORS Pre-chilled seeds in late winter to midsummer, in peat pots.
OUTDOORS Autumn.
DEPTH Surface.

GERMINATING

TIME 60–90 days.
REQUIREMENTS Soak seeds overnight, then place in a plastic bag with moist sand, and refrigerate for 2 months. Provide light and 55°–65°F thereafter.

PLANTING SEEDLINGS OUTDOORS

TIME Spring or autumn.
SPACING 12"–24".
LIGHT Sun or part shade.
SOIL Prefers soil that is sandy, acid (pH level of 4.5–5.5), and infertile, but will tolerate most soils.

CARING FOR PLANTS

Difficult. Water only during extreme drought and do not feed. Plants can be sheared to keep neat and compact. Mulch with pine needles and leave plants undisturbed.

PROPAGATING

Take cuttings in autumn.

Arctostaphylos uva-ursi

Arctotis

African daisy

> TYPE HHP usually grown as HHA
> ZONE A: 3–10; P: 9–10. Performs most successfully in coastal regions and where summer nights are cool. Tolerant of heat and drought, but does not like *humid* heat.
> FLOWERING SEASON Summer through late autumn

Short-lived though long-blooming perennials grown for their abundant, daisylike flowers which range in color from a cool, sophisticated silver to a hot and gaudy orange. Plant tall species (up to 48") at the back of the border, shorter species (12") are ideal for rock gardens. Native to South Africa.

SOWING

INDOORS 6–8 weeks before planting out.
OUTDOORS Early spring, when soil is cool and a light frost is still possible, or late autumn.
DEPTH Just cover seeds.

GERMINATING

TIME 7–35 days.
REQUIREMENTS Easy. 60°–70°F.

PLANTING SEEDLINGS OUTDOORS

TIME After last frost, when temperature remains above 40°F; in autumn where winters are very mild.
SPACING 9"–12".
LIGHT Full sun.
SOIL Prefers sandy, well-drained soil with a pH level of 6.0–7.0, but will tolerate most soils.

CARING FOR PLANTS

Easy. Pinch out young plants to stimulate bushy growth. Water regularly in early spring, but keep fairly dry during summer months. Deadhead regularly. Blooming rapidly diminishes after the first year.

PROPAGATING

Take cuttings. *Arctotis* will self-seed in the South.

A-Annual P-Perennial B-Biennial HHA-Half-hardy annual HA-Hardy annual HB-Hardy biennial HHP-Half-hardy perennial HP-Hardy perennial HHBb-Half-hardy bulb HBb-Hardy bulb

49

Arenaria

Irish moss, Sandwort, Scotch moss

> TYPE HP
> ZONE 3–8: *A. montana*; 4–6:
> *A. tetraquetra*; 4–7: *A. grandiflora*; 5–7: *A. ledebouriana*;
> 6–7: *A. balearica*. Does not like humid summers.
> FLOWERING SEASON Late spring to early summer

Modest, low-growing perennials, under 12", with masses of white or pink flowers hovering above evergreen cushions. Used most often in rock gardens, wall plantings, or between paving stones.

SOWING

INDOORS 6–8 weeks before last frost.
OUTDOORS Early spring, when soil is cool and a light frost is still possible, or late autumn.
DEPTH Surface.

GERMINATING

TIME 8–30 days.
REQUIREMENTS 55°–65°F.

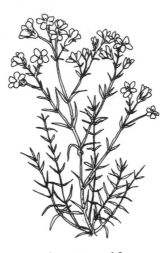

Arenaria grandiflora

PLANTING SEEDLINGS OUTDOORS

TIME After last frost.
SPACING 3"–5".
LIGHT Full sun; will tolerate part shade where summers are very hot.
SOIL Well-drained, gritty or sandy, with a pH level of 6.0–8.0.

CARING FOR PLANTS

Easy. Plants grown in full sun will require frequent watering; give an occasional light feeding.

PROPAGATING

Most successful by seed, but plants may also be increased by taking cuttings in summer, or dividing in early spring.

Argemone

Mexican poppy, Prickly poppy

> TYPE P grown as HA
> ZONE 6–10. Prefers the warm, dry climate of the Southwest.
> FLOWERING SEASON Early summer to midsummer

Upright, short-lived perennials, rather coarse in appearance, grown for their continuous stock of fragrant, poppylike flowers which are usually white or yellow; dangerous looking, spiky foliage. Use in the midsection of the border.

SOWING

INDOORS Not often successful; if attempted, start in peat pots 6 weeks before planting out.
OUTDOORS After last frost.
DEPTH ⅛".

GERMINATING

TIME 14 days.
REQUIREMENTS 55°–60°F.

PLANTING SEEDLINGS OUTDOORS

TIME After last frost.
SPACING Small species: 9"–12". Large species: 24"–36".
LIGHT Full sun.
SOIL Prefers slightly limy soil that is poor and sandy; rich soil produces lush foliage but few flowers. Tolerates dry soil.

CARING FOR PLANTS

Easy. Deadhead regularly to prolong flowering. Stems are easily damaged and should not be tied to supports. Difficult to transplant.

PROPAGATING

Self-seeds.

A-Annual P-Perennial B-Biennial HHA-Half-hardy annual HA-Hardy annual HB-Hardy biennial HHP-Half-hardy perennial HP-Hardy perennial HHBb-Half-hardy bulb HBb-Hardy bulb

50

Arisaema

Dragonroot, Indian turnip, Jack-in-the-pulpit

> TYPE HP
> ZONE 3–8: *A. speciosum*,
>   *A. triphyllum*;
>   4–9: *A. dracontium*;
>   5–9: *A. sikokianum*;
>   7–9: *A. candidissimum*
> FLOWERING SEASON Early summer

Curious-looking woodland plants grown for their mysterious, hooded flowers, which are erect and tubular, in shades of green and palest cream with dark contrasting stripes; 12"–36". Native to woodlands across the globe.

SOWING

INDOORS Any time.
OUTDOORS Late summer or early autumn.
DEPTH Just cover.

Arisaema stewardsonii

GERMINATING

TIME 30–180 days.
REQUIREMENTS Difficult. Place seeds in a plastic bag with moistened growing medium and refrigerate for 6 weeks. Provide 55°–60°F thereafter.

PLANTING SEEDLINGS OUTDOORS

TIME Spring or autumn.
SPACING 8"–10".
LIGHT Part shade.
SOIL Moist, humus-rich, nearly neutral pH.

CARING FOR PLANTS

Easy, if conditions are favorable. *Arisaemas* require plenty of moisture between spring and midautumn, but otherwise prefer to be on the dry side. Apply a mulch of compost in autumn. Attractive to slugs.

PROPAGATING

Divide in autumn south of zone 6, in spring north of zone 7.

Armeria

Sea pink, Thrift

> TYPE HP
> ZONE 3–8: *A. maritima*;
>   4–7: *A. caespitosa*;
>   6–10: *A. plantaginea*,
>   *A. pseudarmeria*
> FLOWERING SEASON Spring
>   through early summer

Dwarf, evergreen perennials and subshrubs native to temperate seaside regions and Alpine meadows. Small globes of pink or white flowers are borne above mounds or rosettes. Use in rock gardens or massed at the front of the border; remarkably tolerant of seaside conditions.

SOWING

INDOORS 8–10 weeks before planting out.
OUTDOORS Early spring or early autumn.
DEPTH Just cover.

GERMINATING

TIME 10–21 days.
REQUIREMENTS Easy. Soak seeds for 6–8 hours in warm water before sowing. Provide darkness and 60°–70°F thereafter.

PLANTING SEEDLINGS OUTDOORS

TIME Early spring, when soil is cool and a light frost is still possible, or early autumn.
SPACING Small species: 6". Large species: 12".
LIGHT Full sun.
SOIL Ordinary, well-drained, fairly sandy, not too rich, with a pH level of 5.5–7.5.

CARING FOR PLANTS

Easy. Deadhead after flowering, water during dry spells, and mulch lightly in winter with straw.

PROPAGATING

Divide or take cuttings in spring.

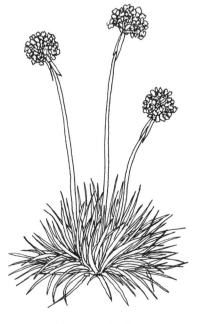

Armeria vulgaris

Arnica

Mountain snuff, Mountain tobacco

> TYPE HP
> ZONE 6–9
> FLOWERING SEASON Summer

Perennials grown for their large, daisylike, orange or yellow flowers with prominent eyes; leaves are narrow, aromatic, sometimes grey. Use low, cushion-forming species at the front of the border or in rock gardens; larger species are useful for cutting.

SOWING

INDOORS Usually sown outdoors, but may be started indoors at any time in individual pots; grow for 1 season before moving outdoors.
OUTDOORS As soon as fresh seed is available, usually late summer.
DEPTH Just cover.

GERMINATING

TIME 25–30 days.
REQUIREMENTS Easy. 55°F.

PLANTING SEEDLINGS OUTDOORS

TIME After last frost.
SPACING 12"–15".
LIGHT Full sun in the North, but prefers shade from afternoon sun where summers are hot.
SOIL Moist, well-drained, acid (pH level of 5.0–6.5), and not too high in nitrogen.

CARING FOR PLANTS

Easy. Do not use high-nitrogen fertilizer, which produces leggy, ungainly plants.

PROPAGATING

Divide in spring or early autumn, or take cuttings in summer.

Artemisia

Estragon, Ghostplant, Mugwort, Southernwood, Summer fir, Tarragon, Wormwood

> TYPE HA, HP, or HHP
> ZONE A: 2–10; P: 4–10:
>   A. absinthium, A. lactiflora,
>   A. schmidtiana, A. stelleriana;
>   5–10: A. dracunculus,
>   A. ludoviciana, A. pontica,
>   A. splendens;
>   6–10: A. abrotanum;
>   8–10: A. pycnocephala;
>   9–10: A. arborescens
> FLOWERING SEASON Late summer

A large and diverse genus of perennials and subshrubs grown mainly for their foliage, which may be grey or green and is often feathery and strongly scented. Large species make excellent specimen plantings, or position one in the border as a foil for plants of contrasting color or texture. 1'–6' tall. Native to Asia, Europe, and North America.

SOWING

INDOORS 10–12 weeks before planting out.
OUTDOORS A: spring or autumn. P: autumn.
DEPTH A: ⅛". P: surface.

GERMINATING

TIME 14–60 days.
REQUIREMENTS 55°–65°F. Perennial seeds require light. *Outdoor sowing:* Sow seeds in flats, sink in the ground against a north-facing wall, and cover with glass. Moisten soil occasionally, if necessary. Remove glass when seeds begin to germinate.

Artemisia 'Silver Mound'

PLANTING SEEDLINGS OUTDOORS

TIME After last frost.
SPACING Small species: 12". Large species: 12"–24".
LIGHT Sun or light shade.
SOIL Most species will be happy in average, well-drained soil that is not too rich and prefer a pH level of 5.5–7.0.

CARING FOR PLANTS

Easy. Cut plants back to ground level in autumn or spring and pinch back new growth to maintain a neat habit. Mulch in winter. Tarragon (*A. dracunculus*) does not grow true from seed and should be bought as a young plant. Grow in very well-drained soil. Apply a 5–10–5 fertilizer in early spring and mulch in winter after the ground has frozen. Divide every 3–4 years in the spring. Harvest leaves at any time for culinary use. To dry, hang in bunches in a dark place, then crush the dried leaves, and store in an airtight container. To grow tarragon indoors, pot up plants in midsummer and give 5 hours sunlight a day.

PROPAGATING

Divide in spring in the North, in autumn south of zone 6; take cuttings in spring.

A-Annual P-Perennial B-Biennial HHA-Half-hardy annual HA-Hardy annual HB-Hardy biennial HHP-Half-hardy perennial HP-Hardy perennial HHBb-Half-hardy bulb HBb-Hardy bulb

Arum

Cuckoopint, Lords-and-ladies

> TYPE HHP or HP
> ZONE 5–8. 7–9: *A. creticum*
>   Does not like humid heat.
> FLOWERING SEASON Early spring
>   to midspring

Upright perennials grown for their distinctive, arrow-shaped leaves and unusual, pitcherlike flowers, which range in appearance from elegant to other-worldly. Use near streams or in other naturalistic settings.

SOWING

INDOORS 10–12 weeks before planting out.
OUTDOORS Autumn.
DEPTH Seed: 1/8". Tuber: 3".

GERMINATING

TIME 30–180 days.
REQUIREMENTS Easy. 55°–65°F.

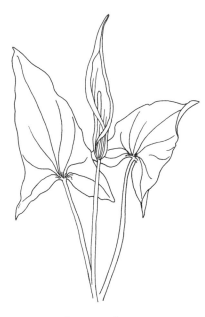

Arum maculatum

PLANTING SEEDLINGS OUTDOORS

TIME Spring or autumn.
SPACING Compact species: 6"–12". Larger species: 12"–18".
LIGHT Sun or part shade. Provide shade from afternoon sun where summers are hot.
SOIL Cool, moist, humus-rich soil that does not remain wet in winter.

CARING FOR PLANTS

Keep soil moist, especially during the growing season. Mulch to keep soil cool and moist and feed ocasionally with a balanced fertilizer. Leaves are attractive to slugs. *Arum* dies back after flowering — mark locations so that plants will not be inadvertently disturbed.

PROPAGATING

Divide tubers in autumn. May self-seed.

Aruncus

Goat's beard, Spiraea

> TYPE HP
> ZONE 3–8
> FLOWERING SEASON Early summer

Bushy perennials grown for their feathery plumes of white flowers borne on long, gracefully arching stalks resembling a shower of tiny white fireworks. Large species, 3'–6' tall, belong at the back of the border; all are useful in naturalistic plantings, wildflower gardens or near streams. Native to Central Europe.

SOWING

INDOORS Late winter to spring.
OUTDOORS After last frost, when soil has warmed.
DEPTH Surface.

GERMINATING

TIME 30–90 days.
REQUIREMENTS 55°–65°F.

PLANTING SEEDLINGS OUTDOORS

TIME Spring or autumn.
SPACING 2'–5'.
LIGHT Part shade; can be grown in full sun where the summer sun is not intensely hot.
SOIL Moist and rich.

CARING FOR PLANTS

Easy. Feed in spring and keep soil moist throughout the growing season. Cut stems to ground level in autumn. Plants will not flower in poor, dry soil.

PROPAGATING

Divide in spring, in autumn in zones 7–8. Allow plants to become well established before dividing.

Aruncus sylvester

A-Annual P-Perennial B-Biennial HHA-Half-hardy annual HA-Hardy annual HB-Hardy biennial HHP-Half-hardy perennial HP-Hardy perennial HHBb-Half-hardy bulb HBb-Hardy bulb

Asarina

(synonymous with *Maurandya*)

Chickabiddy

> TYPE HHP usually treated as
> HHA
> ZONE A: 3–8; P: 9–10. Prefers
> warm temperatures.
> FLOWERING SEASON Late spring
> through late autumn, depending
> on species

Unusual climbers grown for their attractive, rather old-fashioned, trumpet-shaped flowers in varying shades of pink. Heart-shaped leaves are often scented.

Asarina procumbens

SOWING

INDOORS 10–12 weeks before planting out, in peat pots.
OUTDOORS Late winter through early spring.
DEPTH Surface.

GERMINATING

TIME 10–21 days.
REQUIREMENTS 60°–75°F.

PLANTING SEEDLINGS OUTDOORS

TIME Early spring, when temperatures remain above 40°F.
SPACING 12".
LIGHT Sun.
SOIL Moist, fertile, well-drained, neutral or slightly acid.

CARING FOR PLANTS

Easy. Water frequently and feed occasionally. Climbers require a trellis or other support.

PROPAGATING

Take cuttings in summer.

Asarum

Wild ginger

> TYPE HP
> ZONE 2–9: *A. canadense*;
> 4–8: *A. europaeum*;
> 5–9: *A. hartwegii, A. super-*
> *bum*; 6–9: *A. arifolium,*
> *A. caudatum, A. virginicum*;
> 7–9: *A. shuttleworthii*
> FLOWERING SEASON Early spring,
> but flowers sometimes persist
> for several months

Genus of diminutive, low-growing perennials, some of which are evergreen. Grown for their attractive, deep green or variegated heart-shaped leaves; flowers are inconspicuous. Use as a ground cover for small spaces or in woodland plantings.

SOWING

INDOORS As soon as ripe seed is available.
OUTDOORS Autumn, as soon as seed is ripe.
DEPTH Just cover.

GERMINATING

TIME 7–18 days.
REQUIREMENTS Easy. Place seeds in a plastic bag together with moist growing medium and refrigerate for 3 weeks. Provide 60°–65°F after chilling.

PLANTING SEEDLINGS OUTDOORS

TIME After last frost.
SPACING 12–16 plants per square yard.
LIGHT Light to full shade.
SOIL Slightly moist, humus-rich, nearly neutral.

CARING FOR PLANTS

Easy. Water during dry spells. Feed once in spring, then top-dress with peat moss or compost in autumn. Slugs and snails love to feed on these leafy plants.

PROPAGATING

Divide creeping rootstock in spring, late autumn south of zone 6; take cuttings in summer. May self-seed.

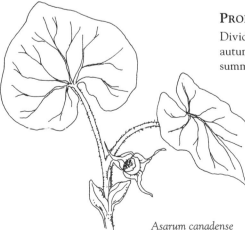

Asarum canadense

A-Annual P-Perennial B-Biennial HHA-Half-hardy annual HA-Hardy annual HB-Hardy biennial HHP-Half-hardy perennial HP-Hardy perennial HHBb-Half-hardy bulb HBb-Hardy bulb

Asclepias

**Butterfly weed, Milkweed,
Orange milkweed, Pleurisy root**

TYPE HP or HHP
ZONE 3–9: *A. incarnata,*
   A. speciosa; 3–10: *A. tuberosa;*
   4–9: *A. hallii, A. syriaca;*
   8–10: *A. curassavica.*
   Prefers warm summers.
FLOWERING SEASON Summer

Large genus of rather coarse, resilient perennials and subshrubs. 12"–6' tall and bearing clusters of sturdy blooms, often in hot colors; many are attractive to butterflies. Use restrainedly in the border, more profligately in wildflower plantings.

SOWING

INDOORS Remove pre-chilled seeds from refrigerator 8–10 weeks before planting.

OUTDOORS Early spring or early autumn.
DEPTH Just cover.

GERMINATING

TIME 30–90 days.
REQUIREMENTS *Indoor sowing:* Sow seeds in peat pots, secure in plastic bags, and refrigerate for 21 days. Provide light and 50°–75°F thereafter.

PLANTING SEEDLINGS OUTDOORS

TIME Early spring, when soil is cool and light frost is still possible, or early autumn.
SPACING 12"–24".
LIGHT Full sun to light shade.
SOIL Prefers average, sandy soil; most species will tolerate dry soil but not heavy clay or chalky conditions.

CARING FOR PLANTS

Easy. Pinch back young plants when 4"–6" tall. Do not move or disturb roots.

Asclepias tuberosa

PROPAGATING

Carefully divide or take root cuttings in spring. Plants are often lost during division due to damage to the delicate taproot.

Asperula

Sweet woodruff, Woodruff

TYPE HA or HP
ZONE A: prefers warm climates;
   P: 3–9: *A. odorata* (synonymous
   with *Galium odoratum*);
   4–8: *A. hirta;* 6–8: *A. lilaciflora;* 7–9: *A. tinctoria*
FLOWERING SEASON A: midsummer; P: late spring

Modest but charming spreading plants bearing tiny white or pink flowers which may be fragrant. A delightful ground cover or rock garden plant.

SOWING

INDOORS Remove pre-chilled seeds from refrigerator 8–10 weeks before planting out.
OUTDOORS A: spring. P: spring through early summer.
DEPTH Surface.

GERMINATING

TIME 21–42 days.
REQUIREMENTS Easy, although seed must be fresh for guaranteed success. *Indoor sowing:* Sow seeds in containers, secure in a plastic bag, and refrigerate for 2 weeks. Provide light and 50°F thereafter.

Asperula odorata

PLANTING SEEDLINGS OUTDOORS

TIME After last frost.
SPACING Small species: 3"–4". Large species: 6"–9".
LIGHT Flowers most profusely in full sun, but will perform quite well in light shade if the soil is kept moist.
SOIL Moist, humus-rich, well-drained, with a pH level of 4.5–5.5. Appreciates the addition of leaf mold.

CARING FOR PLANTS

Easy. Dislikes a wet crown — locate away from dripping overhangs. Leaves can be harvested before flowering and dried for culinary use. Pot up plants in summer to grow indoors, giving at least 5 hours sunlight.

PROPAGATING

Propagate annuals by seed only. Divide perennials in spring or autumn, or take stem cuttings; may self-seed.

A-Annual P-Perennial B-Biennial HHA-Half-hardy annual HA-Hardy annual HB-Hardy biennial HHP-Half-hardy perennial HP-Hardy perennial HHBb-Half-hardy bulb HBb-Hardy bulb

55

Asphodeline

Asphodel, Jacob's rod, King's spear

TYPE HP
ZONE 6–8
FLOWERING SEASON Summer

Genus of clump-forming perennials with sturdy, upright 1'–3' stems bearing terminal clusters of fragrant, bright yellow, star-shaped flowers. Mass for best effect.

SOWING

INDOORS Late winter to early spring.
OUTDOORS Seed: spring through summer. Root: spring or autumn.
DEPTH Seed: just cover. Root: 3"–4".

GERMINATING

TIME 30 days.
REQUIREMENTS 70°–75°F.

PLANTING SEEDLINGS OUTDOORS

TIME After last spring frost or in early autumn.
SPACING Small species: 6"–12". Large species: 15"–18".
LIGHT Sun or part shade, but will flower more freely in sun.
SOIL Ordinary, well-drained, with a pH level of 6.0–8.0.

CARING FOR PLANTS

Easy. Remove flowering stems after last spring frost. Feed once in spring and water during very dry spells. Provide a winter mulch in the North.

PROPAGATING

Divide in early autumn.

Aster

Michaelmas daisy

TYPE HP
ZONE 2–8: A. puniceus,
 A. tataricus;
 3–9: A. divaricatus,
 A. ericoides, A. linariifolius,
 A. linosyris, A. umbellatus;
 4–8: A. x frikartii, A. laevis,
 A. lateriflorus, A. praealtus,
 A. spectabilis, A. tongolensis;
 4–9: A. x alpellus, A. alpinus,
 A. amellus, A. novae-angliae,
 A. novi-belgii;
 5–9: A. thomsonii
FLOWERING SEASON Spring
 through late autumn

Very large group of perennial plants varying in size from 6" to over 4', grown for their daisylike flowers of white or shades of blue, purple, or pink. Indispensable late-bloomer in the border; small species are useful for edging or rock gardens.

Aster novae-angliae

SOWING

INDOORS Remove pre-chilled seeds from refrigerator 6–8 weeks before planting out.
OUTDOORS Early spring, when soil is cool and a light frost is still possible, or late autumn.
DEPTH Just cover.

GERMINATING

TIME 14–36 days.
REQUIREMENTS Easy. *Indoor sowing:* Sow seeds in flats, secure in plastic bags, and refrigerate for 2 weeks. Provide 70°–75°F thereafter.

PLANTING SEEDLINGS OUTDOORS

TIME After last frost.
SPACING Small species: 9"–12". Tall species: 24".
LIGHT Full sun.
SOIL Light, average, with humus added and a pH level of 5.5–7.5. Performs best where soil is neither dry in the summer nor wet in the winter.

CARING FOR PLANTS

Easy. Pinch back young plants to stimulate bushy growth. Encourage larger blooms by pruning young shoots in spring, leaving 6–8 shoots per plant to develop. Feed lightly twice during the summer. Tall species may require staking. Divide every 3 years to maintain vigor. Minimize the risk of powdery mildew by siting in full sun where air circulation is good; keep water off leaves. Hybrids often are more prone to mildew than species.

PROPAGATING

Divide in spring. Species will self-sow, but resulting plants will not have predictable characteristics.

A-Annual P-Perennial B-Biennial HHA-Half-hardy annual HA-Hardy annual HB-Hardy biennial HHP-Half-hardy perennial HP-Hardy perennial HHBb-Half-hardy bulb HBb-Hardy bulb

Astilbe

False goatsbeard, False spiraea, Garden spiraea

> **TYPE** HP
> **ZONE** 4–8: *A. x ardensii,*
>   *A. chinensis, A. simplicifolia,*
>   *A. chinensis* var. *taquetii,*
>   *A. thunbergii;*
>   5–8: *A. biternata;*
>   6–8: *A. rivularis.* Plants lose
>   their vigor in persistently hot
>   weather.
> **FLOWERING SEASON** Late spring to
>   early summer

Neat, airy perennials, 6"–4' tall, with deeply-cut leaves and attractive plume-like flowers in soft pinks and white, or new intense pinks, salmons, and corals. Mass in a cool or shady border; of unrivaled beauty in a woodland planting.

SOWING

INDOORS 6–8 weeks before planting out.
OUTDOORS Early spring, when soil is cool and a light frost is still possible, or late autumn.
DEPTH Surface.

GERMINATING

TIME 25–60 days.
REQUIREMENTS Diffused light and 65°F. Seedlings are very susceptible to damping-off; sow in vermiculite and water only from below.

PLANTING SEEDLINGS OUTDOORS

TIME After last frost.
SPACING Small species: 12". Large species: 20"–30".
LIGHT Shade, or sun where summers are not hot.
SOIL Moist, humus-rich, well-drained, with a pH level of 5.5–7.0. *A. chinensis* var. *tacquetii* grows happily in dry soil.

CARING FOR PLANTS

Easy. Water during dry spells and feed once during the summer. Where summers are very hot, cut plants back hard after blooming. Divide every 3 years.

PROPAGATING

Divide in spring where summers are cool, autumn in the South.

Astilbe astilboides

Astrantia

Masterwort

> **TYPE** HP
> **ZONE** 3–8. Will not tolerate
>   excessive heat and humidity.
> **FLOWERING SEASON** Summer
>   through autumn

Unusual, long-blooming perennials bearing pink or white clover-like blooms surrounded by a spiky collar; 6"–24". Use these European natives in cottage gardens, borders, or cutting beds.

SOWING

INDOORS Late winter.
OUTDOORS Spring or early autumn.
DEPTH Surface.

GERMINATING

TIME 30–180 days.
REQUIREMENTS *Indoor sowing:* Sow seeds in flats, secure in a plastic bag, and refrigerate for 4 weeks. Provide light and 55°–65°F thereafter.

PLANTING SEEDLINGS OUTDOORS

TIME After last spring frost or in autumn.
SPACING 12"–15".
LIGHT Sun or part shade.
SOIL Moist, rich.

CARING FOR PLANTS

Easy. Keep soil moist in summer.

PROPAGATING

Divide in autumn in the South, in spring north of zone 7.

Astrantia major

A-Annual P-Perennial B-Biennial HHA-Half-hardy annual HA-Hardy annual HB-Hardy biennial HHP-Half-hardy perennial HP-Hardy perennial HHBb-Half-hardy bulb HBb-Hardy bulb

Atriplex

French spinach, Mountain spinach, Orach, Salt bush, Sea purslane

> TYPE **HA or HHA**
> ZONE **Prefers warm climates**
> FLOWERING SEASON **Summer**

Large, imposing plants, 4'–6' tall, grown for their striking red or green foliage; tiny green or bronze flowers, often used in dried arrangements, are borne in dense spikes. Makes an unusual screen or background for plants of contrasting color.

SOWING

INDOORS 6 weeks before planting out, in peat pots.
OUTDOORS Early spring, when soil is cool and a light frost is still possible.
DEPTH Just cover.

GERMINATING

TIME 9–21 days.
REQUIREMENTS 50°–55°F.

PLANTING SEEDLINGS OUTDOORS

TIME After last frost.
SPACING 12".
LIGHT Sun.
SOIL Withstands any conditions, even dry soil, although leaves will have best flavor when soil is kept moist.

CARING FOR PLANTS

Shear to maintain shape and neat appearance. May become invasive. Does not like to be moved.

PROPAGATING

Take cuttings; may self-seed.

Aubrieta

False rock cress, Purple rock cress

> TYPE **HP**
> ZONE **4–9. Does not like hot, dry conditions.**
> FLOWERING SEASON **Early spring**

Mat-forming alpines covered at blooming time in a cloak of purple, deepest pink, or blue. Use in rock gardens, to edge borders or paths; essential wall plant. Native of southern Europe and Asia.

SOWING

INDOORS 6–8 weeks before last frost.
OUTDOORS Early spring, when soil is cool and a light frost is still possible, or late autumn.
DEPTH Surface.

GERMINATING

TIME 14–21 days.
REQUIREMENTS Light and 65°–70°F. Very susceptible to damping-off; sow in vermiculite and water only from below.

Aubrieta deltoidea

PLANTING SEEDLINGS OUTDOORS

TIME After last frost.
SPACING 12".
LIGHT Full sun where summers are cool, part shade in the South.
SOIL Average, well-drained, with a pH level of 6.0–7.5.

CARING FOR PLANTS

Easy. Mulch in spring with compost. Deadhead and feed lightly after flowering; where summers are very hot, cut back hard after flowering.

PROPAGATING

Take cuttings in summer.

Aurinia

See *Alyssum* (Perennial)

A-Annual P-Perennial B-Biennial HHA-Half-hardy annual HA-Hardy annual HB-Hardy biennial HHP-Half-hardy perennial HP-Hardy perennial HHBb-Half-hardy bulb HBb-Hardy bulb

Avena

(synonymous with *Helictotrichon*)

Animated oat, Wild oat

> TYPE HA or HP
> ZONE A: 3–9; P: 4–8. Does not like hot, humid summers.
> FLOWERING SEASON Midsummer

European perennial grasses with very stiff, arching, blue leaves 12"–36" long. Use in groupings or as an accent plant.

SOWING

INDOORS Start seeds outdoors only.
OUTDOORS Early spring to midspring.
DEPTH ¼".

GERMINATING

TIME 5–21 days.
REQUIREMENTS Easy. 60°–70°F.

PLANTING SEEDLINGS OUTDOORS

TIME Plant out purchased annual plants in early spring; perennials may be planted out in early spring or autumn.
SPACING Annuals and small perennials: 10"–12". Large perennials: 18"–24".
LIGHT Full sun.
SOIL Dry, well-drained, poor to average, with a pH level of 6.0–7.5. This grass is drought tolerant, but will not do well in clay soil.

CARING FOR PLANTS

Easy. Water regularly for best results. Foliage may be left year-round or cut when seeds are fully developed and dried for indoor decoration. Dry with stalks upright for a natural drooping effect.

PROPAGATING

Self-seeds.

Baptisia

Blue false indigo, False indigo, Rattleweed, Wild indigo

> TYPE HP
> ZONE 4–9; 6–9: *B. perfoliata*
> FLOWERING SEASON Late spring or early summer, depending on species

Upright, branching perennials esteemed for their white, yellow, or blue sweet pea-like flowers scattered along slender stalks of 2'–6'. Plant at the back of the border. Native to North America.

SOWING

INDOORS 6–8 weeks before last frost, in peat pots.
OUTDOORS Early spring or late autumn.
DEPTH ¼".

GERMINATING

TIME 5–36 days.
REQUIREMENTS Soak seeds in warm water for 24 hours, then chip with a knife. Provide 70°–75°F thereafter.

PLANTING SEEDLINGS OUTDOORS

TIME After last spring frost, or in early autumn.
SPACING 2'–3'.
LIGHT Full sun or light shade.
SOIL Well-drained, with a pH level of 5.5–7.0.

CARING FOR PLANTS

Plants grown from seed will take a year or two to become well established. Stake tall plants. Do not disturb roots.

Baptisia australis

PROPAGATING

Divide with care in spring in zones 4–6, autumn in zones 7–9.

A-Annual P-Perennial B-Biennial HHA-Half-hardy annual HA-Hardy annual HB-Hardy biennial HHP-Half-hardy perennial HP-Hardy perennial HHBb-Half-hardy bulb HBb-Hardy bulb

59

Begonia

Very large genus of tropical plants grown for both foliage and flowers. Used extensively in borders and containers; striking when massed in formal and informal displays. Leaves are crisp and glossy in strong shades of green or red, or attractively striped or variegated; blooms are pink, white, or red. 6"–24" tall.

SOWING

INDOORS Seed: 3–4 months before planting out. Tuber: Start tubers indoors in early spring north of zone 10.
OUTDOORS A: start seeds indoors only. P: early spring, when soil is cool and a light frost is still possible, or late autumn.

DEPTH Surface.

GERMINATING

TIME 15–60 days.
REQUIREMENTS 65°–75°F.

PLANTING SEEDLINGS OUTDOORS

TIME After last frost.
SPACING Small species: 9"–12". Large species: 10"–15".
LIGHT Sun where summers are cool, otherwise part shade. Plants grown in sun will require more moisture.
SOIL Rich, moist, slightly acid, with a pH level of 6.0–7.0.

CARING FOR PLANTS

Water regularly, keeping leaves as dry as possible. Feed lightly every month, avoiding fertilizer contact with leaves. In northern zones, cover hardy species thickly with mulch. Where Begonias are not hardy, decrease watering when leaves start to yellow in autumn, lift tubers when leaves drop, carefully remove soil from roots, dry tubers, and store in a cool, frost-free location. Replant in the spring.

PROPAGATING

Take stem or leaf cuttings. Store bulbils over winter and plant in the spring when soil is warm. Tuberous Begonias can be divided. Some species self-seed freely.

Begonia 'Tuberhybrida'

Belamcanda

Blackberry lily, Leopard flower

Charming, rather timid, old-fashioned perennials with sparse, swordlike leaves and flattish, brightly colored, freckled flowers atop sturdy stalks of 18"–36". Now available in a wide range of colors beyond the original orange, including shades of purple, pink, and yellow.

SOWING

INDOORS 8–10 weeks before planting out.
OUTDOORS Early spring or early autumn.
DEPTH Seed: just cover. Roots: 2"–3".

GERMINATING

TIME 14–60 days.
REQUIREMENTS Easy. Place seeds and moistened growing medium in a plastic bag and refrigerate for 7 days. Provide 65°–85°F thereafter.

Belamcanda chinensis

ALISON KOLESAR

PLANTING SEEDLINGS OUTDOORS

TIME Early spring, when soil is cool and a light frost is still possible, or early autumn.
SPACING 6"–8".
LIGHT Full sun to part shade.
SOIL Prefers moist, rich, well-drained soil with a pH level of 5.0–7.0, but is tolerant of a wide variety of conditions.

CARING FOR PLANTS

Easy. Water during dry spells. Cut leaves and flower stalks to the ground in autumn.

PROPAGATING

Divide roots in spring.

Bellis

Bachelor's button, Daisy, English daisy, Meadow daisy

> TYPE P grown as B in zones 3–7, as A in zones 8–9
> ZONE 3–9; 6–9: *B. rotundifolia*. Plants will not flourish in intense heat and will perform best in the Pacific Northwest.
> FLOWERING SEASON Late spring through early summer

Dwarf, carpeting plants of just 6"–8" grown for their cheerful, solitary, white, red, or pink pom-pom flowers. Useful in the rock garden or as edging.

Bellis perennis

SOWING

INDOORS 8–10 weeks before planting out.
OUTDOORS Zones 3–7: midsummer through early autumn for flowering the following year. Zones 8–9: early spring, when soil is cool and a light frost is still possible, or autumn.
DEPTH Surface.

GERMINATING

TIME 10–25 days.
REQUIREMENTS Light and 70°F.

PLANTING SEEDLINGS OUTDOORS

TIME Zones 3–7: October. Zones 8–9: after last frost.
SPACING 6"–8".
LIGHT Sun or part shade.
SOIL Rich, moist loam.

CARING FOR PLANTS

Easy. Feed early in the growing season and water frequently. Where summers are hot, cut plants back hard after flowering. In Northern zones, mulch seedlings lightly before the first frost in autumn.

PROPAGATING

Divide after flowering.

Bergenia

Pig squeak, Siberian tea

> TYPE HP
> ZONE 2–8: *B. crassifolia*;
> 4–8: *B. cordifolia, B. stracheyi*;
> 5–8: *B. ciliata*,
> *B. purpurascens*. Dislikes hot, dry summers.
> FLOWERING SEASON Late spring to early summer

Imposing perennials of strong character grown for their large, glossy, rounded leaves of green or bronze. Plants are mostly 12"–18" tall, with thick, fleshy flowering stems bearing ungainly clusters of small, pink or white, trumpet-shaped flowers which are often removed before blooming. Use judiciously as edging or as a foil for fine-textured plants.

SOWING

INDOORS Pre-chilled seeds 6–8 weeks before last frost.
OUTDOORS Early spring, when soil is cool and a light frost is still possible, or late autumn.
DEPTH Surface.

GERMINATING

TIME 15–180 days.
REQUIREMENTS Place seeds and moistened growing medium in a plastic bag and refrigerate for 2 weeks. Provide 60°–70°F thereafter.

PLANTING SEEDLINGS OUTDOORS

TIME After last frost.
SPACING 12"–18".
LIGHT Full sun where summers are mild, part to full shade elsewhere. Must have moist soil in full sun.
SOIL Performs most successfully in deep, moist, fertile soil with a pH level of 6.0–7.5.

CARING FOR PLANTS

Water regularly and remove dead flowers and leaves to maintain a tidy appearance. Feed once in spring with low-nitrogen fertilizer. Division is only required when plants begin to deteriorate. Slugs will come from miles away to feast on the leaves, especially where soil is damp.

PROPAGATING

Divide every 3–4 years after flowering; take cuttings in spring.

Bergenia cordifolia

A-Annual P-Perennial B-Biennial HHA-Half-hardy annual HA-Hardy annual HB-Hardy biennial HHP-Half-hardy perennial HP-Hardy perennial HHBb-Half-hardy bulb HBb-Hardy bulb

Bletilla

Orchid

TYPE HHP
ZONE 9–10. Some species may survive outdoors in zones 7–8 with a heavy mulch; north of zone 7, lift plants and store in sawdust in a frost-free place over winter, or grow plants in tubs that can be moved indoors.
FLOWERING SEASON Early summer

Perennial orchids grown for their exotic purple or white flowers. Flower stems are erect, 1'–2' tall; leaves are lance-shaped. Grow in containers or near a patio or shaded path where their loveliness can be admired.

SOWING

INDOORS As soon as seed is available.
OUTDOORS Seed: early spring to midsummer. Root: late winter to early spring.
DEPTH Seed: surface. Root: just cover.

GERMINATING

TIME 30–365 days.
REQUIREMENTS Difficult. Sow seeds in a saucer on the surface of a damp paper towel, covering with glass or plastic wrap. Keep soil moist; transplant to individual pots as seeds germinate, giving light and 65°–70°F.

PLANTING SEEDLINGS OUTDOORS

TIME After last frost.
SPACING 6"–12".
LIGHT Part to full shade, with shade from afternoon sun where summers are hot.
SOIL Well-drained, slightly acid, supplemented with peat and leaf mold.

CARING FOR PLANTS

Feed and water regularly during the growing season. Plants may require staking and may attract slugs. Cut back to ground in late autumn. Transplant only in winter, when plants are dormant.

PROPAGATING

Divide large clumps only infrequently, after flowering.

Boltonia

False chamomile, False starwort

TYPE HP
ZONE 3–8. Gratifyingly resistant to humid heat.
FLOWERING SEASON Midsummer through autumn

Unassuming, upright perennials bearing a profusion of guileless daisylike flowers late in the season. Plants grow 2'–4'; blooms are white, soft pink, or lavender with yellow centers. Ideal for the border or cottage garden.

SOWING

INDOORS 6–8 weeks before planting out.
OUTDOORS Early spring, when soil is cool and a light frost is still possible.
DEPTH Just cover.

Boltonia asteroides

GERMINATING

TIME 14–21 days.
REQUIREMENTS 60°F.

PLANTING SEEDLINGS OUTDOORS

TIME After last frost.
SPACING 18"–36".
LIGHT Full sun or light shade.
SOIL Any with a pH level of 5.5–7.0.

CARING FOR PLANTS

Easy. May require staking in windy or shady sites. Short-lived plant; will require renewal by division every 2–4 years.

PROPAGATING

Divide in spring, or after blooming in autumn. *Boltonia* self-seeds and may become invasive.

A-Annual P-Perennial B-Biennial **HHA**-Half-hardy annual **HA**-Hardy annual **HB**-Hardy biennial **HHP**-Half-hardy perennial **HP**-Hardy perennial **HHBb**-Half-hardy bulb **HBb**-Hardy bulb

62

Boussingaultia

(synonymous with *Anredera)*

Madeira vine, Mignonette vine

> TYPE HHP
> ZONE 9–10. May survive in zone 8 with a heavy mulch.
> FLOWERING SEASON Late summer to early autumn

Genus of climbers grown for their thick, lush foliage and clusters of tiny white flowers; 20'. Grow on a trellis near a patio or open window where their sweet scent can be enjoyed.

SOWING
INDOORS 6–8 weeks before planting out.
OUTDOORS Seed: early spring, when soil is cool and a light frost is still possible, or late autumn. Tuber: after last frost.
DEPTH Seed: just cover. Tuber: 2".

GERMINATING
TIME 30 days.
REQUIREMENTS 60°–65°F.

PLANTING SEEDLINGS OUTDOORS
TIME After last frost, when temperatures remain above 45°F.
SPACING 24"–36".
LIGHT Full sun.
SOIL Light, sandy, well-drained, humus-rich.

CARING FOR PLANTS
Soil must be quite dry in autumn and winter, but fairly moist throughout the growing season. Vines require a trellis for support. Cut back by one-half in spring, or to ground level if plants have suffered frost damage. North of zone 9, lift tubers in autumn and store in a frost-free place over winter, replanting after last spring frost.

PROPAGATING
In spring, root the small tubers that form at leaf bases in moist sand; take softwood cuttings in early winter.

Brachycome

Swan river daisy

> TYPE HHA
> ZONE 1–10. Prefers cool temperatures and will perform poorly, or disappear altogether, during prolonged hot spell.
> FLOWERING SEASON Summer through autumn, althoughblooming will cease during very hot weather

Delightful, airy, sprawling perennials bearing masses of dainty daisylike flowers, usually deep blue with black or yellow eyes. Sited near the front door, a display of these 8"–18" charmers will revive your spirits after a day in the ratrace.

SOWING
INDOORS 6–8 weeks before last frost.
OUTDOORS After last frost. Where summers are cool, sow every 3–4 weeks for continuous blooms.
DEPTH Just cover.

GERMINATING
TIME 10–21 days.
REQUIREMENTS Easy. 65°–75°F.

PLANTING SEEDLINGS OUTDOORS
TIME After last frost.
SPACING 9", or 6" for edging.
LIGHT Sun or light shade.
SOIL Deep, rich, well-drained, with a pH level of 6.0–7.0; tolerates dry soil.

CARING FOR PLANTS
Easy. Deadhead regularly to prolong blooming. Support with twiggy branches pushed into the ground when plants are young.

PROPAGATING
Seed only.

JUDY ELIASON

Brachycome iberidifolia

A-Annual P-Perennial B-Biennial HHA-Half-hardy annual HA-Hardy annual HB-Hardy biennial HHP-Half-hardy perennial HP-Hardy perennial HHBb-Half-hardy bulb HBb-Hardy bulb

Brimeura

TYPE HBb
ZONE 3–8
FLOWERING SEASON Late spring

Subtle and charming, these spring bloom-ing bulbs bear narrow, lance-shaped leaves and 6" stalks of china blue bell-shaped flow-ers. An unusual addition to the rock garden or naturalize in the lawn or woodland. Na-tive of northern Spain.

SOWING

INDOORS Late winter to early spring.
OUTDOORS Seed: early to midspring. Bulb: autumn.
DEPTH Seed: just cover. Bulb: 3" where soil is heavy, 5" in light soil.

GERMINATING

TIME 30–60 days.
REQUIREMENTS Easy. *Indoor sowing:* 60°–65°F. *Outdoor sowing:* Sow seeds in flats or individual containers. Lift and over-winter indoors the first year, planting out the following spring.

PLANTING SEEDLINGS OUTDOORS

TIME After last frost, 1 year after sowing.
SPACING 3"–5".
LIGHT Full sun to part shade.
SOIL Well-drained, humus-rich, limy.

CARING FOR PLANTS

Easy. Water throughout the growing season if weather is dry. Apply a complete fertil-izer in spring and mulch with well-rotted manure in autumn. Allow leaves to die back completely before removing. Divide every 3–4 years, if necessary.

PROPAGATING

Divide bulbs in late summer.

Brimeura amethystina

Brittonastrum

See *Agastache*

Briza

Quaking grass

TYPE HA or HP
ZONE A: 5–8; P: 4–8 (prefers cool temperatures)
FLOWERING SEASON Summer

Not showy plants, but a display of these airy grasses is beautiful and restful. 1'–2' tall with fine stalks bearing drooping, silvery spear-heads or tiny, sparsely scattered seed heads. Used mainly in naturalistic plantings.

SOWING

INDOORS 6–8 weeks before last frost. Sow annuals in peat pots.
OUTDOORS After last spring frost or in late summer.
DEPTH 1/8".

GERMINATING

TIME 10–21 days.
REQUIREMENTS Easy. 55°F.

PLANTING SEEDLINGS OUTDOORS

TIME After last frost.
SPACING 12".
LIGHT Full sun to light shade.
SOIL Light, well-drained, rather poor. Most species are drought tolerant, but *B. mi-nor* will die in hot, dry conditions.

CARING FOR PLANTS

Easy. Water plants regularly for best results. Cut back to ground when plants start to look ragged in midsummer. Do not move annuals.

PROPAGATING

Annuals propagate by seed only. Divide perennials in early spring, or allow to self-seed.

A-Annual P-Perennial B-Biennial HHA-Half-hardy annual HA-Hardy annual HB-Hardy biennial HHP-Half-hardy perennial HP-Hardy perennial HHBb-Half-hardy bulb HBb-Hardy bulb

64

Brodiaea

Blue-dicks, Fire-cracker flower, Grassnut, Ithuriel's spear

> TYPE HBb
> ZONE 6–10. Prefers the Pacific Coast and will not thrive where summers are hot and humid.
> FLOWERING SEASON Spring

Lovely bulbs native to the Americas grown for their dazzling star- or funnel-shaped blooms of white or violet-blue. 12"–36" tall with narrow, grassy leaves. Plant in masses under shrubs.

SOWING

INDOORS Early spring.
OUTDOORS Seed: autumn. Bulb: early autumn.
DEPTH Seed: ⅛". Bulb: 3"–4".

GERMINATING

TIME 30–90 days.
REQUIREMENTS 55°–60°F. Seeds are highly susceptible to damping-off; sow in vermiculite and water only from below.

PLANTING SEEDLINGS OUTDOORS

TIME Autumn.
SPACING 3"–6".
LIGHT Full sun.
SOIL Loose, gritty, with very good drainage. *B. peduncularis* requires heavy, wet soil.

CARING FOR PLANTS

Plants grown from seed will flower in about 2 years. Water regularly during growing season, but cease altogether after flowering. Where summers are wet or hot, lift bulbs after flowering and store in a cool, dry place, replanting in the autumn.

PROPAGATING

Plant cormels in autumn.

Brodiaea laxa

Browallia

Bush violet

> TYPE HHP usually grown as HHA
> ZONE A: 3–8; P: 9–10. Prefers warm days with cool nights.
> FLOWERING SEASON Spring through autumn

Useful — and under-used — plants with lush green foliage setting off pretty trumpet-shaped flowers of purple or white. Habit is upright and somewhat bushy; plants grow to 12". Use as an edging for shady borders, in naturalistic plantings as a change from impatiens, or in containers.

SOWING

INDOORS 6–8 weeks before last frost.
OUTDOORS After last frost, but only where summers are very long.
DEPTH Surface.

Browallia speciosa

GERMINATING

TIME 6–21 days.
REQUIREMENTS Light and 65°–75°F.

PLANTING SEEDLINGS OUTDOORS

TIME Spring, when temperatures remain above 40°F.
SPACING Small species: 6"–10". Large species: 12"–18".
LIGHT Sun or part shade.
SOIL Moist, with a pH level of 6.0–7.0.

CARING FOR PLANTS

Mulch plants that are growing in full sun and water often. Pinch back young plants when 6" high to encourage bushiness. Feed only lightly.

PROPAGATING

Self-seeds in the South.

A-Annual P-Perennial B-Biennial HHA-Half-hardy annual HA-Hardy annual HB-Hardy biennial HHP-Half-hardy perennial HP-Hardy perennial HHBb-Half-hardy bulb HBb-Hardy bulb

Brunnera

Forget-me-not anchusa, Siberian
bugloss, Siberian forget-me-not

TYPE HP
ZONE 3–8
FLOWERING SEASON Late spring

Small genus of low-growing perennials bearing attractive green or variegated, heart-shaped leaves and dainty white or blue forget-me-not-like flowers. Stunning when used sensitively in combination with contrasting plants in shady, naturalistic settings.

SOWING

INDOORS Pre-chilled seeds 8–10 weeks before planting out.
OUTDOORS Late summer or early autumn.
DEPTH Just cover.

Brunnera macrophylla

GERMINATING

TIME 30–90 days.
REQUIREMENTS Place seeds and moistened growing medium in a plastic bag, seal, and refrigerate for 4 weeks. Provide 55°–60°F thereafter.

PLANTING SEEDLINGS OUTDOORS

TIME After last frost or in autumn.
SPACING 10"–15"; allow more space in rich soils.
LIGHT Sun or part shade.
SOIL Not fussy, but performs best in moist, rich soil with a pH level of 5.5–7.0.

CARING FOR PLANTS

Keep soil quite moist. *Brunnera* is short-lived and should be divided in autumn or early spring when plants show signs of deteriorating.

PROPAGATING

Divide in early autumn in the South, in spring north of zone 7; take root cuttings in autumn. May self-seed. Propagate cultivars by division only.

Bulbinella

TYPE HP or HHP
ZONE 7–10. Does not like high
heat and humidity.
FLOWERING SEASON Late winter to
early spring

Bright, early-blooming bulbs bearing terminal spikes of small, yellow, star-shaped flowers on erect stalks 1' to 2' tall; leaves are grass-like. Mix with other early blooming bulbs or mass in front of evergreen shrubs.

SOWING

INDOORS Spring.
OUTDOORS Autumn.
DEPTH Seed: just cover. Roots: just below soil level.

GERMINATING

TIME 10–90 days.
REQUIREMENTS 55°F. Grow seedlings indoors for 2 full seasons.

PLANTING SEEDLINGS OUTDOORS

TIME Seedlings: in spring, when nighttime temperatures remain above 50°F. Purchased plants: in spring or autumn.
SPACING 18".
LIGHT Sun or part shade.
SOIL Cool, rich, moist, acid.

CARING FOR PLANTS

Water only occasionally during summer, keeping soil quite moist the rest of the year. Remove dead foliage when plant goes dormant (after flowering); mark location to avoid disturbing roots accidentally. Divide when plants become crowded.

PROPAGATING

Divide in spring.

A-Annual P-Perennial B-Biennial HHA-Half-hardy annual HA-Hardy annual HB-Hardy biennial HHP-Half-hardy perennial HP-Hardy perennial HHBb-Half-hardy bulb HBb-Hardy bulb

Bulbocodium

Spring meadow saffron

Type HBb
Zone 5–10. Plants will not thrive where winters are wet.
Flowering Season Early spring

Genus of bulbs grown for their stemless purple flowers resembling large, open crocuses. Growing only to 1"–2", these little bulbs are at home in the rock garden or massed under shrubs.

SOWING

Indoors Start seeds outdoors.
Outdoors Seed or bulb: autumn.
Depth Seed: surface. Bulb: 3".

GERMINATING

Requirements Division is the most common method of propagation, and little information is available on growing this bulb from seed. Information given here is only a general guideline. Sow seeds in flats, covering first with compost, then a thin layer of fine gravel. Plunge flats into the ground outdoors and cover with glass. Twelve months after germination, transplant corms to a nursery bed, spacing 12" apart. After 2 years, move to final location.

PLANTING SEEDLINGS OUTDOORS

Time Autumn.
Spacing 3"–4".
Light Full sun to very light shade.
Soil Moist, very well-drained, acid, with plenty of organic matter added.

CARING FOR PLANTS

Keep soil moist until after flowering. Feed only if soil is poor. Allow leaves to wither naturally after flowering. Divide every 2–3 years.

PROPAGATING

Divide after flowers and foliage have died back.

Bulbocodium vernum

Buphthalmum

Ox-eye, Ox-eye daisy

Type HP
Zone 3–8
Flowering Season Summer

Summer-blooming perennials grown for their yellow, daisylike flowers, some of which bear unusually fine and delicate petals. Native to Europe and Asia; used in the sunny border.

SOWING

Indoors Spring.
Outdoors Spring or autumn.
Depth Surface.

GERMINATING

Time 14–30 days.
Requirements Light and 70°–75°F.

PLANTING SEEDLINGS OUTDOORS

Time After last frost.
Spacing 8"–12".
Light Full sun or light shade.
Soil Moist, well-drained, rather infertile, with a pH level of 6.0–8.0.

CARING FOR PLANTS

Easy. Plants may require staking. Divide frequently and withhold fertilizer to limit expropriation of your beds.

PROPAGATING

Divide in spring or early autumn; self-seeds.

A-Annual P-Perennial B-Biennial HHA-Half-hardy annual HA-Hardy annual HB-Hardy biennial HHP-Half-hardy perennial HP-Hardy perennial HHBb-Half-hardy bulb HBb-Hardy bulb

Caladium

Angel wings, Elephant's-ear, Mother-in-law plant

> TYPE HHP, usually grown as A
> ZONE A: 4–8; P: 9–10. Will only perform well where summers are very warm.
> FLOWERING SEASON No flower

Heat-loving plants unsurpassed for large, colorful, showy foliage which is mottled, freckled, or striped in shades of pink, green, silver, or red. Growing 1'–2' tall, plants should be massed or planted in containers.

SOWING

INDOORS Short-lived seeds should be sown as soon as available. Where summers are short, start tubers indoors in late winter.
OUTDOORS In zones 9–10 only, as soon as ripe seed is available.
DEPTH Seed: just cover. Tuber: 2".

Caladium humboldtii

GERMINATING

TIME 30–90 days.
REQUIREMENTS 75°–85°F.

PLANTING SEEDLINGS OUTDOORS

TIME When temperatures will not drop below 60°F.
SPACING 8"–10".
LIGHT Leaf colors are most striking when grown in full sun, but in very hot regions, plants need some shade from the afternoon sun.
SOIL Rich, well-drained, acid. Amend with well-rotted cow manure at planting time.

CARING FOR PLANTS

Water and feed frequently throughout the growing season. North of zone 9, ease off watering in autumn and lift tubers before first frost. Store in dry sand over winter in a frost-free location. In zones 9–10, do not water in winter.

PROPAGATING

Divide tubers in spring; each section should contain at least 2 eyes.

Calandrinia

Redmaids, Rock purslane

> TYPE Short-lived HHP usually grown as HHA
> ZONE 3–10; will survive over winter in 8–10. Of about 150 known species, some prefer hot, dry climates while others are at home in mild regions.
> FLOWERING SEASON Midsummer to late summer

Mainly low-growing plants valued for their brightly colored blooms, usually in shades of pink or purple. Makes a stunning edging display or liven up a humdrum rock garden. Native to North and South America.

SOWING

INDOORS 6–8 weeks before last frost.
OUTDOORS After last frost.
DEPTH ⅛".

GERMINATING

TIME 5–14 days.
REQUIREMENTS Easy. 55°–60°F.

PLANTING SEEDLINGS OUTDOORS

TIME After last frost.
SPACING Short species: 6". Tall species: 10".
LIGHT Full sun.
SOIL Sandy or gritty. Withstands dry conditions.

CARING FOR PLANTS

Requires no feeding, but appreciates protection from winter wetness. Plants are short-lived and must be replaced frequently.

PROPAGATING

Take cuttings, or allow to self-seed.

A-Annual P-Perennial B-Biennial HHA-Half-hardy annual HA-Hardy annual HB-Hardy biennial HHP-Half-hardy perennial HP-Hardy perennial HHBb-Half-hardy bulb HBb-Hardy bulb

68

Calendula

English marigold, Pot marigold

> TYPE HA
> ZONE 2–10. Prefers cool temperatures, particularly during early growth stages.
> FLOWERING SEASON Late spring through first frost; in zones 8–10, winter blooming is possible from an autumn sowing

Unsophisticated but cheerful, these bushy annuals are grown for their sturdy orange and yellow, daisylike flowers. Use in the border or cottage garden; 1'–2' tall.

SOWING

INDOORS 6–8 weeks before last frost.
OUTDOORS Early spring, when soil is cool and a light frost is still possible, or late autumn. Where summers are mild, sow in early summer for autumn flowering. In zones 8–10, early autumn sowing is best.
DEPTH ¼".

GERMINATING

TIME 6–14 days.
REQUIREMENTS Darkness and 70°F.

PLANTING SEEDLINGS OUTDOORS

TIME After last frost.
SPACING Dwarf species: 6"–12". Tall species: 18"–24".
LIGHT Full sun; plants will also grow in light shade where summers are very hot.
SOIL Ordinary, with a pH level of 5.5–7.0; tolerates damp soils.

CARING FOR PLANTS

Easy. Pinch back young plants to stimulate bushy growth. Feed occasionally and deadhead and water often, keeping leaves as dry as possible as *Calendulas* are susceptible to mildew. Fresh or dried leaves can be used in cooking. Dig and pot up plants in midsummer to grow indoors over winter.

PROPAGATING

Take cuttings in summer.

Calendula officinalis

CHARLES JOSLIN

Calliopsis

See *Coreopsis*

Callistephus

Annual aster, China aster

> TYPE HA or HHA
> ZONE 1–10. Prefers cool weather, particularly in spring.
> FLOWERING SEASON Summer

Upright, bushy annuals, 8"–24", useful for their chrysanthemumlike blooms in almost every color but yellow. Long bloomers for the border; excellent cut flowers.

SOWING

INDOORS 6–8 weeks before planting out, in peat pots.
OUTDOORS After last frost.
DEPTH Just cover.

GERMINATING

TIME 6–14 days.
REQUIREMENTS 65°–70°F. Very susceptible to damping-off; grow in vermiculite and water only from below.

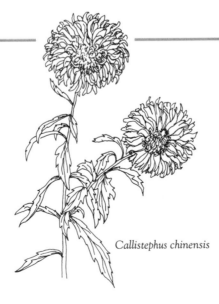

Callistephus chinensis

PLANTING SEEDLINGS OUTDOORS

TIME After last frost.
SPACING Dwarf species: 6"–12". Medium species: 12"–18". Tall species: 18"–24".
LIGHT Sun or light shade.
SOIL Rich, well-drained, with a pH level of 6.0–7.0.

CARING FOR PLANTS

Difficult. Do not pinch back young plants. Feed once or twice during the growing season and water regularly but carefully during droughts (asters are particularly sensitive to overwatering). Keep roots cool in summer with mulch. Weed and deadhead frequently, and stake tall species. For greatest success, grow species that are resistent to aster yellows and change location in the garden every year; do not use high-nitrogen fertilizer, which may encourage disease. Destroy any unhealthy plants immediately before others are infected. Will not flourish if overcrowded, poorly ventilated, or sited close to a heat-reflecting surface.

PROPAGATING

Seed only.

A-Annual P-Perennial B-Biennial HHA-Half-hardy annual HA-Hardy annual HB-Hardy biennial HHP-Half-hardy perennial HP-Hardy perennial HHBb-Half-hardy bulb HBb-Hardy bulb

Calochortus

Butterfly tulip, Cat's ear, Fairy lantern, Globe tulip, Mariposa lily, Sego lily, Star tulip

TYPE HHBb
ZONE 5–10. Performs best in the warm, dry summers and mild winters of the West Coast; particularly dislikes frequent cycles of freezing and thawing.
FLOWERING SEASON Spring

Unusual, wispy bulbs native to western North America. Flowers are generally cup-shaped, pretty and delicate-looking, blooming on stems of 6"–36". Some blooms are nodding, some have backward-curling petals, others are hairy inside; petals may be white, purple, red, or yellow.

SOWING

INDOORS Late summer or early spring.
OUTDOORS Seed or bulb: autumn.
DEPTH Seed: just cover. Bulb: 3"–4".

GERMINATING

TIME 30–180 days.
REQUIREMENTS 55°–65°F. Seedlings started indoors should be left undisturbed for 2 years; pot up and leave for another 2 years before planting outdoors.

Calochortus albus

PLANTING SEEDLINGS OUTDOORS

TIME Seed-grown bulbs: after last frost.
SPACING 4".
LIGHT Sun or part shade.
SOIL Sandy, well-drained, slightly acid loam. Do not add manure.

CARING FOR PLANTS

Easy. Plants grown from seed will flower in 5–6 years. Water in winter and spring, leaving ground quite dry in summer. Do not feed with manure. Mulch in winter in colder zones; north of zone 7, bulbs may require lifting in autumn and storing over winter in a cool, frost-free place. In the East, these lilies are often grown in pots plunged into the ground as heavy Eastern soils do not yield strong bulbs. Bulbs grown this way should rest in a cool place over the summer *outside* their pots; repot in autumn and return to the ground; mulch after the ground freezes.

PROPAGATING

Divide corms in autumn.

Calonyction

Bona nox, Moonflower

TYPE HHP, usually treated as HHA
ZONE A: 3–8; P: 9–10
FLOWERING SEASON July through first frost

Climbing vines with heart-shaped leaves and large, extraordinarily lovely and exotic, white or purple, trumpet-shaped flowers. As flowers open only at night, be sure to place near a porch or patio where they will not be missed.

SOWING

INDOORS 8 weeks before planting out, in peat pots.
OUTDOORS After last frost.
DEPTH Just cover.

GERMINATING

TIME 12–14 days.
REQUIREMENTS Difficult. Chip seeds or soak overnight; provide 70°–75°F thereafter.

PLANTING SEEDLINGS OUTDOORS

TIME After last frost, when temperatures remain above 50°F.
SPACING 6"–12".
LIGHT Full sun or part shade.
SOIL Average.

CARING FOR PLANTS

Vines require a trellis or other support. Pinch out tips once as plants begin to climb. Water frequently during growing season, but do not fertilize. Do not move.

PROPAGATING

Seed only.

A-Annual P-Perennial B-Biennial HHA-Half-hardy annual HA-Hardy annual HB-Hardy biennial HHP-Half-hardy perennial HP-Hardy perennial HHBb-Half-hardy bulb HBb-Hardy bulb

Caltha

Cowslip, Marsh marigold

> **Type** HP
> **Zone** 4–9; 7–10: *C. introloba*
> **Flowering Season** Spring

Mainly low-growing perennials (under 12") thriving near water, grown for their cheerful buttercuplike blooms; flowers are usually yellow, less often white or pink.

Sowing

Indoors Start seeds outdoors only.
Outdoors Sow in peat pots as soon as ripe seed is available (usually early summer).
Depth Just cover.

Caltha palustris

Germinating

Time 30–90 days.
Requirements Seeds must be fresh — old seed is unlikely to germinate. Stand peat pots in a saucer of shallow water and keep soil constantly moist until planted in the garden.

Planting Seedlings Outdoors

Time Transplant peat pots to their permanent location in midsummer.
Spacing Small species: 8"–12". Medium species: 18". Large species: 24"–36".
Light Prefers sun from winter through early spring, but shade thereafter. Requires more moisture when grown in full sun.
Soil Rich, clay soil that is moist or even wet, with a pH level of 5.0–7.0.

Caring for Plants

Easy. Keep soil moist at all times. Mark plant locations as foliage dies back altogether after flowering.

Propagating

Divide after flowering in zones 4–6, in early autumn elsewhere.

Camassia

Camass, Missouri hyacinth, Quamash, Wild hyacinth

> **Type** HBb
> **Zone** 4–8; 5–8: *C. scilloides*;
> 7–9: *C. leichtlinii*
> **Flowering Season** Late spring through summer

Small genus of spring-blooming bulbs bearing blue or white star-shaped flowers along leafless stalks of 1'–6'. Use these dramatic plants as an accent or in a naturalistic setting.

Sowing

Indoors Start seeds outdoors only.
Outdoors Seed: as soon as ripe seed is available (usually in summer). Bulb: autumn.
Depth Seed: just cover. Bulb: 4"–5".

Germinating

Time 30–180 days.
Requirements Easy. Sow seeds in flats, sink flats in the ground against a north-facing wall, and cover with glass. Moisten soil occasionally, if necessary.

Planting Seedlings Outdoors

Time Transplant to the garden in autumn after 2 full growing seasons.
Spacing 6"–8".
Light Full sun or light shade.
Soil Moist, well-drained, fertile, slightly acid.

Caring for Plants

Easy. Plants grown from seed will take up to 5 years to flower. Water frequently and feed once in the early spring. After blooming, cut back flowering stems to ground. Mulch with compost in winter. Plants resent disturbance and should be divided only when overcrowded, replanting bulbs immediately or storing in a cool, dry place until early autumn.

Propagating

Divide bulblets in early autumn.

Camassia quamash

Campanula

Bellflower, Canterbury bells, Harebell, Peach bells

TYPE HP, HB, or, rarely, HA
ZONE A: 3–10; P: 3–8: *C. bononiensis, C. carpatica, C. glomerata, C. persicifolia, C. poscharskyana, C. rapunculoids, C. rotundifolia, C. sarmatica;* 4–8: *C. alliariifolia, C.alpestris, C. betulifolia, C. caespitosa, C. cochleariifolia, C. collina, C. garganica, C. hawkinsiana, C. lactiflora, C. latifolia, C. portenschlagiana, C. punctata;* 5–8: *C. pyramidalis, C. raineri;* 6–8: *C. barbata, C. incurva, C. tommasiniana*
FLOWERING SEASON Spring through summer, depending on species

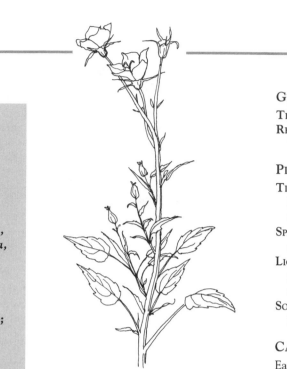

Campanula carpatica

Very large genus of plants of widely differing appearance, but usually bearing bell-shaped flowers of blue, white or, less commonly, pink. Use small species to edge borders or paths or in rock gardens; larger species are at home anywhere from a formal border to a cottage garden.

SOWING

INDOORS 8–10 weeks before planting out.
OUTDOORS Early spring or, where winters are mild, early autumn. B: late spring to early summer.
DEPTH Surface.

GERMINATING

TIME 14–28 days.
REQUIREMENTS Difficult. Light and 60°–70°F. Keep out of strong sunlight.

PLANTING SEEDLINGS OUTDOORS

TIME Early spring, when soil is cool and a light frost is still possible, or early autumn. B: autumn.
SPACING Small species: 5"–10". Tall species: 15"–20".
LIGHT Most *Campanulas* like full sun, but part shade is preferable where summers are very hot.
SOIL Ordinary, with a pH level of 7.0–7.5. Rock garden species need cool, gritty soil.

CARING FOR PLANTS

Easy. Water during dry spells, feed in early spring, deadhead regularly, and you will be repaid with abundant blooms. Mulch with manure in winter. Tall species may need staking.

PROPAGATING

Propagate annuals by seed. Take cuttings or divide perennials in autumn (north of zone 7, divide in the spring).

Canna

Indian shot

TYPE HHP usually grown as HHA
ZONE A: 3–7; P: 8–10
FLOWERING SEASON Summer through early autumn

Tall, stately, substantial plants that demand a large space and dominate the landscape. Big, complex blossoms in shades of pink, red, and yellow bloom in terminal spikes on stiff stalks of 3'–5'. New dwarf plants (2') are suitable for containers.

SOWING

INDOORS 2–3 weeks before last frost.
OUTDOORS Several weeks after last frost, when soil is warm.
DEPTH Seed: ¼". Tuber: 3"–4".

GERMINATING

TIME 21–365 days.
REQUIREMENTS Germination is erratic. Take a small chip off of seeds with a sharp knife and soak in warm water for 48 hours; provide 70°–75°F thereafter.

PLANTING SEEDLINGS OUTDOORS

TIME Several weeks after last frost, when soil is warm and temperatures remain above 50°F.
SPACING 18"–24".
LIGHT Full sun.
SOIL Moist, fertile, well-drained, with a pH level of 6.0–8.0.

CARING FOR PLANTS

Easy. Feed monthly and provide adequate water during dry spells. In zones 4–7, cut back to 6" in autumn, lift tubers, dry, and store in peat moss in a cool, frost-free place. Provide winter mulch for tubers left in the ground over winter.

PROPAGATING

Divide tubers in spring; each new section should contain 2 buds.

Cardiocrinum

Giant Himalayan lily, Giant lily

Type HBb
Zone 5–9. Grows best in the Pacific Northwest where summers are cool and humid and winters are mild.
Flowering Season Summer

Large, lovely, fragrant white trumpets adorn the sturdy 3' stems of these gracious plants. Impossible to misuse, these stunning bulbs work well individually or in masses, in formal or informal settings.

Sowing

Indoors Start seeds outdoors only.
Outdoors Seed: as soon as fresh seed is available in autumn. Bulb: autumn.
Depth Seed: just cover. Bulb: Plant with tip at soil level.

Germinating

Time 90–730 days.
Requirements Difficult. Sow seeds in flats, cover with a sheet of glass, and place containers outdoors against a north-facing wall. Water if necessary to keep growing medium moist but not wet. Bring indoors in spring to 50°F.

Planting Seedlings Outdoors

Time After last frost.
Spacing 24"–36".
Light Part shade.
Soil Deep, moist loam with abundant organic matter added.

Caring for Plants

Difficult. Plants grown from seed will flower in 5–7 years. Apply bulb food in the spring and feed monthly thereafter with a weak fertilizer solution. Mulch with compost to keep soil cool and moist.

Cardiocrinum giganteum

Propagating

Divide bulbs in October.

Cardiospermum

Balloon vine, Heart pea, Heart seed, Love-in-a-puff, Winter cherry

Type HHP usually grown as HHA
Zone A: 3–8; P: 9–10
Flowering Season Summer

Shrubby climbers with lush, feathery foliage, inconspicuous white flowers, and an abundance of showy, round, green fruits. Plants grow to 10', making an excellent cover for a trellis, fence, or pergola.

Sowing

Indoors 6–8 weeks before last frost.
Outdoors After last frost, but only where the growing season is very long.
Depth ½".

Germinating

Time 21–30 days.
Requirements Easy. 65°–70°F.

Planting Seedlings Outdoors

Time In spring, when temperatures remain above 40°F.
Spacing 12"–24" for rapid cover, otherwise 24"–48".
Light Full sun.
Soil Ordinary, well-drained.

Caring for Plants

Requires a trellis or other support. Water frequently.

Propagating

Take cuttings in spring. May self-seed where winters are mild.

A-Annual P-Perennial B-Biennial HHA-Half-hardy annual HA-Hardy annual HB-Hardy biennial HHP-Half-hardy perennial HP-Hardy perennial HHBb-Half-hardy bulb HBb-Hardy bulb

73

Carthamus

False saffron, Safflower, Saffron thistle

TYPE HA
ZONE 3–9. Prefers cool, dry climates and will not tolerate wet summers.
FLOWERING SEASON Midsummer

Upright, stiff, rather prickly-looking annuals grown for use in cooking and dried flower arrangements. Plants grow to 3'; blossoms are tubular, orange or yellow.

SOWING

INDOORS 6–8 weeks before last frost, in peat pots.
OUTDOORS Early spring, when soil is cool and a light frost is still possible, or late autumn.
DEPTH ¼".

GERMINATING

TIME 10–24 days.
REQUIREMENTS 60°–70°F.

PLANTING SEEDLINGS OUTDOORS

TIME After last frost.
SPACING 6"–8".
LIGHT Full sun.
SOIL Poor, light, dry, with a pH level of 6.0–7.0.

CARING FOR PLANTS

Young plants are very attractive to rabbits; screening may be required as protection. Difficult to transplant. Cut flower heads in late summer and dry indoors to use as a substitute for saffron in cooking. For dried flower arrangements, cut stems when flower heads contain both blooms and buds.

PROPAGATING

Self-seeds.

Carum

Caraway

TYPE HB
ZONE 3–8
FLOWERING SEASON Spring to early summer of their second year

Herb grown for its distinctively flavored seed. Plants are upright, 2'–4' tall, with fernlike leaves and flat clusters of tiny white flowers.

SOWING

INDOORS Sow seeds outdoors only.
OUTDOORS 2–3 weeks before last spring frost or early autumn.
DEPTH ⅛".

GERMINATING

TIME Fresh seed will germinate in 14 days; old seed will take considerably longer.
REQUIREMENTS 70°F.

PLANTING SEEDLINGS OUTDOORS

TIME Set out purchased plants after last frost.
SPACING 6"–12".
LIGHT Full sun.
SOIL Light, fertile, well-drained, with a pH level of 6.0–7.0.

CARING FOR PLANTS

Do not move. Feed at planting time and again when rapid growth begins; watering is not necessary. To harvest seeds for cooking, cut flower heads in midsummer when seeds are just turning brown. Hang upside down in a paper bag to collect. Immerse seeds in boiling water to destroy any insects, then dry in the sun for several days. Store in an airtight container.

PROPAGATING

Self-seeds.

A-Annual P-Perennial B-Biennial HHA-Half-hardy annual HA-Hardy annual HB-Hardy biennial HHP-Half-hardy perennial HP-Hardy perennial HHBb-Half-hardy bulb HBb-Hardy bulb

74

Cassia

**American senna, Partridge pea,
Wild senna**

> TYPE HP or HA
> ZONE 6–9
> FLOWERING SEASON Summer

Unusual, shrubby perennials native to North America, with the habit and appearance of a small tree. Leaves are compound; flowers are bright yellow and pealike. This 2'–4' curiosity should be used judiciously, probably in the wild garden.

SOWING

INDOORS 6–8 weeks before planting out.
OUTDOORS Summer through autumn for flowering the following year.
DEPTH ⅛".

GERMINATING

TIME 5–90 days.
REQUIREMENTS Chip seeds with a sharp knife and soak in warm water for 2–3 hours. Provide 70°–75°F thereafter.

PLANTING SEEDLINGS OUTDOORS

TIME After last spring frost or in autumn.
SPACING 24"–36".
LIGHT Full sun to light shade.
SOIL Will grow in most well-drained soils. Particularly tolerant of dry soil.

CARING FOR PLANTS

Easy. Water and feed regularly. Thinning plants in autumn will improve flowering the following year.

PROPAGATING

Take cuttings or divide in spring.

Cassia marilandica

Catananche

**Blue succory, Cupidone,
Cupid's dart**

> TYPE HP often grown as HA
> ZONE 4–9. Does not like intense heat and humidity.
> FLOWERING SEASON Late spring through summer

Rather stiff, upright plants, 12" tall, bearing silvery leaves and upwardly-pointing flower buds; flowers are purple and daisy-like. When used in combination with plants of strongly contrasting shape and harmonizing color, these unimposing perennials can be stunning.

SOWING

INDOORS 6–8 weeks before last frost.
OUTDOORS Early spring, when soil is cool and a light frost is still possible; where winters are mild, late autumn.
DEPTH Just cover.

Catananche caerulea

GERMINATING

TIME 20–25 days.
REQUIREMENTS 65°–75°F.

PLANTING SEEDLINGS OUTDOORS

TIME After last frost.
SPACING 9"–12".
LIGHT Full sun.
SOIL Average, well-drained. Drought tolerant.

CARING FOR PLANTS

Easy. Requires very little care. Cut back to the ground in autumn and mulch for winter. Where summers are very hot, cut plants back hard after flowering. Plants are short-lived and must be renewed regularly.

PROPAGATING

Divide in early spring in the North, early autumn in the South. Take root cuttings in late winter. Self-seeds.

Catharanthus

**Annual vinca,
Madagascar periwinkle**

TYPE P usually grown as HHA
ZONE A: 1–8; P: 9–10. Thrives
where summers are hot and
humid.
FLOWERING SEASON Summer
through first frost

Bushy, 6"–12" annuals with neat, glossy green leaves and a constant display of simple, flattish flowers in white or shades of pink, sometimes with a deeply stained center. A really dependable plant for massing, borders, or containers.

SOWING

INDOORS 12–16 weeks before planting out.
OUTDOORS Late winter, only in zones 9–10.
DEPTH ¼".

GERMINATING

TIME 15–20 days.
REQUIREMENTS Darkness and 70°–75°F.

PLANTING SEEDLINGS OUTDOORS

TIME Spring, when temperatures remain above 40°F.
SPACING 8"–10".
LIGHT Full sun or very light shade.
SOIL Moist, with a pH level of 6.0–7.0.

CARING FOR PLANTS

Easy. Feed lightly in spring and water regularly throughout the year. In zones 9–10, cut plants back occasionally to stimulate new growth.

PROPAGATING

Take cuttings, or allow to self-seed.

Caulophyllum

**Blue cohosh, Papoose root,
Squaw root**

TYPE HP
ZONE 4–7
FLOWERING SEASON May

Two species of erect perennials, one of which is native to eastern North America, grown in woodlands and wild gardens. Leaves are compound and lobed, bluish-green in spring, turning green with maturity. Inconspicuous flowers are followed by attractive blue fruit. Plants grow 18"–36".

SOWING

DEPTH Roots: 1".

GERMINATING

REQUIREMENTS Plants are most successfully propagated by division or cuttings.

PLANTING SEEDLINGS OUTDOORS

TIME Set out purchased plants in autumn.
SPACING 12"–15".
LIGHT Part to full shade.
SOIL Deep, moist, rich woods soil with a pH level of 4.5–7.0.

CARING FOR PLANTS

Mulch with oak leaves and do not allow soil to dry out. Do not disturb established plants.

PROPAGATING

Divide in spring or early autumn. Take cuttings from rhizomes.

A-Annual P-Perennial B-Biennial HHA-Half-hardy annual HA-Hardy annual HB-Hardy biennial HHP-Half-hardy perennial HP-Hardy perennial HHBb-Half-hardy bulb HBb-Hardy bulb

76

Celmisia

Mountain daisy

Celmisia lindsayi

> **TYPE** HHP or HP
> **ZONE** 5–8. Requires mild winters and humid, mild summers.
> **FLOWERING SEASON** Early summer to midsummer

Genus of perennials native to Australia and New Zealand with widely varying foliage that may be green or grey, small and lance-shaped or bold and sword-like; flowers are white and daisylike, borne singly on upright stems of 4"–3'. Grown in rock gardens and borders.

SOWING

INDOORS As soon as ripe seed is available.
OUTDOORS Starting seeds outdoors is not recommended.
DEPTH Surface.

GERMINATING

TIME 30–180 days.
REQUIREMENTS Difficult to grow from seed and it is difficult even to *obtain* seed. Because of its brief viability, seeds must be sown as soon as ripe. Provide light and 60°–65°F.

PLANTING SEEDLINGS OUTDOORS

TIME After last frost, but only after a strong root system is established.
SPACING Small species: 4"–8". Medium species: 12"–24". Spreading species: 4'–6'.
LIGHT Full sun to light shade.
SOIL Acid, peaty, well-drained soil that does not dry out in summer.

CARING FOR PLANTS

Do not allow soil to dry out in summer. Protect furry-leaved species from overhead water, especially in winter. Place stone chippings around plants to improve drainage.

PROPAGATING

Divide or take cuttings in early summer.

Celosia

Cockscomb

> **TYPE** HHA
> **ZONE** 2–10. Prefers warm temperatures.
> **FLOWERING SEASON** Summer through early autumn

Upright plants bearing blossoms in unnatural shades of pink or yellow which resemble either intricately worked chenille or badly dyed dusters. Those who grow this plant seem to prefer it en masse; 12"–4'.

SOWING

INDOORS 6–8 weeks before last frost, in peat pots.
OUTDOORS After last frost.
DEPTH Just cover.

GERMINATING

TIME 6–14 days.
REQUIREMENTS Easy. 70°–75°F.

PLANTING SEEDLINGS OUTDOORS

TIME After last frost.
SPACING Dwarf species: 12". Tall species: 18".
LIGHT Full sun to light shade.
SOIL Ordinary, moist, with a pH level of 6.0–7.0.

CARING FOR PLANTS

Easy. Keep soil moist and fertilize lightly during the growing season.

PROPAGATING

Self-seeds.

A-Annual **P**-Perennial **B**-Biennial **HHA**-Half-hardy annual **HA**-Hardy annual **HB**-Hardy biennial **HHP**-Half-hardy perennial **HP**-Hardy perennial **HHBb**-Half-hardy bulb **HBb**-Hardy bulb

Centaurea

Bachelor's buttons, Basket flower, Blue-bottle, Cornflower, Dusty-miller, Knapweed, Mountain bluet, Ragged robin, Ragged sailor, Royal sweet-sultan, Sweet-sultan

TYPE HA, HB, or HP
ZONE A: 1–10; P: 3–8: *C. hypoleuca*; 4–8: *C. dealbata*, *C. macrocephala*, *C. montana*; 6–8: *C. cineraria*; 6–9: *C. ruthenica*, *C. nigra*. Most species prefer cool temperatures.
FLOWERING SEASON A: late spring through late summer; P: spring or summer, depending on species

Large genus of charming upright plants bearing deeply colored, fine-petalled pom-poms; evocative of carefree summers and country meadows. Use these 12"–36" plants in borders, wild flower plantings, or cottage gardens.

SOWING

INDOORS 6–8 weeks before planting out.
OUTDOORS Just before last frost, or in autumn where winters are mild. Successive sowing will ensure continuous bloom.
DEPTH Just cover.

GERMINATING

TIME 7–30 days.
REQUIREMENTS Provide darkness and 60°–70°F.

PLANTING SEEDLINGS OUTDOORS

TIME A: late spring. B or P: late spring or early autumn.
SPACING Dwarf species: 6". Tall species: 12".
LIGHT Full sun.
SOIL Ordinary, well-drained, with a pH level of 5.5–7.0.

CARING FOR PLANTS

Easy. Water regularly and feed once in the spring. Deadhead frequently to prolong blooming. Where summers are very hot, cut perennials back hard after blooming. Plants may require staking. Do not disturb.

PROPAGATING

Annuals will self-seed. Divide perennials in spring in zones 3–6, in autumn in zones 7–10.

Centaurea montana

Centaurium

(synonymous with *Erythraea*)

Canchalagua, Centaury, Mountain pink

TYPE HA
ZONE 1–9. Performs best where summers are cool.
FLOWERING SEASON Summer

Very low-growing plants, up to 8", with clusters of red or pink blooms. Attractive edging or rock garden or border plants.

SOWING

INDOORS Seeds should be sown *in situ*.
OUTDOORS Very early spring or autumn where winters are mild; after last frost elsewhere.
DEPTH Just cover.

GERMINATING

TIME 21–60 days.
REQUIREMENTS 65°–75°F.

PLANTING SEEDLINGS OUTDOORS

TIME After last frost.
SPACING Small species: 6"–8". Large species: 12".
LIGHT Full sun or part shade; shade from very hot afternoon sun is desirable.
SOIL Light, sandy, very well-drained.

CARING FOR PLANTS

Easy. Requires no special care.

PROPAGATING

Self-seeds.

A-Annual P-Perennial B-Biennial HHA-Half-hardy annual HA-Hardy annual HB-Hardy biennial HHP-Half-hardy perennial HP-Hardy perennial HHBb-Half-hardy bulb HBb-Hardy bulb

78

Centranthus

Fox's brush, Jupiter's beard, Keys of heaven, Pretty Betsy, Valerian

TYPE HP
ZONE 4–9. Does not tolerate excessive heat and humidity.
FLOWERING SEASON Late spring through frost

Shrubby perennials, usually 2'–3', bearing white or deep pink blooms on upright stems. Mediterranean natives grown in rock gardens and borders, or cascading from drystone walls.

SOWING

INDOORS 8 weeks before planting out, in peat pots.
OUTDOORS Early spring when soil is cool and a light frost is still possible.
DEPTH Just cover.

GERMINATING

TIME 21–30 days.
REQUIREMENTS Easy. 60°–70°F.

PLANTING SEEDLINGS OUTDOORS

TIME After last frost.
SPACING 12"–18".
LIGHT Full sun.
SOIL Well-drained, slightly limy. Rich soil will produce large plants, poor soil more compact ones.

CARING FOR PLANTS

Easy. Feed plants in spring and cut back after flowering to encourage a second bloom. Although *Centranthus* is drought-tolerant, more attractive plants will result from regular watering during dry spells. Cut back flowering stems to ground in winter. Plants are short-lived and require frequent renewal. Do not transplant.

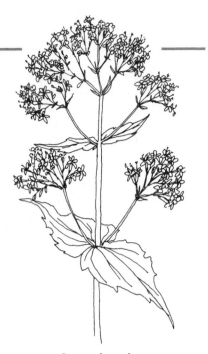

Centranthus ruber

PROPAGATING

Take basal cuttings in early summer. Self-seeds quite freely.

Cephalaria

Scabious

TYPE HP
ZONE 3–9
FLOWERING SEASON Summer

Large, coarse, clump-forming perennials, up to 6', bearing cheerful, cup-shaped, yellow flowers in summer. Allow plenty of room at the back of the border, or set loose in a wild garden; flowers are useful for cutting.

SOWING

INDOORS Late winter to early spring.
OUTDOORS Spring.
DEPTH ¼".

GERMINATING

TIME 21–60 days.
REQUIREMENTS Easy. 55°–65°F. If seeds have not sprouted in 60 days, chill for 3 weeks.

PLANTING SEEDLINGS OUTDOORS

TIME After last frost.
SPACING 24"–36".
LIGHT Sun or part shade.
SOIL Adaptable, but prefers moist soil.

CARING FOR PLANTS

Easy. Water regularly and cut back after flowering. Plants may require staking. Divide every 2–3 years to keep vigorous.

PROPAGATING

Divide in early spring.

A-Annual P-Perennial B-Biennial HHA-Half-hardy annual HA-Hardy annual HB-Hardy biennial HHP-Half-hardy perennial HP-Hardy perennial HHBb-Half-hardy bulb HBb-Hardy bulb

Cephalipterum

Pompoms

> TYPE HHA
> ZONE 1–10. Flowering will be reduced in hot, dry weather.
> FLOWERING SEASON Summer

Annual plants grown for their everlasting flowers. These are small, round and papery, held on wiry 12" stems. Use in the border or cutting bed.

SOWING

INDOORS 6–8 weeks before planting out.
OUTDOORS After last frost.
DEPTH Just cover.

GERMINATING

TIME 14–21 days.
REQUIREMENTS 65°–75°F.

PLANTING SEEDLINGS OUTDOORS

TIME After last frost.
SPACING 12".
LIGHT Full sun or light shade.
SOIL Flowers best in poor soil that is cool and moist, but is fairly drought tolerant.

CARING FOR PLANTS

Mulch to keep soil cool. Water regularly for best results. Watch out for slugs in wet spring weather. For use in dried arrangements, cut stems before flowers are fully open; hang upside down in a cool, shady spot.

PROPAGATING

Seed only.

Cerastium

Snow-in-summer

> TYPE HP
> ZONE 3–9
> FLOWERING SEASON Early spring to summer, depending on species

Delightful, dwarf, mat-forming perennials that are useful ground cover, edging, or rock garden plants. Downy leaves are often grey; small, star-shaped flowers are white.

SOWING

INDOORS 6–8 weeks before planting out.
OUTDOORS Early spring, when soil is cool and a light frost is still possible, or late autumn.
DEPTH Just cover.

GERMINATING

TIME 5–15 days.
REQUIREMENTS 65°–75°F.

PLANTING SEEDLINGS OUTDOORS

TIME After last spring frost or autumn.
SPACING Small species: 4"–6". Tall species: 12"–18".
LIGHT Full sun to light shade.
SOIL Prefers moist soil with a pH level of 6.0–7.0, but will tolerate dry.

CARING FOR PLANTS

Easy. Cut plants back after flowering to maintain a tidy appearance. Divide every 2–3 years.

PROPAGATING

Take cuttings in early summer. Divide in spring in the North, in autumn south of zone 6.

Cerastium tomentosum

A-Annual P-Perennial B-Biennial HHA-Half-hardy annual HA-Hardy annual HB-Hardy biennial HHP-Half-hardy perennial HP-Hardy perennial HHBb-Half-hardy bulb HBb-Hardy bulb

Ceratostigma

Leadwort, Plumbago

> TYPE HP or HHP
> ZONE 5–9: C. *plumbaginoides*;
> 8–9: C. *willmottianum*
> FLOWERING SEASON Summer to
> autumn

Low-growing, spreading, shrubby perennials invaluable for their late summer blooms of intense blue and their clean foliage, which turns a showy bronze in autumn. Use as ground cover, edging plant, or in rock gardens or stone walls; vital players in the autumn garden team.

SOWING

INDOORS Pre-chilled seeds 10–12 weeks before planting out.
OUTDOORS Hardy species: early spring, when soil is cool and a light frost is still possible, or late autumn. Half-hardy species: after last frost.
DEPTH Just cover.

GERMINATING

TIME 30–90 days.
REQUIREMENTS Place seeds together with moistened sand in a plastic bag, seal lightly, and refrigerate for 4–6 weeks. Provide 60°F thereafter.

PLANTING SEEDLINGS OUTDOORS

TIME Hardy species: early spring or early autumn. Half-hardy species: spring, when temperatures remain above 50°F.
SPACING 12"–18".
LIGHT Full sun or part shade.
SOIL Tolerant of many soils, including poor, stony, or heavy, but prefers a rich, well-drained soil with plenty of organic matter.

CARING FOR PLANTS

Water regularly but do not allow soil to become soggy; cut back to ground level in autumn.

Ceratostigma plumbaginoides

PROPAGATING

Divide clumps in autumn or late winter for hardy species, after last spring frost for half-hardy species.

Charieis

(synonymous with *Kaulfussia*)

> TYPE HA
> ZONE 3–10
> FLOWERING SEASON Summer; in
> the South, an autumn sowing
> produces blooms in winter and
> early spring

Pleasing little annuals from South Africa grown for their clear blue, daisylike flowers; 12" tall. Use in borders or containers; excellent cut flower for nosegays.

SOWING

INDOORS 4–6 weeks before last frost.
OUTDOORS Early spring; autumn in zones 9–10.
DEPTH ¼".

GERMINATING

TIME 21–30 days.

PLANTING SEEDLINGS OUTDOORS

TIME After last frost.
SPACING 6".
LIGHT Sun.
SOIL Light, sandy.

CARING FOR PLANTS

No special care required.

PROPAGATING

Seed.

A-Annual P-Perennial B-Biennial HHA-Half-hardy annual HA-Hardy annual HB-Hardy biennial HHP-Half-hardy perennial HP-Hardy perennial HHBb-Half-hardy bulb HBb-Hardy bulb

Cheiranthus

Gillyflower, Wallflower

> **TYPE** HP usually grown as HA or HB
> **ZONE** A: 5–10; P: 8–10. Must have cool, damp summers with night temperatures below 65°F.
> **FLOWERING SEASON** Late spring through early autumn, depending on species

Upright, bushy plants of 6"–30" grown for the tangle of blossoms that covers each stalk for weeks; flowers in almost every color, from subtle to alarming. De rigueur in English gardens, where it has become a cliche.

SOWING

INDOORS 8–10 weeks before planting out.
OUTDOORS A or P: early spring or early autumn. B: midsummer to early autumn for flowers the following years.
DEPTH ¼".

GERMINATING

TIME 5–21 days.
REQUIREMENTS 65°–75°F. Very susceptible to damping-off; sow seeds in vermiculite and water only from below.

PLANTING SEEDLINGS OUTDOORS

TIME A or P: early spring, when soil is cool and a light frost is still possible. B: early summer to midsummer.
SPACING Dwarf species: 6"–9". Medium or tall species: 12"–18".
LIGHT Full sun to light shade.
SOIL Ordinary, very well-drained, neutral or slightly limy.

CARING FOR PLANTS

Easy. Pinch out tips to encourage bushiness. Water during dry spells. Plants may be uprooted and discarded when blooming is finished.

PROPAGATING

Take cuttings in late spring.

Cheiranthus cheiri

Chelidonium

Celandine, Celandine poppy, Greater celandine

> **TYPE** HP or HB
> **ZONE** 4–8
> **FLOWERING SEASON** Spring to summer

Very small genus of rather weedy plants bearing bright green leaves and cheerful yellow blooms; upright habit; 2'–4' tall. Use in wild gardens and areas where its propensity to overrun will not cause heartache.

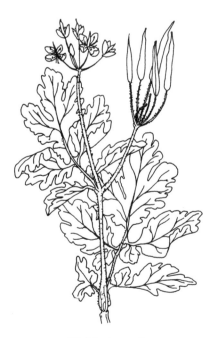

Chelidonium majus

SOWING

INDOORS Start seed outdoors only.
OUTDOORS Early spring or autumn.
DEPTH Surface.

GERMINATING

TIME 30–365 days.
REQUIREMENTS Sow seeds in flats of moistened growing medium, sink flats in the ground against a north-facing wall, and cover with glass. Transplant seedlings as they appear.

PLANTING SEEDLINGS OUTDOORS

SPACING 12".
LIGHT Sun or shade.
SOIL Any that is moist but not wet.

CARING FOR PLANTS

Easy. This wildflower thrives with no care.

PROPAGATING

Divide in spring (autumn in zones 7 and 8). Self-seeds freely.

A-Annual P-Perennial B-Biennial HHA-Half-hardy annual HA-Hardy annual HB-Hardy biennial HHP-Half-hardy perennial HP-Hardy perennial HHBb-Half-hardy bulb HBb-Hardy bulb

Chelone

Snake head, Turtle head

> **Type HP**
> **Zone** 3–9; *C. glabra* and
>   *C. lyonii* will not thrive in high
>   heat and humidity.
> **Flowering Season** Late summer

North American native perennials bearing curiously shaped, pink or white flowers at the tips of stiff, upright stems. Plants are 3'–6'. Grow at the back of the border or near water.

Sowing

Indoors 6–8 weeks before planting out.
Outdoors After last frost.
Depth Just cover.

Chelone glabra

Germinating

Time 14–48 days.
Requirements 55°–65°F.

Planting Seedlings Outdoors

Time After last spring frost or in autumn.
Spacing 7"–12".
Light Sun or light shade.
Soil Moist, rich, with a pH level of 5.0–7.0.

Caring for Plants

Requires little care beyond regular watering. Mulch lightly in spring and autumn with leaf mold. Cut back to ground level after flowering. Susceptible to mildew if air circulation is poor and soil is allowed to remain dry.

Propagating

Divide in early spring where winters are harsh, early autumn in milder climates. Take cuttings in spring or summer.

Chiastophyllum

Silver crown

> **Type HP**
> **Zone** 4–8
> **Flowering Season** Summer

Evergreen, succulent perennial, a mere green blob throughout most of the year, but coming to life in summer when arching wands appear bearing drooping sprays of tiny yellow flowers. Use in rock gardens, drystone walls, and rock crevices.

Sowing

Indoors Pre-chilled seeds 8–10 weeks before planting out.
Outdoors Early spring or late autumn.
Depth Surface.

Germinating

Time 15–60 days.
Requirements Place seeds and moist growing medium in a plastic bag and refrigerate for 2 weeks. Provide 70°–75°F thereafter.

Planting Seedlings Outdoors

Time After last spring frost or in autumn.
Spacing 6".
Light Full sun or part shade.
Soil Tolerant of dry soil but prefers some moisture and light, well-drained soil.

Caring for Plants

Water well during the growing season, but keep plants fairly dry otherwise.

Propagating

Take cuttings in midsummer to late summer; divide in spring, autumn in zones 7–8.

A-Annual P-Perennial B-Biennial HHA-Half-hardy annual HA-Hardy annual HB-Hardy biennial HHP-Half-hardy perennial HP-Hardy perennial HHBb-Half-hardy bulb HBb-Hardy bulb

Chionodoxa

Glory of the snow

> TYPE HBb
> ZONE 4–8
> FLOWERING SEASON Late winter to early spring

Genus of small (3"–8"), pretty, spring-blooming bulbs bearing star-shaped, usually blue flowers; less commonly flowers may be pink or white. Use in rock gardens or naturalize in the lawn or around shrubs; plant thickly to give the effect of a blue carpet.

SOWING

INDOORS There is little need to start plants indoors as *Chionadoxas* self-seed so readily, but for those who wish, seeds may be started at any time.
OUTDOORS Seed: midsummer to late summer. Bulb: autumn.
DEPTH Seed: ¼". Bulb: 3".

GERMINATING

TIME 30–90 days.
REQUIREMENTS 55°F.

PLANTING SEEDLINGS OUTDOORS

TIME Early autumn, after 1 year of growth.
SPACING 3"–6".
LIGHT Sun or part shade.
SOIL Moist, rather fertile, well-drained, with a pH level of 6.0–7.0.

CARING FOR PLANTS

These easy bulbs require very little maintenance. Water regularly, feed every 2 years in early spring, and leave bulbs undisturbed except for division every 4–5 years.

PROPAGATING

Plant bulblets after flowering, or allow to self-seed.

Chlorogalum

Soap plant

> TYPE HBb
> ZONE 8–10. Performs well only on the Pacific Coast.
> FLOWERING SEASON June

This bulb, native to western North America, is something of a botanical curiosity. Growing 2'–8' tall, it has long, thin, grey-green leaves with wavy margins, and white, pink, or blue flowers borne terminally and blooming only in the afternoon. Use judiciously, possibly as a focal point.

SOWING

INDOORS See "Germinating, Requirements."
OUTDOORS Seed: see "Germinating, Requirements." Bulb: autumn.
DEPTH Seed: ⅛". Bulb: Cover with twice its diameter of soil.

GERMINATING

TIME 30–90 days.
REQUIREMENTS *Autumn sowing:* Sow seeds in flats, sink in the ground against a north-facing wall, and cover with glass. Moisten soil occasionally, if necessary. Bring indoors in spring to 55°–60°F. *Spring sowing:* Sow seeds in moistened medium, place containers in plastic bags, and refrigerate for 2–3 weeks. Remove and sink in the ground to the rim in a shady location, covering with glass. Transplant seedlings as they appear.

PLANTING SEEDLINGS OUTDOORS

TIME Autumn.
SPACING 3"–4".
LIGHT Sun or light shade.
SOIL Moist, fertile, and well-drained, especially in winter.

CARING FOR PLANTS

Water frequently and leave bulbs undisturbed, dividing only when they exhibit signs of overcrowding. Cut back flowering stems after blooming. Mulch with compost in winter.

PROPAGATING

Plants offsets in spring or autumn.

A-Annual P-Perennial B-Biennial HHA-Half-hardy annual HA-Hardy annual HB-Hardy biennial HHP-Half-hardy perennial HP-Hardy perennial HHBb-Half-hardy bulb HBb-Hardy bulb

84

Chrysanthemum (Annual)

Corn marigold

Type HA
Zone 3–10
Flowering Season Summer through frost

Long-blooming, easy-care annuals bearing masses of pretty, daisylike flowers in every shade of yellow, red, pink, and white; many have two-toned petals or contrasting eyes. Plants are upright and branching, 4"–36" tall, with feathery or lance-shaped leaves, often grey-green. Dependable in the border or cottage garden; small species make a attractive edging, taller species are excellent cut flowers.

SOWING

INDOORS 6–8 weeks before last frost.
OUTDOORS Just before last frost.
DEPTH ⅛".

GERMINATING

TIME 10–13 days.
REQUIREMENTS 60°–70°F.

PLANTING SEEDLINGS OUTDOORS

TIME After last frost.
SPACING Small species: 6". Medium/tall species: 12"–18".
LIGHT Sun.
SOIL Ordinary, well-drained, with a pH level of 6.0–7.0.

CARING FOR PLANTS

Pinch out seedlings to encourage a bushy habit; deadhead regularly. Tall species may require staking in windy sites.

PROPAGATING

Some species may self-seed.

Chrysanthemum (Perennial)

Feverfew, Painted daisy, Pyrethrum, Shasta daisy

Type HP
Zone 2–9: *C. arcticum*;
3–9: *C. coccineum, C. leucanthemum, C. x morifolium, C. weyrichii*; 5–9: *C. corymbosum, C. frutescens, C. indicum, C. nipponicum, C. parthenium, C. x rubellum, C. x superbum, C. uliginosum*. Most Chrysanthemums prefer a cool growing season and a low humidity. Exceptions are *C. frutescens, C. leucanthemum*, and *C. nipponicum*.
Flowering Season Summer through late autumn, depending on species

Large genus of shrubby annuals and perennials grown for the masses of blooms that cover plants in late summer and autumn. Plants are 4"–36" tall, with daisylike flowers, often double, in shades of red, yellow, orange, pink, and white. Essential part of the autumn garden and useful container plants.

Chrysanthemum maximum

Chrysanthemum x morifolium

SOWING

INDOORS 6–8 weeks before planting out.
OUTDOORS Early spring, when soil is cool and a light frost is still possible, or late autumn.
DEPTH Surface.

GERMINATING

TIME 7–28 days.
REQUIREMENTS Light and 60°–75°F.

PLANTING SEEDLINGS OUTDOORS

TIME After last spring frost or in autumn.
SPACING Small species: 12"–15". Large species: 18"–24".
LIGHT Plants must receive at least 6 hours of sunlight a day to bloom.
SOIL Rich, deep, well-drained, with a pH level of 5.5–7.0.

CARING FOR PLANTS

Feed with a balanced fertilizer 2 weeks after planting and again when plants are 12" tall. Pinch tips when plants are 6" and again after every additional 6" of new growth until early August. Water and deadhead regularly. After blooming, cut back to ground level and mulch lightly. Some species may require division every 1–2 years to maintain strong blooming.

PROPAGATING

Take cuttings. South of zone 6, divide after flowering in autumn; elsewhere, divide in early spring.

A-Annual P-Perennial B-Biennial HHA-Half-hardy annual HA-Hardy annual HB-Hardy biennial HHP-Half-hardy perennial HP-Hardy perennial HHBb-Half-hardy bulb HBb-Hardy bulb

85

Chrysogonum

**Golden knee, Goldenstar,
Green-and-gold**

> TYPE HP
> ZONE 5–9
> FLOWERING SEASON Late spring
> and sporadically through
> summer and autumn

Low-growing American native valued for its bright yellow daisylike flowers borne over a long period. Plant in the rock garden or near a woodland path; possibly useful as a ground cover.

SOWING

INDOORS As soon as fresh seed is available.
OUTDOORS As soon as fresh seed is available.
DEPTH ¼".

GERMINATING

TIME 21 days.
REQUIREMENTS 70°–75°F. Propagation by division or runners is easier and more successful than by seed.

PLANTING SEEDLINGS OUTDOORS

TIME Early spring or autumn.
SPACING 6"–8".
LIGHT Part shade; full sun in northern zones or in moist soil in the South.
SOIL Moist, sandy, well-drained soil that is never very wet or very dry; prefers a pH level of 6.0–7.5.

CARING FOR PLANTS

Mulch to retain soil moisture and water during dry spells. Keep soil on the poor side to maintain compact growth. Flowering is curtailed by very hot weather.

PROPAGATING

Divide in early spring in zones 5 and 6, in early autumn elsewhere or propagate by root runners. *Chrysogonum* will self-seed.

Cimicifuga

**Black cohosh, Black snakeroot,
Bugbane, Snakeroot**

> TYPE HP
> ZONE 3–9
> FLOWERING SEASON Midsummer
> to late summer

Intriguing woodland perennials. Plants are upright, leaves green, sometimes fernlike. Deceptively undistinguished in leaf, but in bloom these plants are magical, bearing long bottle-brushes of tiny white flowers. Most effective when blooming alone or in subtle combination with other low-profile woodland plants.

SOWING

INDOORS Autumn, as soon as seed is ripe.
OUTDOORS Sow fresh seed in autumn.
DEPTH Just cover.

Cimicifuga dahurica

GERMINATING

TIME 30–365 days.
REQUIREMENTS Leave seeds (un-sown) at 55°–60°F for a period of 6–8 weeks, then place in a plastic bag and refrigerate for 8 weeks. Sow seeds and provide 60°F.

PLANTING SEEDLINGS OUTDOORS

TIME After last spring frost or in autumn.
SPACING Small species: 24". Large species: 36".
LIGHT Flowers most profusely in part shade, but will grow quite happily in full shade.
SOIL Moist, humus-rich, with a pH level of 5.0–6.0.

CARING FOR PLANTS

Feed once in the spring and water regularly during dry periods. Mulch with leaf mold or compost. Do not disturb established plants.

PROPAGATING

Divide roots in spring where winters are very cold; in the South, divide in autumn.

A-Annual P-Perennial B-Biennial HHA-Half-hardy annual HA-Hardy annual HB-Hardy biennial HHP-Half-hardy perennial HP-Hardy perennial HHBb-Half-hardy bulb HBb-Hardy bulb

Cineraria

See *Senecio*

Cirsium

Plume thistle, Scotch thistle

> TYPE HP, or B grown as HA
> ZONE 3–9. Prefers cool temperatures.
> FLOWERING SEASON Late summer to early autumn

Erect, spiny, dangerous-looking plants tolerated only for their decorative thistle heads of purple, red, white, or yellow; 3'–4' tall. Use at the back of the border or in the wild garden.

SOWING
INDOORS 2– weeks before last frost.
OUTDOORS After last spring frost or in autumn.
DEPTH ⅛".

GERMINATING
TIME 15–18 days.
REQUIREMENTS 70°–75°F.

PLANTING SEEDLINGS OUTDOORS
TIME After last frost.
SPACING 24".
LIGHT Full sun or part shade.
SOIL Moist, well-drained.

CARING FOR PLANTS
Easy. Requires little maintenance. In congenial surroundings, *Cirsium* can become weedy and effect a hostile takeover of your garden.

PROPAGATING
By seed only.

Cladanthus

Palm Springs daisy

> TYPE HA or HHA
> ZONE 1–9. Flowers best where summers are cool.
> FLOWERING SEASON Summer through first frost

Genus of one species of annual plant growing 24" tall. Golden daisylike flowers peep through a mass of feathery green leaves; both flowers and foliage are fragrant. Very attractive border plant.

SOWING
INDOORS 6–8 weeks before planting out.
OUTDOORS Early spring to midspring.
DEPTH Just cover.

GERMINATING
TIME 30–35 days.
REQUIREMENTS Easy. 70°–75°F.

PLANTING SEEDLINGS OUTDOORS
TIME After last frost.
SPACING 12".
LIGHT Sun.
SOIL Tolerates dry, but prefers moist, well-drained soil.

CARING FOR PLANTS
Easy. Feed in spring and water during dry spells. Deadhead to prolong flowering.

PROPAGATING
Allow to self-seed.

Cladanthus arabicus

A-Annual P-Perennial B-Biennial HHA-Half-hardy annual HA-Hardy annual HB-Hardy biennial HHP-Half-hardy perennial HP-Hardy perennial HHBb-Half-hardy bulb HBb-Hardy bulb

87

Clarkia

(synonymous with *Godetia*)

Farewell-to-spring, Godetia, Rocky Mountain garland, Satin flower

> TYPE HA
> ZONE 2–10. Prefers the cool, damp Pacific Coast; blooming will be reduced where summers are very hot.
> FLOWERING SEASON Summer through early autumn

Genus of bushy, upright annuals, 12"–48" tall. Flowers are rosette-like, often double or semi-double, but even single blooms are wavy and rippling like a full skirt, usually in white or shades of pink or purple. Lovely border plants.

SOWING

INDOORS Stronger plants result when seeds are started outdoors; if indoor sowing is necessary, start 6–8 weeks before last frost, in peat pots.

Clarkia amoena

JUDY ELIASON

OUTDOORS After last frost, then twice more at 2-week intervals to extend the blooming period. In zones 8–10, seeds may be sown in autumn.
DEPTH Surface.

GERMINATING

TIME 5–21 days.
REQUIREMENTS Light and 55°–70°F.

PLANTING SEEDLINGS OUTDOORS

TIME After last frost.
SPACING Small species: 6"–9". Tall species: 9"–12".
LIGHT Full sun in cool climates, otherwise part shade.
SOIL Cool, moist, well-drained, with a pH level of 6.0–7.0. Prefers soil with a low nitrogen content.

CARING FOR PLANTS

Easy. Water regularly and feed lightly in spring. Support with twiggy branches pushed into the ground when plants are young; tall species may require staking. For better blooming, keep plants slightly crowded and do not overfeed. Flowering will be greatly diminished in hot weather. Do not move plants.

PROPAGATING

Some species will self-seed.

Claytonia

Grass flower, Mayflower, Spring beauty

> TYPE HA or HP
> ZONE A: 3–9; P: 5–8. Prefers cool summers.
> FLOWERING SEASON Early spring

Evergreen, rosette-forming perennials with succulent leaves and small, pink or white flowers; usually 3"–6". Grow these American natives in a wildflower, rock, or woodland garden.

SOWING

INDOORS Seeds are best started outdoors.
OUTDOORS As soon as ripe seed is available in summer.
DEPTH ⅛".

GERMINATING

TIME 14–21 days.
REQUIREMENTS Seeds are difficult to collect and rarely available. Sow in flats, sink in the ground against a north-facing wall, and cover with glass. Moisten soil occasionally, if necessary.

PLANTING SEEDLINGS OUTDOORS

TIME Set out purchased plants in spring or autumn.
SPACING 4"–6".
LIGHT Shade.
SOIL Moist, gritty, rich, with a pH level of 5.0–7.0.

CARING FOR PLANTS

Easy if situated correctly, otherwise difficult. Water regularly; plants will not survive in dry soil. Foliage dies back to ground after blooming.

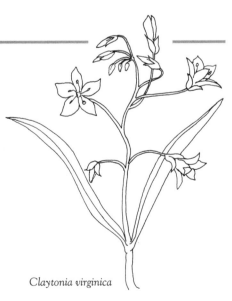

Claytonia virginica

PROPAGATING

Divide perennials very carefully in autumn. Both annuals and perennials may self-seed.

A-Annual P-Perennial B-Biennial HHA-Half-hardy annual HA-Hardy annual HB-Hardy biennial HHP-Half-hardy perennial HP-Hardy perennial HHBb-Half-hardy bulb HBb-Hardy bulb

Clematis

TYPE HP
ZONE 3–9
FLOWERING SEASON Spring,
    summer, or autumn, depending
    on species

Very large genus of climbing vines prized for their eye-catching flowers. Most commonly-grown species flaunt large, flat flower heads of undenied beauty, if little subtlety; lesser-known species bear smaller blooms of simpler colors, upright or pendulous, some resembling *Tulipa*, *Helleborus*, *Campanulas*, and *Browallia*; pink, purple, white, yellow, cream.

SOWING

INDOORS See "Germinating, Requirements."
OUTDOORS See "Germinating, Requirements."
DEPTH Seed: ⅛". Root: 2"–3".

GERMINATING

TIME Usually 30–365 days, but may take up to 3 years.

Clematis lanuginosa

REQUIREMENTS *Autumn sowing*: Sow seeds in flats, sink in the ground next to a north-facing wall, and cover with glass. Moisten soil occasionally, if necessary. Bring indoors in spring to 70°–75°F. *Spring sowing*: Sow seeds in containers and freeze for 3 weeks. Remove and sink in the ground in a shady location, covering with glass. Transplant seedlings as they appear.

PLANTING SEEDLINGS OUTDOORS

TIME Plant purchased vines in autumn.
SPACING 36"–48".

LIGHT Most species prefer full sun, although some will tolerate part shade. All *Clematis* must have shaded roots.
SOIL A cool, rich, sandy loam with a pH level of 6.0–7.5, liberally enriched with organic matter, will produce strong, healthy vines. Prepare planting holes to a depth of 18"–24", adding gravel to the bottom to improve poor drainage.

CARING FOR PLANTS

Easy. Begin feeding 2-year-old plants with a weak 5–10–5 fertilizer in early spring and again every 6 weeks throughout the growing season. Water frequently and mulch liberally. The roots and base of stem are very fragile and should be protected from accidental injury. Provide support, preferably one that encourages branching, thus exposing all parts of the vine to sunlight. To prune vines flowering in spring (on old wood), remove only dead or weak stems in spring, carefully thinning overgrown crowns. Late-blooming vines (flowering on new growth) should be cut back to 12"–18" in late winter, *before* new growth begins.

PROPAGATING

Take cuttings in early summer. Some species may be propagated by seed.

Cleome

Spider flower

TYPE HHA
ZONE 2–10. Prefers warm
    temperatures.
FLOWERING SEASON Summer
    through late autumn

Weedy but carefree, these fast-growing 3'–4' annuals are a haze of open, rounded, spiky flower heads from late spring through frost. Mass at the back of the border or in a neglected corner. Blooms are pink, white, or, recently introduced, an unusual shade of purple. Native of South America.

SOWING

INDOORS 6–8 weeks before last frost.
OUTDOORS After last frost.
DEPTH Surface.

GERMINATING

TIME 10–14 days.
REQUIREMENTS Place seeds and moistened growing medium in a plastic bag and refrigerate for 2 weeks. Seeds require 70°–75°F thereafter.

PLANTING SEEDLINGS OUTDOORS

TIME 2–3 weeks after last frost, when temperatures remain above 40°F.
SPACING 18"–24".
LIGHT Full sun or very light shade.
SOIL Average, with a pH level of 6.0–7.0; tolerant of dry soil.

CARING FOR PLANTS

Easy. Feed and water during the growing season. To avoid self-seeding, pick off seed capsules before they open.

Cleome spinosa

PROPAGATING

Self-seeds wantonly.

A-Annual P-Perennial B-Biennial HHA-Half-hardy annual HA-Hardy annual HB-Hardy biennial HHP-Half-hardy perennial HP-Hardy perennial HHBb-Half-hardy bulb HBb-Hardy bulb

Clintonia

Bluebead, Bride's bonnet, Corn lily, Queen cup

> TYPE HP
> ZONE 3–9. Prefers cool climates.
> FLOWERING SEASON Late spring

Spreading, clump-forming woodland plants native to North America, growing 8"–24" tall. Attractive leaves resemble long, green tongues; petite, bell-shaped flowers of pink, yellow, or white have an elfin quality.

SOWING

INDOORS Late winter to early spring.
OUTDOORS As soon as fresh seed is available (usually midsummer to late summer).
DEPTH Just cover.

GERMINATING

TIME 30–90 days.
REQUIREMENTS *Indoor sowing:* Seeds require 55°–60°F. *Outdoor sowing:* Sow seeds in flats, sink in the ground against a north-facing wall, and cover with glass. Moisten soil occasionally, if necessary. Move seedlings to the garden after 2 growing seasons.

PLANTING SEEDLINGS OUTDOORS

TIME Seedlings started indoors can be moved to the garden in autumn.
SPACING 6"–8".
LIGHT Shade.
SOIL Rich, acid, moist, well-drained soil or sphagnum moss.

CARING FOR PLANTS

Easy. Cover roots with a mulch of leaf mold and keep plants well watered during summer. Do not disturb established plants.

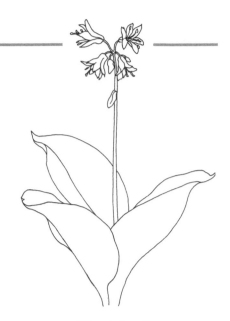

Clintonia borealis

PROPAGATING

Divide in spring.

Cobaea

Cathedral bells, Cup-and-saucer vine, Mexican ivy

> TYPE HHP treated as HHA
> ZONE A: 1–8; P: 9–10. Prefers warm temperatures.
> FLOWERING SEASON Summer through autumn

Sturdy climbing vines grown for their large, showy, bell-shaped flowers of purple, white, or cream; flowers of one species intriguingly start off yellow, then change to purple. 12'–15'.

SOWING

INDOORS 6–8 weeks before last frost, in peat pots.
OUTDOORS Only in zones 9–10, after last frost date.
DEPTH Just cover.

GERMINATING

TIME 10–30 days.
REQUIREMENTS Easy. Nick seeds with a sharp knife before sowing and provide 70°–75°F.

PLANTING SEEDLINGS OUTDOORS

TIME 2–3 weeks after last frost, when temperatures remain above 40°F.
SPACING 24"–36".
LIGHT Full sun, with shade from afternoon sun where summers are hot.
SOIL Ordinary, amended with well-rotted manure.

CARING FOR PLANTS

Easy. Pinch out tips of young plants to encourage branching and provide a trellis for support. Water regularly and feed occasionally. Prune perennials in early spring.

PROPAGATING

Seed only.

A-Annual P-Perennial B-Biennial HHA-Half-hardy annual HA-Hardy annual HB-Hardy biennial HHP-Half-hardy perennial HP-Hardy perennial HHBb-Half-hardy bulb HBb-Hardy bulb

Codonopsis

Bonnet bellflower

> **TYPE** HP
> **ZONE** 5–8
> **FLOWERING SEASON** Summer

Unusual perennial climbers grown for their profuse blooms, which may be pretty blue stars or odd, bell-shaped curiosities of green, yellow, or blue. Grow on a trellis or allow to ramble artistically through shrubs.

SOWING
INDOORS Sow seeds in late winter to early spring, in peat pots.
OUTDOORS Late spring, when soil is cool and a light frost is still possible, or late autumn.
DEPTH Surface.

GERMINATING
TIME 7–24 days.
REQUIREMENTS Light and 60°–70°F.

PLANTING SEEDLINGS OUTDOORS
TIME After last frost.
SPACING 12"–24".
LIGHT Full sun or part shade; plants will be stronger when grown in full sun.
SOIL Acid, well-drained, on the dry side.

CARING FOR PLANTS
Easy. Provide a trellis or other support. Mulch heavily in winter. Do not attempt to move established plants.

PROPAGATING
Divide in spring. Take cuttings in spring or autumn.

Coix

Job's tears

> **TYPE** HHP grown as HHA
> **ZONE** A: 1–8; P: 9–10. Prefers cool temperatures.
> **FLOWERING SEASON** Summer

Stiff, coarse, upright grasses, 3' tall. Leaves are sword-shaped and randomly drooping, giving an unkempt appearance; fruit is green, hard, and beadlike, highly ornamental. Use in naturalistic or meadow plantings.

SOWING
INDOORS 6–8 weeks before last frost, in peat pots.
OUTDOORS After last frost, but only attempt this where the growing season is long.
DEPTH ½".

GERMINATING
TIME 15–28 days.
REQUIREMENTS Soak seeds in warm water overnight and provide 60°–70°F thereafter.

PLANTING SEEDLINGS OUTDOORS
TIME After last frost, when temperatures remain above 45°F.
SPACING 18".
LIGHT Full sun or light shade.
SOIL Rich, well-drained.

CARING FOR PLANTS
Easy. Requires nothing more than watering during dry weather.

PROPAGATING
Self-seeds.

A-Annual P-Perennial B-Biennial HHA-Half-hardy annual HA-Hardy annual HB-Hardy biennial HHP-Half-hardy perennial HP-Hardy perennial HHBb-Half-hardy bulb HBb-Hardy bulb

91

Colchicum

Autumn crocus, Meadow saffron, Naked boys, Naked ladies

> TYPE HBb
> ZONE 4–9
> FLOWERING SEASON Early spring, late summer, or autumn, depending on species

Autumn-blooming bulbs useful for their large, pink, crocuslike flowers which appear without leaves (leaves appear in spring and die in summer). A stunning waterlily-flowered variety should not be missed. Successful use requires some thought: try growing through ground cover or peeping out from under spreading shrubs.

SOWING

INDOORS Start seeds outdoors.
OUTDOORS Seed or bulb: late summer to early autumn.
DEPTH Seed: ⅛". Small bulb: 3"–4". Large bulb: 4"–5".

Colchicum autumnale

GERMINATING

TIME 30–365 days.
REQUIREMENTS Sow seeds in flats, covering first with compost, then a thin layer of fine gravel. Plunge flats into the ground outdoors and cover with glass. Twelve months after germination, transplant corms to a nursery bed, spacing 12" apart. After 2 years, move to their final location.

PLANTING SEEDLINGS OUTDOORS

TIME Late summer to early autumn.
SPACING Small species: 4"–6". Large species: 6"–9".
LIGHT Full sun or part shade.
SOIL Light, rich, well-drained, with a pH level of 5.5–6.5.

CARING FOR PLANTS

Easy. Plants grown from seed will bloom in 4–6 years. Foliage dies back in late spring, reappearing after flowering; allow leaves to wither completely before removing. Water during dry spells, even when foliage is not visible. Do not disturb.

PROPAGATING

Divide cormels in summer. *C. autumnale* will self-seed.

Coleus

Flame nettle, Painted nettle

> TYPE HHP grown as HHA
> ZONE A: 5–9; P: 10. Performs well only where summers are quite warm.
> FLOWERING SEASON Summer, although the flowers are unimportant and are often removed

Low-growing, bushy plants valued for their showy, multicolored leaves in unusual colors: black, scarlet, orange, plum, gold, pink, salmon; 1'–3' high. Mass in a shady spot for best effect.

SOWING

INDOORS 8–12 weeks before last frost.
OUTDOORS Only in zones 9–10, after last frost.
DEPTH Surface.

GERMINATING

TIME 10–20 days.
REQUIREMENTS Easy. Light and 65°–75°F.

PLANTING SEEDLINGS OUTDOORS

TIME Several weeks after last frost, when soil is warm and the temperatures remain above 45°F.
SPACING Dwarf species: 6"–9". Tall species: 12"–20".
LIGHT Part to full shade. Plants grown in sun will have less vivid leaf color.
SOIL Moist, rich loam.

CARING FOR PLANTS

Easy. Pinch back young plants to encourage branching. Feed monthly with a high-nitrogen fertilizer and water during dry spells. Plants grown in sun will require frequent watering.

PROPAGATING

Take stem cuttings in summer or autumn, or root in water in a warm location.

Coleus blumei

A-Annual P-Perennial B-Biennial HHA-Half-hardy annual HA-Hardy annual HB-Hardy biennial HHP-Half-hardy perennial HP-Hardy perennial HHBb-Half-hardy bulb HBb-Hardy bulb

92

Collinsia

Blue-eyed Mary, Bluelips, Chinese houses, Innocence

> TYPE HA or HHA
> ZONE 3–10. Prefers mild days and cool nights and will not tolerate intense heat.
> FLOWERING SEASON Midsummer

Graceful, delicate, little annuals native to western North America. Willowy stalks hold clusters of small, pink flowers resembling parted lips. Blooms may be white, purple, pink, or blue. Plants are 12"–24" high. Grow in borders or containers.

SOWING

INDOORS Seeds are best started *in situ*.
OUTDOORS Where summers are cool: early spring, when soil is cool and a light frost is still possible; make successive plantings for continuous blooming. Where winters are mild: autumn.
DEPTH ¼".

GERMINATING

TIME 14–21 days.
REQUIREMENTS 65°–70°F.

PLANTING SEEDLINGS OUTDOORS

TIME Set out purchased plants after last frost.
SPACING 6"–12".
LIGHT Full sun where summers are mild, elsewhere provide afternoon shade.
SOIL Prefers moist, fertile, well-drained, with a pH level of 5.0–8.0; tolerates dry soil.

CARING FOR PLANTS

Easy. Deadhead regularly. Weak stems may necessitate staking. High summer temperatures will reduce blooming considerably.

PROPAGATING

Self-seeds.

Consolida

Annual delphinium, Larkspur

> TYPE HA
> ZONE Must have cool temperatures and may fail altogether where summers are too hot
> FLOWERING SEASON Summer to early autumn

Narrow, upright annuals with feathery, insignificant leaves but tall spires of blossoms that pack a punch all summer. Flowers are pink, purple, blue, or white; height is 12"–48". Exquisite when seen towering at the back of the border.

SOWING

INDOORS Pre-chilled seeds 6–8 weeks before planting out, in peat pots, but outdoor sowing is preferable.
OUTDOORS 2 weeks before last frost or in late autumn.
DEPTH Just cover.

GERMINATING

TIME 14–21 days.
REQUIREMENTS Place seeds and moistened growing medium in a plastic bag and refrigerate for 2 weeks. Provide darkness and 50°–55°F thereafter.

PLANTING SEEDLINGS OUTDOORS

TIME After last spring frost.
SPACING 18"–24".
LIGHT Full sun.
SOIL Rich, amended with well-rotted cow manure.

CARING FOR PLANTS

Feed once or twice during the growing season. Stake tall species and deadhead to avoid self-seeding. Do not transplant.

PROPAGATING

Self-seeds.

Consolida ambigua

Convallaria

Lily of the valley

TYPE HP
ZONE 2–9. Leaves will turn brown and die back during prolonged hot weather.
FLOWERING SEASON Late spring to early summer

Convallaria majalis

Much-loved, deeply-scented, spring-blooming perennials grown for their tiny, white, bell-shaped flowers and rich green, broadly lance-shaped leaves. 6"–8" tall. Marvelous shady ground cover.

SOWING

INDOORS Autumn.
OUTDOORS Seed or rhizome: late winter or early spring.
DEPTH Seed: just cover. Rhizome: 2"–3".

GERMINATING

TIME 60–365 days.
REQUIREMENTS Sow seeds in flats and cover with compost, then a layer of fine gravel. Plunge flats in the ground outdoors and cover with glass. Transplant seedlings to individual pots when they are big enough to handle. When plants are sufficiently strong, move to a nursery bed for 2 years before finally planting in a permanent location.

PLANTING SEEDLINGS OUTDOORS

TIME Early spring or autumn.
SPACING 4"–6".
LIGHT Part to full shade, although flowering will be diminished in full shade.
SOIL Fertile, moist, well-drained, enriched with plenty of organic matter.

CARING FOR PLANTS

Water deeply during dry spells to avoid developing a scorched look. Top-dress with 2" of leaf mold in autumn or apply a complete fertilizer in early spring, taking care to wash residual fertilizer from leaves. Regular applications of liquid seaweed during the growing season will greatly improve the look of plants in summer. Divide after flowering every 4–6 years to maintain good blooming.

PROPAGATING

Divide in autumn in the South, in early spring north of zone 7.

Convolvulus

Dwarf morning-glory, Silverbush

TYPE HA or HP
ZONE A: 3–9; P: 7–9. Morning glories like warm weather, but do not thrive where summers are very hot and humid.
FLOWERING SEASON A: summer to first frost. P: summer.

Scourge or boon? That depends on the species. The best are twining vines with large, heart-shaped leaves and showy, trumpet-shaped flowers that bloom for just one day; the worst are identical in description, but are pernicious, ineradicable weeds. Flowers are shades of blue, purple, pink, or white. Grow climbers on trellises; dwarf varieties make excellent edging plants.

SOWING

INDOORS 5–6 weeks before last frost, in peat pots.
OUTDOORS In spring, when soil is warm and nighttime temperatures remain above 50°F, but only where summers are long.
DEPTH ⅛".

GERMINATING

TIME 5–14 days.
REQUIREMENTS Chip seeds or soak in warm water for 24 hours before sowing. Leave flats where temperature is a constant 70°–80°F.

PLANTING SEEDLINGS OUTDOORS

TIME After last frost.
SPACING Small species: 6"–12". Large species: 12"–24".
LIGHT Full sun.
SOIL Tolerant of most, but prefers well-drained soil with a pH level of 6.0–8.0.

CARING FOR PLANTS

Easy. Prefers regular watering, but tolerates considerable neglect. Do not move. *C. arvensis* is highly invasive and should not be planted.

PROPAGATING

Take cuttings in late spring or summer, or allow to self-seed.

A-Annual P-Perennial B-Biennial HHA-Half-hardy annual HA-Hardy annual HB-Hardy biennial HHP-Half-hardy perennial HP-Hardy perennial HHBb-Half-hardy bulb HBb-Hardy bulb

94

Coreopsis

Calliopsis, Tickseed

TYPE HHA, HHP, or HP
ZONE A: 2–10; P:
  3–10: *C. verticillata;*
  4–9: *C. auriculata, C. grandi-*
  flora, C. rosea, C. tripteris;
  5–9: *C. lanceolata;*
  9–10: *C. gigantea, C. maritima*
  (does not perform well in hot,
  humid climates). Highly tolerant
  of hot, humid weather.
FLOWERING SEASON Summer
  through early autumn

Versatile, carefree plants grown for the reliable abundance of yellow or orange daisylike blooms borne over a long period; 8"–30" tall. Use small species in the rock garden; mix different species in the border for spots of lively color.

SOWING

INDOORS A: 6–8 weeks before last frost. P: 8–10 weeks before planting out.
OUTDOORS After last frost or, where winter are mild, in late autumn.
DEPTH Surface.

GERMINATING

TIME 5–25 days.
REQUIREMENTS Light and 55°–70°F.

PLANTING SEEDLINGS OUTDOORS

TIME A: after last frost. P: after last frost or in autumn.
SPACING Dwarf species: 6". Tall species: 12"–18".
LIGHT Full sun.
SOIL Withstands a wide range of conditions but prefers rich, well-drained soil with a pH level of 5.5–7.0.

CARING FOR PLANTS

Easy. Deadhead often and feed only lightly as excessive fertilizing decreases flowering. Tall species may need support.

Coreopsis tinctoria

PROPAGATING

Annuals self-seed. Divide hardy perennial species after blooming in zones 3–6, in autumn in the South; half-hardy perennials can be divided in spring.

Coriandrum

Chinese parsley, Cilantro, Coriander

TYPE HA
ZONE 2–9
FLOWERING SEASON Early summer

Culinary herb of 1'–2' bearing tiny white, pink, or lavender flowers in lacy umbels; leaves are toothed and fernlike.

SOWING

INDOORS 6–8 weeks before planting out, in peat pots.
OUTDOORS After last frost and at 2-week intervals for a constant supply of fresh leaves; autumn in southern states.
DEPTH ½".

GERMINATING

TIME 10 days.
REQUIREMENTS Darkness and 55°–65°F.

PLANTING SEEDLINGS OUTDOORS

TIME Early spring.
SPACING 8"–10".
LIGHT Full sun or light shade.
SOIL Rich, very well-drained, with a pH level of 6.0–7.0.

CARING FOR PLANTS

Shelter plants from winds and do not move; feed only with low-nitrogen fertilizer. Plants can be potted and brought indoors for winter use. Cut fresh leaves for cooking; leaves do not freeze successfully. To harvest seeds, cut flowering stalks when seeds are light brown and hang upside-down in a paper bag in a warm spot to dry. Rub fruit gently to release seeds and store in an airtight container. One plant will produce ¼ cup of seeds in 2 months.

PROPAGATING

Self-seeds.

A-Annual P-Perennial B-Biennial HHA-Half-hardy annual HA-Hardy annual HB-Hardy biennial HHP-Half-hardy perennial HP-Hardy perennial HHBb-Half-hardy bulb HBb-Hardy bulb

95

Coronilla

Crown vetch, Scorpion senna

> TYPE HP or HHP
> ZONE 3–10: *C. varia*;
>   7–10: *C. cappadocica*
> FLOWERING SEASON Summer

Somewhat weedy, sprawling, shrubby perennials used as low-maintenance ground cover in difficult sites. Yellow, pink, purple, or white, pealike flowers cover plants over a long period.

SOWING

INDOORS More practical to start *in situ*.
OUTDOORS Midspring. Sow at the rate of 1 pound per 1000 square feet.
DEPTH ⅛".

GERMINATING

TIME 30 days.
REQUIREMENTS Chip or soak seeds to hasten germination.

PLANTING SEEDLINGS OUTDOORS

TIME Set out purchased plants in late spring or autumn.
SPACING 8"–12".
LIGHT Full sun or very light shade.
SOIL Well-drained, with a pH level of 6.5–7.5. Tolerant of dry conditions.

CARING FOR PLANTS

Easy. Feed with a low-nitrogen fertilizer and water only during droughts. Cut back hardy species to ground level in late autumn.

PROPAGATING

Divide in spring where winters are very cold, autumn in the South; or take cuttings in autumn.

Coronilla varia

Cortaderia

Pampas grass

> TYPE HP
> ZONE 8–10. Can be grown as an
>   annual north of zone 8.
> FLOWERING SEASON Late summer
>   through early autumn

Ornamental grasses bearing dramatic 8'–12' spires of cream or pink plumes. Excellent specimen; also effective in groups in a very large garden.

SOWING

INDOORS 8–10 weeks before planting out.
OUTDOORS Early spring or early autumn.
DEPTH Surface.

GERMINATING

TIME 14–21 days.
REQUIREMENTS Light; prefers 60°–75°F. Highly susceptible to damping-off; grow seedlings in vermiculite and water only from below.

PLANTING SEEDLINGS OUTDOORS

TIME Early spring, when soil is cool and a light frost is still possible, or early autumn.
SPACING Allow 4'–5' between plants, although this enormous grass is most effective when grown singly.
LIGHT Full sun.
SOIL Moist, rich, well-drained.

CARING FOR PLANTS

Easy. Trim off dead leaves occasionally to keep plants looking tidy. North of zone 8, dig roots in autumn and store in a cool, dry, frost-free location.

PROPAGATING

Divide in early spring.

Cortaderia selloana

A-Annual P-Perennial B-Biennial HHA-Half-hardy annual HA-Hardy annual HB-Hardy biennial HHP-Half-hardy perennial HP-Hardy perennial HHBb-Half-hardy bulb HBb-Hardy bulb

Corydalis

Fumewort, Fumitory

> **Type** HA, HB, or HP
> **Zone** A: 3–7; P: 4–9. Plants are severely weakened by excessive heat and humidity.
> **Flowering Season** Early spring to autumn, depending on species

Delicate, low-growing plants with fernlike leaves and small clusters of tubular flowers, most commonly yellow but also blue or deep pink; 6"–24" high. Useful in stone walls, rock gardens, or borders.

Sowing

Indoors Seeds are best started *in situ*.
Outdoors A: early spring; spring or autumn, where winters are mild. B: early summer. P: as soon as ripe seed is available.
Depth Seed: surface. Tuber: 3".

Corydalis aurea

Germinating

Time 30–365 days.
Requirements Difficult. Keep seeds at 60°–65°F for 6–8 weeks, then chill for 2 weeks, and finally sow and keep at 60°–65°F. Seeds require light to germinate.

Planting Seedlings Outdoors

Time Set out purchased plants after last frost, or autumn.
Spacing Small species: 4"–6". Large species: 10"–15".
Light Part shade.
Soil Prefers moist, rich, well-drained, with a pH level of 6.0–8.0, but will tolerate poor soil.

Caring for Plants

Easy. Survives considerable neglect. Water regularly and mulch with leaf mold. Trim plants after flowering to keep tidy and prevent self-seeding. Do not disturb established plants.

Propagating

Divide after flowering. Some species will self-seed.

Cosmos

Cosmea

> **Type** HHP or HHA
> **Zone** A: 2–10; P: 7–10 (C. *atrosanguineus* is the only commonly available perennial form). Prefers warm temperatures.
> **Flowering Season** Late spring through early autumn

Useful in any garden, these cheerful, carefree, airy plants add lightness and color to borders and wildflower plantings. Flowering stems of 12"–48" and feathery foliage are topped with good-sized, daisylike flowers in pinks, reds, oranges, yellows, and white.

Sowing

Indoors 4–5 weeks before last frost.
Outdoors After last frost.
Depth ⅛".

Germinating

Time 3–10 days.
Requirements Easy. 70°–75°F.

Planting Seedlings Outdoors

Time After last frost.
Spacing Small species: 8"–10". Tall species: 18"–36".
Light Full sun.
Soil Plants will flower more abundantly in poor soil than rich. Prefers a pH level of 5.0–7.0.

Caring for Plants

Easy. Pinch out tips when plants are 18" high; stake tall species. Water during very dry spells. Provide winter mulch in zones 7–8. Perennials can be lifted, stored over winter, and replanted after the last frost in the North.

Propagating

Seed only.

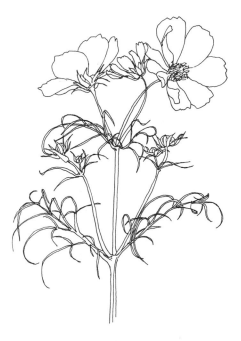

Cosmos bipinnatus

A-Annual P-Perennial B-Biennial HHA-Half-hardy annual HA-Hardy annual HB-Hardy biennial HHP-Half-hardy perennial HP-Hardy perennial HHBb-Half-hardy bulb HBb-Hardy bulb

Cotula

Brass buttons, Pincushion plant

TYPE HHA, HHP, or HP
ZONE A: 1–9; P: 9–10;
7–10: *C. coronopifolia.* Prefers cool, dry summers and mild winters.
FLOWERING SEASON Midsummer

Annuals and perennials usually grown for their fragrant, bright orange, buttonlike flowers, which are everlasting. Plants are 6"–2' tall and grown in rock gardens and cutting beds.

SOWING

INDOORS 6–8 weeks before planting out.
OUTDOORS After last frost.
DEPTH Just cover.

GERMINATING

TIME 14–21 days.
REQUIREMENTS Easy. 50°F.

PLANTING SEEDLINGS OUTDOORS

TIME After last frost.
SPACING 4"–6".
LIGHT Full sun or part shade, except C. *coronopifolia*, which will grow only in full sun.
SOIL Most species require moist soil; some will grow in standing water. May become invasive if grown in rich soil.

CARING FOR PLANTS

Water regularly. May become invasive.

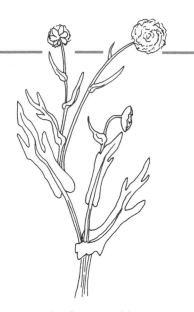

Cotula coronopifolia

PROPAGATING

Annuals are propagated by seed. Divide perennials in spring.

Cracca

See *Tephrosia*

Crambe

Colewort, Seakale

TYPE HA, HB, or HP
ZONE 5–9
FLOWERING SEASON Summer

Enormous (3'–7') perennials with large, ruffled leaves and tall, woody, flowering stems bearing a profusion of surprisingly airy and delicate white blooms resembling a cloud of smoke. Carefully placed, these giants are stunning in the border.

SOWING

INDOORS Most successfully started *in situ.* Indoor sowing may be attempted 8–10 weeks before last frost, in peat pots.
OUTDOORS A: after last spring frost. B: late summer. P: early spring, when soil is cool and a light frost is still possible, or in autumn.
DEPTH ½".

GERMINATING

TIME 21–180 days.
REQUIREMENTS Seed started indoors must be kept cool and moist at 60°–65°F.

PLANTING SEEDLINGS OUTDOORS

TIME A: after last frost. B: autumn. P: autumn, or after last spring frost.
SPACING 24"–36".
LIGHT Sun to light shade.
SOIL Fertile, well-drained, slightly alkaline.

CARING FOR PLANTS

Plants grown from seed will not bloom well until their third year. *Crambe* is susceptible to many insect pests and may require frequent spraying with insecticidal soap. Tall species will need staking. Cut plants back to ground level in autumn and mulch where winters are cold. Do not move plants unnecessarily.

PROPAGATING

Divide or take root cuttings in spring, or allow to self-seed.

A-Annual P-Perennial B-Biennial HHA-Half-hardy annual HA-Hardy annual HB-Hardy biennial HHP-Half-hardy perennial HP-Hardy perennial HHBb-Half-hardy bulb HBb-Hardy bulb

Crepis

Dandelion, Hawk's beard

> **TYPE** HA, HP, or HB
> **ZONE** A: 3–9; P: 4–9. Blooming will be greatly diminished in hot, humid weather.
> **FLOWERING SEASON** Midsummer to late summer

Domesticated species of the dandelion family, 12"–18" tall, with lance-shaped leaves and an abundance of solitary flowers that do indeed look like pink, red, orange, or white dandelions. Pretty plants for the rock garden or front of the border.

SOWING

INDOORS 6–8 weeks before last frost.
OUTDOORS A: early spring; where winters are mild, seeds may be sown in autumn. P: early spring, when soil is cool and a light frost is still possible.
DEPTH Just cover.

GERMINATING

TIME 5–14 days.
REQUIREMENTS 70°–80°F.

PLANTING SEEDLINGS OUTDOORS

TIME After last frost.
SPACING 4"–6".
LIGHT Full sun.
SOIL Well-drained.

CARING FOR PLANTS

Easy. Support with twiggy branches pushed into the ground when plants are young; deadhead regularly to prolong blooming.

PROPAGATING

Take root cuttings of perennials in late winter. Both annuals and perennials will self-seed.

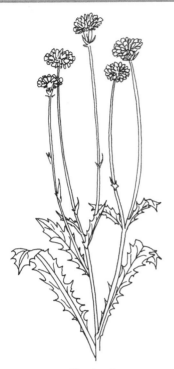

Crepis rubra

Crinum

Bengal lily, Cape lily, Crinum lily, Milk-and-wine lily, Spider lily, Swamp lily

> **TYPE** HHBb often grown as A
> **ZONE** A: 3–7; 8–10;
>   10: *C. amoenum, C. asiaticum, C. macowanii*
> **FLOWERING SEASON** Late summer

Genus of bulbs grown for their funnel-shaped, lilylike flowers borne in terminal whorls on stiff, leafless, upright stems 18"–36" tall. Blooms may be pink, red, or white and are often fragrant. Best grown on their own in front of walls and shrubs.

SOWING

INDOORS As soon as seed is ripe.
OUTDOORS Seed: as soon as seed is ripe. Bulb: late spring when the temperatures remain above 60°F.
DEPTH Seed: ¼". Bulb: 8".

GERMINATING

TIME 7–21 days.
REQUIREMENTS Easy. 60°–70°F.

PLANTING SEEDLINGS OUTDOORS

TIME Late spring.
SPACING Small species: 12"–24". Large species: 24"–36".
LIGHT Full sun, with afternoon shade where summers are very hot.
SOIL Moist, humus-rich, with excellent drainage.

CARING FOR PLANTS

Plants grown from seed flower in 4–5 years. Water frequently during dry weather and feed 2–3 times per year. Remove faded blooms and dead leaves to keep plants tidy. In zones 3–7, lift bulbs in autumn and store over winter in a cool, frost-free location; provide a winter mulch in zone 8. Disturb as little as possible and divide only very rarely.

PROPAGATING

Plant offsets.

Crinum x powellii

A-Annual P-Perennial B-Biennial HHA-Half-hardy annual HA-Hardy annual HB-Hardy biennial HHP-Half-hardy perennial HP-Hardy perennial HHBb-Half-hardy bulb HBb-Hardy bulb

Crocosmia

Copper tip, Montbretia

> TYPE HHBb often grown as A
> ZONE A: 3–6; P: 7–10
> FLOWERING SEASON Summer

Small genus of plants from Africa forming clumps of sword-shaped leaves out of which stiff, arching branches of 2'–4' emerge bearing bright red or orange, funnel-shaped flowers. Interesting foliage and flowers make these plants useful in the border.

SOWING

INDOORS 6–8 weeks before planting out.
OUTDOORS Seed: in zones 9–10, sow as soon as ripe in early autumn; early spring is preferable in zones 7–8. Corm: autumn in zones 9–10; well after last frost in zones 3–8.
DEPTH Seed: just cover. Corm: Plant 6" deep in zones 7–10, 3" in zones 3–6.

Crocosmia 'Lucifer'

GERMINATING

TIME 30–90 days.
REQUIREMENTS Easy. 55°–60°F.

PLANTING SEEDLINGS OUTDOORS

TIME After last frost.
SPACING 4"–8".
LIGHT Sun or light shade.
SOIL Average, well-drained. Tolerant of dry conditions, but prefers adequate moisture.

CARING FOR PLANTS

Easy. Plants grown from seed will flower in 2–3 years. Water and feed regularly in summer; mulch in winter. Divide every 3 years. Provide a heavy winter mulch in zone 7. In zones 3–6, lift corms and store in a cool, frost-free place, replanting in spring.

PROPAGATING

Plant offsets in spring.

Crocus

Saffron, Spring crocus

> TYPE HBb
> ZONE 3–9: C. etruscus;
>   4–9: C. chrysanthus, C. flavus,
>   C. tommasinianus, C. vernus;
>   5–9: C. biflorus, C. longiflorus,
>   C. versicolor; 6–9: C. imperati,
>   C. medius; 7–9: C. niveus;
>   8–10: C. goulimyi
> FLOWERING SEASON Late winter,
>   early spring, or autumn,
>   depending on species

Much-loved harbingers of spring, these little bulbs have grassy leaves and purple, yellow, or white upturned, funnel-shaped flowers. Ideal for filling naked winter beds, naturalizing in the lawn, or under shrubs.

SOWING

INDOORS Not recommended.
OUTDOORS Seed: early spring, preferably in a cold frame. Leave undisturbed for 2 growing seasons. Bulb: Plant spring-blooming bulbs in autumn, autumn-bloomers in July or August.
DEPTH Seed: ⅛". Bulb: 2"–3".

GERMINATING

TIME 30–180 days.
REQUIREMENTS 55°–65°F.

PLANTING SEEDLINGS OUTDOORS

SPACING 2"–4".
LIGHT Leaves must receive full sun during growing season, but can take light shade throughout the rest of the year.
SOIL Rich, light, well-drained, with a pH level of 6.0–8.0.

CARING FOR PLANTS

Easy. *Crocuses* grown from seed will flower in 3–4 years. Feed annually in early spring; use manure only sparingly. Allow leaves to wither before removing or mowing. Where rodents are a problem, plant bulbs in wire cages.

PROPAGATING

Divide bulbs in autumn. Some *Crocuses* will self-seed.

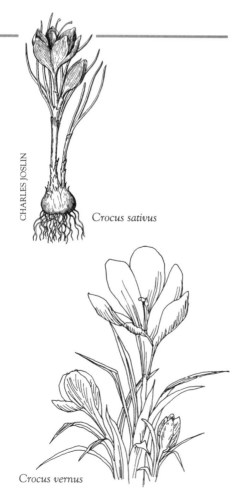

CHARLES JOSLIN

Crocus sativus

Crocus vernus

A-Annual P-Perennial B-Biennial HHA-Half-hardy annual HA-Hardy annual HB-Hardy biennial HHP-Half-hardy perennial HP-Hardy perennial HHBb-Half-hardy bulb HBb-Hardy bulb

Crucianella

See *Phuopsis*

Cucurbita

Gourd, Luffa

TYPE HHA
ZONE 5–10. Must have hot weather and a long growing season to produce satisfactory fruit.
FLOWERING SEASON Summer

Genus of annual runners grown for their fruits, which are often displayed as well as eaten. Leaves are large and plants require considerable space; fruit may be round, oblong, or pear-shaped, orange, yellow, green, white, or multicolored. Don't miss the 'Choose Your Weapon' series.

SOWING
INDOORS 3–4 weeks before planting out, in peat pots.
OUTDOORS 2 weeks after last frost.
DEPTH ¼".

GERMINATING
TIME 8–28 days.
REQUIREMENTS Soak seeds in warm water for 48 hours and sow where temperature is 70°–80°F.

PLANTING SEEDLINGS OUTDOORS
TIME Several weeks after last frost, when soil is warm.
SPACING 24".
LIGHT Full sun.
SOIL Rich, well-drained, with a pH level of 6.0–7.0.

CARING FOR PLANTS
Water frequently and do not move. Vines require support and fruit must be kept off the ground to avoid rot. Harvest gourds when they no longer respond to light pressure. Clean fruit well and store singly in a warm, airy place, turning from time to time. After 2–3 weeks, fully dried gourds will rattle when shaken (very large gourds may take up to 6 months to dry completely). Glaze with floor wax. Gourds will rot if bruised or scratched at any time or if not fully mature when harvested. To make luffa sponges, soak ripe luffa gourds in warm water for 2–3 days, after which skins should come away easily. Wash well to remove all seeds and loose pulp. Allow to dry for one week before using.

PROPAGATING
Seed only.

Cuminum

Cumin

TYPE HHA
ZONE 5–10
FLOWERING SEASON Midsummer

Low-growing (4"–6"), feathery-leaved annual herb grown for its piquant seeds. Tiny white or pink flowers are held in umbels. Perfect for edging the herb bed.

SOWING
INDOORS 6–8 weeks before planting out, in peat pots.
OUTDOORS South of zone 6 only, 2–3 weeks after last frost, when soil has warmed.
DEPTH ¼".

GERMINATING
TIME 10–14 days.
REQUIREMENTS Easy. 70°F.

PLANTING SEEDLINGS OUTDOORS
TIME When nighttime temperatures remain above 55°F.
SPACING 4"–6"; plants grown close together will support each other.
LIGHT Full sun.
SOIL Well-drained, fertile.

CARING FOR PLANTS
Feed once at planting time and water regularly during hot, dry weather to ensure a good seed crop. Harvest seeds when pods turn brown. Dry thoroughly, then rub pods gently to release seed. Store in an airtight container.

PROPAGATING
Seed only.

A-Annual P-Perennial B-Biennial HHA-Half-hardy annual HA-Hardy annual HB-Hardy biennial HHP-Half-hardy perennial HP-Hardy perennial HHBb-Half-hardy bulb HBb-Hardy bulb

Cuphea

Cigar plant, Firecracker plant, Mexican cigar flower

> TYPE HHP grown as HHA
> ZONE 6–10. Requires long, hot growing season.
> FLOWERING SEASON Summer to frost

Genus of widely varying plants native to the Americas. Flowers may be deep purple and orchidlike, long, deep red tubes, or bright pink pinwheels. Use in containers or borders.

SOWING

INDOORS 10–12 weeks before planting out.
OUTDOORS Not recommended, as flowering takes 4–5 months from sowing.
DEPTH Surface.

GERMINATING

TIME 8–10 days.
REQUIREMENTS Light and 70°–75°F.

PLANTING SEEDLINGS OUTDOORS

TIME Late spring, when soil is warm and temperatures remain above 40°F.
SPACING 9"–12".
LIGHT Sun or part shade.
SOIL Somewhat heavy, humus-rich.

CARING FOR PLANTS

Very easy. Pinch out tips to induce branching. Water plants regularly. May be potted up in autumn and overwintered indoors.

PROPAGATING

Take stem or root cuttings in spring or autumn.

Cyclamen

Sow bread

> TYPE HP. Cultural information for tender *Cyclamen* species is not included here.
> ZONE 5–9. *Will not flourish where summer temperatures are hot.*
> FLOWERING SEASON Any time from late winter through autumn, depending on species

Genus of low-growing perennials, 3"–6", with heart-shaped leaves sometimes patterned with white. Graceful flowers with reflexed petals that have the appearance of hovering butterflies. Plant near a woodland path or use as a ground cover.

SOWING

INDOORS See "Germinating, Requirements."
OUTDOORS See "Germinating, Requirements."
DEPTH Seed: ¼". Tuber: 1"–2".

GERMINATING

TIME 21–380 days.
REQUIREMENTS Difficult. Soak seeds in hot water for 24 hours before sowing. *Autumn sowing:* Sow seeds in flats, plunge in the ground against a north-facing wall, and cover with glass. Moisten soil occasionally, if necessary. Bring indoors in spring to 55°–60°F. *Spring sowing:* Sow seeds in flats, place in a plastic bag, and refrigerate. Remove after 2–3 weeks and sink flats in the ground in a shady location, covering with glass. Transplant seedlings as they emerge.

PLANTING SEEDLINGS OUTDOORS

TIME After last frost.
SPACING 6"–8".
LIGHT Full sun to part shade.
SOIL Cool, well-drained, very rich, slightly limy.

CARING FOR PLANTS

Very easy. Water regularly only during growing period; top-dress with leaf mold in late summer. In cold climates, provide a winter mulch. Do not disturb established plants.

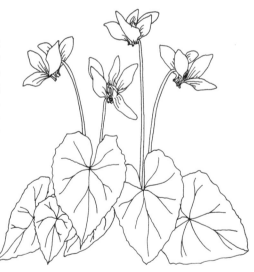

Cyclamen hederaefolium

PROPAGATING

Divide tubers in late summer, or allow to self-seed.

Cymbalaria

Coliseum ivy, Ivy-leaved toadflax, Kenilworth ivy

TYPE HHP usually grown as
  HHA
ZONE 6–9
FLOWERING SEASON Midsummer

Creeping plants grown for their neat, ivylike leaves and masses of tiny, purple, yellow-throated, tubular flowers resembling snapdragons. Useful ground cover or container plant.

SOWING
INDOORS 8–10 weeks before planting out.
OUTDOORS After last frost.
DEPTH Surface.

GERMINATING
TIME 14–30 days.
REQUIREMENTS Easy. Light and 60°–65°F.

PLANTING SEEDLINGS OUTDOORS
TIME After last frost.
SPACING 5"–7".
LIGHT C. *pilosa* prefers full sun, but all other species must have shade where afternoon sun is very hot.
SOIL Moist, gritty, slightly alkaline, not too rich.

CARING FOR PLANTS
Water frequently but feed only sparingly. May become invasive.

PROPAGATING
Divide in autumn, or take cuttings. Self seeds in the South and may be a nuisance.

Cynara

Wild artichoke, Cardoon

TYPE HHP often grown as HHA
ZONE A: 6–7; P: 8–10
FLOWERING SEASON Summer
  through autumn

Small group of coarse, prickly plants grown for their architectural form and purple, thistlelike flowers. Foliage is silvery green; flower stalks grow up to 6'.

SOWING
INDOORS Very early spring.
OUTDOORS In zones 9–10 only, after last frost date.
DEPTH ⅛".

GERMINATING
TIME 14–30 days.
REQUIREMENTS 50°–55°F.

PLANTING SEEDLINGS OUTDOORS
TIME Just before last frost.
SPACING 2'–3'.
LIGHT Full sun, with some protection from afternoon sun in very hot locations.
SOIL Rich, moist, well-drained. Add plenty of manure or compost if growing for food.

CARING FOR PLANTS
Water regularly and deeply. Plants grown for food will respond well to a top-dressing of 5-10-10 every 3–4 weeks. Harvest artichokes when fruit is green but still unopened. Cut plants back to ground level in autumn and mulch.

PROPAGATING
Propagation by seed is most successful, but plants can also be increased by division in early spring.

A-Annual P-Perennial B-Biennial HHA-Half-hardy annual HA-Hardy annual HB-Hardy biennial HHP-Half-hardy perennial HP-Hardy perennial HHBb-Half-hardy bulb HBb-Hardy bulb

Cynoglossum

Chinese forget-me-not, Hound's tongue

> TYPE B usually grown as HA
> ZONE 2–10. Requires cool temperatures.
> FLOWERING SEASON Summer through late autumn

Genus of long-blooming, rather weedy plants grown for their dainty, blue, purple, or white forget-me-not flowers; leaves are small and lance-shaped, sometimes greyish-green. Plants grow 18"–36". Use with care in the border.

SOWING

INDOORS 6–8 weeks before planting out.
OUTDOORS Several weeks before last frost, or in autumn where winters are mild.
DEPTH ¼".

Cynoglossum amabile

GERMINATING

TIME 5–10 days.
REQUIREMENTS Darkness and 65°–75°F.

PLANTING SEEDLINGS OUTDOORS

TIME Late spring.
SPACING 10"–12".
LIGHT Full sun or light shade.
SOIL Ordinary, well-drained, with a pH level of 6.0–7.0. Tolerant of both wet and dry conditions. Rich soil produces weak plants.

CARING FOR PLANTS

Easy. Support plants with twiggy branches pushed into the ground when young. Remove flowers before seeds set to prevent self-seeding; cut back to ground level in autumn.

PROPAGATING

Divide in spring, or take root cuttings in autumn. Also self-seeds.

Cyperus

Bulrush, Chufa, Galingale, Paper plant, Papyrus, Umbrella grass

> TYPE HHP
> ZONE 9–10; 8–10: C. *esculentus*, C. *longus*
> FLOWERING SEASON Autumn

Very large genus of ornamental grasses with thick, erect stems, 18"–48", topped with an umbrella of leaves and tiny green or cream-colored flowers. Grow in or near water.

SOWING

INDOORS 6–8 weeks before planting out.
OUTDOORS Spring or early autumn.
DEPTH Just cover.

GERMINATING

TIME 25–30 days.
REQUIREMENTS 70°–75°F.

PLANTING SEEDLINGS OUTDOORS

TIME Late spring, when temperatures remain above 45°F, or early autumn.
SPACING Dwarf species: 12". Medium species:24"–36". Large species: 48".
LIGHT Full sun, with light shade from afternoon sun where summers are hot.
SOIL Rich, moist. Some species prefer to grow in shallow water that is a constant 65°–70°F.

CARING FOR PLANTS

Potted plants can be submerged in outdoor pools in summer, then brought indoors in autumn when temperatures fall into the low 50s°F. C. *esculentus* and C. *longus* may survive in zone 7 with a heavy winter mulch.

PROPAGATING

Divide in early spring.

A-Annual P-Perennial B-Biennial HHA-Half-hardy annual HA-Hardy annual HB-Hardy biennial HHP-Half-hardy perennial HP-Hardy perennial HHBb-Half-hardy bulb HBb-Hardy bulb

Cypripedium

Lady's slipper orchid, Moccasin flower

TYPE HP
ZONE 4–8; 3–7: *C. montanum*;
5–9: *C. californicum*
FLOWERING SEASON Late spring

Genus of wild orchids native to North America. Flowers are usually bicolored, the pouched lower lip (the "slipper") being one color and the petals another; pink, white, yellow, brown, and purple are the most common colors. Plants grow from 12"–30" and are best suited to in the woodland garden.

SOWING

INDOORS Spring or autumn.
OUTDOORS Do not attempt outdoors.
DEPTH Surface.

GERMINATING

TIME 30–365 days.
REQUIREMENTS At the risk of sounding defeatist, I must say that propagation from seed is virtually impossible. For the determined: Sterilize a margarine tub with boiling water and half-fill with crumpled paper towels; soak towels with cooled boiled water. Cut 5–6 pieces of paper towel to fit the tub, place over the crumpled towels and moisten. Sterilize seeds by placing in a jar filled with 1 cup water and ¾ teaspoon vinegar; shake well and drain. With a sterilized instrument, place seeds on the damp towels in the tub. Cover with a clear plastic lid that has been sterilized, place tub in plastic bag, and seal with a rubber band. Leave in a light location at 65°–75°F. Transplant seedlings to peat pots after germination.

PLANTING SEEDLINGS OUTDOORS

TIME After last spring frost, or autumn.
SPACING 12"–18".
LIGHT Part to full shade.
SOIL Cool, rich, moist, acid, woods soil with plenty of humus.

CARING FOR PLANTS

Difficult to establish, but fairly easy thereafter. Keep soil very moist even during dormancy; this is especially important the first season after planting. Mulch with leaf mold in early spring. Do not disturb roots. If moving is necessary, do so with a very large root ball.

Cypripedium acaule

PROPAGATING

Divide in autumn where winters are mild, in early spring north of zone 7. Keep at least 1 bud per new plant and set this just below the surface.

Dahlia

TYPE HHP usually grown as
  HHA
ZONE A: 3–8; P: 9–10. Prefers
  warm summers.
FLOWERING SEASON Midsummer
  to frost, depending on species

Showy plants that often dominate the summer border, dahlias are grown for their showy (sometimes downright gaudy), usually double flowers. Plants are sturdy, branched, and erect, 1'–5' tall; flower colors range from demure pastels to deep, unnatural neons. *Dahlias* are the Ethel Mermans of the perennial bed: often lacking in subtlety, but you've got to admire their chutzpa.

SOWING

INDOORS 8–10 weeks before planting out.
OUTDOORS Seed: 1–2 weeks before last frost. Tuber: after last frost.
DEPTH Seed: just cover. Tuber: 6", with eye pointing upward.

GERMINATING

TIME 5–20 days.
REQUIREMENTS 65°–70°F. Sow in individual pots, not in flats.

PLANTING SEEDLINGS OUTDOORS

TIME 4 weeks after last frost, when soil and air temperatures are consistently warm.
SPACING Dwarf species: 12"–15". Medium species: 18"–24". Tall species: up to 36".
LIGHT Full sun.
SOIL Deeply prepared, enriched with humus and bonemeal, with a pH level of 6.0–7.5. Excessive nitrogen will produce leggy plants with few blooms.

CARING FOR PLANTS

Easy. Site plants where air circulation is unrestricted. Pinch out small species to increase branching; stake tall species occasionally as plants grow taller. Feed with bonemeal in June and early August. Water only during very dry weather until flowering begins; give ground a good soaking once a week while plants are in bloom. Deadhead regularly. Cut back to ground level in autumn and, north of zone 9, lift tubers. Store over winter in a cool, frost-free location.

PROPAGATING

Divide clumps in autumn, or take cuttings from new shoots in late winter.

Dahlia hybrid

A-Annual P-Perennial B-Biennial HHA-Half-hardy annual HA-Hardy annual HB-Hardy biennial HHP-Half-hardy perennial HP-Hardy perennial HHBb-Half-hardy bulb HBb-Hardy bulb

105

Darlingtonia

California pitcher plant, Cobra lily

> TYPE HP
> ZONE 8–10. May survive farther north if sited carefully and protected with a thick winter mulch.
> FLOWERING SEASON Spring to early summer

One of those carnivorous plants that looks like it came from another planet, but which is actually native to the western United States. 1'–3' tall plants bear ominous-looking, veined and pitted, hooded, greenish purple flowers. A few of these plants grown against a moist, shady wall of the house will give your friends something to think about.

SOWING

INDOORS Late winter to early summer.
OUTDOORS Spring.
DEPTH Surface.

GERMINATING

TIME 30–90 days.
REQUIREMENTS Difficult. Light and 75°–80°F required. Sow seeds in sphagnum moss in 6" pots and stand in water at all times. Plant seedlings out after 1 year.

PLANTING SEEDLINGS OUTDOORS

TIME Late spring.
SPACING 6"–12".
LIGHT Full shade.
SOIL Cool, fine, peaty, very moist or even wet (plants will live happily in up to 1" of water).

CARING FOR PLANTS

Difficult. Plants grown from seed will not bloom for 3–5 years. Keep soil constantly moist; mulch in late autumn with leaf mold.

PROPAGATING

Divide in spring in the North, autumn in the South.

Datura

(synonymous with *Brugmansia*)

Angel's trumpet, Floripondio, Horn of plenty, Trumpet flower

> TYPE HHP grown as HHA
> ZONE A: 3–8; P: 9–10. Prefers warm temperatures.
> FLOWERING SEASON Late summer to autumn

Bushy plants of 3'–5' with bluish foliage and achingly beautiful flowers. Blooms are 4"–8" long white trumpets, some delicately edged in palest lavender, some lightly scented. A stunning container plant.

SOWING

INDOORS 2–3 months before planting out.
OUTDOORS Start seeds outdoors only in zones 9–10, after last frost date.
DEPTH 1/8".

GERMINATING

TIME 21–42 days.
REQUIREMENTS Easy. 65°–70°F.

Datura suaveolens

PLANTING SEEDLINGS OUTDOORS

TIME 2–3 weeks after last frost, when temperatures remain above 45°F.
SPACING 3'–4'.
LIGHT Sun.
SOIL Prefers rich and moist; will tolerate poor soil.

CARING FOR PLANTS

Easy. Water well in winter.

PROPAGATING

Allow to self-seed, or take cuttings of side shoots when temperature is above 60°F.

A-Annual P-Perennial B-Biennial HHA-Half-hardy annual HA-Hardy annual HB-Hardy biennial HHP-Half-hardy perennial HP-Hardy perennial HHBb-Half-hardy bulb HBb-Hardy bulb

Delphinium

Type HP or HHP
Zone 3–9: *D. elatum*,
  D. grandiflorum;
  4–9: *D. x belladona*,
  D. nudicaule; 6–9: *D. cardi-
  nale*, *D. tatsienense*;
  7–9: *D. x ruysii*;
  8–9: *D. semibarbatum*, (synonymous with *D. zalil*)
Flowering Season Late spring
  through autumn, depending on
  species

Statuesque perennials of unequalled beauty, evocative of medieval gardens. Tall spires are cloaked in spurred blooms of blue, white, purple, pink, or yellow; green foliage resembles the cut-leaf maple. Growing from a dwarf 6" to a towering 7', these plants will add grace to any border.

Sowing

Indoors 8–10 weeks before planting out.
Outdoors Early spring or early autumn.
Depth Just cover.

Germinating

Time 14–28 days.
Requirements Place seeds and moistened growing medium in a plastic bag and refrigerate for 2 weeks. Provide darkness and 50°–55°F thereafter.

Planting Seedlings Outdoors

Time Early spring, when soil is cool and a light frost is still possible, or early autumn.
Spacing Small species: 12"–18". Large species: 24"–36".
Light Full sun to light shade.
Soil Deep, rich, well-drained, with a pH level of 5.5–7.0.

Caring for Plants

Easy. Fertilize in early spring. Water well throughout the growing season. Remove faded blooms immediately after first flowering and feed again. When new growth reaches 9", cut off old growth completely. Plants over 18" tall will require staking. *Delphiniums* are short-lived and should be replaced regularly.

Delphinium 'Giant Pacific'

Propagating

Divide in spring. May self-seed.

Dianthus (Annual)

(includes *D. chinensis*)

Annual carnation, Annual pink, China pink, Indian pink

Type HHP grown as HHA
Zone 2–10. Flowers most freely
  in cool weather.
Flowering Season Late spring
  through early summer

Neat, fine-textured, shrubby plants grown for an abundance of saucer-shaped flowers borne throughout the season. Blooms are red, white, or pink, often bicolored, with pinked edges; 6"–12" tall. Excellent edging plant that is useful in both formal and informal plantings.

Sowing

Indoors 8–10 weeks before last frost.
Outdoors Early spring, when soil is cool and a light frost is still possible, or late autumn.
Depth Just cover.

Germinating

Time 5–21 days.
Requirements 60°–70°F.

Planting Seedlings Outdoors

Time After last frost.
Spacing 8"–10".
Light Full sun.
Soil Rich, moist, well-drained, with a pH level of 6.0–7.5.

Caring for Plants

Easy. Pinch back young plants to stimulate bushy growth and deadhead frequently to prolong blooming. Where summers are very hot, cut back hard after blooming. A good mulch may bring plants through winter, but those that survive should be discarded after their second year of blooming.

Propagating

Take cuttings in summer.

A-Annual P-Perennial B-Biennial HHA-Half-hardy annual HA-Hardy annual HB-Hardy biennial HHP-Half-hardy perennial HP-Hardy perennial HHBb-Half-hardy bulb HBb-Hardy bulb

107

Dianthus (Biennial)

(includes *D. armeria, D. barbatus, D. caryophyllus, D. superbus*)

Sweet William

TYPE HB or P grown as B
ZONE 2–10. Performs best where summers are mild.
FLOWERING SEASON Midspring to frost, depending on species

Bushy, plants, 6"–18" tall, with cushiony tufts of lance-shaped leaves and tightly-packed bouquets of blooms borne on rather floppy stems. Flowers are red, white, violet, or pink, bi- or tricolored, flat or double, often with prettily serrated edges. Mass in the border for best effect.

SOWING

INDOORS 6–8 weeks before planting out.
OUTDOORS Any time from April to July for blooms the following year.
DEPTH ¼".

GERMINATING

TIME 10 days.
REQUIREMENTS 70°F.

PLANTING SEEDLINGS OUTDOORS

TIME After last spring frost, or in autumn.
SPACING 9".
LIGHT Sun; *D. barbatus* will grow in light shade.
SOIL Deep, rich, well-drained, with a pH level of 6.0–7.5.

CARING FOR PLANTS

Easy. Water regularly and feed once or twice during the growing season. Shear back after flowering to prolong the life of the plant. Mulch in winter.

PROPAGATING

Take root cuttings.

Dianthus (Perennial)

(includes *D. × allwoodii, D. caryophyllus, D. deltoides, D. gratianopolitanus, D. knappii, D. plumarius*)

Perennial carnation, Cheddar pink, Cottage pink, Maiden pink, Sand pink

TYPE HP
ZONE 3–9; 5–9: *D. gratianopolitanus*
FLOWERING SEASON Late spring or summer, depending on species

True carnation flowers in every shade of pink, red, yellow, and white held on slender stems of 6"–24"; distinctive lanceshaped leaves are midgreen or silvery blue. Use different species with abandon in rock gardens, borders, or along stone walls.

SOWING

INDOORS 8–10 weeks before planting out.
OUTDOORS Early spring or early autumn.
DEPTH Just cover.

Dianthus barbatus

GERMINATING

TIME 14–21 days.
REQUIREMENTS 60°–70°F.

PLANTING SEEDLINGS OUTDOORS

TIME Early spring, when soil is cool and a light frost is still possible, or early autumn.
SPACING Small species: 6". Tall species: 9".
LIGHT Full sun.
SOIL Rich, well-drained, with a pH level of 6.0–7.5.

CARING FOR PLANTS

Easy. Water only during very dry spells. Cut back stems after flowering. Mulch in winter in coldest zones. Renew plants every 2–3 years.

PROPAGATING

Divide in early spring in zones 3–6, in autumn in zones 7–9. Take stem cuttings in summer.

Diascia

Twinspur

Pretty, unusual, low-growing plants resembling a diminutive foxglove. Shell pink flowers are borne on 9"–12" stems all summer. Suitable for borders, rock gardens, or containers. Native to South Africa.

SOWING

INDOORS 6–8 weeks before last frost.
OUTDOORS Early spring to midspring.
DEPTH Just cover.

GERMINATING

TIME 14–30 days
REQUIREMENTS Easy. 60°F.

PLANTING SEEDLINGS OUTDOORS

TIME After last frost.
SPACING Low species: 5"–8". Spreading species: 12"–14".
LIGHT Full sun, with protection from very hot afternoon sun.
SOIL Humus-rich, well-drained, but not too dry.

CARING FOR PLANTS

Pinch tips of young plants to establish a bushy habit. Mulch plants with rock chips to ensure excellent drainage, but do not allow soil to dry out. Cut back after first blooms fade to stimulate further flowering.

PROPAGATING

Take cuttings in late spring.

Diascia barberae

Dicentra

Bleeding heart, Dutchman's breeches, Lady-in-the-bath

Shrubby perennials, 3"–24" tall, bearing dainty flowers of white or pink, some resembling lilliputian britches hanging out to dry, others a string of tiny hearts; foliage is deeply cut and fernlike. Indispensable in any shady garden.

SOWING

INDOORS Midsummer.
OUTDOORS Late autumn or early winter.
DEPTH Seed: just cover. Roots: 2"–3".

GERMINATING

TIME 30–365 days.
REQUIREMENTS Place seeds together with moistened growing medium in a plastic bag and freeze for 6 weeks. Provide 55°–60°F thereafter.

PLANTING SEEDLINGS OUTDOORS

TIME Spring or autumn.
SPACING Small species: 12"–15". Large species: 24".
LIGHT Full sun to part shade. More shade is required where summers are very hot.
SOIL Light, rich, moist, with a pH level of 5.0–6.0.

CARING FOR PLANTS

Easy. Feed lightly during the growing season and water regularly. Do not move established plants. Where summers are very hot, cut back to ground level after flowering and divide every 3–4 years.

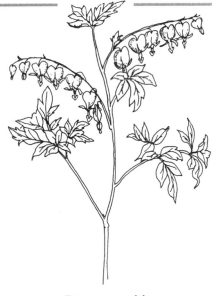

Dicentra spectabilis

PROPAGATING

Take root cuttings at any time, or carefully divide in early spring.

Dictamnus

Burning bush, False dittany, Fraxinella, Gas plant

> TYPE HP
> ZONE 3–8. Dislikes extreme heat and humidity.
> FLOWERING SEASON Late spring to summer

Upright perennials grown for their pink or white, star-shaped flowers borne in stiff terminal spikes; foliage is fragrant and glossy green, 3' tall. Useful in the midsection of the border.

SOWING

INDOORS Late autumn.
OUTDOORS Autumn.
DEPTH Just cover.

GERMINATING

TIME 30–180 days.
REQUIREMENTS Difficult. Sow seeds in flats, seal in a plastic bag, and leave at 60°–65°F for 2 weeks. Refrigerate for 3–6 weeks, then return to 60°–65°F. If seeds do not germinate after 6–10 weeks, chill again for 5–6 weeks, removing from the refrigerator as soon as germination begins.

PLANTING SEEDLINGS OUTDOORS

TIME After last spring frost, or autumn.
SPACING 24"–36".
LIGHT Full sun or part shade.
SOIL Tolerates dry soil that is very rich; poor soil must be kept moist. Prefers a pH level of 5.5–7.0.

CARING FOR PLANTS

Easy. Plants grown from seed will flower in 3–4 years. Prepare the planting hole deeply, adding plenty of compost, and your *Dictamnus* will almost take care of itself. Where summers are very hot, prune severely after blooming. Cut back stems in autumn and mulch for winter.

Dictamunus albus

PROPAGATING

Division may be successful, although seed is preferable as plants resent disturbance.

Didiscus

See *Trachymene*

Dierama

Angels'-fishing-rods, Wand flower

> TYPE HP
> ZONE 7–9. Will not thrive in hot, humid conditions.
> FLOWERING SEASON Summer

Unusual, clump-forming plants with grassy foliage and drooping, funnel- or bell-shaped flowers in shades of pink borne loosely on long, arching stems; 3'–5' tall. Native to South Africa.

SOWING

INDOORS Spring.
OUTDOORS Autumn or spring.
DEPTH Seed: surface. Corm: 4"–6".

Dierama pulcherrimum

GERMINATING

TIME 30–180 days.
REQUIREMENTS Light and 60°–65°F.

PLANTING SEEDLINGS OUTDOORS

TIME Spring or autumn.
SPACING Small species: 6"–8". Large species: 12"–20".
LIGHT Sun. Plant in a location that will be warm and sheltered in winter.
SOIL Rich, well-drained.

CARING FOR PLANTS

Easy. Plants grown from seed will flower in 3 years. Keep soil moist during the growing season and mulch in winter in zones 7–8. Do not lift corms unless absolutely necessary as they take 2–3 years to recover.

PROPAGATING

Plant offsets.

A-Annual P-Perennial B-Biennial HHA-Half-hardy annual HA-Hardy annual HB-Hardy biennial HHP-Half-hardy perennial HP-Hardy perennial HHBb-Half-hardy bulb HBb-Hardy bulb

Digitalis

Foxglove

Majestic yet unpretentious, this Old World standard adds a touch of class, whether used in the border, woodland planting, or allowed to self-seed at random. From a demure 2' to a towering 6', spires carry tubular flowers in subtle shades of pink, salmon, orange, yellow, and cream, often innocently freckled.

SOWING

INDOORS 8–10 weeks before planting out for blooms first year.
OUTDOORS After last spring frost for flowering the following year. Where winters are mild, late summer or autumn.
DEPTH Surface.

Digitalis purpurea

GERMINATING

TIME 14–21 days.
REQUIREMENTS Light and 60°–65°F.

PLANTING SEEDLINGS OUTDOORS

TIME 2–3 weeks before last frost.
SPACING 18"–24".
LIGHT Full sun to part shade; afternoon shade is necessary in hot climates. *D. lutea* will thrive in full shade.
SOIL Cool, moist, rich, with well-rotted manure added at planting time; pH level of 6.0–7.5.

CARING FOR PLANTS

Easy. Water plants deeply and often. Cut flowering stems to ground after blooming if self-seeding is not desired. Mulch after the ground freezes to minimize the chance of crown rot. Foxgloves do not like heat or drought and will languish in unfavorable conditions; where summers are very hot, early-blooming species stand a better chance of surviving. Even under ideal conditions, foxgloves may require renewal every 2–3 years. Much loved by slugs.

PROPAGATING

Divide in early spring in the North, autumn in the South. May self-seed.

Dimorphotheca

African daisy, Cape marigold, Star of the Veldt

Long-blooming annuals (12"–18" tall) covered in delightful, daisylike flowers in every color but blue with strongly contrasting eyes. Use in containers or borders. Native to South Africa.

SOWING

INDOORS 6–8 weeks before planting out.
OUTDOORS Early autumn for winter flowering, winter for spring blooms, but only in zones 9–10.
DEPTH Just cover.

GERMINATING

TIME 10–15 days.
REQUIREMENTS Difficult. 60°–70°F.

PLANTING SEEDLINGS OUTDOORS

TIME Late spring, when soil is warm.
SPACING 8"–12".
LIGHT Full sun.
SOIL Prefers rich, well-drained, but will tolerate dry soil.

CARING FOR PLANTS

Water frequently early in the day; keep water off of leaves as plants are susceptible to fungal diseases in wet or humid conditions. Cut stems to ground after flowering. Do not move.

Dimorphotheca aurantiaca

PROPAGATING

Take cuttings in late summer.

A-Annual P-Perennial B-Biennial HHA-Half-hardy annual HA-Hardy annual HB-Hardy biennial HHP-Half-hardy perennial HP-Hardy perennial HHBb-Half-hardy bulb HBb-Hardy bulb

111

Dioscorea

Chinese yam, Cinnamon vine

TYPE HHP grown as A in the North
ZONE A: 4–8; P: 9–10
FLOWERING SEASON Spring to autumn, depending on species

Genus of mainly tropical climbers sometimes grown on porches or pergolas for their handsome, shiny, heart-shaped leaves (some with an attractive mosaic pattern of dark green, pale green, and white) and clusters of small, white, cinnamon-scented flowers.

SOWING
INDOORS Late winter to early spring.
OUTDOORS Seed: September to October. Tuber: after last frost date.
DEPTH Seed: ⅛". Tuber: 3".

GERMINATING
TIME 21–36 days.
REQUIREMENTS 70°–75°F.

PLANTING SEEDLINGS OUTDOORS
TIME When temperatures remain above 45°F.
SPACING Climbers: 12". Others: 24"–36".
LIGHT Full sun to light shade.
SOIL Deep, well-drained.

CARING FOR PLANTS
Water well during the growing season. Provide a trellis for climbers. North of zone 9, lift tubers in the autumn and store in a cool, frost-free place, replanting in spring.

PROPAGATING
Take cuttings or divide in spring or autumn.

Diosphaera

See *Trachelium*

Dipsacus

Teasel

TYPE HB
ZONE 3–9
FLOWERING SEASON Summer

Coarse, prickly, plants, 3'–6' tall, with pink, white, or purple thistlelike flowers. Grown as a curiosity or for textural interest.

SOWING
INDOORS Seeds should be started outdoors.
OUTDOORS Late spring to early summer.
DEPTH ¼".

GERMINATING
TIME 4–30 days.
REQUIREMENTS 60°–65°F.

PLANTING SEEDLINGS OUTDOORS
TIME Set out purchased plants in autumn.
SPACING 24"–36".
LIGHT Prefers sun, but will tolerate shade.
SOIL Moist.

CARING FOR PLANTS
The problem here is how to keep plantings within bounds. Teasels must be controlled ruthlessly and should only be grown by responsible gardeners. Cut off flower heads before seeds ripen and pull up unwanted plants as soon as they emerge. Older plants are susceptible to mildew.

PROPAGATING
Just stand back and watch your teasels self-seed all over the garden.

A-Annual P-Perennial B-Biennial HHA-Half-hardy annual HA-Hardy annual HB-Hardy biennial HHP-Half-hardy perennial HP-Hardy perennial HHBb-Half-hardy bulb HBb-Hardy bulb

Dodecatheon

American cowslip, Prairie pointer, Shooting star

> TYPE HP or HHP
> ZONE 3–8: *D. pulchellum;* 4–8: *D. alpinum, D. meadia;* 5–8: *D. jeffreyi;* 8–10: *D. clevelandii*
> FLOWERING SEASON Spring to early summer

Small woodland perennials, most no more than 6"–18" tall. Pink, green, or purple star-shaped flowers with reflexed petals on leafless stalks look as though they are battling a strong wind, with petals streaming behind them. Use this North American native in the woodland garden.

SOWING

INDOORS Spring.
OUTDOORS Late autumn to early winter.
DEPTH Surface.

Dodecatheon meadia

GERMINATING

TIME 90–365 days.
REQUIREMENTS Difficult. *Autumn sowing:* Sow seeds in flats, sink these in the ground outdoors, and cover with glass. Transplant seedlings to beds when they are large enough to handle. *Spring sowing:* Place seeds in a plastic bag together with moist growing medium and refrigerate for 3 weeks. Provide light and 60°–70°F thereafter.

PLANTING SEEDLINGS OUTDOORS

TIME After last spring frost, or in autumn.
SPACING Small species: 6"–8". Large species: 18"–20".
LIGHT Part to full shade.
SOIL Rich, moist, woodland soil, with a pH level of 5.0–7.0.

CARING FOR PLANTS

Easy, when planted in a suitable location. Apply mulch in spring and do not allow soil to dry out during the growing season. Foliage dies back in the heat of summer. Do not move established plants.

PROPAGATING

Divide in autumn.

Dolichos

Bonavist, Hyacinth bean, Lablab, Sarawak bean

> TYPE HHP grown as HHA
> ZONE A: 3–8; P: 9–10. Performs most successfully where there is a long, warm growing season.
> FLOWERING SEASON Summer through frost

Woody-stemmed, rather shrubby climbers with purple, white, or yellow pealike flowers, followed by ornamental pods; foliage may be midgreen or a very showy purple; grows to 30'.

SOWING

INDOORS 6–8 weeks before last frost, in peat pots.
OUTDOORS After last frost.
DEPTH Just cover.

GERMINATING

TIME 14–30 days.
REQUIREMENTS Soak seeds for 24 hours in warm water and provide 70°F thereafter.

PLANTING SEEDLINGS OUTDOORS

TIME Several weeks after last frost, when temperatures remain above 45°F.
SPACING 24"–36".
LIGHT Full sun.
SOIL Rich, moist, warm.

CARING FOR PLANTS

Easy. Provide a trellis for support and do not attempt to transplant.

PROPAGATING

Seed only.

A-Annual P-Perennial B-Biennial HHA-Half-hardy annual HA-Hardy annual HB-Hardy biennial HHP-Half-hardy perennial HP-Hardy perennial HHBb-Half-hardy bulb HBb-Hardy bulb

113

Dondia

See *Hacquetia*

Doronicum

Leopard's bane

> TYPE HP
> ZONE 4–8. **Prefers cool summers.**
> FLOWERING SEASON **Spring to early summer, depending on species**

Cheerful perennials grown for their showy, yellow, daisylike flowers; 12"–36". Useful in the border and for cutting.

SOWING

INDOORS 8–10 weeks before planting out.
OUTDOORS Early spring or early autumn.
DEPTH Surface.

Doronicum plantagineum

GERMINATING

TIME 15–20 days.
REQUIREMENTS Light and 70°F.

PLANTING SEEDLINGS OUTDOORS

TIME Early spring, when soil is cool and a light frost is still possible, or early autumn.
SPACING Small species: 9"–12". Large species: 12"–18".
LIGHT Full sun where summers are cool; elsewhere plant in part shade.
SOIL Moist, humus-rich.

CARING FOR PLANTS

Water plants frequently in summer and cut back to ground level in autumn (where summers are hot this will not be necessary as leaves will die back naturally). Mulch in spring and again in winter to protect shallow roots. Plants are short-lived and require dividing every 2–4 years.

PROPAGATING

Divide in late summer or autumn.

Dorotheanthus

See *Mesembryanthemum*

Doryanthes

Gymea lily

> TYPE HHP
> ZONE 10
> FLOWERING SEASON **Summer**

Massive succulent plants (6'–12') with sword-shaped leaves and large flowers, red outside and white inside, borne terminally on stiff stalks. Use as a specimen or in a desert garden.

SOWING

INDOORS As soon as fresh seed is available.
OUTDOORS As soon as fresh seed is available.
DEPTH Surface.

GERMINATING

TIME 30–90 days.
REQUIREMENTS Soak seeds for 3 hours in warm water. Provide light and 65°–70°F thereafter. As soon as seeds germinate, surround gently with pea gravel to provide support and good drainage.

PLANTING SEEDLINGS OUTDOORS

TIME After last frost, when temperatures will remain above 50°F.
SPACING Usually planted singly, as plants have a spread of 4'–6'.
LIGHT Sun.
SOIL Prefers well-drained, humus-rich soil.

CARING FOR PLANTS

Difficult. Water abundantly during the growing season; taper off watering in winter, but do not allow soil to dry out completely.

PROPAGATING

Plant rooted suckers, or plant mature bulbils, after flowering.

A-Annual P-Perennial B-Biennial HHA-Half-hardy annual HA-Hardy annual HB-Hardy biennial HHP-Half-hardy perennial HP-Hardy perennial HHBb-Half-hardy bulb HBb-Hardy bulb

Douglasia

(synonymous with *Vitaliana*)

Yellow rock jasmine

TYPE HP
ZONE 5–7. Requires cool, moist summers.
FLOWERING SEASON Spring

Prostrate, rosette-forming perennials bearing tight clusters of tiny oblong leaves and masses of yellow or pink tubular flowers. Rock garden plants.

SOWING
INDOORS Late winter to early spring.
OUTDOORS Autumn.
DEPTH Surface.

GERMINATING
TIME 30 days to 2 years.
REQUIREMENTS *Outdoor sowing:* Sow seeds in flats, sink in the ground against a north-facing wall, and cover with glass. Moisten growing medium occasionally, as necessary. In the spring, bring indoors to 50°–55°F. *Indoor sowing:* Place seeds in a plastic bag together with moist growing medium. Refrigerate for 3–5 weeks, then provide 50°–55°F.

PLANTING SEEDLINGS OUTDOORS
TIME Early spring, when soil is cool and a light frost is still possible, or late autumn.
SPACING 8".
LIGHT Full sun or light shade.
SOIL Moist, very well-drained, neutral or slightly acid.

CARING FOR PLANTS
Difficult. Plants grown from seed will flower in 2 years. Water frequently during dry spells, taking care to keep water off of leaves. Protect crowns from heavy rain. Mulch lightly in winter.

PROPAGATING
Divide in autumn, or take softwood cuttings in summer.

Draba

Whitlow grass

TYPE HP
ZONE 3–8: *D. mollissima*, *D. sibirica*; 4–8: *D. lasiocarpa*, *D. densiflora*; 5–8: *D. aizoides*; 6–8: *D. rigida* var. *bryoides*
FLOWERING SEASON Early spring

Compact, mounding plants for the rock garden growing 1"–8" tall. Flowers are diminutive stars of yellow, white, pink, or purple borne in terminal clusters on leafless stems.

SOWING
INDOORS 8–10 weeks before planting out.
OUTDOORS After last frost.
DEPTH Just cover.

Draba aizoides

GERMINATING
TIME 30–90 days.
REQUIREMENTS 60°–70°F. For *D. rigida* var. *bryoides* refrigerate seeds for 4–6 weeks.

PLANTING SEEDLINGS OUTDOORS
TIME After last frost.
SPACING 3"–5".
LIGHT Prefers full sun but will tolerate light shade.
SOIL Gritty or sandy. Add a little lime to acid soil.

CARING FOR PLANTS
Protect plants from overhead water in winter. Mulch in autumn where winters are very cold.

PROPAGATING
Divide in spring.

A-Annual P-Perennial B-Biennial HHA-Half-hardy annual HA-Hardy annual HB-Hardy biennial HHP-Half-hardy perennial HP-Hardy perennial HHBb-Half-hardy bulb HBb-Hardy bulb

115

Dracocephalum

See *Physostegia*

Dracunculus

Dragon arum, Dragon plant

> TYPE HP
> ZONE 7–10. Requires warm
> temperatures.
> FLOWERING SEASON Early summer

Exotic perennials bearing large, blood-red, arum-type flowers of alien appearance and noxious odor; 18"–36". Grown as a curiosity.

SOWING

INDOORS Late winter to early spring.
OUTDOORS Autumn.
DEPTH Seed: just cover. Tuber: 3".

GERMINATING

TIME 30–180 days.
REQUIREMENTS 55°–65°F.

PLANTING SEEDLINGS OUTDOORS

TIME After last frost.
SPACING 10"–12".
LIGHT Part to full shade.
SOIL Rich, well-drained, with abundant organic matter.

CARING FOR PLANTS

Mulch in spring. Keep soil moist during growing season, fairly dry at all other times.

PROPAGATING

Divide in autumn.

Dracunculus vulgaris

Dryas

Mountain avens

> TYPE HP
> ZONE 2–6
> FLOWERING SEASON Late spring to
> summer

Creeping evergreen perennials with small, dark green leaves and cup-shaped flowers of white or palest yellow, followed by ornamental, feathery seeds. Use in the rock garden or as a ground cover for small spaces.

SOWING

INDOORS See "Germinating, Requirements."
OUTDOORS See "Germinating, Requirements."
DEPTH Just cover.

GERMINATING

TIME 50–365 days.
REQUIREMENTS *Autumn sowing:* Sow seeds in flats, sink in the ground against a north-facing wall, and cover with glass. Moisten soil occasionally, if necessary. Bring indoors in spring to 60°–70°F. *Spring sowing:* Place seeds in a plastic bag together with moist growing medium and refrigerate for 2–3 weeks. Sow seeds in flats, plunge in the ground in a shady location, and cover with glass. Transplant seedlings as they emerge.

PLANTING SEEDLINGS OUTDOORS

TIME Spring or autumn.
SPACING 12"–15".
LIGHT Sun or part shade.
SOIL Moist, peaty, sandy or gritty, slightly alkaline.

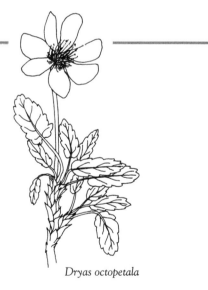
Dryas octopetala

CARING FOR PLANTS

Difficult. Mulch in spring with a mixture of one-half leaf mold and one-half rock chips. Cut back creeping stems as they emerge — these do not flower as well as the parent plant.

PROPAGATING

Divide in spring, or take cuttings in late summer.

A-Annual P-Perennial B-Biennial HHA-Half-hardy annual HA-Hardy annual HB-Hardy biennial HHP-Half-hardy perennial HP-Hardy perennial HHBb-Half-hardy bulb HBb-Hardy bulb

116

Eccremocarpus

Chilean glory flower, Glory flower

TYPE HP, or HHP grown as HHA
ZONE A: warm climates; P: 8–10
FLOWERING SEASON Summer

Shrubby climbers grown for their decorative, tubular flowers of bright orange, yellow, or scarlet. Grows to 12'. Native to Chile and Peru.

SOWING

INDOORS 4–6 weeks before planting out.
OUTDOORS Early spring, when soil has warmed.
DEPTH Just cover.

GERMINATING

TIME 14–60 days.
REQUIREMENTS 60°–70°F.

PLANTING SEEDLINGS OUTDOORS

TIME 2–3 weeks after last frost.
SPACING 12"; most effective when grown singly.
LIGHT Sun.
SOIL Prefers light, rich, moist, well-drained; will tolerate poor soil.

CARING FOR PLANTS

Requires a trellis or other form of support. Lightly prune perennials in early spring.

PROPAGATING

Self-seeds.

Echinacea

Coneflower, Hedgehog coneflower

TYPE HP
ZONE 3–9
FLOWERING SEASON Summer through early autumn

Rugged but beautiful upright perennials bearing white or raspberry-colored, daisy-like flowers with large pincushion eyes throughout the summer; 2'–4' tall. Essential in any border or wildflower garden.

SOWING

INDOORS 8–10 weeks before planting out.
OUTDOORS Early spring or early autumn.
DEPTH ⅛".

Echinacea purpurea

GERMINATING

TIME 10–21 days.
REQUIREMENTS Darkness and 70°–75°F.

PLANTING SEEDLINGS OUTDOORS

TIME Early spring, when soil is cool and a light frost isstill possible, or early autumn.
SPACING Small species: 12"–15". Large species: 18"–24".
LIGHT Full sun or very light shade.
SOIL Prefers average, well-drained, with a pH level of 5.5–7.0; will tolerate poor, dry soil.

CARING FOR PLANTS

Easy. Water plants regularly and leave undisturbed once established. Susceptible to powdery mildew, which can be minimized by regular watering during dry spells, keeping leaves as dry as possible. Cut flowering stems to the ground in late autumn.

PROPAGATING

Divide in spring north of zone 7, early autumn in the South. Or take root cuttings in spring.

A-Annual P-Perennial B-Biennial HHA-Half-hardy annual HA-Hardy annual HB-Hardy biennial HHP-Half-hardy perennial HP-Hardy perennial HHBb-Half-hardy bulb HBb-Hardy bulb

Echinops

Globe thistle

TYPE HP
ZONE 3–9
FLOWERING SEASON Summer to late autumn, depending on species

Unusual perennials grown for their display of spiky purple or white globes borne atop fleshy, white wands; leaves are coarse and spiny. Plants are 3'–5' tall and useful at the back of the border where their unusual flowers provide an interesting contrast to many other plants.

SOWING

INDOORS 2–3 weeks before last frost.
OUTDOORS After last frost.
DEPTH Just cover.

GERMINATING

TIME 15–60 days.
REQUIREMENTS 65°–75°F.

Echinops ritro

PLANTING SEEDLINGS OUTDOORS

TIME After last frost.
SPACING 24"–36".
LIGHT Full sun or part shade.
SOIL Tolerant of almost any soil, but must have good drainage. A pH level of 5.5–7.0 is preferred.

CARING FOR PLANTS

Easy. Water during very dry weather and cut back to ground level in autumn. Tall species and plants grown in very rich soil will require staking. Replace every 3–4 years when plants begin to deteriorate.

PROPAGATING

Divide in spring, autumn in zones 7–9; take root cuttings in spring.

Echium

Pride of Madeira, Viper's bugloss

TYPE HHP or HB grown as HA
ZONE A: 1–8; P: 9–10. Prefers mild, dry climates.
FLOWERING SEASON Summer

Shrublike plants growing 1'–4' tall, the best species having an interesting, spiky texture. Flowers may be stunning bottlebrushes of deepest blue or pretty cups in shades of purple or pink. Edging or border plants.

SOWING

INDOORS 6–8 weeks before planting out, in peat pots.
OUTDOORS Autumn in zones 9–10, elsewhere in spring.
DEPTH ¼".

GERMINATING

TIME 7–21 days.
REQUIREMENTS 60°–70°F.

PLANTING SEEDLINGS OUTDOORS

TIME Spring, when temperatures remain above 40°F.
SPACING Small species: 8"–10". Large species: 18"–24".
LIGHT Full sun.
SOIL Tolerant of wet or dry soil, but prefers good drainage and a pH level of 6.5–7.0. Rich soil produces lush foliage with few flowers.

CARING FOR PLANTS

Water during very dry spells. Bugloss is short-lived and needs to be replaced regularly, but may become invasive if allowed to self-seed. Do not move established plants.

PROPAGATING

Take cuttings, or allow to self-seed.

A-Annual P-Perennial B-Biennial HHA-Half-hardy annual HA-Hardy annual HB-Hardy biennial HHP-Half-hardy perennial HP-Hardy perennial HHBb-Half-hardy bulb HBb-Hardy bulb

Emilia

Devil's paintbrush, Flora's paintbrush, Tassel flower

TYPE HA or HHA
ZONE 3–10. Prefers cool temperatures.
FLOWERING SEASON Summer to early autumn

Wiry, unkempt annuals of 18"–24" grown for the small scarlet balls that bloom all summer on long thin stems. Colorful plants for the border; ideal cut flowers.

SOWING

INDOORS 6–8 weeks before planting out, in peat pots.
OUTDOORS Zones 3–7: 2–3 weeks before last frost. Zones 8–10: autumn.
DEPTH Just cover.

GERMINATING

TIME 8–15 days.
REQUIREMENTS Darkness and 60°–70°F.

PLANTING SEEDLINGS OUTDOORS

TIME 2–3 weeks after last frost.
SPACING 8"–10".
LIGHT Full sun.
SOIL Average to dry, well-drained.

CARING FOR PLANTS

Easy. For more abundant blooms, keep plants somewhat crowded and deadhead often. Do not move.

PROPAGATING

Seed only.

Emilia coccinea

Epigaea

Ground laurel, Mayflower, Trailing arbutus

TYPE HP
ZONE 3–9
FLOWERING SEASON Early spring

Prostrate, evergreen perennials with large, dark, oval leaves making an elegant backdrop for clusters of cup-shaped, white or shell pink flowers. Charming plants for the woodland garden.

SOWING

INDOORS Start seeds outdoors.
OUTDOORS As soon as ripe seeds are available, usually in July.
DEPTH ¼".

GERMINATING

TIME 30+ days.
REQUIREMENTS Extremely difficult. It is essential to use a sterile growing medium.

PLANTING SEEDLINGS OUTDOORS

TIME Set out purchased plants in early spring or early autumn.
SPACING 8"–12".
LIGHT Part to full shade.
SOIL Slightly sandy or gritty, very acid (pH level of 4.0–5.0).

CARING FOR PLANTS

Difficult to establish, but easy to maintain once this is done. Plants grown from seed will bloom in 3 years. Provide a permanent mulch of pine needles or oak leaves. Do not allow young plants to dry out, and do not disturb roots.

PROPAGATING

Take softwood cuttings in late summer. Or divide in spring in the North, in autumn south of zone 6 (this method may be less successful).

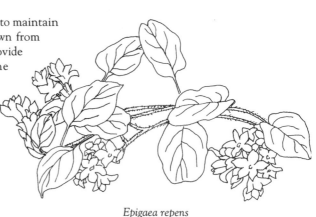

Epigaea repens

Epilobium

Fireweed, French willow, Rosebay, Willow herb

> TYPE HP or HHP
> ZONE 2–8: *E. latifolium*; 3–8: *E. angustifolium, E. dodonaei*; 8–9: *E. chloraefolium, E. glabellum*
> FLOWERING SEASON Midsummer

Very large genus of perennials, many of which are too weedy for the garden. Desirable species are either erect clumps, 4"–8" high, with neat, attractive leaves and white or red funnel-shaped flowers, or large upright plants of 4'–5' bearing terminal spikes of tiny pink or white blooms. Use small species for edging rock gardens, tall species for borders or wildflower gardens.

SOWING

INDOORS Start seeds outdoors only.
OUTDOORS Autumn, as soon as ripe seed is available.
DEPTH ⅛".

GERMINATING

TIME 14–30 days.
REQUIREMENTS Sow seeds in flats, sink in the ground against a north-facing wall, and cover with glass. Moisten soil occasionally, if necessary. Transplant seedlings 6 weeks after germinating.

PLANTING SEEDLINGS OUTDOORS

TIME Spring.
SPACING 12"–24".
LIGHT Sun or part shade.
SOIL Dry, stony, with a pH level of 6.0–7.0. Plants grown in moist soil develop a coarse appearance.

CARING FOR PLANTS

Easy. Deadhead diligently to avoid unwanted self-seeding; ungroomed plants will take over the garden.

PROPAGATING

Divide in early spring, or take softwood cuttings in spring. Many species will self-seed.

Epilobium angustifolium

Epimedium

Barrenwort, Bishop's hat

> ZONE 4–9
> FLOWERING SEASON May to June

Shy and lovely, these modest perennials bear midgreen, heart-shaped leaves and clusters of complex flowers, both held on the slenderest of stems; 6"–18" tall. Blooms may be white, pink, red, or yellow. Use as a ground cover for small shady spots, in rock gardens, or in mixed shady plantings.

GERMINATING

REQUIREMENTS Not successfully propagated by seed.

PLANTING SEEDLINGS OUTDOORS

TIME Set out purchased plants after last frost in spring or early autumn.
SPACING 6"–12".
LIGHT Part to full shade. Tolerates sun if soil is rich, moist, and acid.
SOIL Prefers moist, well-drained, with a pH level of 5.5–7.0; will tolerate dry soil. Add generous amounts of organic matter.

CARING FOR PLANTS

A very slow grower that requires patience. It will be many years before your plants resemble the photographs in nursery catalogues. Cut back straggly growth in early spring, water during dry spells, and cover with a light straw mulch in winter.

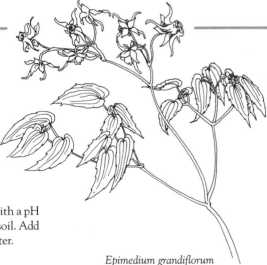

Epimedium grandiflorum

PROPAGATING

Divide in spring north of zone 7 or in autumn in the South.

A-Annual P-Perennial B-Biennial HHA-Half-hardy annual HA-Hardy annual HB-Hardy biennial HHP-Half-hardy perennial HP-Hardy perennial HHBb-Half-hardy bulb HBb-Hardy bulb

Eragrostis

Lace grass, Love grass

> TYPE HA or HP
> ZONE A: 3–10; P: 7–10; 5–9: *E. spectabilis*
> FLOWERING SEASON Late spring to autumn, depending on species

Graceful ornamental grasses with fine, arching leaves of pale green and airy flower spikes 3'–4' tall. Used in plantings of mixed grasses or in contrast with coarse-textured plants.

SOWING

INDOORS 6–8 weeks before planting out.
OUTDOORS After last frost.
DEPTH Surface.

GERMINATING

TIME 21 days.
REQUIREMENTS Light and 60°–75°F.

PLANTING SEEDLINGS OUTDOORS

TIME After last frost.
SPACING 24". Allow very large species more room or plant singly.
LIGHT Full sun.
SOIL Fertile, well-drained.

CARING FOR PLANTS

Easy. Site plants in a sheltered location to avoid damage to the delicate flowers from wind and rain. Water regularly for best results; keep direct spray off of plants. In late winter, cut back perennials to no less than 8"–12" — more than this will weaken plants. Cut flowers for drying before seeds are fully ripe.

PROPAGATING

Annuals will self-seed. Divide perennials in spring.

Eranthis

Winter aconite

> TYPE HP
> ZONE 4–9
> FLOWERING SEASON Late winter to early spring

Low-growing, mat-forming perennials bearing solitary, stalkless, cup-shaped, bright yellow flowers on a whorl of green, leaflike bracts. Mass under shrubs or throughout a woodland garden.

SOWING

INDOORS See "Germinating, Requirements."
OUTDOORS See "Germinating, Requirements."
DEPTH Seed: just cover. Tuber: soak for 24 hours and plant at a depth of 3"–5".

Eranthis hyemalis

GERMINATING

TIME 30–365 days.
REQUIREMENTS *Autumn sowing:* Sow seeds in flats, sink in the ground against a north-facing wall, and cover with glass. Moisten soil occasionally, if necessary. Bring indoors in spring to 60°–70°F. *Spring sowing:* Sow seeds in flats with moistened medium, secure in plastic bags, and refrigerate for 2–3 weeks. Sink flats in the ground in a shady location, covering with glass. Transplant seedlings as they appear.

PLANTING SEEDLINGS OUTDOORS

TIME Late summer to early autumn.
SPACING 3"–4".
LIGHT Likes full sun in winter and early spring, but prefers light shade the rest of the year.
SOIL Ordinary, humus-rich, slightly moist.

CARING FOR PLANTS

Plants grown from seed will not flower for 3–4 years. Keep soil moist during the growing season. Mark plant locations as aconites die back completely in summer. Do not disturb.

PROPAGATING

Divide clumps immediately after flowering, or allow to self-seed.

A-Annual P-Perennial B-Biennial HHA-Half-hardy annual HA-Hardy annual HB-Hardy biennial HHP-Half-hardy perennial HP-Hardy perennial HHBb-Half-hardy bulb HBb-Hardy bulb

121

Eremurus

Desert candle, Foxtail lily, King's spear

> TYPE HP
> ZONE 5–8: *E. himalaicus*;
>   6–9: *E. stenophyllus*,
>   *E. x isabellinus, E. robustus*
> FLOWERING SEASON Late spring to
>   early summer.

Interesting perennials with tufts of narrow, straplike leaves and 2'–6' stalks bearing thick, showy racemes of tiny white, pink, or yellow flowers. Contrasts nicely in the border with more horizontal plants.

SOWING

INDOORS Late winter to early spring.
OUTDOORS Autumn.
DEPTH Seed: just cover. Roots: 4"–6".

GERMINATING

TIME 30–365 days.
REQUIREMENTS Difficult. *Indoor sowing:* Sow seeds in peat pots, secure in plastic bags, and refrigerate for 2–3 weeks. Provide 55°–60°F thereafter. *Outdoor sowing:* Sow seeds in flats, sink in the ground against a north-facing wall, and cover with glass. Remove glass when seeds sprout.

PLANTING SEEDLINGS OUTDOORS

TIME Autumn.
SPACING Small species: 12"–18". Large species: 36".
LIGHT Full sun.
SOIL Prepare an 18" planting hole for each plant and backfill with ⅓ good soil, ⅓ well-rotted cow manure, ⅓ peat, well mixed.

CARING FOR PLANTS

Plants grown from seed take up to 6 years to flower. Site plants away from damaging winds. Water well during the growing season, ceasing during dormancy. Top-dress in

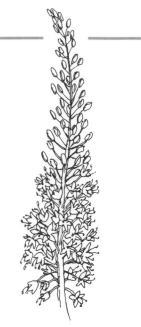

Eremurus stenophyllus 'Bungei'

spring with manure. Mark location of plants after flowering as foliage dies back completely. Divide carefully every 5 years to rejuvenate, but otherwise disturb roots as little as possible.

PROPAGATING

Carefully divide in late summer.

Erigeron

Fleabane

> TYPE HP or HHP
> ZONE 2–9: *E. compositus*,
>   *E. speciosus*; 3–8: *E. aureus*,
>   *E. glaucus, E. pulchellus*;
>   4–8: *E. aurantiacus*;
>   8–9: *E. karvinskianus*
> FLOWERING SEASON Early summer
>   to early autumn, depending on
>   species

Genus of North American plants resembling the aster in appearance, with neat foliage and fine-petalled, daisylike flowers of pink, purple, white, yellow, or orange and yellow eyes; 4"–36". Excellent edging and border plants.

Erigeron speciosus

SOWING

INDOORS 8–10 weeks before planting out.
OUTDOORS Early spring or early autumn.
DEPTH Surface.

GERMINATING

TIME 15–50 days.
REQUIREMENTS 55°F.

PLANTING SEEDLINGS OUTDOORS

TIME Early spring, when soil is cool and a light frost is still possible, or early autumn.
SPACING Dwarf species: 9". Larger species:12"–18".
LIGHT Full sun or very light shade.
SOIL Ordinary, well-drained.

CARING FOR PLANTS

Easy. Feed lightly, deadhead regularly, and cut back stems to ground in autumn. Divide every 3 years.

PROPAGATING

Divide in spring in zones 2–6, or early autumn in zones 7–9.

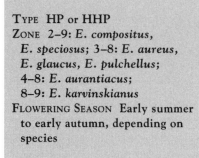

A-Annual P-Perennial B-Biennial HHA-Half-hardy annual HA-Hardy annual HB-Hardy biennial HHP-Half-hardy perennial HP-Hardy perennial HHBb-Half-hardy bulb HBb-Hardy bulb

Erinus

Fairy foxglove

TYPE Short-lived HP
ZONE 4–9. Not tolerant of high heat and humidity.
FLOWERING SEASON Late winter to summer, depending on species

Small species of low-growing, tufted perennials with tiny leaves and masses of small, flat, pink, white, or red flowers. Adds color to rock gardens or drystone walls.

SOWING

INDOORS 6–8 weeks before planting out.
OUTDOORS Early spring.
DEPTH Surface.

GERMINATING

TIME 20–25 days.
REQUIREMENTS Easy. 65°–75°F.

Erinus alpinus

PLANTING SEEDLINGS OUTDOORS

TIME After last frost.
SPACING Small species: 3"–4". Large species: 6"–8".
LIGHT Sun, but with some shade in the afternoon where summers are hot.
SOIL Well-drained, sandy or gritty. Poor drainage is often the cause of plants failing in winter.

CARING FOR PLANTS

Easy. Improve drainage by mulching with fine gravel or rock chips. Grow early-blooming species where summers are hot. These short-lived plants require frequent replacing.

PROPAGATING

Divide in autumn in the South, in spring north of zone 7. Take cuttings in early summer. Will self-seed, although rampant cross-fertilization results in unpredictable offspring.

Eriophorum

Cotton grass

TYPE HP
ZONE 7–10; 4–10: *E. angustifolium*; 6–10: *E. x polystachion, E. scheuchzeri*
FLOWERING SEASON Summer

Ornamental grasses, 1'–3' tall, grown for their long-lasting, cottony white flowers held on stiff stems. Used in bog or waterside plantings.

SOWING

INDOORS Best started *in situ.*
OUTDOORS Early spring to midspring.
DEPTH Surface.

GERMINATING

TIME 21 days.
REQUIREMENTS Light and 60°–75°F.

PLANTING SEEDLINGS OUTDOORS

TIME Early spring.
SPACING 12"–18".
LIGHT Full sun or shade.
SOIL Acid and always moist. Will grow in shallow water.

CARING FOR PLANTS

Keep soil moist at all times. Cut back severely in early spring.

PROPAGATING

Divide in spring.

Erodium

Alfilaria, Filaree, Heron's bill, Pin clover, Storksbill

Low-growing perennials, 3"–18" tall, similar to the *Geranium*. Leaves are finely dissected, sometimes with a silver or bluish cast; flowers are cup-shaped, pink, white, or yellow, often veined. Rock garden and border plants.

Erodium glutinosum

SOWING

INDOORS Start seed outdoors.
OUTDOORS Autumn, as soon as seed is ripe.
DEPTH ⅛".

GERMINATING

TIME 14–21 days.
REQUIREMENTS Easy. 55°F.

PLANTING SEEDLINGS OUTDOORS

TIME After last frost.
SPACING Small species: 6"–8". Large species: 12"–18".
LIGHT Sun or light shade.
SOIL Sandy or gritty, slightly sweet.

CARING FOR PLANTS

Improve drainage by mulching with fine gravel; provide additional organic mulch in autumn where winters are cold. Protect hairy species from overhead water. *Erodium* can become weedy.

PROPAGATING

Divide in spring, or take cuttings in summer.

Eryngium

Eryngo, Sea holly

Large genus of prickly perennials with spiny leaves that are sometimes silver or blue, and spiky blue or white blooms that are made up of a small cone-shaped flower surrounded by pointy bracts. Plants are 1'–4' tall and add an unusual texture to the border.

SOWING

INDOORS See "Germinating, Requirements."
OUTDOORS See "Germinating, Requirements."
DEPTH Surface.

GERMINATING

TIME 5–90 days.
REQUIREMENTS *Autumn sowing:* Sow seeds in flats, sink in the ground against a north-facing wall, and cover with glass. Moisten soil occasionally, if necessary. Bring indoors in spring to 65°–75°F. *Spring sowing:* Sow seeds in flats with moistened medium, place in a plastic bag, and refrigerate. After 2–3 weeks, remove and sink in the ground in a shady location, covering with glass. Transplant seedlings as they appear.

PLANTING SEEDLINGS OUTDOORS

TIME After last frost.
SPACING Small species: 12"–18". Larger species: 24"–36".
LIGHT Full sun.
SOIL Light, very well-drained, rather poor, with a pH level between 5.0 and 7.0.

CARING FOR PLANTS

Easy. Requires very little care. Water only during very dry spells. Large species grown in rich soil may require staking. Mulch with gravel in winter to keep crowns dry. Long taproots make transplanting difficult.

PROPAGATING

Take root cuttings in spring.

Eryngium amethystinum

Erysimum

Alpine wallflower, Blister cress, Coastal wallflower, Fairy wallflower, Siberian wallflower

> TYPE HA, HB, or HP
> ZONE 3–9. Flowering inhibited by hot weather.
> FLOWERING SEASON Spring

Genus of plants resembling wall flowers, 6"–3' tall, with lance-shaped leaves and fragrant, bright orange or yellow, 4-petalled flowers. Satisfying plants for the rock garden or borders.

SOWING

INDOORS Not recommended.
OUTDOORS A: in autumn where winters are mild, elsewhere in spring. B: spring, moving to permanent location in autumn. P: spring or autumn.
DEPTH ¼".

GERMINATING

TIME 14–30 days.

PLANTING SEEDLINGS OUTDOORS

TIME Set out purchased plants in spring or autumn.
SPACING 4"–10".
LIGHT Sun.
SOIL Ordinary, well-drained, with a pH level of 5.0–8.0. Withstands dry soil.

CARING FOR PLANTS

Easy. Deadhead regularly. Mulch in autumn north of zone 9.

PROPAGATING

Take cuttings in midspring, or allow to self-seed.

Erythronium

Adam-and-Eve, Adder's tongue, Avalanche lily, Chamise lily, Dogs-tooth violet, Fawn lily, Trout lily

> TYPE HP
> ZONE 4–9: E. americanum, E. dens-canis, E. revolutum, E. tuolumnense; 6–9: E. californicum, E. citrinum, E. grandiflorum, E. hendersonii, E. montanum
> FLOWERING SEASON Early spring

Lovely North American natives with brindled basal leaves and small, pendant, pink, white, or yellow lilylike flowers with reflexed petals; 6"–12" high. Stunning in the wild garden or rock garden.

SOWING

INDOORS See "Germinating, Requirements."
OUTDOORS Seed: see "Germinating, Requirements." Corm: autumn.
DEPTH Seed: ⅛". Corm: 3"–4".

GERMINATING

TIME 1–18 months.
REQUIREMENTS Difficult. *Autumn sowing:* Sow seeds in flats, sink in the ground against a north-facing wall, and cover with glass. Check soil moisture occasionally. Bring indoors in spring to 50°–60°F. *Spring sowing:* Sow seeds in containers, secure in plastic bags, and refrigerate. After 2–3 weeks, remove flats and sink in the ground in a shady location, covering with glass. Transplant seedlings as they appear.

PLANTING SEEDLINGS OUTDOORS

TIME After last frost.
SPACING 3"–6".
LIGHT Part to full shade.
SOIL Moist, rich, woodland soil that is not too acid.

CARING FOR PLANTS

Easy. Do not allow roots to dry out in summer or winter. Plants disappear shortly after blooming and their locations should be marked to avoid unintentional disturbance. Top-dress in late summer with leaf mold. Divide every 3–4 years, but otherwise leave undisturbed.

PROPAGATING

Plant offsets in early autumn.

Erythronium americanum

A-Annual P-Perennial B-Biennial HHA-Half-hardy annual HA-Hardy annual HB-Hardy biennial HHP-Half-hardy perennial HP-Hardy perennial HHBb-Half-hardy bulb HBb-Hardy bulb

125

Eschscholzia

California poppy

TYPE P treated as HA
ZONE A: 1–10; P: 8–10. Performs most successfully in the moderate temperatures of the Pacific Coast.
FLOWERING SEASON Midspring to midautumn

Genus of poppies native to the western United States with feathery foliage and slim stalks bearing cup-shaped flowers, most commonly orange, yellow, or white; 1'–2 tall'. Cheerful plants exuding optimism; grow in the border or wildflower meadow.

Eschscholzia californica

SOWING

INDOORS 2–3 weeks before last frost, in peat pots. Most successful when started outdoors.
OUTDOORS After last frost, or autumn through early spring where winters are mild.
DEPTH ¼".

GERMINATING

TIME 14–21 days.
REQUIREMENTS 60°–65°F.

PLANTING SEEDLINGS OUTDOORS

TIME After last frost.
SPACING 8"–10".
LIGHT Full sun.
SOIL Ordinary, well-drained; tolerant of dry soil.

CARING FOR PLANTS

Easy. Water and deadhead regularly to prolong blooming. Difficult to transplant.

PROPAGATING

Self-seeds.

Eucomis

Pineapple flower, Pineapple lily

TYPE HHBb
ZONE A: 3–7; P: 8–10
FLOWERING SEASON Summer

Genus of bulbs, most of which have wide, sword-shaped leaves and thick, erect stems bearing bottle-brushes of small, star-shaped flowers of green or white; 2'–3' tall. Use in the border.

SOWING

INDOORS Early spring.
OUTDOORS Seed: spring. Bulb: spring.
DEPTH Seed: just cover. Bulb: 4"–6".

GERMINATING

TIME 20–25 days.
REQUIREMENTS Easy. 70°–75°F.

PLANTING SEEDLINGS OUTDOORS

TIME Spring.
SPACING 10"–12".
LIGHT Sun.
SOIL Average, well-drained.

CARING FOR PLANTS

Easy. Plants grown from seed will flower in 5–6 years. During growing season, keep soil moist and feed occasionally with a weak fertilizer. Reduce watering during dormancy, but do not allow soil to dry out completely. Alternate periods of wet and dry may induce repeat blooming. North of zone 7, lift bulbs and store over winter in vermiculite in a cool, dry place.

PROPAGATING

Divide in spring.

Eucomis comosa

A-Annual P-Perennial B-Biennial HHA-Half-hardy annual HA-Hardy annual HB-Hardy biennial HHP-Half-hardy perennial HP-Hardy perennial HHBb-Half-hardy bulb HBb-Hardy bulb

Eupatorium

Boneset, Hardy ageratum, Joe pye weed, Mist flower, Thoroughwort, White snakeroot

TYPE HP
ZONE 3–8: *E. purpureum,*
  E. rugosum; 4–8: *E. perfolia-*
  tum; 5–8: *E. hyssopifolium;*
  6–8: *E. coelestinum*
FLOWERING SEASON Summer to
  autumn

Late-flowering perennials grown for their purple, pink, or white flowers which are fuzzy, rounded, or flat-topped clusters held above dense, midgreen foliage; 2'–10'. Use in the border or wildflower garden.

SOWING

INDOORS 8–10 weeks before planting out.
OUTDOORS Autumn, as soon as ripe seed is available.
DEPTH Just cover.

Eupatorium perfoliatum

GERMINATING

TIME 30–90 days.
REQUIREMENTS 55°F.

PLANTING SEEDLINGS OUTDOORS

TIME After last spring frost or in early autumn.
SPACING Small species: 12"–24". Large species: 24"–48".
LIGHT Sun or light shade.
SOIL Ordinary, somewhat moist, with a pH level of 5.0–6.0.

CARING FOR PLANTS

Easy. Keep plants mulched in summer. Cut back to ground in autumn. Divide every 3 years.

PROPAGATING

Divide in spring, in autumn in zones 7 and 8, or allow to self-seed.

Euphorbia (Annual)

Annual poinsettia, Crown of thorns, Fire on the mountain, Ghost weed, Mexican fire plant, Mole plant, Painted leaf, Snow on the mountain, Spurge

TYPE HA or HHA
ZONE 3–10. Prefers warm
  temperatures.
FLOWERING SEASON Midsummer

Shrubby plants grown for their distinctively colored foliage of green and red or green and white. Plants are 18"–24" and make useful foils for contrasting colors and textures.

SOWING

INDOORS 6–8 weeks before last frost.
OUTDOORS After last frost, but only where summers are long and hot.
DEPTH ¼".

GERMINATING

TIME 10–28 days.
REQUIREMENTS 70°–75°F.

PLANTING SEEDLINGS OUTDOORS

TIME After last frost; with half-hardy species, wait until the temperatures remain above 50°F.
SPACING 12"–18".
LIGHT Full sun.
SOIL Tolerant of many conditions, but prefers moist soil.

CARING FOR PLANTS

Easy. Water well during the growing season, otherwise allow soil to remain fairly dry. Do not plant near ponds as the juice of *Euphorbia* may be poisonous to fish.

PROPAGATING

Self-seeds.

A-Annual P-Perennial B-Biennial HHA-Half-hardy annual HA-Hardy annual HB-Hardy biennial HHP-Half-hardy perennial HP-Hardy perennial HHBb-Half-hardy bulb HBb-Hardy bulb

Euphorbia (Perennial)

Flowering spurge, Scarlet plume, Spurge, Wood spurge

TYPE HP or HHP
ZONE 3–9: *E. corollata*,
E. cyparissias; 4–9: *E. poly-chroma* (does not like hot, humid climates);
5–9: *E. griffithii, E. myrsinites* (does not like hot, humid climates); 5–10: *E. sikkimensis*;
6–10: *E. nicaeensis*,
E. seguieriana spp. *niciciana* (does not like hot, humid climates); 7–9: *E. amygdaloides*,
E. palustris (does not like hot, humid climates), *E. robbiae*;
8–10: *E. characias*,
E. x martini; (does not like hot, humid climates), *E. rigida* (does not like hot, humid climates)
FLOWERING SEASON Spring, summer, or autumn, depending on species

Very large species of perennials, many of which are useful for their strongly horizontal foliage and the brightly colored bracts surrounding insignificant flowers. Plants are 6"–36" tall and useful as edging, in borders, and in rock gardens.

SOWING

INDOORS Pre-chilled seeds 6–8 weeks before last frost, in peat pots.
OUTDOORS After last frost.
DEPTH ⅛".

Euphorbia characias

GERMINATING

TIME 10–28 days.
REQUIREMENTS Chill seeds in refrigerator for 7 days, soak in warm water for 2 hours, then sow and place where temperatures remain a constant 65°–70°F.

PLANTING SEEDLINGS OUTDOORS

TIME After last frost.
SPACING Small species: 12". Large species: 12"–24".
LIGHT Full sun to part shade.
SOIL Most will do well in average to poor soil with a pH level of 6.0–7.0. *E. palustris* requires moist soil.

CARING FOR PLANTS

Easy. Water well during growing season, but allow soil to remain fairly dry otherwise. Do not plant near ponds as the plant's juice may be poisonous to fish.

PROPAGATING

Carefully divide in spring in the North, in autumn south of zone 6. Take cuttings after flowering, or allow to self-seed.

Eustoma

(synonymous with *Lisianthus*)

Prairie gentian

TYPE HHA, HHP, or B grown as HHA
ZONE A: 5–10; P: 9–10.
Performs most successfully where summers are hot.
FLOWERING SEASON Summer

North American native with upright stems holding bell-shaped flowers, often double, in shades of purple, pink, and cream. Extraordinary cut flowers, border, or containers plants. 6"–24".

SOWING

INDOORS 10–12 weeks before planting out, in peat pots.
OUTDOORS Early spring, only where growing season is very long.
DEPTH Surface.

GERMINATING

TIME 10–21 days.
REQUIREMENTS Difficult. Light and 65°–75°F.

PLANTING SEEDLINGS OUTDOORS

TIME Transplant 6" seedlings in spring when temperatures remain above 40°F.
SPACING 12".
LIGHT Full sun.
SOIL Moist, well-drained.

CARING FOR PLANTS

Pinch out young plants to increase flower production. Water sparingly, keeping blossoms dry; plants will not flourish where summer rainfall is heavy. Dislikes transplanting.

PROPAGATING

Seed.

Felicia

**Blue daisy, Blue marguerite,
Kingfisher daisy**

> **TYPE** HHP usually grown as
> HHA
> **ZONE** A: 1–10; P: 9–10. Must
> have mild temperatures and
> performs most successfully on
> the West Coast and in the
> Northern states.
> **FLOWERING SEASON** Summer
> through autumn

Blue, daisylike flowers with yellow eyes
cover these pretty 6"–18" annuals all summer, making them useful for edging or
borders.

SOWING

INDOORS Pre-chilled seeds 6–8 weeks be-
fore last frost.
OUTDOORS After last frost.
DEPTH Just cover.

GERMINATING

TIME 30 days.
REQUIREMENTS Place seeds together with
moistened growing medium in a plastic
bag, seal lightly, and refrigerate for 3
weeks. Provides 60°–70°F thereafter.

PLANTING SEEDLINGS OUTDOORS

TIME 2–3 weeks after last frost, when temperatures remain above 40°F.
SPACING Small species: 6". Large species:
12"–18".
LIGHT Full sun.
SOIL Ordinary, well-drained; withstands dry
soil.

CARING FOR PLANTS

Easy. Water often during dry weather and
protect from harsh winds.

PROPAGATING

Take cuttings in summer or early autumn.

Festuca

Fescue

> **TYPE** HP
> **ZONE** 4–9. Will not thrive where
> summers are hot and humid.
> **FLOWERING SEASON** Late spring to
> midsummer

Tufted ornamental grasses, many with airy
blue or grey foliage; 6"–18" tall. Mass for
best effect.

SOWING

INDOORS Sow seeds *in situ*.
OUTDOORS Early spring to midspring.
DEPTH Surface.

GERMINATING

TIME 21 days.

PLANTING SEEDLINGS OUTDOORS

TIME Plant out purchased plants in spring
or autumn.
SPACING Small species: 8"–12". Large species: 18"–24".
LIGHT Sun or part shade. Blue species will
be a deeper blue when grown in full sun
with dry soil.
SOIL Rather dry, infertile soil will produce
neater plants, although fescues are highly
adaptive as long as they have good drainage.

CARING FOR PLANTS

Easy. Water regularly for best results. Divide every 2–3 years. Where soil is heavy,
plants will die back in center and require
more frequent division. Susceptible to rust.

PROPAGATING

Divide in spring.

Festuca ovina

A-Annual P-Perennial B-Biennial HHA-Half-hardy annual HA-Hardy annual HB-Hardy biennial HHP-Half-hardy perennial HP-Hardy perennial HHBb-Half-hardy bulb HBb-Hardy bulb

129

Filipendula

**Dropwort, Meadowsweet,
Queen of the meadows,
Queen of the prairie, Spiraea**

TYPE HP
ZONE 3–9
FLOWERING SEASON Summer

A small genus of lovely and unique perennials with highly decorative foliage and flowers. Pink or white plumes are held above fernlike leaves; plants grow from 2' to a towering 10'. Use in any moist situation, from borders to woodlands.

SOWING

INDOORS 8–10 weeks before planting out.
OUTDOORS As soon as ripe seed is available (usually autumn).
DEPTH Just cover.

GERMINATING

TIME 30–90 days.
REQUIREMENTS 55°–60°F. *Outdoor sowing:* Sow seeds in flats, sink in ground against a north-facing wall, and cover with glass. Moisten soil occasionally, if necessary. Transplant seedlings to pots as they germinate; plant out in the garden in autumn.

Filipendula ulmaria

PLANTING SEEDLINGS OUTDOORS

TIME After last frost.
SPACING 12"–24".
LIGHT Sun or part shade. *F. ulmaria* must have shade; *F. palmata* and *F. purpurea* should be planted in full sun only where soil is very moist.
SOIL Moist, slightly alkaline, enriched with compost or manure. *F. vulgaris* will tolerate dry soil.

CARING FOR PLANTS

Easy. Plants grown from seed will take 2 years to flower. Mulch with organic matter in spring to keep soil moist, and again in autumn to protect roots. Support with twiggy branches pushed into the ground when spring growth begins; cut back to ground in autumn.

PROPAGATING

Divide in early spring in the North, in autumn south of zone 6.

Foeniculum

Fennel

TYPE HP often grown as HA
ZONE 4–10. Prefers cool climates.
FLOWERING SEASON Late summer to midautumn

One of the many herbs that resembles Queen Anne's lace, with feathery leaves and clusters of tiny yellow flowers in umbels atop 3'–4' stalks.

SOWING

INDOORS 4–6 weeks before last frost, in peat pots. May not survive transplanting.
OUTDOORS Early spring, when soil is cool and a light frost is still possible.
DEPTH ⅛".

GERMINATING

TIME 10–14 days.
REQUIREMENTS Darkness and 65°F.

PLANTING SEEDLINGS OUTDOORS

TIME Spring or autumn.
SPACING 18".
LIGHT Prefers full sun but will accept light shade.
SOIL Well-drained, somewhat dry, with a pH level between 6.0 and 8.0.

CARING FOR PLANTS

Easy. Remove flower heads after blooming to stimulate leaf production; cut back stems in autumn. Use either fresh or dried leaves in cooking, cutting any time after flower heads form. Harvest ripe seeds in autumn, dry thoroughly, and store in an airtight container. Do not grow near dill in the herb garden as cross-pollination will result.

Foeniculum vulgare

PROPAGATING

Divide in early spring, or allow to self-seed.

A-Annual P-Perennial B-Biennial HHA-Half-hardy annual HA-Hardy annual HB-Hardy biennial HHP-Half-hardy perennial HP-Hardy perennial HHBb-Half-hardy bulb HBb-Hardy bulb

130

Francoa

Bridal wreath, Maiden's wreath

TYPE HHP
ZONE 7–10. Requires a temperate climate and is best suited to the West Coast.
FLOWERING SEASON Summer

Rarely seen, clump-forming perennials bearing wiry stalks with bottle-brushes of tiny pink or white flowers. Foliage hugs the ground, but flowering stems are 2'–3' tall. Use in borders.

SOWING
INDOORS See "Germinating, Requirements."
OUTDOORS See "Germinating, Requirements."
DEPTH Surface.

GERMINATING
TIME 14–30 days.
REQUIREMENTS *Autumn sowing:* Sow seeds in flats, sink flats in ground against a north-facing wall, and cover with glass. Moisten soil occasionally, if necessary. Bring indoors in spring to 50°–55°F. *Spring sowing:* Sow seeds in flats of moistened medium, place in plastic bags, and refrigerate. Remove after 2–3 weeks and sink in the ground in a shady location, covering with glass. Transplant seedlings as they appear.

PLANTING SEEDLINGS OUTDOORS
TIME After last frost.
SPACING 12".
LIGHT Full sun to light shade.
SOIL Average, moist, with good drainage.

CARING FOR PLANTS
Easy. Mulch in spring to keep soil cool and moist.

PROPAGATING
Divide in the spring.

Freesia

TYPE HHBb
ZONE 9–10. Requires dry summers and cool, moist winters.
FLOWERING SEASON Winter and spring

Tender corms grown for their deliciously fragrant funnel-shaped flowers held in clusters on slender stalks. Plants are 12"–18" high, flowers bright or subtle shades of yellow, orange, pink, red, purple, blue, or white. Usually grown in containers.

SOWING
INDOORS Early spring.
OUTDOORS Start seeds or corms outdoors *only* in zones 9–10. Seed: after last frost. Corm: autumn.
DEPTH Seed: ¼". Corm: 1"–2".

GERMINATING
TIME 25–30 days.
REQUIREMENTS Easy. Soak seeds for 24 hours in warm water; provide 65°–75°F thereafter.

PLANTING SEEDLINGS OUTDOORS
TIME Early autumn.
SPACING 4"–6".
LIGHT Sun.
SOIL Moist, well-drained, amended with manure.

CARING FOR PLANTS
Easy. Water well before flowering begins, decrease watering significantly while plants are in bloom, and discontinue altogether after flowering. Plant *Freesias* close together to support each other, or support with twiggy branches pushed into the ground when plants are young.

PROPAGATING
Plant offsets in autumn.

A-Annual P-Perennial B-Biennial HHA-Half-hardy annual HA-Hardy annual HB-Hardy biennial HHP-Half-hardy perennial HP-Hardy perennial HHBb-Half-hardy bulb HBb-Hardy bulb

Fritillaria

Checkered lily, Crown imperial,
Fritillary, Guinea-hen flower,
Snake's head fritillary,
Snake's head lily, Toad lily

TYPE HBb
ZONE 3–8: *F. meleagris;*
4–9: *F. persica, F. pudica;*
5–9: *F. imperialis, F. pallidi-
flora;* 6–9: *F. verticillata.*
Most species do not like cold,
wet winters.
FLOWERING SEASON Spring

Large genus of unusual and enchanting bulbs. Small species are 4"–12", large species 2'–3'; all sport delicate, downward-facing, bell-shaped flowers, giving the appearance of shyness which inspires subtle placement in the garden. Flowers are orange, yellow, white, green, or deep plum. Some are suited to borders, others most effective when massed near the woodland edge.

SOWING

INDOORS See "Germinating, Requirements."
OUTDOORS Seed: see "Germinating, Requirements." Bulb: late summer to early autumn.
DEPTH Seed: just cover. Small bulb: 3"–4". Large bulb: 6"–8".

GERMINATING

TIME 11–18 months.
REQUIREMENTS Difficult. *Autumn sowing:* Sow seeds in flats, sink in the ground against a north-facing wall, and cover with glass. Moisten soil occasionally, if necessary. Bring indoors in spring to 55°–60°F. *Spring sowing:* Sow seeds in moistened medium, place in a plastic bag, and refrigerate. After 2–3 weeks, remove and sink in the ground in a shady location, covering with glass. Transplant seedlings as they appear.

PLANTING SEEDLINGS OUTDOORS

TIME Late summer to early autumn.
SPACING Small species: 4"–6". Large species: 9"–12".
LIGHT Sun to light shade.
SOIL Prefers rich, well-drained soil. Surround bulb with coarse sand when planting.

CARING FOR PLANTS

Difficult. Plants grown from seed will flower in 4–5 years. Mark location as plants die down after flowering. Mulch in winter. Divide every 3–5 years when crowding necessitates.

PROPAGATING

Plant bulblets in autumn.

Fritillaria meleagris

Gaillardia (Annual)

Blanket flower, Indian blanket

TYPE HA or HHA
ZONE 1–10. Performs well in *dry*
heat, but not *moist* heat.
FLOWERING SEASON Summer
through early autumn

Long-blooming plants with cheerful, daisylike flowers of bright yellow and/or orange and large eyes; 6"–30". Use as edging, in borders, or wildflower gardens.

SOWING

INDOORS 4–6 weeks before last frost.
OUTDOORS After last frost; in autumn where winters are mild.
DEPTH Surface.

GERMINATING

TIME 7–20 days.
REQUIREMENTS Light and 70°F.

PLANTING SEEDLINGS OUTDOORS

TIME After last frost.
SPACING 12".
LIGHT Full sun.
SOIL Ordinary, with a pH level of 6.0–7.0; tolerates poor, dry soil.

CARING FOR PLANTS

Feed when flowering begins; top-dress with manure once in summer. Deadhead regularly.

PROPAGATING

Self-seed.

A-Annual P-Perennial B-Biennial HHA-Half-hardy annual HA-Hardy annual HB-Hardy biennial HHP-Half-hardy perennial HP-Hardy perennial HHBb-Half-hardy bulb HBb-Hardy bulb

132

Gaillardia (Perennial)

Blanket flower, Indian blanket

TYPE HP
ZONE 3–9. *G. x grandiflora* will not tolerate hot, humid summers.
FLOWERING SEASON Summer through autumn

Long-blooming, short-lived plants with grey-green leaves and cheerful, daisylike flowers of bright yellow, red, and orange and large, colorful, prominent eyes; 15"–36" tall. Use as edging, in borders, or wildflower gardens.

SOWING

INDOORS 6–8 weeks before planting out.
OUTDOORS Spring.
DEPTH Surface.

GERMINATING

TIME 15–20 days.
REQUIREMENTS Light and 70°F.

PLANTING SEEDLINGS OUTDOORS

TIME Late spring, when soil is warm.
SPACING 12"–18".
LIGHT Full sun.
SOIL Prefers a moist, well-drained loam, but will tolerate soil that is poor and dry. Short-lived in heavy soil.

CARING FOR PLANTS

Easy. Feed just once in the spring with manure; overfertilizing will weaken plants. Deadhead often and cut back completely in late summer to stimulate a second blooming. Provide support for tall species. Divide regularly to maintain vigor.

Gallardia x grandiflora

PROPAGATING

Divide in autumn in the South, in spring north of zone 7. Take root cuttings in spring, or allow to self-seed.

Galanthus

Snowdrop

TYPE HBb
ZONE 2–8: *G. nivalis;*
5–9: *G. byzantinus, G. elwesii*
FLOWERING SEASON Midwinter to late winter

Genus of bulbs grown for their very early, nodding, white flowers. Leaves are narrow and straplike; plants grow 2"–10" tall. Use in abundance in the lawn, under shrubs, or in the woodland.

SOWING

INDOORS As soon as seed is ripe in spring.
OUTDOORS Seed: as soon as ripe seed is available in spring. Bulb: late summer.
DEPTH Seed: ¼". Bulb: 3".

GERMINATING

TIME Seed should germinate within 4 weeks.
REQUIREMENTS 60°–65°F.

PLANTING SEEDLINGS OUTDOORS

TIME Summer, 1 year after sowing seeds.
SPACING 3"–4".
LIGHT Sun in winter, light shade throughout the rest of the year.
SOIL Cool, moist, rich, somewhat heavy, with a pH level of 6.0–8.0.

CARING FOR PLANTS

Easy. Bulbs grown from seed will flower in 3–4 years. Feed with bonemeal in early spring and water regularly, particularly while plants are in bloom. Allow leaves to wither before removing. Divide when plants begin to deteriorate, but do not disturb otherwise.

PROPAGATING

Divide bulbs immediately after flowering, in early autumn south of zone 6, or allow to self-seed.

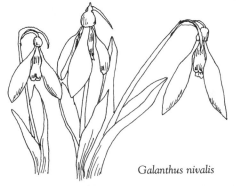

Galanthus nivalis

A-Annual P-Perennial B-Biennial HHA-Half-hardy annual HA-Hardy annual HB-Hardy biennial HHP-Half-hardy perennial HP-Hardy perennial HHBb-Half-hardy bulb HBb-Hardy bulb

133

Galega

Goat's rue

TYPE HP
ZONE 3–9. Does not like the intense heat and humidity of the South.
FLOWERING SEASON Summer

Unusual, vigorous, upright perennials. Overall appearance is rather untidy, with compound leaves growing at awkward angles along 3'–4' stems, but sprays of lilac, pink, or white flowers are pretty. Use with discretion at the back of the border.

SOWING

INDOORS Seeds are best started outdoors.
OUTDOORS Early spring, when soil is cool and a light frost is still possible, or late autumn.
DEPTH ¼".

Galega officinalis

GERMINATING

TIME 14–60 days.

PLANTING SEEDLINGS OUTDOORS

TIME Set out purchased plants in spring or autumn.
SPACING 8"–36".
LIGHT Full sun to light shade.
SOIL Ordinary, not too rich.

CARING FOR PLANTS

Easy. Be sparing with fertilizer to avoid lanky plants that require staking. Cut back flowering stems after blooming. Divide every 2–3 years.

PROPAGATING

Divide in spring, in autumn in zones 7–9.

Galtonia

**Giant summer hyacinth,
Summer hyacinth**

TYPE HBb
ZONE 6–9. May be grown as an annual north of zone 6.
FLOWERING SEASON Midsummer to autumn

Dazzlingly white, bell-shaped flowers adorn these summer-blooming bulbs for 3 months. Leaves are straplike, with 3'–4' flower stalks towering above. Use in borders or massed in front of shrubs.

SOWING

INDOORS 6–8 weeks before planting out.
OUTDOORS Seed: early spring through summer. Bulb: early spring.
DEPTH Seed: just cover. Bulb: 5"–6".

GERMINATING

TIME 15–20 days.
REQUIREMENTS 70°F.

PLANTING SEEDLINGS OUTDOORS

TIME Early spring or autumn.
SPACING Small species: 6"–8". Tall species: 15"–18".
LIGHT Sun.
SOIL Prefers moist, well-drained soil.

CARING FOR PLANTS

Easy. Plants grown from seed will flower in 4–5 years. Water well during dry spells. Provide mulch where winters are cold; north of zone 6, lift plants, store in a cool, dry place over winter, and replant in the spring.

PROPAGATING

Plant offsets in early spring or late autumn.

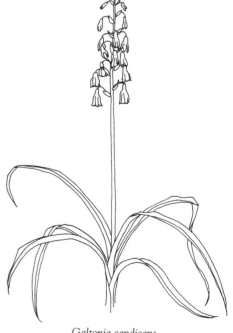

Galtonia candicans

A-Annual P-Perennial B-Biennial HHA-Half-hardy annual HA-Hardy annual HB-Hardy biennial HHP-Half-hardy perennial HP-Hardy perennial HHBb-Half-hardy bulb HBb-Hardy bulb

Gaura

Type HHP or HHA
Zone A: 3–10; P: 6–9. Prefers warm climates and is well suited to hot, humid conditions.
Flowering Season Summer through autumn

Recently rediscovered by the gardening world, this native to Mexico and the southern United States is useful in hot, dry regions. Plants are shrubby, 2'–5' tall, with white or pink flowers on coarse spikes. Use in informal borders, cutting beds, or wildflower gardens.

Sowing

Indoors A: 4–6 weeks before last frost. P: 8–10 weeks before planting out.
Outdoors A: after last frost. P: early spring or early autumn.
Depth Just cover.

Germinating

Time 14–30 days.
Requirements 65°–75°F.

Planting Seedlings Outdoors

Time A: after last frost. P: early spring, when soil is cool and a light frost is still possible, or autumn.
Spacing 24"–36".
Light Sun.
Soil Ordinary, very well-drained.

Caring for Plants

Easy. Drought tolerant. Water only during very dry weather. Deadhead to prolong flowering. Annuals may be short-lived, but perennials take 2–3 years to become established. Midseason of their second year, cut back plants to 8" to encourage bushiness. Provide winter mulch north of zone 7.

Propagating

Divide perennials in autumn, in spring in zone 6. Propagate annuals by seed.

Gazania

Treasure flower

Type HHP often grown as HHA
Zone A: 5–8; P: 9–10. Likes hot, dry weather, and will not perform well where the growing season is short and nights are cool.
Flowering Season Summer to early autumn

Compact plants, 8"–15" high, bearing bright, daisylike flowers in hot yellows, oranges, reds, and dusky pinks, often striped. Useful edging, border, or container plants.

Sowing

Indoors 6–8 weeks before planting out.
Outdoors After last frost.
Depth ⅛".

Germinating

Time 8–21 days.
Requirements Darkness and 60°–65°F.

Planting Seedlings Outdoors

Time 2 weeks after last frost, when soil is beginning to warm.
Spacing Plant at intervals equal to the ultimate height of the plant.
Light Full sun.
Soil Light, sandy, with a pH level of 5.5–7.0. Withstands dry soil.

Caring for Plants

Easy. Once plants are established, water only during very dry spells. Do not overfertilize. Deadhead regularly to maintain a tidy appearance.

Propagating

Take basal cuttings in late summer.

A-Annual P-Perennial B-Biennial HHA-Half-hardy annual HA-Hardy annual HB-Hardy biennial HHP-Half-hardy perennial HP-Hardy perennial HHBb-Half-hardy bulb HBb-Hardy bulb

Gentiana

Gentian

TYPE HP
ZONE 3–9: *G. acaulis,*
G. andrewsii, G. angustifolia,
G. asclepiadea, G. dahurica,
G. dinarica, G. lutea,
G. pneumonanthe, G. septem-
fida, G. verna; 4–8: *G. crinita;*
6–9: *G. triflora.* Prefers the
temperate climate of the Pacific
Northwest.
FLOWERING SEASON Summer
through autumn, depending on
species

Mostly low-growing, mat-forming plants; some are evergreen, bearing clusters of flowers that are usually an intense blue, but may be white, pink, purple, or yellow.

SOWING

INDOORS Spring.
OUTDOORS Autumn.
DEPTH Just cover.

GERMINATING

TIME 14–180 days.
REQUIREMENTS Difficult. *Autumn sowing:* Sow seeds in flats, sinking these in ground against a north-facing wall, and cover with glass. Moisten soil, as necessary. Transplant to peat pots after the first growing season, to the garden after the second. *Spring sowing:* Sow seeds in moistened medium in flats. Cover with plastic and refrigerate for 8 weeks. Provide darkness and 70°–75°F thereafter to stimulate germination. Transplant seedlings to pots as they appear.

PLANTING SEEDLINGS OUTDOORS

TIME Spring or autumn.
SPACING Small species: 6"–9". Medium species: 12"–15". Tall species: 18"–24".
LIGHT Full sun or part shade, except for *G. lutea,* which must have full sun.
SOIL Cool, moist, humus-rich, with a pH level of 5.0–7.5.

CARING FOR PLANTS

Difficult. Must have cultural requirements met precisely in order to flower, and it is often difficult to analyze the reason for poor flowering. Keep soil moist but not wet; plants growing in full sun must be watered regularly. Do not disturb roots.

PROPAGATING

Divide roots after flowering, early spring is preferable in zones 3–6.

Geranium

**Cranesbill, Hardy geranium,
Mourning widow**

TYPE HP or HHP
ZONE 4–8: *G. clarkei, G. dalmaticum, G. maculatum,*
G. x magnificum, G. pratense,
G. psilostemon, G. sylvaticum,
G. wallichianum; 4–9: *G. argenteum, G. cinereum, G. endressii,*
G. himalayense, G. phaeum;
4–10: *G. sanguineum;*
5–9: *G. macrorrhizum;*
5–10: *G. 'Johnson's Blue';*
6–8: *G. renardii;* 7–9: *G. x riversleaianum;* 9–10: *G. incanum, G. maderense.* Not tolerant of extreme heat and humidity.
FLOWERING SEASON Spring
through late summer, depending
on species

Carefree and underused in American gardens, these perennials have a place in any border and make a wonderful deciduous ground cover. Size ranges from 4"–24"; leaves are lobed and often deeply cut, flowers saucer-shaped and plentiful, usually in purples and pinks.

SOWING

INDOORS Spring.
OUTDOORS Late autumn.
DEPTH Just cover.

GERMINATING

TIME 3–90 days.
REQUIREMENTS Easy. *Autumn sowing:* Sow seeds in flats; sink flats in ground against a north-facing wall, and cover with glass. Moisten soil occasionally, if necessary. Bring indoors in spring to 70°–75°F. *Spring sowing:* Sow seeds in flats of moistened medium, secure in plastic bags, and refrigerate for 2–3 weeks. Then sink flats in the ground in a shady location, covering with glass. Transplant seedlings as they appear.

PLANTING SEEDLINGS OUTDOORS

TIME After last frost.
SPACING 8"–12".
LIGHT *G. sanguineum* and *G. incanum* must be sited in full sun; other species will take full sun or part shade, but appreciate some shade where summers are very hot.
SOIL Average, well-drained, with a pH level of 5.5–7.0. Where summers are hot, soil must be moist. Plants grown in rich soil will spread rapidly.

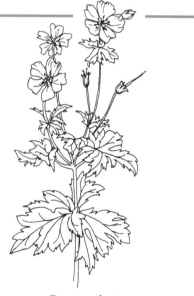

Geranium ibericum

CARING FOR PLANTS

Easy. Cut back hard after blooming to encourage further flowering. Tall species may require the support of twiggy branches pushed into the ground when plants are young. Provide a good winter mulch in northern zones.

PROPAGATING

Divide in spring in zones 4–6, in autumn in the South.

A-Annual P-Perennial B-Biennial HHA-Half-hardy annual HA-Hardy annual HB-Hardy biennial HHP-Half-hardy perennial HP-Hardy perennial HHBb-Half-hardy bulb HBb-Hardy bulb

136

Gerbera

African daisy, Barberton daisy, Transvaal daisy

> **TYPE** HHP usually grown as HHA
> **ZONE** Performs most successfully where days are warm and nights cool
> **FLOWERING SEASON** Summer

Elegant plants, 8"–24", grown for their many-petalled, daisylike flowers. In some species these are borne singly on long stems, others form mounds of blooms; coloring ranges from simple pinks, yellows, and reds to sophisticated mustard, ocher, or burnt umber. Use in borders and cutting beds.

SOWING

INDOORS 12 weeks before planting out, in peat pots.
OUTDOORS Not recommended.
DEPTH Surface.

GERMINATING

TIME 15–30 days.
REQUIREMENTS Difficult. Always start with fresh seed; provide light and 70°–75°F.

PLANTING SEEDLINGS OUTDOORS

TIME Late spring, when soil is quite warm.
SPACING 12"–18".
LIGHT Full sun; part shade where summers are very hot.
SOIL Prefers a rich, moist, fertile, and slightly acid soil.

CARING FOR PLANTS

Easy. Water regularly, particularly during hot weather. Fertilize lightly every 6 weeks during the growing season. Deadhead to keep plants tidy.

PROPAGATING

Divide in summer or autumn, or take cuttings in summer.

Geum

Avens

> **TYPE** HP
> **ZONE** 2–9: *G. rossii;*
> 3–8: *G. rivale;* 4–8: *G. x borisii,*
> *G. montanum, G. reptans;*
> 5–9: *G. elatum, G. quellyon*
> **FLOWERING SEASON** Summer

Genus of rather delicate perennials bearing long, slender stems topped with red or yellow saucer-shaped flowers; 6"–36". Plant in groups and site carefully as *Geums* are easily lost in a crowd.

SOWING

INDOORS 8–10 weeks before planting out.
OUTDOORS Early spring or early autumn.
DEPTH Just cover.

GERMINATING

TIME 21–28 days.
REQUIREMENTS 65°–70°F.

PLANTING SEEDLINGS OUTDOORS

TIME Early spring, when soil is cool and a light frost is still possible, or early autumn.
SPACING 12"–18".
LIGHT Full sun; light shade where summers are very hot.
SOIL Rich, well-drained, with a pH level of 5.5–7.0.

CARING FOR PLANTS

Easy. Deadhead regularly. Mulch in winter north of zone 7. Divide every 3–4 years to maintain vigor.

PROPAGATING

Divide in autumn.

Geum coccineum

A-Annual P-Perennial B-Biennial HHA-Half-hardy annual HA-Hardy annual HB-Hardy biennial HHP-Half-hardy perennial HP-Hardy perennial HHBb-Half-hardy bulb HBb-Hardy bulb

137

Gilia

(synonymous with *Leptosiphon*)

Bird's eyes, Queen Anne's thimble, Standing cypress, Thimble flower

> TYPE HA
> ZONE 6–10. Prefers the temperate climate of the West Coast.
> FLOWERING SEASON Summer to autumn, depending on species

Genus of little-used, rather sloppy annuals bearing globe- or funnel-shaped flowers of pink, white, blue, or yellow. Flowers close up on cloudy days. Plants are 6"–30" and useful in borders or cutting beds.

SOWING

INDOORS 6–8 weeks before last frost. Most successful started outdoors.
OUTDOORS 2–3 weeks before last frost; autumn in mild climates.
DEPTH ⅛".

GERMINATING

TIME 17–21 days.
REQUIREMENTS 55°–65°F.

PLANTING SEEDLINGS OUTDOORS

TIME After last frost.
SPACING Small species: 9"–15". Large species: 24"–36".
LIGHT Full sun.
SOIL Average, well-drained. Will grow in very sandy soil.

CARING FOR PLANTS

Easy. Support tall species with twiggy branches pushed into the ground when plants are young.

PROPAGATING

Self-seeds.

Gillenia

(synonymous with *Porteranthus*)

Bowman's root

> TYPE HP
> ZONE 4–8. Tolerant of hot, humid weather.
> FLOWERING SEASON Summer

Small genus of loose, shrubby, 4' perennials scattered with white, star-shaped flowers. Use this North American native in a woodland planting or mixed with shade-loving shrubs.

SOWING

INDOORS When ripe seed is available in autumn.
OUTDOORS As soon as seed is ripe in autumn.
DEPTH ¼".

GERMINATING

TIME 14–21 days.
REQUIREMENTS Difficult. *Indoor sowing:* Refrigerate seeds for 3 months before sowing. *Outdoor sowing:* Sow seeds in flats, sink in the ground in a sheltered location, and cover with glass. Remove glass when seeds sprout.

PLANTING SEEDLINGS OUTDOORS

TIME Autumn.
SPACING 18"–24".
LIGHT Sun or shade; G. *trifoliata* requires full sun, except where summers are very hot.
SOIL Rich, moist, well-drained woods soil, with a pH level of 5.0–6.0.

CARING FOR PLANTS

Easy. Mulch well and keep soil moist throughout the growing season. Do not disturb roots. Plants may require staking. Cut back flowering stems after blooming.

PROPAGATING

Divide in early spring in zones 4–6, in autumn in zones 7 and 8.

A-Annual P-Perennial B-Biennial HHA-Half-hardy annual HA-Hardy annual HB-Hardy biennial HHP-Half-hardy perennial HP-Hardy perennial HHBb-Half-hardy bulb HBb-Hardy bulb

Gladiolus

Corn flag, Corn lily, Sword lily

TYPE HHBb or HBb
ZONE A: 2–10; P:
   5–10: *G. byzantinus*;
   7–10: *G. x colvillei*, *G. segetum*,
   G. tristis; 9–10: *G. carneus*,
   G. x gandavensis, *G. x hortu-
   lanus*, *G. illyricus*
FLOWERING SEASON Summer
   through early autumn

Much-loved and much-used summer bulbs. Leaves are erect swords; sturdy flowering stems from 1' to a towering 5' bear elegant if somewhat stiff flowers in ravishing shades of every color. Stunning in an informal summer planting or cottage garden, essential member of the cutting garden, always at home in a formal border.

SOWING

INDOORS Late winter.
OUTDOORS Seed: not recommended. Bulb: For continuous blooms, plant every 10–14 days starting 4 weeks after last frost, continuing until 90 days before first frost.
DEPTH Seed: ⅛". Corm: 4" in clay soil, 6" in sandy soil.

Gladiolus byzantinus

GERMINATING

TIME 20–40 days.
REQUIREMENTS 70°F.

PLANTING SEEDLINGS OUTDOORS

TIME 2–3 weeks after last frost, when soil is warming.
SPACING Short species: 4"–6". Tall species: 6".
LIGHT Sun.
SOIL Rich, well-drained, with a pH level of 6.0–7.0.

CARING FOR PLANTS

Easy. Plants grown from seed will flower in 3 years. Fertilize lightly when flower buds first appear, once again when plants are in bloom, and once when flowering is finished. Water frequently. Shallowly planted corms produce stalks that are likely to require staking. Where plants are not hardy, lift corms in autumn, separate cormels, and store in a cool, dark, frost-free place.

PROPAGATING

Plant cormels during resting period.

Glaucium

Horned poppy, Sea poppy

TYPE HA, HB, or HP grown as
   HA
ZONE 3–9
FLOWERING SEASON All summer

Upright plants of 12"–36" grown for their papery, poppylike flowers of golden yellow or orange and ornamental seed pods. Foliage may be an attractive silvery green. Use in borders and cutting beds.

SOWING

INDOORS Most successful when started outdoors. If sown indoors, use peat pots. A or P: 6–8 weeks before planting out. B: late spring to early summer.
OUTDOORS A or P: after last frost, or in autumn where winters are mild. B: late spring to early summer.
DEPTH Just cover.

GERMINATING

TIME 14–21 days, possibly up to 365 days.
REQUIREMENTS Darkness and 60°–65°F.

PLANTING SEEDLINGS OUTDOORS

TIME Several weeks after last frost, when soil has warmed.
SPACING 12"–24".
LIGHT Sun.
SOIL Tolerates hot, dry soil, but must have good drainage.

CARING FOR PLANTS

Fertilize only lightly; overfeeding stimulates lush foliage but fewer flowers. Do not move.

PROPAGATING

Self-seeds.

A-Annual P-Perennial B-Biennial HHA-Half-hardy annual HA-Hardy annual HB-Hardy biennial HHP-Half-hardy perennial HP-Hardy perennial HHBb-Half-hardy bulb HBb-Hardy bulb

139

Globularia

Globe daisy

> TYPE HP
> ZONE 5–9
> FLOWERING SEASON Late spring to early summer; some may bloom again sparsely in autumn

Small group of mounding perennials, often evergreen, bearing small, round, fluffy blue flowers. Most are edging or rock garden plants of just 4"–8", though larger 2' species are grown in the border.

SOWING

INDOORS Pre-chilled seeds 6–8 weeks before last frost.
OUTDOORS Late autumn or early spring.
DEPTH Surface.

GERMINATING

TIME 10–50 days.
REQUIREMENTS Place seeds together with moistened growing medium in a plastic bag and refrigerate for 3 weeks. Provide light and 55°F thereafter.

PLANTING SEEDLINGS OUTDOORS

TIME After last frost.
SPACING Small species: 5"–8". Tall species: 12".
LIGHT Full sun or part shade.
SOIL Moist, well-drained, with a pH level of 5.5–7.0.

CARING FOR PLANTS

Easy. Feed occasionally, water regularly, and trim lightly after blooming to maintain shape.

PROPAGATING

Divide in spring in zones 6–7, in early autumn in the South.

Gloriosa

Climbing lily, Gloriosa lily, Glory lily

> TYPE HHP, usually grown as HHA
> ZONE A: 6–8; P: 9–10. Prefers high humidity and a daytime temperature of at least 75°F, with a night temperature of 60°–70°F, although *Gloriosas* will survive where the night temperature drops as low as 50°F.
> FLOWERING SEASON Summer

Compact climbers (4'–6') grown for their, exotic lilylike flowers, which are crimson and yellow, wavy-edged, and deeply reflexed. Site near an entrance or patio where friends can admire and envy.

SOWING

INDOORS Late winter, in peat pots.
OUTDOORS Seed: spring, in zones 9–10 only. Tuber: spring, when the temperatures remain above 50°F.
DEPTH Seed: just cover. Tuber: 2".

GERMINATING

TIME 30 days.
REQUIREMENTS Easy. Soak seeds overnight and provide 70°–75°F.

PLANTING SEEDLINGS OUTDOORS

TIME When spring temperatures remain above 50°F.
SPACING 12".
LIGHT Sun.
SOIL Well-drained, humus-rich.

CARING FOR PLANTS

Easy. Provide a trellis or other support for vines. Feed with a liquid fertilizer every 2 weeks in summer. Gradually taper off watering after blooming has finished. North of zone 9, dig and store bulbs at 55°–60°F.

PROPAGATING

Divide tubers after last spring frost.

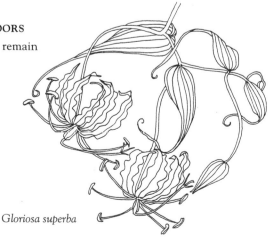

Gloriosa superba

Godetia

See *Clarkia*

Gomphrena

Globe amaranth

TYPE HHA
ZONE 3–10
FLOWERING SEASON Summer to early autumn

Compact, upright bedding plants, 10"–18" tall, with dense foliage and masses of bright little everlasting balls of violet, white, or red. Use dwarf species as edging or in containers; taller species are useful in the border.

SOWING

INDOORS 6–8 weeks before last frost.
OUTDOORS After last frost.
DEPTH Just cover.

GERMINATING

TIME 6–15 days.
REQUIREMENTS Easy. Soak seeds in warm water for 24 hours; leave flats in a dark location at 70°–75°F.

PLANTING SEEDLINGS OUTDOORS

TIME After last frost.
SPACING 9"–12".
LIGHT Full sun.
SOIL Average, well-drained, not too rich, with a pH level of 6.0–7.0; tolerant of dry soil.

CARING FOR PLANTS

Easy. Pinch out young plants to increase bushiness; feed lightly when first flowers appear.

Gomphrena globosa

PROPAGATING

Seed only.

Gunnera

Prickly rhubarb

TYPE HP
ZONE 6–9
FLOWERING SEASON Midsummer through early autumn

Weird and wonderful South American natives grown for their exotic foliage. Lobed and toothed leaves are up to 6' wide, held on prickly stems up to 6' tall; small yellow, red, or green blooms form thick cones 3' tall. 1" dwarf species is a miniature version of its giant cousins. Use in large waterside plantings or wild gardens.

SOWING

INDOORS 6–8 weeks before planting out.
OUTDOORS After last frost.
DEPTH Just cover.

GERMINATING

TIME 14–60 days.
REQUIREMENTS 60°–70°F.

Gunnera chilensis

PLANTING SEEDLINGS OUTDOORS

TIME Late spring, when soil has warmed.
SPACING Large species: 4'–6'. Gigantic species: 8'–10'.
LIGHT Sun or part shade.
SOIL Rich, moist, deeply prepared.

CARING FOR PLANTS

Water well during dry weather and feed regularly with liquid fertilizer throughout the growing season. Cut back leaves to the ground in autumn and cover crowns with leaf mold.

PROPAGATING

Divide in spring.

A-Annual P-Perennial B-Biennial HHA-Half-hardy annual HA-Hardy annual HB-Hardy biennial HHP-Half-hardy perennial HP-Hardy perennial HHBb-Half-hardy bulb HBb-Hardy bulb

Gypsophila (Annual)

Annual baby's breath

> TYPE HA
> ZONE 2–10. Most successful where summers are not extremely hot.
> FLOWERING SEASON Late spring through summer

Erect, bushy plants, 1'–2' tall, with inconspicuous, lance-shaped leaves and a haze of tiny white flowers on branching stems. Use to soften the border or for cutting.

SOWING

INDOORS 6–8 weeks before last frost. Seeds are normally started outdoors, as plants bloom quickly from seed.

OUTDOORS Early spring, when soil is cool and a light frost is still possible. Sow every 3–4 weeks until July for continuous blooms. Sow in late autumn where winters are mild.

DEPTH Just cover.

GERMINATING

TIME 10–20 days.
REQUIREMENTS 70°F.

PLANTING SEEDLINGS OUTDOORS

TIME After last frost.
SPACING 8"–12".
LIGHT Full sun, with afternoon shade where summers are hot.
SOIL Ordinary, not too rich, with a pH level close to 7.0.

CARING FOR PLANTS

Easy. For best blooming, do not overwater or overfertilize and keep plants slightly crowded. Cut back after flowering to encourage a second bloom. Support tall species with wire frames or twiggy branches pushed into the ground when plants are young.

PROPAGATING

Seed only.

Gypsophila (Perennial)

Baby's breath

> TYPE HP
> ZONE 3–8: G. oldhamiana, G. pacifica, G. repens; 4–8: G. paniculata; 6–9: G. cerastioides
> FLOWERING SEASON Late spring through summer

Large genus of bushy plants with thin, wiry stems and masses of tiny white flowers, the overall effect being airy and dainty. Plants grow 6"–3' and are used in the border, rock garden, or cutting bed.

SOWING

INDOORS 8–10 weeks before planting out, in peat pots.
OUTDOORS Early spring or early autumn.
DEPTH Just cover.

Gypsophila paniculata

GERMINATING

TIME 10–15 days.
REQUIREMENTS 70°F.

PLANTING SEEDLINGS OUTDOORS

TIME Early spring, when soil is cool and a light frost is still possible, or early autumn.
SPACING Small species: 15"–24". Large species: 24"–48".
LIGHT Full sun.
SOIL Average, well-drained, with a pH level of 6.5–7.5.

CARING FOR PLANTS

Easy. Keep plants well watered. Trim lightly after flowering to restrict size and encourage further blooming; cut back to ground level in autumn. Do not disturb roots. Large plants are most discretely supported with a wire frame.

PROPAGATING

Take cuttings in early summer.

A-Annual P-Perennial B-Biennial HHA-Half-hardy annual HA-Hardy annual HB-Hardy biennial HHP-Half-hardy perennial HP-Hardy perennial HHBb-Half-hardy bulb HBb-Hardy bulb

142

Hacquetia

(synonymous with *Dondia*)

Type HP
Zone 4–9
Flowering Season Late winter to early spring

Genus of one species of perennial grown in the rock garden. This unusual little plant is just 2"–8" tall; umbels of yellow blooms, which appear before leaves, are surrounded by showy, bright green bracts.

Sowing

Indoors Pre-chilled seeds 10–12 weeks before planting out.
Outdoors When seed is fresh in autumn.
Depth Surface.

Germinating

Time 30–180 days.
Requirements Place seeds and moistened growing medium in a plastic bag, seal loosely, and refrigerate for 2–3 weeks. Sow in flats and leave at 55°F.

Planting Seedlings Outdoors

Time Early spring, when soil is cool and a light frost is still possible.
Spacing 8"–10".
Light Sun or shade.
Soil Moist, well-drained.

Caring for Plants

Mulch in spring to keep roots cool. Do not move established plants.

Propagating

Divide in spring.

Hacquetia epipactis

Hardenbergia

Australian sarsparilla, Coral pea, Vine lilac

Type HHP
Zone 9–10. Prefers the climate of California and the Southwest.
Flowering Season Spring

Evergreen climbers grown for their dense foliage and racemes of purple or white pea-like flowers. This Australian native grows to 10'.

Sowing

Indoors 8–10 weeks before planting out.
Outdoors After last frost.
Depth 1/8".

Germinating

Time 30–90 days.
Requirements Soak seeds in warm water for 24 hours; provide 55°–65°F thereafter.

Planting Seedlings Outdoors

Time After last frost, when temperatures remain above 45°F.
Spacing Plant singly.
Light Sun or shade.
Soil Prefers moist, peaty, well-drained, and lime-free soil.

Caring for Plants

Easy. Feed monthly with a weak liquid fertilizer and water regularly during dry spells.

Propagating

Take stem cuttings in summer or autumn.

A-Annual P-Perennial B-Biennial HHA-Half-hardy annual HA-Hardy annual HB-Hardy biennial HHP-Half-hardy perennial HP-Hardy perennial HHBb-Half-hardy bulb HBb-Hardy bulb

143

Hedychium

**Butterfly lily, Garland lily,
Ginger lily**

TYPE HHP often grown as A
ZONE A: 3–8; P: 9–10 (with a
good mulch, plants may survive
as far north as zone 7)
FLOWERING SEASON Summer

Genus of half-hardy plants with broad,
lance-shaped leaves and abundant spikes of
fragrant, white, yellow, orange, red, or bicolored flowers; in some species foliage is
highly ornamental. Plants grow 2'–12'. Use
in the border or near patios and decks where
their fragrance can be appreciated.

SOWING

INDOORS 6–8 weeks before last frost.
OUTDOORS Early spring, when soil is cool
and light frost is still possible, or late autumn.
DEPTH Just cover.

GERMINATING

TIME 20–25 days.
REQUIREMENTS Soak seeds for 2 hours in
warm water; provide 70°–75°F thereafter.

PLANTING SEEDLINGS OUTDOORS

TIME 2–3 weeks after last frost, when temperatures remain above 40°F.

SPACING 24"–36".
LIGHT Sun; part shade where summers are
hot.
SOIL Humus-rich, very moist (or even wet),
and very well-drained.

CARING FOR PLANTS

Easy. Water well during the growing season and cut back stems after flowers fade.
Mulch well in autumn, or lift rhizomes and
store in a cool, dry place over winter.

PROPAGATING

Divide rhizomes, each containing 1 eye, in
late winter.

Hedyotis

(synonymous with *Houstonia*)

**Bluets, Innocence, Quaker bonnets,
Quaker-ladies**

TYPE HP
ZONE 3–8. Not tolerant of arid
heat.
FLOWERING SEASON Late spring to
early summer

Genus of perennials grown for their tiny,
bright green leaves and blue, white, or
purple, star-shaped flowers. Most commonly
used species are 4"–6" and grown mainly in
rock gardens; taller species of up to 18" are
useful in shady plantings or wildflower
gardens.

SOWING

INDOORS Seeds are best started outdoors.
OUTDOORS As soon as fresh seed is avail-
able, usually around late summer.
DEPTH Just cover.

GERMINATING

TIME 15–20 days.
REQUIREMENTS Sow seeds thinly in vermiculite, sink containers in the ground
against a north-facing wall, and cover
with glass. Moisten soil occasionally, if
necessary. Allow 1 season of growth before transplanting to the garden.

PLANTING SEEDLINGS OUTDOORS

TIME Spring or autumn.
SPACING 12"–18".
LIGHT Full sun, with shade from the after-
noon sun where summers are very hot.
SOIL Moist, with a pH level of 5.0–6.0.

CARING FOR PLANTS

Water throughout the growing season. Allow foliage to die back naturally before removing. Plants are short-lived and require
regular division.

PROPAGATING

Divide in early spring (autumn in zones 7–8).

A-Annual P-Perennial B-Biennial HHA-Half-hardy annual HA-Hardy annual HB-Hardy biennial HHP-Half-hardy perennial HP-Hardy perennial HHBb-Half-hardy bulb HBb-Hardy bulb

144

Hedysarum

French honeysuckle, Sulla clover

> TYPE HP; often grown as A or B
> ZONE 4–9. Prefers the temperate climate of the Pacific Northwest.
> FLOWERING SEASON All summer

Genus of perennials grown for their fragrant, pealike flowers of crimson, violet, yellow, or purple. Plants are somewhat shrubby, 24"–48", and used in borders or cutting beds.

SOWING

INDOORS 6–8 weeks before last frost.
OUTDOORS Early spring, when soil is cool and a light frost is still possible, or late autumn.
DEPTH Just cover.

GERMINATING

TIME 14–90 days.
REQUIREMENTS Easy. 55°–65°F.

PLANTING SEEDLINGS OUTDOORS

TIME Spring or autumn.
SPACING 24"–36".
LIGHT Sun or shade.
SOIL Tolerates poor soil, but prefers a rich loam; must be well drained.

CARING FOR PLANTS

Easy. Cut plants to ground level in autumn. The leaves are attractive to slugs.

PROPAGATING

Take root cuttings or divide in spring (zones 4–6) or autumn (zones 7–9).

Helenium

False sunflower, Sneezeweed, Yellow star

> TYPE HP
> ZONE 3–8: *H. autumnale*, *H. hoopesii*; 5–9: *H. flexuosum*; 7–9: *H. bigelovii*
> FLOWERING SEASON Late summer to frost

Dependable, late summer-blooming perennials native to North America, growing 2'–4'. Abundant flowers are daisylike with prominent pincushion centers; colors are autumnal: golden yellow, flame red, orange, russet. Mass in the border for greatest impact.

SOWING

INDOORS 8–10 weeks before planting out.
OUTDOORS Early spring or early autumn.
DEPTH Just cover.

Helenium autumnale

GERMINATING

TIME 7–10 days.
REQUIREMENTS 70°F.

PLANTING SEEDLINGS OUTDOORS

TIME Early spring, when soil is cool and a light frost is still possible, or early autumn.
SPACING Small species: 12"–18". Tall species: 24"–36".
LIGHT Sun.
SOIL Will tolerate any soil, but is happiest in rich soil, with a pH level of 5.5–7.0.

CARING FOR PLANTS

Pinch back tall species in spring to inhibit growth (this will delay flowering) and/or support unruly plants with twiggy branches pushed into the ground when plants are young. Deadhead regularly and do not allow soil to dry out during the growing season. Cut back to the ground in autumn. Divide every 3–4 years to maintain vigor.

PROPAGATING

Divide in spring north of zone 7, in autumn in the South.

A-Annual P-Perennial B-Biennial HHA-Half-hardy annual HA-Hardy annual HB-Hardy biennial HHP-Half-hardy perennial HP-Hardy perennial HHBb-Half-hardy bulb HBb-Hardy bulb

145

Helianthemum

Frostweed, Rock rose, Sun rose

> TYPE HP or HHP
> ZONE 6–9. Not tolerant of extreme heat and humidity.
> FLOWERING SEASON Spring to autumn, depending on species

Shrubby, evergreen perennials growing to 1' and bearing long-blooming flowers, many of which are everlasting. Foliage is silver or green and flowers orange, yellow, bronze, or scarlet. Plant in rock gardens, drystone walls, or between paving stones.

SOWING

INDOORS 6–8 weeks before last frost.
OUTDOORS Early spring, when soil is cool and a light frost is still possible, or late autumn.
DEPTH Surface.

Helianthemum oelandicum

GERMINATING

TIME 15–20 days.
REQUIREMENTS 70°–75°F.

PLANTING SEEDLINGS OUTDOORS

TIME After last frost.
SPACING Small species: 5"–8". Large species: 12"–18".
LIGHT Full sun.
SOIL Tolerant of poor, dry soil. Will not stand wet feet in winter and must have excellent drainage.

CARING FOR PLANTS

Difficult. Remove faded blossoms, which open for just 1 day. After flowering, cut back lanky growth by one-third to maintain size and shape and to encourage a second blooming.

PROPAGATING

Take cuttings in late summer.

Helianthus

Sunflower

> TYPE HA, HP, or HHP
> ZONE A: 1–10; P:3–10:
> H. x multiflorus, H. rigidus;
> 4–9: H. maximilianii,
> H. salicifolius;
> 5–9: H. decapetalus;
> 6–9: H. angustifolius;
> 8–10: H. atrorubens
> FLOWERING SEASON Midsummer to midautumn

Large genus of coarse, erect plants native to North America, grown for their showy, daisylike flowers in yellows, oranges, and creams, usually with very large, flat eyes. Dwarf species are 18", but most tower between 5' and 10'. Grow at the back of the border, in wildflower gardens, or individually as a curiosity.

SOWING

INDOORS Seeds may be started indoors in peat pots 2–3 weeks before planting out, but little time is gained as sunflowers grow very quickly outdoors.
OUTDOORS After last frost.
DEPTH ¼".

GERMINATING

TIME 10–14 days.
REQUIREMENTS 70°–85°F.

PLANTING SEEDLINGS OUTDOORS

TIME After last frost.
SPACING Dwarf species: 12". Large species: 36".
LIGHT Full sun to light shade.
SOIL Tolerant of both wet and dry soils, but stronger plants will be produced in deep, rich, well-drained soil with a pH level of 5.0–7.0.

CARING FOR PLANTS

Easy. Pinch back small species when young to produce bushier plants; stake tall species. Water regularly and fertilize lightly several times during the summer; overfertilization will increase leaf production but reduce flowering. If seeds are to be harvested, cover flower heads with cheesecloth to protect from birds. Cut back perennials to ground level in autumn. Caution: Neighboring plants may be harmed by a substance emitted by sunflower roots.

Helianthus debilis

PROPAGATING

Annual sunflowers are propagated by seed. Divide perennials in spring north of zone 7, in autumn elsewhere.

A-Annual P-Perennial B-Biennial HHA-Half-hardy annual HA-Hardy annual HB-Hardy biennial HHP-Half-hardy perennial HP-Hardy perennial HHBb-Half-hardy bulb HBb-Hardy bulb

Helichrysum

Curry plant, Immortelle,
Licorice plant, Strawflower

TYPE HHA or HP
ZONE A: 2–10; P: 9–10; 5–10:
H. *arenarium*, H. 'Drakensberg
Mountains', H. 'Sulfur Light',
H. 'Sussex Silver';
7–10: H. *bellidoides*,
H. *milfordiae*, H. *orientale*,
H. *plicatum*, H. *sibthorpii*.
Prefers warm, dry climates.
Most *Helichrysums* are particu-
larly intolerant of wet winters.
FLOWERING SEASON Summer to
frost

Genus of mainly upright, branching annuals and perennials grown for their papery,
everlasting flowers. Plants are 1'–4' tall;
flowers are bright white, orange, yellow, or
red, often bicolored. Use in rock gardens,
borders, and cutting beds.

SOWING
INDOORS 6–8 weeks before planting out.
OUTDOORS After last frost, only where sum-
mers are very long.
DEPTH Surface.

Helichrysum bracteatum

GERMINATING
TIME 5–20 days.
REQUIREMENTS Easy. Light and 65°–75°F.

PLANTING SEEDLINGS OUTDOORS
TIME 2–3 weeks after last frost, when tem-
peratures remain above 40°F.
SPACING Small species: 8"–10". Tall spe-
cies: 15"–18".
LIGHT Full sun.
SOIL Average, sandy, with a pH level of
6.0–7.0; tolerant of poor, dry soils.

CARING FOR PLANTS
Easy. Water sparingly. To produce very large
flowers, remove all but 1 bud from each
flower stem. Excellent in dried arrangements: Cut stems before flowers are fully
open and hang upside-down to dry in a
shady place; remove leaves.

PROPAGATING
Take cuttings in summer, or allow to self-
seed.

Helictotrichon

See *Avena*

Heliophila

Cape stock, Sun lovers

TYPE HA or HHA
ZONE Cool temperatures
FLOWERING SEASON Late spring
through early summer, or into
early autumn with successive
plantings

Genus of annuals native to South Africa
grown for their racemes of bright blue, pink,
white, or yellow (often bicolored) flowers.
Plants are 12"–36"; small species make attractive container plants, larger species suit
the border.

SOWING
INDOORS 6–8 weeks before last frost.
OUTDOORS Early spring, when soil is cool
and a light frost still possible, or late autumn. Make successive plantings for a
longer display of blooms.
DEPTH Just cover.

GERMINATING
TIME 14–21 days.
REQUIREMENTS 60°–65°F.

PLANTING SEEDLINGS OUTDOORS
TIME After last frost.
SPACING Small species: 6"–10". Medium
species: 12"–18". Large species: 24"–36".
LIGHT Full sun.
SOIL Well-drained.

CARING FOR PLANTS
Support plants with twiggy branches pushed
into the ground in spring. Water during dry
spells.

PROPAGATING
Seed only.

A-Annual P-Perennial B-Biennial HHA-Half-hardy annual HA-Hardy annual HB-Hardy biennial HHP-Half-hardy perennial HP-Hardy perennial HHBb-Half-hardy bulb HBb-Hardy bulb

147

Heliopsis

False sunflower, Orange sunflower

TYPE HP
ZONE 4–9. Not tolerant of humid heat.
FLOWERING SEASON Summer through early autumn

Tall, upright, long-blooming perennials, many being rather coarse and weedy but useful for their cheerful yellow or orange daisylike flowers; selected varieties are more desirable than the species. Plants grow from 3'–5', and should be used judiciously in the border or with abandon in the wildflower garden.

SOWING
INDOORS 8–10 weeks before planting out.
OUTDOORS Early spring or early autumn.
DEPTH Just cover.

Heliopsis helianthoides

GERMINATING
TIME 10–15 days.
REQUIREMENTS 70°F.

PLANTING SEEDLINGS OUTDOORS
TIME Early spring, when soil is cool and a light frost is still possible, or early autumn.
SPACING 24"–36".
LIGHT Full sun.
SOIL Prefers a rich, moist loam with a pH level of 5.5–7.0; will tolerate poor, dry soil.

CARING FOR PLANTS
Easy. Plants appreciate water during dry spells and a light feeding midseason. Cut back to ground level in autumn.

PROPAGATING
Divide in spring, or take stem cuttings in summer.

Heliotropium

Cherry pie, Heliotrope

TYPE HHP usually grown as HHA
ZONE A: 3–10; P: 9–10
FLOWERING SEASON Late spring to late autumn, depending on species

Genus of plants grown for their fragrant, deep blue, purple, or white flowers which are trumpet-shaped or clustered in umbels. Plants grow from 8" to 4'. Use small species in containers, larger species in the border.

SOWING
INDOORS 10–12 weeks before planting out.
OUTDOORS Start seed indoors.
DEPTH Just cover.

GERMINATING
TIME 2–42 days.
REQUIREMENTS 70°–75°F.

PLANTING SEEDLINGS OUTDOORS
TIME 2–3 weeks after last frost, when temperatures remain above 40°F.
SPACING 12"–24".
LIGHT Full sun, with afternoon shade where summers are hot.
SOIL Rich, well-drained.

CARING FOR PLANTS
Keep soil evenly moist and feed once a month. Pinch back young plants to encourage bushiness and deadhead regularly to prolong blooming. Grow plants indoors with 4 hours sunlight a day; feed lightly every 2 weeks.

PROPAGATING
Take root or stem cuttings in autumn.

A-Annual P-Perennial B-Biennial HHA-Half-hardy annual HA-Hardy annual HB-Hardy biennial HHP-Half-hardy perennial HP-Hardy perennial HHBb-Half-hardy bulb HBb-Hardy bulb

148

Helipterum

(synonymous with *Acroclinium* and *Rhodanthe*)

Australian everlasting, Everlasting, Immortelle, Mangles everlasting, Strawflower, Swan River everlasting

> TYPE HA or HHA
> ZONE Prefers warm temperatures.
> 3–10
> FLOWERING SEASON Summer

Group of upright annuals with papery, many-petaled, daisylike blooms held on wiry stems; flowers may be red, pink, or white and are everlasting when dried. Plants grow to 12" and are useful in the border or cutting bed.

SOWING
INDOORS 4–6 weeks before last frost, or 6–8 weeks before last frost where summers are short, in peat pots.
OUTDOORS 4 weeks after last frost.
DEPTH Just cover.

GERMINATING
TIME 14–20 days.
REQUIREMENTS 65°–75°F.

PLANTING SEEDLINGS OUTDOORS
TIME After last frost.
SPACING 6"–8".
LIGHT Sun.
SOIL Light, somewhat sandy; tolerates dry soil.

CARING FOR PLANTS
Easy. Plants may require staking and are susceptible to aphids. For dried arrangements, pull up entire plant when flowering is at its peak.

PROPAGATING
Seed.

Helleborus

Christmas rose, Hellebore, Lenten rose

> TYPE HP
> ZONE 3–9: *H. foetidus, H. niger, H. viridis*; 4–9: *H. atrorubens*;
> 5–9: *H. orientalis*;
> 6–8: *H. argutifolius, H. viridis*;
> 7–9: *H. lividus*. Does not like excessive heat.
> FLOWERING SEASON Winter to late spring, depending on species

Striking but subtle perennials grown for their imposing foliage and unusual anemone-like flowers in funereal shades of murky pink, brown, green, plum, or cream. Best suited to woodland plantings.

SOWING
INDOORS See "Germinating, Requirements."
OUTDOORS Seed: see "Germinating, Requirements." Roots: early spring or early autumn.
DEPTH Seed: ⅛". Roots: 3".

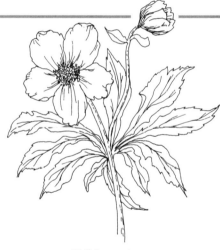

Helleborus niger

GERMINATING
TIME 1–18 months.
REQUIREMENTS Very difficult. *Autumn sowing:* Sow seeds in peat pots, sink in the ground against a north-facing wall, and cover with glass. Moisten soil occasionally, if necessary. Bring indoors in spring to 60°–65°F. *Spring sowing:* Sow seeds in peat pots, place in plastic bags, and refrigerate for 3 weeks. Sink pots in the ground in a shady location, covering with glass; remove glass when seedlings emerge.

PLANTING SEEDLINGS OUTDOORS
TIME Spring or autumn, when plants are at least 1 year old.
SPACING Small species: 6"–12". Large species: 12"–18".
LIGHT Can take a little sun in winter, but must have shade in summer.
SOIL Rich, moist, well-drained, with a pH level of 6.0–7.5.

CARING FOR PLANTS
Easy. Water regularly and feed lightly twice a year. Remove faded flowers and dead leaves in autumn. Do not disturb established plants.

PROPAGATING
Very carefully divide after flowering to retain a large root ball. Give extra attention to newly divided plants.

A-Annual P-Perennial B-Biennial HHA-Half-hardy annual HA-Hardy annual HB-Hardy biennial HHP-Half-hardy perennial HP-Hardy perennial HHBb-Half-hardy bulb HBb-Hardy bulb

Hemerocallis

Daylily

TYPE HP
ZONE 3–9; 5–9: *H. multiflora;*
6–9: *H. aurantiaca*
FLOWERING SEASON Midspring to early autumn, depending on species

Irresistible, long-stemmed perennials bearing straplike leaves and large, trumpet-shaped flowers in an ever-increasing range of colors, mainly in the yellow/orange/apricot range. Flower stems are 12"–5'. Use in the border, massed in a bed of their own, or singly in naturalistic plantings. No summer is complete without these carefree charmers.

SOWING

INDOORS 8–10 weeks before planting out.
OUTDOORS Early spring, when soil is cool and a light frost is still possible; late summer, where winters are mild.
DEPTH Seed: ⅛". Roots: 4"–6".

GERMINATING

TIME 15–49 days.
REQUIREMENTS Place seeds together with moistened growing medium in a plastic bag and refrigerate for 6 weeks; provide 60°–70°F thereafter.

PLANTING SEEDLINGS OUTDOORS

TIME After last frost.
SPACING 12" for quick cover, 24" if you prefer not to divide plants frequently.
LIGHT Full sun in the North, part shade where summers are very hot. Pastels will retain their color best in light shade, but blooming probably will be sparser.
SOIL Prefers rich, moist, with a pH level of 5.5–7.0, but famously tolerant of a wide range of conditions.

CARING FOR PLANTS

Very easy. Fertilize in late winter and again in early spring with 5–10–10. Water well during dry spells to maintain flowering. Cut flower stems to ground after blooming to keep plants looking neat.

Hemerocallis flava

PROPAGATING

Divide at any time.

Hepatica

Liverleaf, Liverwort

TYPE HP
ZONE 4–8. Happiest in cool climates.
FLOWERING SEASON Late winter to spring

Diminutive (2"–9"), slow-growing perennials producing a mass of charming anemone-like blooms in blue, white, or pink on sturdy stems. Grow in shady rock gardens or woodland settings.

SOWING

INDOORS Pre-chilled seeds 12–14 weeks before planting out, in peat pots. Starting seeds outdoors is usually more successful.
OUTDOORS When seed is fresh, usually May or June.
DEPTH ¼".

GERMINATING

TIME 30–360 days.
REQUIREMENTS Place seeds in a plastic bag together with moist growing medium and refrigerate for 3 weeks. Provide 50°–55°F thereafter.

Hepatica americana

PLANTING SEEDLINGS OUTDOORS

TIME Autumn.
SPACING 6"–12".
LIGHT Part to full shade.
SOIL Moist, humus-rich, and well-drained.

CARING FOR PLANTS

Easy. Feed occasionally for better flowering and do not allow soil to dry out in summer. Mulch with oak leaves in autumn. Leave plants undisturbed.

PROPAGATING

Carefully divide in spring, autumn in zones 7 and 8, or allow to self-seed.

A-Annual P-Perennial B-Biennial HHA-Half-hardy annual HA-Hardy annual HB-Hardy biennial HHP-Half-hardy perennial HP-Hardy perennial HHBb-Half-hardy bulb HBb-Hardy bulb

150

Heracleum

**American cow parsley,
Cartwheel flower, Cow parsnip,
Giant hogweed, Masterwort**

TYPE HP
ZONE 3–9
FLOWERING SEASON Midsummer

Towering, coarse perennials, 9'–12', resembling enormous Queen Anne's lace. White or pink flowers are held in umbels on thick, fleshy stems. Mass near water, at the woodland's edge, or in a wildflower garden.

SOWING
INDOORS See "Germinating, Requirements."
OUTDOORS See "Germinating, Requirements."
DEPTH ¼".

Heracleum villosum

GERMINATING
TIME 30–90 days.
REQUIREMENTS *Autumn sowing:* Sow seeds in peat pots, sink pots in the ground against a north-facing wall, and cover with glass. Moisten soil occasionally, if necessary. Bring indoors in spring. *Spring sowing:* Sow seeds in moistened medium in peat pots, seal loosely in plastic bags, and refrigerate for 2–3 weeks. Sink pots in the ground outdoors against a north-facing wall and cover with glass; remove glass when seedlings emerge. Transplant to the garden in autumn.

PLANTING SEEDLINGS OUTDOORS
TIME Autumn.
SPACING 36"–48".
LIGHT Sun or light shade.
SOIL Rich, moist.

CARING FOR PLANTS
Remove flowering stems as soon as they appear; this will result in healthier foliage and will prevent a complete takeover of your flower beds by this invasive plant. Do not disturb roots. Contact with foliage may cause skin rash.

PROPAGATING
Very carefully divide in spring or autumn, or allow to self-seed.

Herniaria

Rupture-wort

TYPE HP
ZONE 3–9
FLOWERING SEASON Summer

Diminutive, trailing, mat-forming perennials useful for their finely-textured, durable, evergreen foliage. Plants grow 4"–18"; tiny flowers are green. Useful rock garden plant or ground cover for difficult areas.

SOWING
INDOORS 6–8 weeks before last frost.
OUTDOORS Early spring, when soil is cool and a light frost is still possible, or late autumn.
DEPTH Just cover.

GERMINATING
TIME 10–12 days.
REQUIREMENTS 70°F.

PLANTING SEEDLINGS OUTDOORS
TIME After last frost.
SPACING Small species: 4"–6". Large species: 12"–18".
LIGHT Full sun or part shade.
SOIL Average to dry, well-drained.

CARING FOR PLANTS
No special care required.

PROPAGATING
Divide in spring north of zone 7, in autumn elsewhere.

A-Annual P-Perennial B-Biennial HHA-Half-hardy annual HA-Hardy annual HB-Hardy biennial HHP-Half-hardy perennial HP-Hardy perennial HHBb-Half-hardy bulb HBb-Hardy bulb

151

Hesperis

Dame's rocket, Dames violet, Garden rocket, Sweet rocket

> TYPE **HP often grown as HB**
> ZONE **3–9**
> FLOWERING SEASON **Summer**

Woody, upright perennials bearing a hazy mass of white, lilac, or purple blossoms with a heavenly, nocturnal fragrance; plants grow 1'–4'. Mass in the shady border, or near a patio where their scent can be enjoyed.

SOWING

INDOORS 8–10 weeks before planting out.
OUTDOORS Midsummer; cover seedbeds in winter with a mulch of straw.
DEPTH Surface.

GERMINATING

TIME 20–25 days.
REQUIREMENTS Light and 70°–85°F.

PLANTING SEEDLINGS OUTDOORS

TIME After last frost.
SPACING 12"–20".
LIGHT Full sun or part shade; full shade where summers are hot.
SOIL Rich, moist, well-drained, with a pH level of 5.0–8.0; tolerates poor soil.

CARING FOR PLANTS

Easy. Feed regularly and cut back stems after flowering to prolong blooming. Plants are short-lived and require regular replacement.

PROPAGATING

Take cuttings, or allow to self-seed.

Hesperis matronalis

Heuchera

Alum root, Coral bells

> TYPE **HP**
> ZONE **3–9 (except H. *maxima*, which grows only in zones 9–10)**
> FLOWERING SEASON **Late spring to early autumn, depending on species**

Compact, clump-forming, mainly evergreen perennials bearing attractive, toothed or scalloped, green, bronze, or silvery leaves and delicate sprays of flowers on long, wiry stems. Commonly grown species are 6"–12", larger species grow to 3'. Attractive edging plant, ground cover, or woodland plant.

SOWING

INDOORS 8–10 weeks before planting out.
OUTDOORS Early spring or late autumn.
DEPTH Surface.

GERMINATING

TIME 10–60 days.
REQUIREMENTS Light and 60°–70°F.

Heuchera sanguinea

PLANTING SEEDLINGS OUTDOORS

TIME After last frost.
SPACING 9"–12".
LIGHT Sun where summers are cool, otherwise part shade.
SOIL Light, fertile, well-drained, with a pH level of 6.0–7.0; intolerant of wet soil.

CARING FOR PLANTS

Mulch well in early spring. Remove flowering stems after blooming to maintain neat appearance. Divide every 3–4 years, enriching the soil with organic matter at that time.

PROPAGATING

Divide in spring north of zone 7, or autumn.

Hibiscus

Flower-of-an-hour,
Goodnight-at-noon, Rose mallow,
Sea hollyhock, Swamp mallow

> **TYPE** HHA or HHP that is often grown as a HHA
> **ZONE** A: 3–10; P: 9–10; 4–10: *H. militaris,* *H. moscheutos;* 5–10: *H. lasiocarpos;* 6–10: *H. coccineus*
> **FLOWERING SEASON** Summer to frost, depending on species

Tall, upright perennials and annuals prized for their large, showy, trumpet-shaped flowers with a decidedly tropical look. Plants grow from 18" to 8'; blooms are hot pink, fiery red, or white. Mass in borders or use in containers; gaudy, large-flowered cultivars make an unusual hedge.

Hibiscus moscheutos

SOWING

INDOORS A: 8 weeks before last frost. P: 12 weeks before last frost.
OUTDOORS After last frost. *H. trionum* should be started *in situ* only.
DEPTH Surface.

GERMINATING

TIME 10–30 days.
REQUIREMENTS Chip seeds and soak in hot water for 1 hour. Provide 70°–80°F thereafter.

PLANTING SEEDLINGS OUTDOORS

TIME After last frost, when temperatures remain above 45°F.
SPACING Small species: 12"–18". Large species: 24"–48".
LIGHT Full sun to light shade.
SOIL Prefers rich, moist soil, but will tolerate dry.

CARING FOR PLANTS

Water frequently. Prune lightly after flowering. Do not transplant.

PROPAGATING

Divide in spring; often self-seeds.

Hieracium

Devil's-paintbrush, Hawkweed

> **TYPE** HP
> **ZONE** 3–9
> **FLOWERING SEASON** Late spring to autumn

Large genus of weedy plants, only a handful of which are useful in the garden, these being grown primarily for their silvery grey foliage. Plants are 12"–18"; dandelionlike flowers are bright orange or yellow, borne singly on upright stems. Use with caution in the rock garden.

SOWING

INDOORS 7–9 weeks before planting out.
OUTDOORS Early spring, when soil is cool and a light frost is still possible, or late autumn.
DEPTH Just cover.

GERMINATING

TIME 21–30 days.
REQUIREMENTS 50°–60°F.

PLANTING SEEDLINGS OUTDOORS

TIME Early spring, when soil is cool and a light frost is still possible, or late autumn.
SPACING 10"–12".
LIGHT Full sun.
SOIL Poor, dry, well-drained.

CARING FOR PLANTS

Not called hawkweed for nothing! This unassuming plant will swoop down on any unguarded square of earth and devour your flower beds completely if you are not ever-vigilant and prepared to be ruthless. *H. x rubrum* is less invasive than other species. Do not move once established.

PROPAGATING

Divide in spring. Self-seeds to the point of being a nuisance.

A-Annual P-Perennial B-Biennial HHA-Half-hardy annual HA-Hardy annual HB-Hardy biennial HHP-Half-hardy perennial HP-Hardy perennial HHBb-Half-hardy bulb HBb-Hardy bulb

153

Hordeum

Fox-tail barley, Squirreltail barley, Squirreltail grass

> TYPE **HA**
> ZONE **3–10. Prefers warm temperatures.**
> FLOWERING SEASON **Late spring to early summer**

Genus of grasses, only one of which has ornamental value. This unremarkable grass comes to life in summer when it displays a mass of beautiful, silky, silver-grey inflorescences on 2' stems. Useful in mixed grass plantings or naturalistic gardens.

SOWING

INDOORS Most successfully started outdoors.
OUTDOORS Early spring, when soil is cool and a light frost is still possible, or late autumn.
DEPTH ⅛".

GERMINATING

TIME 21–50 days.
REQUIREMENTS 70°F.

PLANTING SEEDLINGS OUTDOORS

SPACING 12".
LIGHT Sun.
SOIL Well-drained, somewhat dry, and limy.

CARING FOR PLANTS

Site carefully as grass is easily damaged by wind and rain. May become invasive.

PROPAGATING

Self-seeds.

Hosta

Funkia, Plantain lily

> TYPE **HP**
> ZONE **3–9**
> FLOWERING SEASON **Summer**

Surely one of the most widely grown plants in the United States, these useful and elegant shade-lovers come in all sizes, from a dainty 3"–4" to an imposing 3'. Leaf color ranges from acid green to true blue, with numerous gradations in between. Stunning shady ground cover, edging, border, container, or woodland plants.

SOWING

INDOORS 6–8 weeks before planting out.
OUTDOORS Spring or summer.
DEPTH Seed: just cover. Roots: 3"–5".

GERMINATING

TIME 15–90 days.
REQUIREMENTS Difficult. 50°F.

PLANTING SEEDLINGS OUTDOORS

TIME Early spring.
SPACING Dwarf species: 12". Medium species: 18"–24". Large species: 36"–48".
LIGHT Most prefer light to heavy shade, but some will tolerate sun.
SOIL Moist, with a pH level of 5.5–7.0. Will tolerate dry soil, but will languish if left to dry out completely.

CARING FOR PLANTS

Easy. Water regularly and feed twice a year. Very attractive to slugs, which will leave plants with a Swiss cheese look if not controlled. Divide no more than every 2 years.

PROPAGATING

Divide in early spring or autumn.

Hosta x 'Royal Standard'

Hosta x 'August Moon'

ALISON KOLESAR

A-Annual P-Perennial B-Biennial HHA-Half-hardy annual HA-Hardy annual HB-Hardy biennial HHP-Half-hardy perennial HP-Hardy perennial HHBb-Half-hardy bulb HBb-Hardy bulb

154

Houstonia

See *Hedyotis*

Humulus

Hop, Japanese hop

Type HP, usually grown as HHA
Zone 3–9
Flowering Season Late spring through autumn, depending on sowing time

Unusual rampant climber with deeply lobed foliage, sometimes variegated, and showy "hops" in autumn. Quickly covers unsightly structures.

Sowing

Indoors 6–8 weeks before planting out.
Outdoors For summer flowers, sow in early spring, when a light frost is still possible; Sow in summer for flowering in autumn. Sow in autumn for late spring blooms the following year.
Depth ¼".

Humulus lupulus

Germinating

Time 25–30 days.
Requirements 70°–75°F.

Planting Seedlings Outdoors

Time After last frost.
Spacing 24"–36".
Light Full sun or light shade.
Soil Prefers moist, rich, well-drained; will tolerate dry soil.

Caring for Plants

Water well during dry weather and provide a sturdy support.

Propagating

Take tip cuttings, or divide in spring.

Hunnemannia

Golden cup, Mexican tulip poppy

Type HHA or P grown as HHA
Zone A: 6–8; P: 9–10. Prefers warm climates.
Flowering Season Summer to early autumn

Fast-growing Mexican native bearing yellow poppylike blooms on 2' tall stems; fernlike foliage has a grey cast. Use in borders and wildflower plantings.

Sowing

Indoors 6–8 weeks before last frost, in peat pots.
Outdoors When nighttime temperatures reach 50°F; where winters are mild, seeds also may be sown in late autumn.
Depth Just cover.

Germinating

Time 15–20 days.
Requirements 70°–75°F.

Planting Seedlings Outdoors

Time After last frost.
Spacing 8"–12".
Light Full sun.
Soil Average, well-drained, neutral to slightly alkaline; tolerant of dry soil.

Caring for Plants

Easy. Do not overwater or attempt to transplant.

Propagating

Self-seeds.

Hutchinsia

Small group of diminutive, tufted alpine plants with deep green, lobed leaves (although some species have almost no leaves at all), and racemes of small, white flowers. Grown in containers and rock gardens.

SOWING

Indoors Most successful when started outdoors.
Outdoors When fresh seed is available in summer.
Depth ¼".

GERMINATING

Time 14–30 days.
Requirements Easy.

PLANTING SEEDLINGS OUTDOORS

Spacing 3"–6".
Light Full sun where summers are cool, otherwise part to full shade. Flowers more abundant in sun.
Soil Cool, moist, well-drained, with a pH level of 6.0–7.5.

CARING FOR PLANTS

Mulch to keep soil cool and moist, and water regularly during dry spells. These delicate plants are short-lived and require regular division.

PROPAGATING

Divide in early spring, or take cuttings in summer.

Hyacinthus

Hyacinth

Genus of bulbs grown for their showy, highly fragrant blooms. Flower stalks are strong and upright, 6" tall, covered in trumpets of blue, purple, white, red, yellow, or pink. Mass for a striking color effect, or use in mixed bulb plantings or containers.

SOWING

Indoors Start seeds outdoors only.
Outdoors Seed: late summer to early autumn. Bulb: early autumn.
Depth Seed: ½". Bulb: Plant tip of bulb 3" deep where soil is heavy, 5" in light soil.

Hyacinthus orientalis

GERMINATING

Time 30–365 days.
Requirements Because of the difficulty of propagating hyacinths from seed, starting with purchased bulbs is more practical. But for the adventurous: Sow seeds in flats, plunge flats to the rims against a north-facing wall, and cover with glass. Moisten soil occasionally, if necessary. May not come true from seed.

PLANTING SEEDLINGS OUTDOORS

Time Transplant seed-grown bulbs in the autumn of their second year.
Spacing 8"–10".
Light Full sun to light shade.
Soil Rich, very well-drained, with a pH level of 6.0–7.0.

CARING FOR PLANTS

Easy. Plants grown from seed will flower in 3–6 years. Feed in early spring and again in autumn. Water during dry spells until flowering has ended, then discontinue. Remove flowers after blooming, allowing leaves to die back naturally. Mulch the first winter after planting, and annually in cold climates. Discard old plants when they begin to decline, every 3–4 years.

PROPAGATING

Hyacinths can be propagated with limited success by offsets, but starting with purchased bulbs is recommended.

Hypericum

**Aaron's beard, Rose of Sharon,
St.-John's-wort**

> TYPE HP
> ZONE 5–9. Prefers cool weather.
> FLOWERING SEASON Summer or
> autumn, depending on species

Genus of subshrubs and perennials grown
for their large, saucer-shaped, bright yellow
flowers sporting many fluffy stamens; some
are evergreen. Plants grow from 6"–6'.
Small species are useful in rock gardens or
as ground cover; grow larger species in the
border.

SOWING

INDOORS 8–10 weeks before planting out.
OUTDOORS Early spring or early autumn.
DEPTH Just cover.

GERMINATING

TIME 20–90 days.
REQUIREMENTS 50°–55°F.

PLANTING SEEDLINGS OUTDOORS

TIME 2–3 weeks before last spring frost, or
early autumn.
SPACING Small species: 6"–9". Medium species: 18"–24". Large species: 24"–36".
LIGHT Full sun to part shade.
SOIL Highly adaptable. Prefers well-drained
soil with a pH level of 5.5–7.0.

CARING FOR PLANTS

Easy. Generally trouble-free, except for a
susceptibility to rust. Prune hard in early
spring.

PROPAGATING

Divide in autumn after blooming, or take
cuttings in spring or summer.

Hypericum aureum

Hyssopus

Hyssop

> TYPE HP
> ZONE 3–10. Does not like
> extreme heat and humidity
> FLOWERING SEASON Late summer

Shrubby perennial herb of 18"–24", grown
singly as a specimen or massed to form an
unusual hedge. Flowers are tiny, fragrant
tubes of pink, white, or blue grown high on
slender stalks amid lance-shaped leaves.

SOWING

INDOORS 8–10 weeks before planting out.
OUTDOORS Early spring, when soil is cool
and a light frost is still possible.
DEPTH Just cover.

GERMINATING

TIME 14–42 days.
REQUIREMENTS 60°–70°F.

PLANTING SEEDLINGS OUTDOORS

TIME Spring.
SPACING 18"–36".
LIGHT Full sun to part shade.
SOIL Light, somewhat dry.

CARING FOR PLANTS

Easy. Cut back to the ground in autumn or
spring and divide every 3–4 years to maintain vigorous growth.

PROPAGATING

Take cuttings in summer. Carefully divide
in spring in the North, in autumn in the
South.

CHARLES JOSLIN

Hyssopus officinalis

A-Annual P-Perennial B-Biennial HHA-Half-hardy annual HA-Hardy annual HB-Hardy biennial HHP-Half-hardy perennial HP-Hardy perennial HHBb-Half-hardy bulb HBb-Hardy bulb

157

Iberis (Annual)

Annual candytuft, Globe candytuft, Hyacinth-flowered candytuft, Rocket candytuft

TYPE HA
ZONE 1–10. Prefers cool weather.
FLOWERING SEASON Early summer to frost

Small group of upright plants growing 12"–16". Flowers, which may be in racemes or umbels, are white, pink, purple, or red, and are sometimes fragrant; leaves are lance-shaped. Use in rock gardens or at the front of the border.

SOWING

INDOORS 6–8 weeks before last frost, in peat pots.
OUTDOORS For continuous blooms, sow every 10 days from last frost date to mid-July. In zones 8–10 seeds may also be sown in late summer.
DEPTH 1/8".

GERMINATING

TIME 10–20 days.
REQUIREMENTS Easy. 70°–85°F.

PLANTING SEEDLINGS OUTDOORS

TIME After last frost.
SPACING 6"–12".
LIGHT Full sun, with some afternoon shade where summers are hot.
SOIL Ordinary, well-drained, with a pH level of 6.0–7.0.

CARING FOR PLANTS

Easy. Water plants regularly, allowing soil to dry out between waterings. After flowering, trim plants lightly to extend the blooming period; discard plants as they begin to decline. Do not move established plants.

PROPAGATING

Self-seeds.

Iberis (Perennial)

Candytuft

TYPE HP
ZONE 3–9: *I. saxatilis, I. sempervirens*; 7–9: *I. gibraltarica*
FLOWERING SEASON Midspring

Low-growing and evergreen, these spreading, woody perennials are covered in tiny white flowers in spring and make a neat green mound of 6"–12" throughout the rest of the year. Plant in rock gardens, cascading over walls, or edging borders.

SOWING

INDOORS 6–8 weeks before last frost.
OUTDOORS Early spring, when soil is cool and a light frost is still possible, or late autumn.
DEPTH 1/4".

GERMINATING

TIME 10–60 days.
REQUIREMENTS Easy. 55°–65°F.

PLANTING SEEDLINGS OUTDOORS

TIME After last frost.
SPACING Small species: 12". Large species: 24".
LIGHT Sun or part shade.
SOIL Rich, well-drained, with a pH level of 6.0–7.5.

CARING FOR PLANTS

Easy. Flowering will be diminished or may stop altogether if soil is too dry. Trim lightly after blooming to keep plants looking tidy.

PROPAGATING

Divide after flowering where summers are mild, in autumn south of zone 6. Take cuttings after flowering.

Iberis sempervirens

A-Annual P-Perennial B-Biennial HHA-Half-hardy annual HA-Hardy annual HB-Hardy biennial HHP-Half-hardy perennial HP-Hardy perennial HHBb-Half-hardy bulb HBb-Hardy bulb

158

Impatiens

Balsam, Busy lizzie, Lady's slipper, Patience plant, Patient Lucy, Sultana, Touch-me-not

> **TYPE** HHA or P grown as HHA
> **ZONE** A: 3–9; P: 10
> **FLOWERING SEASON** Late spring through first frost

Genus of annuals and, less commonly, perennials, the most widely grown species prized for their vibrantly colored flowers which bloom even in deep shade. Most are 12"–24", with midgreen leaves and flat, open blossoms in rich pinks, oranges, reds, purples, and white; some species have flowers that are hooded and lipped. Mass under trees, use in woodland plantings, or in containers.

SOWING

INDOORS 8–10 weeks before last frost.
OUTDOORS After last frost.
DEPTH Surface.

GERMINATING

TIME 7–30 days.
REQUIREMENTS Light, high humidity, and 70°–75°F. Highly susceptible to damping-off; sow seeds in vermiculite and water only from below.

PLANTING SEEDLINGS OUTDOORS

TIME Several weeks after last frost, when temperatures remain above 50°F.
SPACING 8"–12".
LIGHT Most species prefer full shade, but all are more tolerant of sun where summers are cool. Some 'New Guinea' impatiens require full sun.
SOIL Rich, moist, with a pH level of 6.0–7.0. Supplement with well-rotted manure.

CARING FOR PLANTS

Easy. Pinch back young plants once or twice to increase branching. Fertilize twice during the growing season. Keep watered for an unbeatable display of color all season.

Impatiens balsamina

PROPAGATING

Take cuttings in spring or autumn, or allow to self-seed.

Incarvillea

Chinese trumpet flower, Hardy gloxinia, Trumpet flower

> **TYPE** HP
> **ZONE** 3–8. Will not thrive in humid heat.
> **FLOWERING SEASON** Late spring to summer

Genus of Asian perennials grown for their exotic, trumpet-shaped flowers of red, pink, or yellow. Plants are clump-forming, 1'–4', with fernlike foliage and strong flower-bearing stems. Use in rock gardens and borders.

SOWING

INDOORS 8–10 weeks before last frost.
OUTDOORS Early spring, when soil is cool and a light frost is still possible, or early autumn.
DEPTH Surface.

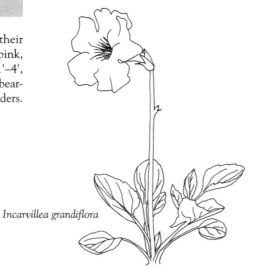

Incarvillea grandiflora

GERMINATING

TIME 25–60 days.
REQUIREMENTS 60°–70°F.

PLANTING SEEDLINGS OUTDOORS

TIME After last frost.
SPACING Small species: 8"–12". Tall species: 18"–24".
LIGHT Full sun, with afternoon shade where summers are very hot.
SOIL Rich, sandy, slightly acid.

CARING FOR PLANTS

Keep soil moist during the growing season and deadhead regularly. North of zone 6 provide a heavy winter mulch. Plants may be attractive to slugs. Divide and move very carefully to avoid damaging the taproot.

PROPAGATING

Very carefully divide in late spring.

A-Annual P-Perennial B-Biennial HHA-Half-hardy annual HA-Hardy annual HB-Hardy biennial HHP-Half-hardy perennial HP-Hardy perennial HHBb-Half-hardy bulb HBb-Hardy bulb

Inula

Elecampane, Horseheal

TYPE HP
ZONE 3–7: *I. royleana*;
  3–9: *I. acaulis, I. ensifolia,*
  I. helenium, I. hookeri,
  I. orientalis; 5–8: *I. magnifica*
FLOWERING SEASON Summer

Large genus of coarse, upright perennials, 1'–7' tall, bearing showy, daisylike flowers with large eyes surrounded by thin, spidery bracts. Useful in wildflower gardens; some are suitable for sunny borders.

SOWING

INDOORS 6–8 weeks before last frost.
OUTDOORS Early spring, when soil is cool and a light frost is still possible, or early autumn.
DEPTH Just cover.

GERMINATING

TIME 14–42 days.
REQUIREMENTS 55°–65°F.

PLANTING SEEDLINGS OUTDOORS

TIME After last frost.
SPACING Small species: 6"–12". Medium species: 18"–24". Large species: 24"–48".
LIGHT Full sun; *I. ensifolia* can be planted in part shade.
SOIL Ordinary, well-drained.

CARING FOR PLANTS

Easy. Top-dress with well-rotted manure in early spring. Keep soil moist in summer. Cut back flowering stems in autumn. Divide every 3 years to maintain healthy plants.

PROPAGATING

Divide in spring (zones 3–6) or early autumn (zones 7–9).

Inula helenium

Ionopsidium

Diamond flower, Violet cress

TYPE HA
ZONE Cool climates
FLOWERING SEASON Spring through autumn, depending on sowing time

Genus of annuals, only one species of which is commonly grown. These fast-growing 2"–3" plants bear a profusion of lilac or white blooms over a long period. Use in rock gardens, drystone walls, between pavers, or as edging.

SOWING

INDOORS Start seeds outdoors only.
OUTDOORS Early spring for midsummer blooms, summer for autumn blooms, autumn for spring blooms. Or sow at intervals from early spring to early summer, then again in autumn for continuous flowering.
DEPTH Just cover.

GERMINATING

TIME 14–21 days.
REQUIREMENTS 55°–60°.

PLANTING SEEDLINGS OUTDOORS

SPACING 4"–5".
LIGHT Sun to part shade, with shade from hot afternoon sun.
SOIL Prefers cool, moist soil, but will tolerate dry.

CARING FOR PLANTS

Mulch to keep soil cool and moist, and water during dry spells. Plants will languish in hot weather.

PROPAGATING

Self-seeds.

A-Annual P-Perennial B-Biennial HHA-Half-hardy annual HA-Hardy annual HB-Hardy biennial HHP-Half-hardy perennial HP-Hardy perennial HHBb-Half-hardy bulb HBb-Hardy bulb

160

Ipomoea

Cardinal climber, Cypress vine, Moonflower, Morning glory

> TYPE HHA or P usually grown as A
> ZONE A: 3–8; P: 9–10. Performs most successfully where temperatures are warm.
> FLOWERING SEASON Summer through early autumn

Genus of climbing plants grown for their charming trumpet-shaped flowers. Blooms may be small and dainty or large and exotic, pink, white, blue, purple, red, or bicolored; some are fragrant. Grow on a trellis or post, through shrubs, or in containers. Sadly, *Ipomoea* is often avoided by gardeners who confuse it with *Convolvulus arvensis*, a weed of alarming tenacity.

SOWING

INDOORS Starting seeds *in situ* is usually more successful, but may be attempted 3–4 weeks before last frost, in peat pots.
OUTDOORS 1–2 weeks after last frost.
DEPTH ¼".

GERMINATING

TIME 5–21 days.
REQUIREMENTS Easy. Chip seeds and soak in warm water for 24 hours; provide 70°–85°F thereafter.

PLANTING SEEDLINGS OUTDOORS

TIME 3–4 weeks after last frost, when temperatures remain above 45°F.
SPACING 12"–18".
LIGHT Full sun.
SOIL Moist, loose soil that is not too high in nitrogen, with a pH level of 6.0–7.5; tolerates dry soil.

CARING FOR PLANTS

Easy. Provide a trellis for support and pinch tips once as plants begin to climb. Do not fertilize.

PROPAGATING

Seed only.

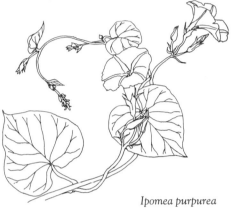

Ipomea purpurea

Iris

(for *Iris kaempferi*, see next entry)

> TYPE HP, HHP, or HBb
> ZONE 2–8: *I. setosa*; 3–8: *I. missouriensis*; 3–9: *I. versicolor*, bearded iris; 4–9: *I. germanica**, *I. laevigata*, *I. pumila*, *I. sibirica*; 5–8: *I. aphylla*, *I. hollandica*; 5–9: *I. brevicaulis*, *I. danfordiae*, *I. histrio*, *I. histrioides*, *I. pseudacorus*, *I. reticulata*, *I. tectorum*, *I. xiphioides*; 6–9: *I. cristata*, *I. pallida**, *I. xiphium*; 7–9: *I. chrysographes*, *I. foetidissima*, *I. unguicularis**; 7–10: *I. fulva*, *I. hexagona*; 8–10: *I. confusa*, *I. douglasiana**
> *Does not perform well where the climate is excessively hot and humid
> FLOWERING SEASON Spring through winter, depending on species

Large genus of justly popular, bulbous or rhizomatous perennials, usually with swordlike leaves and intricate, exquisite flowers. Plants grow from a dwarf 4" to a stately 6'; flower color ranges from pure pastels in every shade to deepest purple, maroon, and even brown. Uses are limitless: in borders, formal or naturalistic plantings, massed or singly.

SOWING

INDOORS See "Germinating, Requirements."
OUTDOORS Seed: see "Germinating, Requirements." Bulb: early autumn.
DEPTH Seed: ¼". Bulb: *I. cristata*: 2"–3". *I. hollandica*: 4"–5". Others: plant rhizomes level with soil surface.

GERMINATING

TIME 1–18 months.
REQUIREMENTS Difficult. Soak seeds for 24 hours in warm water. *Autumn to winter sowing:* Sow in flats, sink these in the ground against a north-facing wall, and cover with glass. Moisten soil occasionally, if necessary. Bring indoors in spring to 60°–70°F. *Spring to summer sowing:* Sow seeds in moistened medium in flats, place flats in plastic bags, and refrigerate for 2–3 weeks. Then remove and sink in the ground in a shady location; cover with glass. Remove glass when seeds germinate. Grow for 2 seasons before transplanting to the garden.

PLANTING SEEDLINGS OUTDOORS

TIME Bulb: early autumn. Purchased rhizome: spring.
SPACING Dwarf species: 4"–8". Medium species: 12". Large species: 15"–18".
LIGHT *I. germanica*, *I. pallida*, *I. pumila*, and bearded irises require full sun, while *I. chrysographes*, *I. cristata*, and *I. douglasiana* will take up to halfshade.
SOIL Bearded iris and *I. laevigata* require a pH level of 7.0–8.0. *I. sibirica* requires a pH level of 5.5–7.0. Whereas bearded irises do well in quite dry soil, *I. sibirica* will grow in very wet soils. For the preferences of more obscure species, a good text devoted to *Iris* cultivation should be consulted.

CARING FOR PLANTS

Easy. Feed in spring with a low-nitrogen fertilizer; add a little lime around bearded irises. Water during dry spells. Deadhead regularly. Tall species may require staking. Divide bearded irises every 3–4 years.

PROPAGATING

Divide rhizomes just after flowering ceases. Divide bulbs in autumn.

A-Annual P-Perennial B-Biennial HHA-Half-hardy annual HA-Hardy annual HB-Hardy biennial HHP-Half-hardy perennial HP-Hardy perennial HHBb-Half-hardy bulb HBb-Hardy bulb

Iris (kaempferi)

(synonymous with *Iris ensata*)

Japanese iris, Oriental iris

TYPE HP
ZONE 5–9
FLOWERING SEASON Summer

This native of eastern Asia is a beardless iris with swordlike leaves and white, purple, or blue flowers on 2'–3' stems; flowers often have contrasting centers.

SOWING

INDOORS Any time.
OUTDOORS Autumn or winter.
DEPTH ¼".

GERMINATING

TIME 1–18 months.
REQUIREMENTS *Indoor sowing:* Place seeds in a plastic bag together with moist growing medium. Refrigerate for 5 weeks, then provide 60°–70°F. *Outdoor sowing:* Sow seeds in flats and sink into the ground against a north-facing wall. Bring inside after 4–5 weeks, then return to the ground in early spring. Feed regularly. Move to a permanent location in late spring or early autumn.

PLANTING SEEDLINGS OUTDOORS

TIME Spring or autumn.
SPACING 9"–12".
LIGHT Full sun to part shade.
SOIL Prefers rich soil with a pH level of 5.5–7.0. Moist — or even wet — soil produces best results.

CARING FOR PLANTS

Feed with liquid manure during the growing season. Divide every 3–4 years in autumn to maintain good flowering.

PROPAGATING

Divide tubers after flowering. Japanese iris must be hand-pollinated to produce seeds.

Isatis

Dyer's woad, Woad

TYPE HB
ZONE 3–10
FLOWERING SEASON Summer

Genus of vigorous, summer-blooming plants of upright, branching habit. Small yellow flowers grow in terminal panicles; plants grow 1'–3' tall. Usually restricted to cutting beds. This is the plant from which the famous Celtic war paint, woad, was made, but, sadly, its common use today is in the more prosaic art of flower arranging.

SOWING

INDOORS Start seeds outdoors only.
OUTDOORS Late summer.
DEPTH Just cover.

GERMINATING

TIME 14–42 days.
REQUIREMENTS 50°F.

PLANTING SEEDLINGS OUTDOORS

SPACING 6"–12".
LIGHT Sun or part shade.
SOIL Rich; can be either moist or dry, as long as it is well drained.

CARING FOR PLANTS

No special care required. Transplant only in early spring.

PROPAGATING

Self-seeds.

A-Annual P-Perennial B-Biennial HHA-Half-hardy annual HA-Hardy annual HB-Hardy biennial HHP-Half-hardy perennial HP-Hardy perennial HHBb-Half-hardy bulb HBb-Hardy bulb

162

Ixia

African corn lily, African iris, Corn lily

> TYPE HHBb
> ZONE A: 3–6; P: 7–10
> FLOWERING SEASON Spring to summer, depending on planting time

South African natives with grassy leaves and spikes of star-shaped flowers held on wiry, 1'–3' stems; flowers may be light blue, red, purple, or white.

SOWING

INDOORS Autumn.
OUTDOORS Seed: after last frost. Corm: In zones 3–6, plant in spring for late summer bloom. In zones 7–10, plant in late November for spring to early summer bloom.
DEPTH Seed: just cover. Corm: 4", on a cushion of sand.

Ixia maculata

GERMINATING

REQUIREMENTS Not often grown from seed, and little literature exists; information given here is only a general guideline. Bulb seeds usually require 60°–65°F for germination.

PLANTING SEEDLINGS OUTDOORS

TIME After 2 seasons of growth: spring in the North, autumn in the South.
SPACING 4".
LIGHT Sun or part shade, but the flowers close up in full sun.
SOIL Rich, well-drained.

CARING FOR PLANTS

Plants grown from seed will flower in 3 years. Water regularly from early spring until blooming has ceased. Provide a good winter mulch in zones 7 and 8. North of zone 7, lift corms when leaves die back in autumn and store in a dry, frost-free place over winter; replant in spring.

PROPAGATING

Divide cormels at planting time. Allow to self-seed in areas where no rain falls during the summer.

Ixiolirion

Lily-of-the-Altai, Siberian lily, Tartar lily

> TYPE HBb sometimes grown as A
> ZONE A: 3–6; P: 7–10
> FLOWERING SEASON Summer

Bulbous Asian plants growing 12"–16", bearing clusters of blue funnel-shaped flowers and grassy leaves. Dainty plants for rock gardens and drystone walls.

SOWING

INDOORS 8–10 weeks before planting out.
OUTDOORS Seed: early spring, when soil is cool and a light frost is still possible. Bulb: spring.
DEPTH Seed: just cover. Bulb: 2"–3".

GERMINATING

TIME 30–90 days.
REQUIREMENTS 50°F.

PLANTING SEEDLINGS OUTDOORS

TIME After last frost.
SPACING 4".
LIGHT Sun.
SOIL Hot, dry, sandy.

CARING FOR PLANTS

Top-dress with well-rotted cow manure in spring. North of zone 7, lift bulbs after leaves die back and store over winter in a cool, frost-free place.

PROPAGATING

Plant offsets in autumn.

Ixiolirion pallasii

A-Annual P-Perennial B-Biennial HHA-Half-hardy annual HA-Hardy annual HB-Hardy biennial HHP-Half-hardy perennial HP-Hardy perennial HHBb-Half-hardy bulb HBb-Hardy bulb

Jasione

Shepherd's scabious, Sheep's bit, Sheep's scabious

> TYPE HP, HB, or HA
> ZONE 5–9
> FLOWERING SEASON Summer

Genus of little-known summer-flowering plants, usually 9"–12", bearing blue or white pom-pom flowers in summer. Useful in rock gardens and borders.

SOWING

INDOORS 8–10 weeks before planting out, in peat pots.
OUTDOORS Early spring, when soil is cool and a light frost is still possible, or early autumn.
DEPTH Just cover.

GERMINATING

TIME 10–25 days.
REQUIREMENTS Easy. 70°F.

PLANTING SEEDLINGS OUTDOORS

TIME Early spring, when soil is cool and a light frost is still possible, or early autumn.
SPACING 8"–12".
LIGHT Full sun or light shade.
SOIL Well-drained, acid, not overly rich.

CARING FOR PLANTS

Easy. Mulch lightly in spring to keep the soil moist and remove flowering stems in autumn. Feed only sparingly, as overfertilizing results in lanky growth. Do not move established plants.

PROPAGATING

Divide in spring, or allow to self-seed.

Jeffersonia

Manchuria, Rheumatism root, Twinleaf

> TYPE HP
> ZONE 5–8. Prefers cool temperatures.
> FLOWERING SEASON Spring

Unusual and enchanting small woodland plants bearing distinctive two-lobed leaves and white or purple cup-shaped flowers held singly on rigid stems. Use in shady borders or mixed woodland plantings.

SOWING

INDOORS Start seeds outdoors only.
OUTDOORS As soon as fresh seed is available in late summer/early autumn.
DEPTH Just cover.

GERMINATING

TIME Up to 2 years.
REQUIREMENTS Sow seeds sparsely in flats, sink in the ground against a north-facing wall, and cover with glass. Moisten soil occasionally, if necessary. Transplant seedlings in the autumn of their second growing season.

PLANTING SEEDLINGS OUTDOORS

TIME Autumn.
SPACING 6"–10".
LIGHT Part to full shade.
SOIL Moist, rich, peaty, lime-free woods soil.

CARING FOR PLANTS

Mulch with compost to keep soil cool and moist; water during dry spells. Do not disturb. Will not tolerate hot, dry conditions.

PROPAGATING

Divide in spring (zones 5–6) or autumn (zones 7–8).

Jeffersonia diphylla

A-Annual P-Perennial B-Biennial HHA-Half-hardy annual HA-Hardy annual HB-Hardy biennial HHP-Half-hardy perennial HP-Hardy perennial HHBb-Half-hardy bulb HBb-Hardy bulb

164

Kaulfussia

See *Charieis*

Kirengeshoma

Yellow waxbells

TYPE HP
ZONE 5–8. Does not like hot, humid summers.
FLOWERING SEASON Late summer to autumn

Charming late-blooming perennials with attractive, lobed, maplelike leaves and clusters of cream, funnel-shaped flowers held on slim purple stems, 3'–4' tall. Subtle but stunning in the woodland garden.

SOWING

INDOORS Any time.
OUTDOORS After last frost.
DEPTH Just cover.

GERMINATING

TIME 30–300 days.
REQUIREMENTS 55°–65°F.

PLANTING SEEDLINGS OUTDOORS

TIME After last frost.
SPACING 24"–36".
LIGHT Part shade.
SOIL Cool, moist, rich, acid, and well-drained. Amend with organic matter at planting time.

CARING FOR PLANTS

Performs admirably when given the soil conditions it prefers. Allow plants to become established for 3–4 years before moving or dividing.

PROPAGATING

Divide in spring in zones 5–6, autumn in zones 7–8.

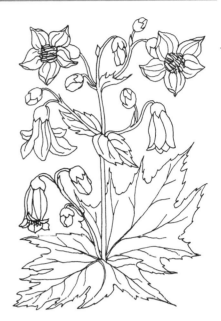

Kirengeshoma palmata

Kniphofia

(synonymous with *Tritoma*)

Red-hot-poker, Torch lily

TYPE HP
ZONE 5–9: K. *uvaria*; 7–9: K. *caulescens*, K. *triangularis*
FLOWERING SEASON Summer through autumn, depending on species

Genus of light-hearted perennials with coarse and rather messy, grasslike leaves and insolent flowers held on sturdy 2'–4' stems, the horticultural equivalent of the Swatch watch. Flower heads consist of a dense cluster of tiny downward-drooping tubes of yellow, orange, or green, sometimes more than one color appearing on each flowering head. Use in the border for dramatic interest.

SOWING

INDOORS 6–8 weeks before planting out, in peat pots.
OUTDOORS Seed: early spring, when soil is cool and a light frost is still possible, or late autumn. Rhizome: spring or autumn.
DEPTH Seed: ¼". Rhizome: 2"–3".

GERMINATING

TIME 10–30 days.
REQUIREMENTS 70°–75°F.

PLANTING SEEDLINGS OUTDOORS

TIME After last spring frost or in autumn.
SPACING Small species: 12"–15". Large species: 18"–24".
LIGHT Sun, or part shade where summers are very hot.
SOIL Rich, deep, moist, well-drained, with a pH level of 6.0–7.5.

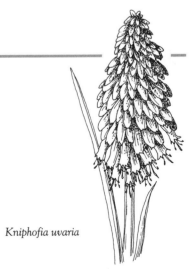

Kniphofia uvaria

CARING FOR PLANTS

Easy. Water well while buds are setting in spring. Cut back flower stems to base after blooming. Plants resent root disturbance; divide very carefully no more than every 4–5 years.

PROPAGATING

Divide in spring; propagate cultivars by division rather than seed.

A-Annual P-Perennial B-Biennial HHA-Half-hardy annual HA-Hardy annual HB-Hardy biennial HHP-Half-hardy perennial HP-Hardy perennial HHBb-Half-hardy bulb HBb-Hardy bulb

165

Kochia

Belvedere, Burning bush, Firebush, Mexican firebush, Summer cypress

> TYPE HA or HHA
> ZONE 2–10. Prefers warm temperatures and will perform well in very hot weather.
> FLOWERING SEASON Summer

Upright, shrubby annuals grown for their fine, lance-shaped leaves which are intense green in summer, turning to deep red in autumn. These 24"–36" plants are most often used to form hedges, but also make unusual container plants.

SOWING

INDOORS 6–8 weeks before planting out, in peat pots.
OUTDOORS 1–2 weeks before last frost.
DEPTH Surface.

GERMINATING

TIME 10–15 days.
REQUIREMENTS Soak seeds for 24 hours; provide light and 70°–75°F thereafter.

PLANTING SEEDLINGS OUTDOORS

TIME Late spring.
SPACING 8" for hedging, otherwise 18"–24".
LIGHT Full sun.
SOIL Average, with a pH level of 6.0–7.0; tolerant of dry soil.

CARING FOR PLANTS

Easy. Water regularly and feed with a high-nitrogen fertilizer several times during the summer.

PROPAGATING

Often self-seeds and may become invasive.

Koeleria

(not to be confused with *Kohleria*)

Blue hair grass, Blue June grass, Blue meadow grass

> TYPE HP
> ZONE 4–9. Does not like hot climates.
> FLOWERING SEASON Spring to early summer

Genus of annual and perennial grasses, only a few of which are of ornamental interest. Flat leaves are 6"–18" long, midgreen or deep blue; neat, close-cropped inflorescences are held on long stems above the foliage. Use in mixed grass plantings.

SOWING

INDOORS Start seeds outdoors.
OUTDOORS Early spring to midspring.
DEPTH Seed: surface. Tuber: 2".

GERMINATING

TIME 4–21 days.
REQUIREMENTS 60°–75°F.

PLANTING SEEDLINGS OUTDOORS

SPACING 6"–12".
LIGHT Full sun.
SOIL Sandy, well-drained, neither too acid nor too fertile.

CARING FOR PLANTS

Water occasionally during dry spells. Plants are short-lived and will need replacing every 1–2 years.

PROPAGATING

Divide in spring (zones 4–6) or autumn (zones 7–9).

A-Annual P-Perennial B-Biennial HHA-Half-hardy annual HA-Hardy annual HB-Hardy biennial HHP-Half-hardy perennial HP-Hardy perennial HHBb-Half-hardy bulb HBb-Hardy bulb

166

Lagerstroemia

Crape myrtle, Crape myrtlette

> TYPE HHP
> ZONE 7–10
> FLOWERING SEASON July through frost

These crape myrtles are actually dwarf shrubs grown as half-hardy perennials. Plants are 12" mounds covered from summer through frost in panicles of ruffled blossoms in shades of pink, purple, or white. Excellent container or specimen plants.

SOWING

INDOORS 6–8 weeks before planting out.
OUTDOORS After last frost.
DEPTH Surface.

GERMINATING

TIME 14–21 days.
REQUIREMENTS Easy. Light and 70°–75°F.

PLANTING SEEDLINGS OUTDOORS

TIME 2–3 weeks after last frost, when temperatures remain above 40°F.
SPACING 12"–24".
LIGHT Full sun.
SOIL Fertile, moist.

CARING FOR PLANTS

Easy. Keep soil moist and feed monthly during the growing season. Prune in spring.

PROPAGATING

Take hardwood cuttings in autumn.

Lagurus

Hare's tail, Rabbit-tail grass

> TYPE HA
> ZONE 3–10. Prefers warm climates.
> FLOWERING SEASON Summer

Genus of one annual ornamental grass bearing short 4" leaves and masses of slender 1' stems tipped with silky inflorescences. This Mediterranean native is sufficiently compact to be used in the border.

SOWING

INDOORS 6–8 weeks before last frost.
OUTDOORS 3 weeks before last spring frost, or early autumn.
DEPTH ¼".

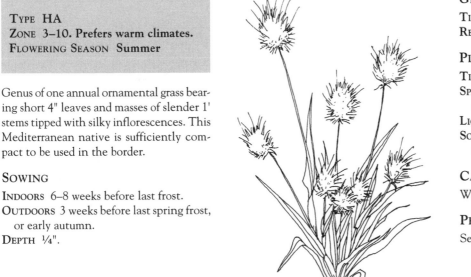

Lagurus ovatus

GERMINATING

TIME 15–21 days.
REQUIREMENTS 55°F.

PLANTING SEEDLINGS OUTDOORS

TIME After last frost.
SPACING Small species: 4"–6". Large species: 12".
LIGHT Sun.
SOIL Light, well-drained; tolerates dry conditions.

CARING FOR PLANTS

Water regularly for best results.

PROPAGATING

Self-seeds.

A-Annual P-Perennial B-Biennial HHA-Half-hardy annual HA-Hardy annual HB-Hardy biennial HHP-Half-hardy perennial HP-Hardy perennial HHBb-Half-hardy bulb HBb-Hardy bulb

Lamium

Cobbler's bench, Dead nettle, Yellow archangel

TYPE HP
ZONE 3–8
FLOWERING SEASON Late spring to early summer

Large genus of plants that are mainly weedy, although those that are of horticultural interest are quite beautiful. Low-growing, trailing or mounding plants have attractive foliage (sometimes silver or variegated) and short spikes of white or purple flowers reminiscent of snapdragons. Handsome ground cover or member of a mixed shady planting.

SOWING

INDOORS 8–10 weeks before planting out.
OUTDOORS White and purple species: spring. Yellow species: autumn.
DEPTH Just cover.

GERMINATING

TIME 30–60 days.
REQUIREMENTS Easy. 65°–70°F.

PLANTING SEEDLINGS OUTDOORS

TIME Spring or autumn.
SPACING 12"–18".
LIGHT Full sun or part shade.
SOIL Prefers a fairly poor soil that is well drained, particularly in winter.

CARING FOR PLANTS

Easy. May become invasive. Feed once in spring; shear back after flowering to maintain a tidy appearance. Leaves may be attractive to slugs.

PROPAGATING

Take root cuttings in spring. Divide in spring (autumn zones 7–8).

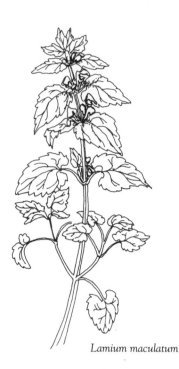

Lamium maculatum

Lampranthus

TYPE HHP
ZONE 9–10. Not tolerant of high heat combined with humidity.
FLOWERING SEASON Spring

Genus of low-growing, succulent perennials prized for the stunning, brightly colored, daisylike flowers that clothe them in spring; blooms may be orange, purple, white, or pink. Use in containers or dry, sunny beds.

SOWING

INDOORS 6–8 weeks before planting out.
OUTDOORS After last frost.
DEPTH Just cover.

GERMINATING

TIME 15–30 days.
REQUIREMENTS Darkness and 65°–75°F.

PLANTING SEEDLINGS OUTDOORS

TIME Spring, when temperatures remain steadily above 40°F.
SPACING Small species: 6"–8". Large species: 18"–24".
LIGHT Full sun.
SOIL Dry, stony, very well-drained, and amended with well-rotted manure.

CARING FOR PLANTS

Easy. Water only during prolonged dry spells and remove dead stems in autumn. Renew every few years when plants become woody.

PROPAGATING

Take cuttings in spring.

A-Annual P-Perennial B-Biennial HHA-Half-hardy annual HA-Hardy annual HB-Hardy biennial HHP-Half-hardy perennial HP-Hardy perennial HHBb-Half-hardy bulb HBb-Hardy bulb

Lantana

Red sage, Yellow sage

> **Type** HHP usually grown as HHA
> **Zone** A: must have warm temperatures; P: 8–10
> **Flowering Season** July to frost

Evergreen where it is hardy, some species of this bushy plant are widely grown as annuals for their neat clusters of red, yellow, pink, lilac, white, or orange blooms; 12"–24". Grow in containers or warm, sunny beds.

SOWING

Indoors 6–8 weeks before planting out.
Outdoors Start seeds outdoors in the South only, in late winter or early spring.
Depth ⅛".

GERMINATING

Time 30–90 days.
Requirements Soak seeds for 24 hours in warm water and provide a constant 70°–75°F thereafter.

PLANTING SEEDLINGS OUTDOORS

Time In the spring, when temperatures remain above 50°F.
Spacing 12"–18".
Light Full sun or light shade.
Soil Average.

CARING FOR PLANTS

Easy. Pinch back young plants to encourage bushiness. Water deeply in summer. Plants can be potted up in autumn and overwintered indoors; replant outdoors in spring. Susceptible to red spider mites and whitefly.

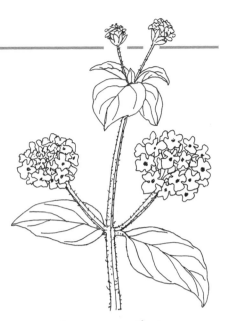

Lantana montevidensis

PROPAGATING

Take cuttings in spring or summer.

Lapageria

Chilean bell flower, Copihue

> **Type** HHP
> **Zone** 8–10
> **Flowering Season** Midsummer to autumn

Genus of one species of exotic vine bearing long, luscious, deep pink trumpets; leaves are leathery and sharply pointed. This native of Chile is suitable only for warm outdoor locations.

SOWING

Indoors As soon as ripe seed is available, usually early autumn.
Outdoors Start seeds indoors only.
Depth ⅛".

GERMINATING

Time 30–90 days.
Requirements Difficult. 65°–75°F.

PLANTING SEEDLINGS OUTDOORS

Time Grow indoors for 2 years, planting out after last spring frost.
Spacing Singly.
Light Prefers full shade; at the least, must be shaded from hot afternoon sun.
Soil Humus-rich, very well-drained.

CARING FOR PLANTS

Water well during dry spells. Mulch lightly in winter with straw.

PROPAGATING

Take cuttings in spring or autumn.

A-Annual P-Perennial B-Biennial HHA-Half-hardy annual HA-Hardy annual HB-Hardy biennial HHP-Half-hardy perennial HP-Hardy perennial HHBb-Half-hardy bulb HBb-Hardy bulb

Lapeirousia

(synonymous with *Anomatheca*)

> TYPE HBb sometimes grown as A
> ZONE A: 3–6; P: 7–10
> FLOWERING SEASON Late summer
> to autumn

Small, upright bulbs with narrow, sword-shaped leaves, and spikes of red, white, or pink tubular flowers, some spotted; 6"–12" tall. Flowers are followed by egg-shaped seed pods. Use in the rock garden or border.

SOWING
INDOORS 8–10 weeks before planting out.
OUTDOORS Seed: early spring, when soil is cool and a light frost is still possible, or late autumn in zones 9–10. Corm: early autumn.
DEPTH Seed: ⅛". Corm: 2"–4".

GERMINATING
TIME 30–90 days.
REQUIREMENTS 55°–60°F.

PLANTING SEEDLINGS OUTDOORS
TIME Early spring.
SPACING 3"–5".
LIGHT Sun; part shade where summers are very hot.
SOIL Well-drained, acid, dry.

CARING FOR PLANTS
Do not allow soil to dry out during spring and summer. Divide every few years to maintain vigor. North of zone 7, dig up corms and store in trays in a cool, frost-free location over winter.

PROPAGATING
Divide cormels in spring. Allow to self-seed in the South.

Lathyrus (Annual)

(includes *L. chloranthus*, *L. odoratus*, *L. tingitanus*)

Sweetpea

> TYPE HA
> ZONE 1–10. Prefers long, cool
> summers.
> FLOWERING SEASON Early spring
> to autumn, depending on species

Genus of erect or climbing plants reaching 2'–10', grown for their prolific butterflylike flowers in both intense and delicate shades; some are gloriously fragrant. Allow plants to sprawl along the ground or grow on a fence or trellis; small species are attractive in the border or cottage garden.

SOWING
INDOORS 6–8 weeks before last frost.
OUTDOORS Early spring, when soil is cool and a light frost is still possible. Where winters are mild, a second sowing in late autumn will produce winter blooms.
DEPTH ½".

GERMINATING
TIME 10–20 days.
REQUIREMENTS Chip seeds or soak in warm water for 24 hours. Inoculate with nitrogen-fixing bacteria. Provide 55°–65°F.

PLANTING SEEDLINGS OUTDOORS
TIME After last frost.
SPACING Vine: 6". Bush: 12".
LIGHT Full sun.
SOIL Prepare ground in autumn to a depth of 12"–18", adding plenty of compost and bonemeal. Prefers a pH level of 6.0–7.0.

CARING FOR PLANTS
Water during dry spells and mulch to keep soil cool. Fertilize with a weak solution several times during the growing season. Deadhead often to prolong blooming. Provide a trellis for large species or stake plants when 4" tall. Change location every year to avoid disease problems.

PROPAGATING
Seed only.

A-Annual P-Perennial B-Biennial HHA-Half-hardy annual HA-Hardy annual HB-Hardy biennial HHP-Half-hardy perennial HP-Hardy perennial HHBb-Half-hardy bulb HBb-Hardy bulb

Lathyrus (Perennial)

(includes *L. grandiflorus, L. japonicus, L. latifolius, L. gmelinii, L. nervosus, L. rotundifolius, L. sylvestris, L. vernus*)

Everlasting pea, Lord Anson's blue pea, Perennial pea, Spring vetch, Sweetpea

TYPE HP
ZONE 4–9; 6–9: *L. nervosus*
FLOWERING SEASON Late spring to summer

Genus of erect or climbing plants reaching 2'–10', grown for their prolific butterflylike flowers in both intense and delicate shades; some are gloriously fragrant. Allow plants to sprawl along the ground or grow on a fence or trellis; small species are attractive in the border or cottage garden.

SOWING

INDOORS 6–8 weeks before planting out, in peat pots.

OUTDOORS Early spring, when soil is cool and a light frost is still possible, or late summer to early autumn where winters are mild. Seeds can be sown earlier in spring if soil is heated by stretching black landscaping plastic over beds in late winter. To sow seeds, make slits in the plastic. When seedlings reach 4"–6", apply mulch over the plastic to keep plants cool.
DEPTH ¼".

GERMINATING

TIME 20–30 days.
REQUIREMENTS Chip seeds or soak for 24 hours in warm water. Inoculate with nitrogen-fixing bacteria. Provide a constant 55°–65°F.

PLANTING SEEDLINGS OUTDOORS

TIME After last frost.
SPACING 6"–10".
LIGHT Full sun to light shade.

Lathyrus latifolius

SOIL Prepare beds deeply, adding well-rotted manure and bonemeal. A pH level of 6.0–7.5 is preferred.

CARING FOR PLANTS

Easy. Water and deadhead regularly while plants are in bloom. Mulch to keep soil cool.

PROPAGATING

Most successfully propagated by seed.

Lavandula

Lavender

TYPE HP
ZONE 5–9
FLOWERING SEASON Late spring to summer

Genus of 1'–3' tall evergreen shrubs widely used in borders and herb gardens. Narrow, somewhat fleshy leaves are often fragrant; tiny, tubular flowers colored blue or shades of purple are clustered at the ends of long, slim stems. Attractive container or hedge plants for informal gardens.

SOWING

INDOORS 6–8 weeks before planting out.
OUTDOORS Early spring, when soil is cool and a light frost is still possible, or early autumn.
DEPTH Just cover.

GERMINATING

TIME 15–90 days.

REQUIREMENTS Place seeds together with moistened growing medium in a plastic bag and refrigerate for 4–6 weeks. Requires 55°–65°F thereafter.

CHARLES JOSLIN

Lavendula officinalis

PLANTING SEEDLINGS OUTDOORS

TIME After last frost.
SPACING 15"–18".
LIGHT Full sun.
SOIL Ordinary, well-drained, somewhat poor, with a pH level of 6.5–7.5.

CARING FOR PLANTS

Easy. Prune back hard in early spring and cut off all dead flower stalks after blooming. Fertilizing will decrease flowers' fragrance. Harvest flowers when buds are barely open and dry in a warm place for several weeks; remove flowers from stems before storing. Try growing *L. dentata* or *L. stoechas* indoors: Add lime to commercial potting soil, feed occasionally with half-strength fertilizer, water sparingly, and give at least 4 hours sunlight a day.

PROPAGATING

Take cuttings in spring or summer.

A-Annual P-Perennial B-Biennial HHA-Half-hardy annual HA-Hardy annual HB-Hardy biennial HHP-Half-hardy perennial HP-Hardy perennial HHBb-Half-hardy bulb HBb-Hardy bulb

171

Lavatera

Annual mallow, Mallow, Tree mallow

> TYPE HA, HB, or HP; usually grown as HA
> ZONE A: 2–10; P: 8–10; 4–10: *L. cachemiriana*, *L. thuringiaca*. Prefers the mild West Coast climates.
> FLOWERING SEASON Perennial: summer. Annual: summer to frost, if sown continuously

Erect, somewhat shrubby plants grown for their charming cup- or trumpet-shaped flowers in shades of pink, purple, or white, blooming over a long period. Leaves are handsome, often maple-shaped; plants grow from 2'–6'. At home in cottage gardens and borders.

SOWING

INDOORS 6–8 weeks before last frost, in peat pots.
OUTDOORS Early spring, when soil is cool and a light frost is still possible. For continuous blooming, sow annuals at intervals throughout the spring until nighttime temperatures become warm. Seeds may also be sown in early autumn in the South.
DEPTH Just cover.

GERMINATING

TIME 15–20 days.
REQUIREMENTS Easy. 70°F.

PLANTING SEEDLINGS OUTDOORS

TIME After last frost.
SPACING Small species: 12"–18". Large species: 24"–36".
LIGHT Full sun.
SOIL Moist, well-drained. Soil that is too rich will produce lush foliage but few flowers.

CARING FOR PLANTS

Easy. Water and deadhead regularly. Feed monthly with a low-nitrogen fertilizer. Leave plants undisturbed.

PROPAGATING

Take cuttings in early summer, or allow to self-seed.

Layia

Tidy tips

> TYPE HA
> ZONE 3–10. Prefers cool temperatures.
> FLOWERING SEASON Late spring to autumn

Genus of annuals native to western North America that are fast-growing and long-blooming. Grey-green foliage is smothered in yellow daisylike flowers with white, serrated edges. Plants are bushy, 18"–24" tall.

SOWING

INDOORS 6–8 weeks before planting out.
OUTDOORS After last frost, or late summer where winters are mild.
DEPTH ⅛".

GERMINATING

TIME 8–36 days.
REQUIREMENTS 70°–75°F.

PLANTING SEEDLINGS OUTDOORS

TIME After last frost.
SPACING Small species: 4"–8". Large species: 12"–15".
LIGHT Full sun or part shade.
SOIL Light, well-drained, with a pH level of 5.0–8.0.

CARING FOR PLANTS

Easy. Water regularly and feed monthly.

PROPAGATING

Seed only; *Layia* will self-seed in its native habitat.

A-Annual P-Perennial B-Biennial HHA-Half-hardy annual HA-Hardy annual HB-Hardy biennial HHP-Half-hardy perennial HP-Hardy perennial HHBb-Half-hardy bulb HBb-Hardy bulb

172

Leontopodium

Edelweiss

TYPE HP
ZONE 4–7. All edelweiss prefer
cool temperatures, although
L. leontopodioides is somewhat
heat tolerant.
FLOWERING SEASON Late spring to
summer

Compact 12" perennials bearing bright white, star-shaped flowers above woolly, lance-shaped leaves. Native to the mountains of Asia, Europe, and South America, these short-lived plants are suited only to rock gardens.

SOWING

INDOORS 8–10 weeks before last frost.
OUTDOORS Early spring, when soil is cool and a light frost is still possible.
DEPTH Surface.

Leontopodium alpinum

GERMINATING

TIME 10–42 days.
REQUIREMENTS Easy. Place seeds and moistened growing medium in a lightly sealed plastic bag and refrigerate for 3 weeks. Provide light and 50°F thereafter.

PLANTING SEEDLINGS OUTDOORS

TIME After last frost.
SPACING Small species: 3"–6". Large species: 6"–12".
LIGHT Part shade.
SOIL Gritty, loose soil, with a pH level of 6.5–7.5.

CARING FOR PLANTS

Plants prefer a winter mulch of snow; where there is no constant snow cover, mulch lightly, removing mulch in early spring. Shield from winter rains. Edelweiss is short-lived, requiring division every 2 years.

PROPAGATING

Carefully divide plants in spring.

Leucojum

Loddon lily, Snowflake, Summer snowflake

TYPE HBb
ZONE 4–9: *L. aestivum*,
L. vernum; 6–9: *L. autumnale*
FLOWERING SEASON Late winter,
late spring, or autumn, depending on species

Spring- and autumn-blooming bulbs grown for their showy white flowers resembling clusters of tiny bells. Leaves are grassy or strap-shaped; plants grow from 4" to 3'. Effective when massed under shrubs; woodland species brighten up shady plantings.

SOWING

OUTDOORS Bulb: October to early November.
DEPTH Bulb: 3"–4".

GERMINATING

REQUIREMENTS Growing from seed not recommended.

PLANTING SEEDLINGS OUTDOORS

SPACING 6".
LIGHT Full sun to part shade.
SOIL Woodsy, rather damp but well drained.

CARING FOR PLANTS

Easy. Allow leaves to wither naturally before removing. Do not disturb except to divide every 5–8 years.

PROPAGATING

Plant bulblets in autumn.

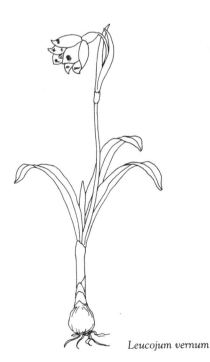
Leucojum vernum

A-Annual P-Perennial B-Biennial HHA-Half-hardy annual HA-Hardy annual HB-Hardy biennial HHP-Half-hardy perennial HP-Hardy perennial HHBb-Half-hardy bulb HBb-Hardy bulb

Levisticum

Lovage

TYPE HP
ZONE 4–8
FLOWERING SEASON Midsummer

Imposing herb growing 3'–7'. Foliage is dark green, resembling flat parsley; tiny yellow flowers growing in umbels resemble Queen Anne's lace. Allow plenty of room in the herb garden.

SOWING

INDOORS 6–8 weeks before planting out, in peat pots.
OUTDOORS As soon as seed is ripe (late summer to early autumn).
DEPTH ¼".

GERMINATING

TIME 10–20 days.
REQUIREMENTS Sow seeds thickly, as the germination rate is poor; provide 60°–70°F.

PLANTING SEEDLINGS OUTDOORS

TIME After last frost.
SPACING 24"–36"; 1 or 2 plants will be sufficient for a household.
LIGHT Full sun to light shade.
SOIL Rich, moist, well-drained, with a pH level of 6.0–7.0. Amend with compost or cow manure at planting time.

CARING FOR PLANTS

Feed once in spring with compost, manure, or 5–10–5. Discard any leaves infested with leaf miner. If growing to use leaves, cut back flowering stems before blooms form. Harvest leaves of 2-year-old plants 3 times throughout the season. Leaves can be used either fresh, dried, or frozen (blanch before freezing). Harvest seeds when fruit begins to open. Cut seed head, and hang in a cool, dark place to dry.

PROPAGATING

Divide in early spring.

Lewisia

Bitterroot

TYPE HP
ZONE 4–7: *L. nevadensis;*
4–8: *L. columbiana,*
L. cotyledon. **Does not perform well where summers are hot and humid.**
FLOWERING SEASON Spring through early summer

Genus of rosette-forming perennials with succulent leaves; some species are evergreen. Cup-shaped flowers of white, red, pink, or purple are held on stiff stems. Best suited to rock gardens or moist drystone walls.

SOWING

INDOORS 10–12 weeks before planting out.
OUTDOORS As soon as seeds are ripe, in late autumn or early winter.
DEPTH Surface.

Lewisia cotyledon

GERMINATING

TIME 1–2 years.
REQUIREMENTS Difficult. Place seeds together with moistened growing medium in a plastic bag and refrigerate for 5 weeks. Provide light and 50°–60°F thereafter.

PLANTING SEEDLINGS OUTDOORS

TIME Plant out in spring after 1 year of growth.
SPACING Small species: 2"–4". Larger species: 6"–8".
LIGHT Full sun or light shade.
SOIL Prefers moist, rich, rather gritty, with a pH level of 5.0–8.0; tolerant of dry soil.

CARING FOR PLANTS

Difficult. To avoid crown rot, set crowns 1" above the soil level and surround with stone chips. Keep soil moist during flowering, but protect plants from overhead water.

PROPAGATING

Root detached rosettes in summer.

Liatris

Blazing star, Button snake root, Gay feather, Prairie pine, Prairie snake root

TYPE HP
ZONE 3–10
FLOWERING SEASON Summer to early autumn

Cheerful perennials that lift the spirits with their mass of purple- or white-tipped flowering stems that erupt from a base of hairy leaves like fireworks shooting skyward. Plants grow from 2' to 6' and are invaluable in the summer border or wildflower garden.

Liatris spicata

SOWING

INDOORS 6–8 weeks before last frost.
OUTDOORS Early spring when soil is cool and a light frost still possible, or early autumn.
DEPTH Just cover.

GERMINATING

TIME 20–25 days.
REQUIREMENTS 55°–75°F.

PLANTING SEEDLINGS OUTDOORS

TIME After last frost.
SPACING 12"–15".
LIGHT Full sun to light shade.
SOIL Prefers a sandy, rich loam with a pH level of 5.5–7.5; will tolerate poor, dry soil. Excellent winter drainage is essential.

CARING FOR PLANTS

Easy. Water during dry spells. Remove flowering stems after blooming. Mulch with well-rotted manure in spring; surround plants with fine gravel where soil is wet.

PROPAGATING

Divide in spring.

Libertia

TYPE HP or HHP
ZONE 8–10. *Libertia* only grows successfully on the Pacific Coast.
FLOWERING SEASON Summer

Clump-forming perennials with grassy foliage out of which emerge stiff spikes topped with clusters of dainty white flowers followed by showy orange seed pods; plants are 1'–3' tall and are useful in the border.

SOWING

INDOORS See "Germinating, Requirements."
OUTDOORS See "Germinating, Requirements."
DEPTH ⅛".

GERMINATING

TIME 1–6 months.
REQUIREMENTS *Autumn sowing:* Sow seeds in flats, sink in the ground against a north-facing wall, and cover with glass. Moisten soil occasionally, if necessary. Bring flats indoors in spring to 50°F. *Spring sowing:* Sow seeds in flats of moistened medium, place in a plastic bags, and refrigerate for 2–3 weeks. Sink flats in the ground in a shady location, covering with glass. Transplant seedlings as they appear.

PLANTING SEEDLINGS OUTDOORS

TIME After last frost.
SPACING 18"–24".
LIGHT Sun.
SOIL Sandy, moist, well-drained loam.

CARING FOR PLANTS

Shelter plants from wind and keep soil moist to prevent leaf tips from browning. Leaves become ragged wtih age; remove unkempt plants to make room for volunteers.

PROPAGATING

Divide in spring, or allow to self-seed.

A-Annual P-Perennial B-Biennial HHA-Half-hardy annual HA-Hardy annual HB-Hardy biennial HHP-Half-hardy perennial HP-Hardy perennial HHBb-Half-hardy bulb HBb-Hardy bulb

175

Ligularia

Goldenray, Leopard plant

TYPE HP
ZONE 4–8
FLOWERING SEASON Summer

Genus of coarse but intriguing perennials growing 2'–6' tall. Yellow flowers held on tall stalks may grow singly like large daisies or in long, dramatic racemes; leaves are generally large and leathery. Most effective when massed near water or in shady beds; contrast well with fine-textured plants.

SOWING

INDOORS 6–8 weeks before planting out.
OUTDOORS Early spring, when soil is cool and a light frost is still possible, or early autumn.

DEPTH Surface.

GERMINATING

TIME 14–42 days.
REQUIREMENTS 55°–65°F.

PLANTING SEEDLINGS OUTDOORS

TIME Spring.
SPACING 24"–36".
LIGHT Full sun; sun or part shade where summers are hot.
SOIL Ordinary, moist.

CARING FOR PLANTS

Easy. Water well during dry weather and feed occasionally in spring and summer. Remove flower stalks after blooming to maintain a neat appearance, and cut back to ground level in autumn. Divide every 3 years.

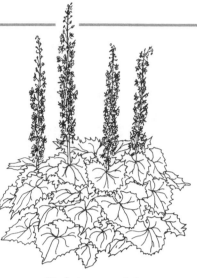

Ligularia stenocephala

PROPAGATING

Divide in spring.

Lilium

Annunciation lily, Bamboo lily, Bulbil lily, Golden-rayed lily of Japan, Japanese lily, Lemon lily, Leopard lily, Lily, Madonna lily, Martagon lily, Meadow lily, Regal lily, Royal lily, Turk's-cap lily

TYPE HBb or HHBb
ZONE 4–7: Asiatic hybrids, Aurelian hybrids; 4–8: American hybrids; 4–9: *L. amabile*, *L. canadense*, *L. candidum*, *L. hansonii*, *L. henryi*, *L. lancifolium*, *L. martagon*, *L. monadelphum*, *L. regale*; 5–9: Candidum hybrids, Oriental hybrids, *L. auratum*, *L. concolor*, *L. × hollandicum*, *L. maculatum*, *L. michiganense*, *L. philadelphicum*, *L. pyrenaicum*, *L. speciosum*, *L. superbum*; 6–9: *L. formosanum*, *L. japonicum*; 7–9: *L. columbianum*, *L. parryi*, *L. washingtonianum*; 8–9: *L. longiflorum*. Most lilies perform poorly in extreme heat.
FLOWERING SEASON Late spring through late summer, depending on species

Genus of bulbs prized for their exquisite trumpet-shaped blooms. Stems are strong, upright, and unbranched, 1'–6' tall, usually bearing whorled, lance-shaped leaves; flowers are large and beautifully colored, often fragrant. Mass or grow individually in formal or naturalistic plantings; small species make excellent container plants. A perfect addition to any border.

SOWING

INDOORS Any time.
OUTDOORS Seed: early spring, when soil is cool and a light frost is still possible, or early autumn. Bulb: early spring or autumn.
DEPTH Seed: ¼". Bulb: *L. candidum*: 2"–3". *L. auratum*: 6". *L. regale*: 8"–9". A good rule of thumb is to plant bulbs with their bottoms resting at a depth 3 times the diameter of the bulb.

GERMINATING

TIME 1–8 months.
REQUIREMENTS Soak seeds for 24 hours, then place in a bag together with moist growing medium, and seal lightly. Leave at around 70°F. After 4 weeks begin to check for growth. Move the bag to the refrigerator when first bulblets appear and chill for 2–3 months. Plant bulblets in individual pots.

PLANTING SEEDLINGS OUTDOORS

TIME Plant out seed-grown bulbs in their second spring, after last frost.
SPACING Small species: 9"–12". Large species: 12"–24".
LIGHT Full sun to light shade, depending on species. Plant *L. hansonii*, *L. japonicum*, and *L. martagon*, only in a partly shady location.
SOIL Most lilies require moist, well-drained, slightly acid soil. *L. canadense* requires moist to wet soil; *L. henryi* and *L. monadelphum* prefer limy soil.

CARING FOR PLANTS

Plants grown from seed will bloom in 2–4 years. Mulch soil in spring and water well during the growing season, tapering off towards winter. Feed in early spring and again after flowering. Stake tall species individually. Deadhead regularly to maintain a neat appearance and cut back stems to soil line after first frost. Many lilies do not bloom well in extreme heat; some are short-lived and require regular replacing.

PROPAGATING

Plant bulbils or bulb scales in late summer or early autumn.

Limnanthes

Fried eggs, Marsh flower, Meadow foam

> TYPE HA
> ZONE Prefers the cool temperatures of the Pacific Northwest.
> FLOWERING SEASON Spring through late summer, depending on sowing time

Genus of annuals, only one of which is commonly grown. This is a spreading plant, 1' tall, covered in fragrant, cup-shaped flowers that are yellow, deeply edged with a white border. Use in rock gardens, at the front of the border, or edging a path.

SOWING

INDOORS Best started outdoors.
OUTDOORS For summer blooms sow in early spring, when soil is cool and a light frost is still possible. Sow in late autumn for early spring flowers.
DEPTH Just cover.

GERMINATING

TIME 14–21 days.
REQUIREMENTS 50°–60°F.

PLANTING SEEDLINGS OUTDOORS

TIME After last frost.
SPACING 4".
LIGHT Sun or part shade.
SOIL Cool, moist, well-drained. Tolerates wet soil. Maintain pH level of 5.5–6.5.

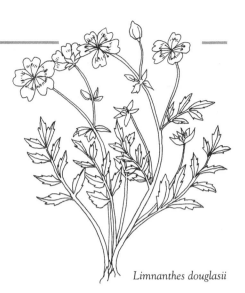

Limnanthes douglasii

CARING FOR PLANTS

Easy. Water regularly during dry spells. After first heavy spring flowering, allow seeds to mature and disburse, then remove plants and replace with summer bloomers. New seedlings will bloom in autumn.

PROPAGATING

Self-seeds.

Limonium

Sea lavender, Sea pink, Statice

> TYPE HHA, HHP, or HP
> ZONE A: 2–10; P: 4–9; *L. latifolium, L. tataricum*; 9–10: *L. perezii*
> FLOWERING SEASON Late spring to autumn, depending on species

Large genus of annuals and perennials grown for their flowers, which vary considerably among species. Plants grow from 8"–36", often having coarse woody stems. Flowers grow in panicles or spikes; many resemble tiny papery trumpets, often in rather unnatural colors; the most commonly grown species are everlasting. More refined specimens are attractive in the front of the border; mass coarser plants in a distant border or cutting bed.

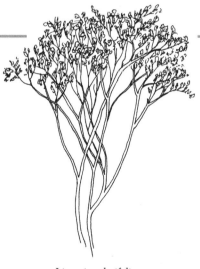

Limonium latifolium

SOWING

INDOORS 6–8 weeks before last frost.
OUTDOORS A: after last frost. P: early spring, when soil is cool and a light frost is still possible.
DEPTH Just cover.

GERMINATING

TIME 10–20 days.
REQUIREMENTS 65°–75°F.

PLANTING SEEDLINGS OUTDOORS

TIME After last frost, plant out half-hardy species when the temperatures remain above 45°F.
SPACING Small species: 12"–15". Large species: 12"–24".
LIGHT Full sun.
SOIL Light, sandy. Tolerant of very dry soil.

CARING FOR PLANTS

Easy. Water only when soil is dry and feed once annually. Plants grown in fertile soil may require staking. Cut plants back to ground level in autumn. Do not move.

PROPAGATING

Sow seeds for annuals. Divide perennial spring bloomers in autumn; divide autumn-blooming species in early spring.

A-Annual P-Perennial B-Biennial HHA-Half-hardy annual HA-Hardy annual HB-Hardy biennial HHP-Half-hardy perennial HP-Hardy perennial HHBb-Half-hardy bulb HBb-Hardy bulb

Linaria

**Baby snapdragon, Butter and eggs,
Spurred snapdragon,
Three-birds-flying, Toadflax**

> **TYPE** HA or HP
> **ZONE** A: 2–10; P: 4–9: *L. alpina,*
> *L. dalmatica, L. nevadensis,*
> *L. pupurea, L. vulgaris;*
> 8–10: *L. triornithophora.* Prefers
> cool temperatures.
> **FLOWERING SEASON** Late spring to
> summer; midsummer where
> climate is cool

Upright plants with lance-shaped leaves out of which shoot stiff spikes bearing small, snapdragonlike flowers in an incredible range of colors: violet, orange, yellow, white, purple, pink, maroon, and gold, to name just a few. Plants grow from 6" to 4'. Small species are useful in rock gardens, drystone walls, or between paving stones; larger species are invaluable in the spring border.

Linaria maroccana

SOWING

INDOORS Pre-chilled seeds 6–8 weeks before planting out.
OUTDOORS 2–3 weeks before last frost, and at intervals to extend the blooming period; where winters are mild, sow in early autumn.
DEPTH Just cover.

GERMINATING

TIME 10–15 days.
REQUIREMENTS Easy. Place seeds in a plastic bag together with moist growing medium and refrigerate for 3 weeks. Provide light and a constant temperature of 55°–60°F thereafter.

PLANTING SEEDLINGS OUTDOORS

TIME After last frost.
SPACING Small species: 8"–10". Large species: 24"–36".
LIGHT Full sun.
SOIL Any.

CARING FOR PLANTS

Easy. Water during dry spells. Cut back annuals after blooming to stimulate a more abundant second bloom. Perennials bloom more successfully if thinned occasionally, but intense summer heat will stop blooming altogether. Some species can become invasive.

PROPAGATING

Allow annuals to self-seed. Take cuttings of perennials in early summer, or divide in spring.

Linnaea

Twin-flower

> **TYPE** HP
> **ZONE** 1–5
> **FLOWERING SEASON** Late spring to
> early summer

Delightful little woodland subshrubs whose diminutive proportions give them a fairyland quality. Leaves are small, rounded, and evergreen. Flowers are bell-shaped, fragrant, pink or white, borne in pairs on thin, wiry stems high above the foliage. Use as a shady ground cover for small areas or in rock gardens.

SOWING

INDOORS Sow seed outdoors only.
OUTDOORS As soon as ripe seed is available.
DEPTH Just cover.

GERMINATING

TIME Very slow.
REQUIREMENTS Difficult; seed is rarely available commercially. Sow in flats, sink in the ground against a north-facing wall, and cover with glass. Moisten soil occasionally, if necessary. Transplant seedlings as they appear.

PLANTING SEEDLINGS OUTDOORS

TIME Set out purchased plants in spring or autumn.
SPACING 12".
LIGHT Part to full shade.
SOIL Moist, peaty woods soil with a pH level of 4.0–5.0.

CARING FOR PLANTS

Keep soil very moist and do not disturb roots. Plants will not survive in hot weather, but otherwise will spread rapidly when their cultural needs are satisfied.

PROPAGATING

Divide in early spring, or root cuttings under glass.

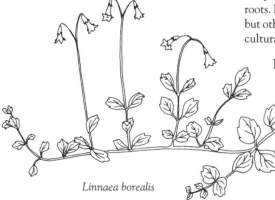

Linnaea borealis

A-Annual P-Perennial B-Biennial HHA-Half-hardy annual HA-Hardy annual HB-Hardy biennial HHP-Half-hardy perennial HP-Hardy perennial HHBb-Half-hardy bulb HBb-Hardy bulb

178

Linum

Flax

Very large genus of annuals and perennials grown for their cheerful, abundant, funnel- or cup-shaped flowers. Fine, deep green foliage provides a strong foil for clear blue, red, yellow, or white blooms. Plants are 2"–4' tall. Use in borders and rock gardens.

SOWING

INDOORS Starting seeds outdoors is recommended, but seed may be sown indoors 6–8 weeks before last frost, in peat pots.

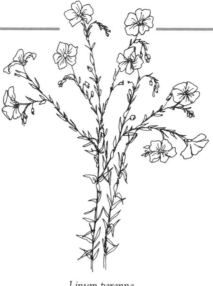

Linum perenne

OUTDOORS Early spring, when soil is cool and a light frost is still possible. Make successive plantings every 2–3 weeks for continuous blooming. Sow in early autumn where winters are mild.
DEPTH ⅛".

GERMINATING

TIME 20–25 days.
REQUIREMENTS 65°–70°F.

PLANTING SEEDLINGS OUTDOORS

TIME After last frost.
SPACING Small species: 4"–6". Medium species: 6"–12". Large species: 12"–18".
LIGHT Full sun.
SOIL Ordinary, well-drained, not too rich, with a pH level of 5.0–7.0.

CARING FOR PLANTS

Easy. Cut back one-half of the flowering stalks early in the growing season to extend the blooming period. Trim perennials to the ground in autumn. Plants resent root disturbance and are short-lived.

PROPAGATING

Annuals will self-seed. Take cuttings of perennials, divide in spring (zones 5–6) or autumn (zones 7–9).

Liriope

Lily turf

Useful but overused evergreen perennials, 12"–18", grown for their resilient, grasslike foliage and pretty spikes of purple or white flowers. Attractive ground cover, path edging, or border plants.

SOWING

INDOORS 6–8 weeks before planting out.
OUTDOORS Early spring, when soil is cool and a light frost is still possible, or late autumn.
DEPTH ¼".

GERMINATING

TIME 30 days.
REQUIREMENTS Soak seeds in warm water for 24 hours before planting; provide a constant 65°–70°F thereafter.

PLANTING SEEDLINGS OUTDOORS

TIME After last frost.
SPACING 12"–18".
LIGHT Part shade; full sun where soil is sufficiently moist.
SOIL Prefers moist, fertile, and well-drained soil, but will perform quite well in dry.

CARING FOR PLANTS

Easy. A most obliging plant with almost no faults. Water during dry spells. Remove flowering stems after blooming to keep plants looking neat and prevent self-seeding. Tidy throughout winter by removing dead leaves. Cut back plants to 3"–6" in late winter.

Liriope muscari

PROPAGATING

Divide at any time. Many species will self-seed.

Lisianthus

See *Eustoma*

A-Annual P-Perennial B-Biennial HHA-Half-hardy annual HA-Hardy annual HB-Hardy biennial HHP-Half-hardy perennial HP-Hardy perennial HHBb-Half-hardy bulb HBb-Hardy bulb

Lithodora

(synonymous with *Lithospermum*)

Gromwell, Indian Paint, Puccoon

> TYPE HHP or HP
> ZONE 3–9
> FLOWERING SEASON Most species bloom in midsummer; some bloom in spring and again in autumn, others in summer, then sporadically into autumn

Genus of perennials and subshrubs grown for their charming blue, purple, white, or yellow, funnel-shaped flowers and strong, tidy foliage. Plants grow from 6" to 4'. Useful in rock gardens and borders.

GERMINATING

REQUIREMENTS Not successfully grown from seed.

PLANTING SEEDLINGS OUTDOORS

SPACING Small species: 6"–8". Medium species: 12". Large species: 18".

LIGHT Full sun to part shade.

SOIL Grows in a wide range of conditions, but produces more flowers in poor soil. Most species prefer moist, well-drained soil. *L. diffusa* hates lime.

CARING FOR PLANTS

Water frequently during hot weather, trim back after flowering, and mulch with straw in winter. Do not disturb.

PROPAGATING

Take cuttings in midsummer.

Lithodora diffusa

Lithospermum

See **Lithodora**

Lobelia

Cardinal flower, Edging lobelia

> TYPE HHA or HHP
> ZONE A: 1–10; P: 2–9:
>   *L. cardinalis*; 3–9: *L.* x *speciosa*;
>   4–8: *L. siphilitica*;
>   5–8: *L.* x *gerardii*;
>   7–9: *L. splendens*;
>   8–10: *L. tupa*; 9–10: *L. erinus*,
>   *L. pendula, L. tenuior,*
>   *L. vallida.* Annual *Lobelia*
>   performs most successfully
>   where summers are not too hot.
> FLOWERING SEASON Summer

Annual and perennial plants grown for their intensely colored flowers. Perennials are usually tall (3') and erect, bearing tiny scarlet, blue, or yellow flowers in terminal spikes; annuals are low (4"–12") with frothy green foliage and masses of tiny blooms in strong shades of purple, blue, purple-red, and white. Grow perennials in borders; use annuals in baskets, containers, rock gardens, or for edging borders and paths.

SOWING

INDOORS A: 6–8 weeks before planting out. P: Pre-chilled seeds 8–10 weeks before last frost.

OUTDOORS Most successful when started indoors.

DEPTH Surface.

GERMINATING

TIME 15–21 days.

REQUIREMENTS Light and 65°–75°F. Highly susceptible to damping-off; sow in vermiculite and water only from below. P: Place seeds in a plastic bag together with moist growing medium and refrigerate for 3 months.

PLANTING SEEDLINGS OUTDOORS

TIME 2–3 weeks after last frost, when temperatures remain above 40°F.

SPACING Small species: 4"–6". Medium species: 9"–12". Large species: 18"–25".

LIGHT Full sun or part shade, with shade from hot afternoon sun in the South.

SOIL Moist, humus-rich, with a pH level of 6.0–7.5.

Lobelia cardinalis

CARING FOR PLANTS

Easy. For best results, water frequently during dry periods and keep mulched all year. Deadhead regularly. Plants will survive hot summers if given good drainage, afternoon shade, and abundant water.

PROPAGATING

Take cuttings of perennials or divide in spring (zones 2–6) or autumn (zones 7–10). Both annuals and perennials may self-seed.

A-Annual P-Perennial B-Biennial HHA-Half-hardy annual HA-Hardy annual HB-Hardy biennial HHP-Half-hardy perennial HP-Hardy perennial HHBb-Half-hardy bulb HBb-Hardy bulb

Lobularia

(synonymous with *Alyssum maritinum*)

Snowdrift, Sweet alyssum

> TYPE P usually grown as HA
> ZONE A: 3–8 (requires cool
> weather to flower effectively);
> P: 9–10
> FLOWERING SEASON Summer to
> autumn

Fast-growing, compact, carefree annuals grown for the clusters of tiny, scented, deep pink, purple, or white flowers that adorn them in summer. Plants are 3"–12" high, leaves small, lance-shaped, and tidy. Useful edging or container plants.

Lobularia maritima

SOWING

INDOORS 6–8 weeks before last frost.
OUTDOORS Early spring, when soil is cool and a light frost is still possible, or early autumn.
DEPTH Surface.

GERMINATING

TIME 5–14 days.
REQUIREMENTS Easy. Light and 55°–70°F.

PLANTING SEEDLINGS OUTDOORS

TIME After last frost.
SPACING Small species: 6"–8". Large species: 8"–12".
LIGHT Full sun or light shade.
SOIL Prefers a moist loam with a pH level of 6.0–7.0; tolerates dry soil.

CARING FOR PLANTS

Easy. If flowering is lessened due to hot weather, cut plants back by one-half to rejuvenate; water regularly.

PROPAGATING

Self-seeds.

Lonas

African daisy, Golden ageratum, Yellow ageratum

> TYPE HA or HHA
> ZONE Prefers cool temperatures
> FLOWERING SEASON Summer
> through autumn

Mediterranean native grown for its everlasting yellow flowers borne in clusters above feathery, deep green foliage; 12" tall. Grow in a sunny border or cutting bed.

SOWING

INDOORS 6–8 weeks before last frost.
OUTDOORS After last frost.
DEPTH Just cover.

GERMINATING

TIME 5–7 days.
REQUIREMENTS Darkness and 70°F.

PLANTING SEEDLINGS OUTDOORS

TIME After last frost.
SPACING 6"–12".
LIGHT Sun.
SOIL Light, well-drained, not too rich.

CARING FOR PLANTS

Easy. Deadhead regularly and feed only sparingly. For use in dried flower arrangements, cut and dry flowering stems when heads are fully open.

PROPAGATING

Seed only.

A-Annual P-Perennial B-Biennial HHA-Half-hardy annual HA-Hardy annual HB-Hardy biennial HHP-Half-hardy perennial HP-Hardy perennial HHBb-Half-hardy bulb HBb-Hardy bulb

Lunaria

Honesty, Money plant, Moonwort, Satin flower, Satin pod

> TYPE HP or HB grown as HA
> ZONE A: 3–10; P: 6–9. Prefers cool temperatures.
> FLOWERING SEASON Summer

Upright, bushy plants of 18"–36" bearing purple or white flowers followed by showy, silver, papery seed pods. Simple but charming plants, most effective when scattered through woodland plantings. Seed pods are used in dried flower arrangements.

SOWING

INDOORS 6–8 weeks before last frost, but best started *in situ*.

OUTDOORS Early spring, when soil is cool and a light frost is still possible, or early autumn where winters are mild.

DEPTH ⅛".

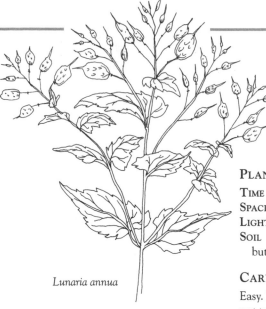

Lunaria annua

GERMINATING

TIME 10–14 days.

REQUIREMENTS Easy. 70°F.

PLANTING SEEDLINGS OUTDOORS

TIME After last frost.

SPACING 12"–18".

LIGHT Full sun or part shade.

SOIL Plants thrive in reasonably good soil, but will tolerate dry.

CARING FOR PLANTS

Easy. Mulch well before first winter and do not transplant. Remove plants after blooming if self-seeding is not desired. *Lunaria* are short-lived.

PROPAGATING

Self-seeds once established.

Lupinus

Bluebonnet, Lupin or Lupine, Texas bluebonnet

> TYPE HA, HHA, or HP
> ZONE A: 1–9; P: 4–8: *L. latifolius*; 4–9: Russell hybrids, *L. perennis* (best species for East Coast), *L. polyphyllus*; 7–9: *L. argenteus*. Prefers cool, rather humid summers, and may stop blooming altogether in extreme heat. Performs most gratifyingly in the cool zones of the East Coast and the warm zones of the West Coast.
> FLOWERING SEASON A: flower from seed in 2 months, blooming for just a few weeks. P: early summer to midsummer.

Stunning if not subtle, these brightly colored garden favorites epitomize summer. Strongly architectural plants with stiff, erect flower spikes of 1'–5' emerging from horizontal foliage. Flowers are pealike, growing in large, crowded racemes of deep blue, purple, yellow, pink, or white; some are fragrant. Mass in the border, or scatter through the cottage garden or wildflower meadow.

SOWING

INDOORS 6–8 weeks before last frost, in peat pots.

OUTDOORS A: after last frost. P: early spring, when soil is cool and a light frost is still possible, or in early autumn where winters are mild.

DEPTH ⅛".

GERMINATING

TIME 14–60 days.

REQUIREMENTS Chip seeds or soak in warm water for 24 hours, provide 55°–65°F thereafter.

PLANTING SEEDLINGS OUTDOORS

TIME After last frost or early autumn.

SPACING A: 12". Small perennial species: 12"–18". Large perennial species: 24"–36".

LIGHT Full sun to light shade.

SOIL Moist, well-drained, with a pH level of 5.5–7.0.

CARING FOR PLANTS

Easy. Water and deadhead regularly. Feed with a low-nitrogen, high-phosphorus fertilizer. After flowering, cut stems down to base. Leave plants undisturbed.

Lupinus x regalis

PROPAGATING

Sow seeds for annuals. Divide perennials in early spring, or take cuttings in spring or early summer.

A-Annual P-Perennial B-Biennial HHA-Half-hardy annual HA-Hardy annual HB-Hardy biennial HHP-Half-hardy perennial HP-Hardy perennial HHBb-Half-hardy bulb HBb-Hardy bulb

Lychnis

(synonymous with *Viscaria*)

Campion, Catchfly, Flower-of-Jove, Jerusalem cross, Maltese cross, Mullein pink, Ragged robin, Rose campion, Rose-of-heaven, Scarlet lightning

> **Type** HHA or HP
> **Zone** A: 2–10; P: 3–9; 6–9: *L. fulgens*. Most species prefer warm, dry climates.
> **Flowering Season** Summer to autumn

Clump-forming annuals and perennials, some being rather coarse, with clusters of flowers in hot shades of orange, red, or purple; others are more refined with soft green or grey foliage and rose or pale pink blossoms; 12"–48" tall. Use in borders, cottage, or wildflower gardens.

Lychnis chalcedonica

SOWING

Indoors Pre-chilled seeds 8–10 weeks before planting out.
Outdoors Early spring or early autumn.
Depth Surface.

GERMINATING

Time 21–30 days.
Requirements Place seeds in a plastic bag together with moist growing medium and refrigerate for 2 weeks. Provide light and 70°F thereafter.

PLANTING SEEDLINGS OUTDOORS

Time After last frost.
Spacing Small species: 8"–10". Large species: 12"–15".
Light Full sun or part shade.
Soil Prefers moist, well-drained soil, with a pH level of 5.0–7.0; tolerates dry soil.

CARING FOR PLANTS

Easy. Shearing plants after flowering may result in a second bloom in autumn. Cut back to ground level in autumn and mulch heavily north of zone 6. Most species are short-lived.

PROPAGATING

Divide in spring in the North, in autumn south of zone 6, or allow to self-seed.

Lycoris

Hardy amaryllis, Magic lily, Spider lily

> **Type** HBb
> **Zone** 7–10
> **Flowering Season** Late summer to autumn

Late-blooming bulbs bearing large clusters of miniature lilylike flowers of red, white, pink, or yellow held high on thick, leafless, 1'–3' stems. Grow in borders, massed in front of shrubs, or scattered through light woodland gardens.

SOWING

Indoors Start seed outdoors.
Outdoors Seed: as soon as ripe seed is available, usually late summer to autumn. Bulb: early August.
Depth Seed: just cover. Bulb: small species: 3"–4". Large species: 6"–8".

GERMINATING

Requirements Not often grown from seed and little literature is available on the subject. Information given here is a general guideline only. Sow seeds in shallow containers, plunge in the ground against a north-facing wall, and cover with glass.

PLANTING SEEDLINGS OUTDOORS

Time Early autumn. Plant seed-grown bulbs shallowly their first year; replant at their proper depth the following autumn.
Spacing Small species: 4"–6". Large species: 12"–18".
Light Sun or part shade.
Soil Rich, moist, well-drained, and either acid or neutral.

CARING FOR PLANTS

Keep soil moist at all times. Feed every other year during the growing season. Do not disturb roots too often.

PROPAGATING

Plant bulblets after flowering.

Lycoris squamigera

A-Annual P-Perennial B-Biennial HHA-Half-hardy annual HA-Hardy annual HB-Hardy biennial HHP-Half-hardy perennial HP-Hardy perennial HHBb-Half-hardy bulb HBb-Hardy bulb

Lysichiton

Skunk cabbage

Type HP
Zone 6–9
Flowering Season April to July

Small genus of primeval-looking bog plants, 2'–4' tall, whose yellowish green flowers are borne on short, thick spikes (called a spadix), surrounded by a white hoodlike spathe.

Sowing

Indoors 10–12 weeks before planting out; probably more successful when started outdoors.
Outdoors As soon as ripe seed is available, usually late summer.
Depth ¼".

Lysichiton americanum

Germinating

Time 30–60 days.
Requirements 55°–65°F. *Indoors:* stand flats in a pan of water to keep soil constantly moist. *Outdoors:* do not allow soil to become dry.

Planting Seedlings Outdoors

Time After last frost.
Spacing 36"–48".
Light Prefers full sun, but will tolerate part shade.
Soil Deep, rich, wet. Prepare to a depth of 12".

Caring for Plants

Easy. Keep soil moist at all times; apply mulch if plants are not growing in standing water.

Propagating

Divide in early spring.

Lysimachia

Creeping Charlie, Creeping Jenny, Loosestrife, Moneywort

Type HP
Zone 3–9: *L. ciliata,*
L. clethroides, L. nummularia;
5–9: *L. punctata;*
6–9: *L. ephemerum*
Flowering Season Summer

Vigorous, mainly upright, strongly architectural, summer-flowering annuals and perennials. Leaves are lance-shaped, growing horizontally; flowers may be small and white, borne in crooked, pointed clusters, or yellow and star-shaped, growing in terminal whorls. Plants normally grow 1'–3', with a prostrate species reaching only 3". Dwarfs make good rock garden or edging plants; taller species need plenty of space in a border or bog garden.

Sowing

Indoors Start seeds outdoors.
Outdoors Autumn.
Depth Surface.

Germinating

Time 30–90 days.
Requirements Sow seeds in flats, sink these into the ground against a north-facing wall, and cover with glass. Moisten soil occasionally, if necessary. Transplant to the garden when seedlings begin to trail.

Planting Seedlings Outdoors

Time After last frost.
Spacing 15"–20".
Light Full sun or part shade.
Soil Moist is ideal; will generally tolerate dry if sited in part shade.

Lysimachia punctata

Caring for Plants

Easy. For best results keep soil moist. Cut plants back to ground level in autumn. May become invasive.

Propagating

Divide in spring in the North, in autumn south of zone 6.

A-Annual P-Perennial B-Biennial HHA-Half-hardy annual HA-Hardy annual HB-Hardy biennial HHP-Half-hardy perennial HP-Hardy perennial HHBb-Half-hardy bulb HBb-Hardy bulb

184

Lythrum

Loosestrife, Purple loosetrife, Purple willow-herb, Red Sally

> TYPE HP
> ZONE 3–9
> FLOWERING SEASON Summer to
> early autumn

Beautiful, invasive, summer-blooming perennials grown for their carefree 2'–4' spikes of pink or purple blooms. Light and airy addition to the border or wildflower garden.

SOWING

INDOORS 6–8 weeks before planting out.
OUTDOORS Early spring, when soil is cool and a light frost is still possible, or late autumn.
DEPTH Just cover.

GERMINATING

TIME 5–30 days.
REQUIREMENTS 65°–70°F.

PLANTING SEEDLINGS OUTDOORS

TIME After last frost.
SPACING Small species: 18"–24". Large species: 24"–36".
LIGHT Full sun or part shade.
SOIL Most prefer moist soil with a pH level of 5.0–7.0. *L. salicaria* 'Robert' is tolerant of quite wet soil, and *L. salicaria* 'Morden's pink' will stand very dry.

CARING FOR PLANTS

Easy. Deadhead frequently to prevent self-seeding and encourage abundant flowering. Divide every 3 years.

PROPAGATING

Divide in early spring, or allow to self-seed.

Lythrum salicaria

> NOTE: Lythrum has invaded and choked great expanses of Northern wetlands. It has been banned in some states; check with your local Cooperative Extension Service before planting. 'Morden's Pink' is the least invasive cultivar.

Machaeranthera

Tahoka daisy

> TYPE HHA
> ZONE Prefers a cool, dry climate, but will flower for a short period in a hot, humid location.
> FLOWERING SEASON Summer through autumn

Genus of annuals native to the American Midwest. Blue, daisylike flowers are borne on 2' stems. Useful for borders and cutting.

SOWING

INDOORS Pre-chilled seeds 6–8 weeks before planting out.
OUTDOORS Early spring, when soil is cool and a light frost is still possible, or early autumn.
DEPTH Surface.

GERMINATING

TIME 25–30 days.
REQUIREMENTS Place seeds in a plastic bag together with moist growing medium and refrigerate for 2 weeks. Provide light and 70°F thereafter.

PLANTING SEEDLINGS OUTDOORS

TIME After last frost.
SPACING 9"–12".
LIGHT Full sun or light shade.
SOIL Average, well-drained, with a pH level of 6.0–7.0.

CARING FOR PLANTS

No special care required. Tahoka daisies are short-lived in hot, humid climates.

PROPAGATING

Seed only.

A-Annual P-Perennial B-Biennial HHA-Half-hardy annual HA-Hardy annual HB-Hardy biennial HHP-Half-hardy perennial HP-Hardy perennial HHBb-Half-hardy bulb HBb-Hardy bulb

Macleaya

Plume poppy

> TYPE **HP**
> ZONE **3–9**
> FLOWERING SEASON **Summer**

Unusual, attractive perennials with highly ornamental, deeply lobed leaves and tall, airy sprays of tiny, pink or white flowers; 5'–8' tall. Use in place of deciduous shrubs.

SOWING

INDOORS Start seeds outdoors.
OUTDOORS Early spring, when soil is cool and a light frost is still possible.
DEPTH Just cover.

GERMINATING

TIME 14 days.
REQUIREMENTS Propagation by division or root cutting is more successful than growing from seed.

PLANTING SEEDLINGS OUTDOORS

TIME After last frost.
SPACING 3'–5' or singly.
LIGHT Sun in cool climates, part shade where summers are hot.
SOIL Average, moist, well-drained. Plants may spread rampantly in rich soil.

CARING FOR PLANTS

Easy. Water during dry spells, deadhead after blooming, and cut back to the ground in autumn. Divide every 3–4 years. M. cordata is fairly restrained, but other species can be invasive.

PROPAGATING

Take root cuttings in winter, carefully divide in early spring, or allow to self-seed.

Macleaya cordata

Majorana

See Origanum

Malcolmia

Virginia stock

> TYPE **HA or HHA**
> ZONE **Requires cool temperatures**
> FLOWERING SEASON **Blooms from spring through midautumn with successive sowings**

Small genus of fast-growing, quick-to-bloom, erect annuals growing 8"–12". Flowers are 4-petalled, small and dainty, but profuse. Flower color is purple, pink, or white; some are fragrant. Foliage may have a grey tinge. Grow in the border or cottage garden.

SOWING

INDOORS Best started outdoors.
OUTDOORS For continuous blooming, sow at 4-week intervals from early spring, when a light frost is still possible, through late summer. Where winters are mild, sow in autumn for spring blooms.
DEPTH Surface.

GERMINATING

TIME 10–14 days.
REQUIREMENTS Light and 55°–60°F.

PLANTING SEEDLINGS OUTDOORS

TIME Set out purchased plants after last frost.
SPACING 3"–4".

LIGHT Sun or part shade.
SOIL Will grow in any soil, but prefers one that is rich and moist. Add manure at planting time.

CARING FOR PLANTS

Easy. Water frequently; *Malcolmia* will die back during prolonged hot spells. Plants may be discarded after flowering, but if self-seeding is desired, allow seed to mature and disburse before uprooting.

PROPAGATING

Self-seeds, although colors may not come true.

A-Annual P-Perennial B-Biennial HHA-Half-hardy annual HA-Hardy annual HB-Hardy biennial HHP-Half-hardy perennial HP-Hardy perennial HHBb-Half-hardy bulb HBb-Hardy bulb

186

Malope

Mallow-wort

> **Type** HA
> **Zone** Prefers cool temperatures
> **Flowering Season** All summer

Upright, branching annuals native to the Mediterranean, grown for their attractive, lobed foliage and large, open, trumpet-shaped flowers. Blooms are held singly and may be deep pink or white; plants grow to 3'. Use in the border or cottage garden.

Sowing

Indoors Pre-chilled seeds 4–6 weeks before last frost, in peat pots.
Outdoors 2–3 weeks before last frost.
Depth Just cover.

Germinating

Time 14–30 days.
Requirements Place seeds in a plastic bag together with moist growing medium and refrigerate for 3 weeks. Provide 65°–75°F thereafter.

Planting Seedlings Outdoors

Time After last frost.
Spacing Small species: 9"–12". Large species: 24".
Light Sun or light shade.
Soil Light, well-drained. High fertility will result in abundant leaves but few flowers.

Caring for Plants

Stake young plants individually, being careful not to damage roots. Do not disturb.

Propagating

Self-seeds.

Malva

Curled mallow, Hollyhock mallow, Musk mallow, Musk rose

> **Type** HA or HP
> **Zone** 3–9. Prefers cool temperatures.
> **Flowering Season** Summer to early autumn

Bushy, upright annuals and perennials of great charm and beauty. Plants stand 2'–4', spattered with 2" cup-shaped blooms of pink, white, or purple. A good choice for the summer border or cottage garden.

Sowing

Indoors 6–8 weeks before planting out.
Outdoors Early spring, when soil is cool and a light frost is still possible, or early autumn.
Depth Just cover.

Malva moschata

Germinating

Time 5–21 days.
Requirements Easy. 70°F.

Planting Seedlings Outdoors

Time After last frost.
Spacing Small species: 10"–15". Large species: 12"–24".
Light Full sun, or part shade where summers are hot.
Soil Prefers dry, well-drained soil; quite tolerant of a wide range of conditions.

Caring for Plants

Easy. Feed and water regularly and cut back to ground level in autumn. Plants require more frequent watering during very hot spells.

Propagating

Take cuttings in spring. Divide in spring north of zone 7, autumn in the South. Or allow to self-seed.

A-Annual P-Perennial B-Biennial HHA-Half-hardy annual HA-Hardy annual HB-Hardy biennial HHP-Half-hardy perennial HP-Hardy perennial HHBb-Half-hardy bulb HBb-Hardy bulb

Martynia

Unicorn plant

Unusual, upright annuals, 2'–6', with large, rather coarse leaves. Plants are redeemed by their intricately tinted blooms which resemble miniature orchids; spiky fruits are used in dried arrangements. Grow in borders and containers.

SOWING
INDOORS 6–8 weeks before last frost.
OUTDOORS After last frost, but only where summers are long.
DEPTH ¼".

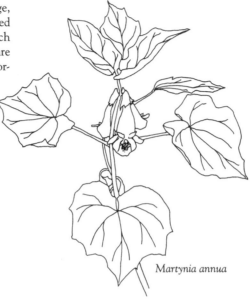

Martynia annua

GERMINATING
TIME 20 days.
REQUIREMENTS 70°–75°F.

PLANTING SEEDLINGS OUTDOORS
TIME After last frost.
SPACING 12".
LIGHT Full sun or part shade.
SOIL Rich, well-drained; tolerates dry conditions.

CARING FOR PLANTS
Easy. No special care is required.

PROPAGATING
Seed only.

Matricaria

Feverfew, False chamomile, Sweet chamomile

Genus of plants grown for their abundance of flowers produced over an extremely long period. Blooms may be sunny, gold pompoms or yellow daisies with large eyes and short petals; some are very fragrant. Foliage is handsome and deep green. Plants grow from 4" to 24". Useful for edging, borders, or containers.

SOWING
INDOORS 6–8 weeks before last frost.
OUTDOORS Early spring, when soil is cool and a light frost is still possible, or early autumn.
DEPTH Surface.

GERMINATING
TIME 5–21 days.
REQUIREMENTS Light and 65°–75°F.

PLANTING SEEDLINGS OUTDOORS
TIME After last frost.
SPACING Small species: 6"–12". Large species: 12"–15".
LIGHT Full sun or light shade.
SOIL Ordinary or poor, well-drained.

CARING FOR PLANTS
Easy. Feed with all-purpose fertilizer in spring and pinch back young plants to encourage bushiness. Cut back in autumn. Susceptible to spider mites in hot, dry weather, which can be controlled with a forceful spray of water. Chamomile tea is made from *Matricaria* flowers: Harvest flowers on a sunny day when blooms are fully open, dry in the sun, remove stems and leaves, and store in an airtight container.

CHARLES JOSLIN

Matricaria chamomilla

PROPAGATING
Self-seeds.

Matthiola

Brompton stock, Common stock,
Evening stock, Gillyflower,
Grecian stock, Night-scented stock,
Stock, Ten-weeks stock

> **TYPE** HP, HA, HHA, or HB
> **ZONE** 2–10. Performs best where temperatures are cool; must have a night temperature below 60°F.
> **FLOWERING SEASON** Late spring to summer

Erect, bushy plants, 12"–30", bearing highly fragrant flowers clustered thickly on long spikes; blooms are red, purple, pink, blue, or white. Lance-shaped leaves have a grey cast. Stunning in the border.

Matthiola incana

SOWING

INDOORS A or P: 6–8 weeks before last frost. B: summer.
OUTDOORS After last frost. Seeds may also be sown in late summer through early autumn in zones 9–10 for early spring blooms.
DEPTH Surface.

GERMINATING

TIME 3–20 days.
REQUIREMENTS Light and 55°–65°F. Very susceptible to damping-off; sow in vermiculite and always water from below.

PLANTING SEEDLINGS OUTDOORS

TIME A or P: after last frost in the North, autumn in the South. B: autumn.
SPACING Dwarf species: 6"–9". Large species: 12"–18".
LIGHT Full sun, except where summers are very hot.
SOIL Moist, well-drained, very fertile, neutral or alkaline.

CARING FOR PLANTS

Pinch out lateral shoots to produce taller specimens and keep plants somewhat crowded to induce earlier blooming. Water regularly and fertilize monthly.

PROPAGATING

Take cuttings from perennials in summer.

Maurandya

See **Asarina**

Mazus

> **TYPE** HP
> **ZONE** 6–9: *M. reptans*; 7–9: *M. pumilio*
> **FLOWERING SEASON** Spring or summer, depending on species

Creeping perennials, 2"–4" tall, with delicate, tubular flowers of blue or white and attractive, healthy green foliage. Use as ground cover, pathway edging, or in woodland or rock gardens.

GERMINATING

REQUIREMENTS Propagate plants by division.

PLANTING SEEDLINGS OUTDOORS

TIME Set out purchased plants in spring or autumn.
SPACING 8"–10".
LIGHT Part to full shade, or full sun in cool climates.
SOIL Cool, moist, peaty.

CARING FOR PLANTS

Mulch in spring to keep soil cool and moist, and again in winter.

PROPAGATING

Divide in spring.

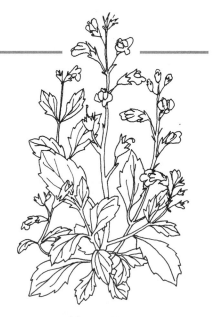

Mazus reptans

Meconopsis

Asiatic poppy, Blue poppy, Harebell poppy, Himalayan poppy, Welsh poppy

TYPE HP
ZONE 6–9. Performs most successfully in the cool, damp climate of the Pacific Northwest.
FLOWERING SEASON Spring to early autumn, depending on species

Genus of alpine plants best known for their enchanting, blue, poppylike blooms, although lesser-known species bear yellow, orange, white, red, pink, or purple flowers. Plants grow from 12" to 5', and flowers are held singly on slender stems. Their charm is only enhanced by the brevity of their lives. Use in borders or rock gardens.

SOWING

INDOORS 6–8 weeks before last frost.
OUTDOORS Early spring, when soil is cool and a light frost is still possible, or late autumn.
DEPTH Surface.

Meconopsis cambrica

GERMINATING

TIME 14–28 days.
REQUIREMENTS Difficult. Very susceptible to damping-off; sow seeds in vermiculite and water from below. Keep seeds at 55°–65°F.

PLANTING SEEDLINGS OUTDOORS

TIME After last frost.
SPACING Small species: 12"–18". Large species: 24"–36".
LIGHT Part to full shade, or sun in areas where summers are cool.
SOIL Rich, acid, moist in summer but dry in winter.

CARING FOR PLANTS

Difficult. Water during dry spells and cut back to the ground in autumn. Plants will be plagued by mildew where summers are dry. Short-lived.

PROPAGATING

Carefully divide in early spring.

Melica

Melic, Pearl grass

TYPE HP
ZONE 5–9
FLOWERING SEASON Summer

Large genus of grasses, two of which are grown ornamentally. Leaves are flat or rolled, 12"–24"; inflorescences are like tight wads of silvery silk. Use in wildflower gardens or mixed grass plantings.

SOWING

INDOORS Best started *in situ*.
OUTDOORS Early spring to midspring.
DEPTH Just cover.

GERMINATING

TIME 21 days.
REQUIREMENTS 60°–75°F.

PLANTING SEEDLINGS OUTDOORS

TIME Set out purchased plants in spring.
SPACING 8"–12".
LIGHT Sun or part shade.
SOIL Moist.

CARING FOR PLANTS

Water during dry spells. Cut back hard in spring.

PROPAGATING

Divide in spring.

Melica uniflora

Melissa

Balm, Lemon balm, Sweet balm

Type HP
Zone 4–9
Flowering Season Early summer through autumn

Upright, perennial herbs grown for culinary use or ornament. Leaves are toothed and opposite, similar to mint in appearance; one species has golden foliage. Plants grow to 2'. Native to North America, Europe, and Asia.

Sowing

Indoors 8–10 weeks before planting out.
Outdoors Late autumn.
Depth Surface.

Germinating

Time 14–21 days.
Requirements Light and 70°F.

Planting Seedlings Outdoors

Time After last frost.
Spacing 18"–24".
Light Full sun to light shade.
Soil Sandy, dry, with a pH level of 6.5–7.5. Leaves will be more aromatic in poor soil.

Caring for Plants

Ensure healthy air circulation to avoid powdery mildew. If balm is grown for culinary use, cut back hard periodically to stimulate a fresh supply of new leaves. Cut back to ground level in autumn. Use fresh or dried leaves in cooking. To dry, harvest leaves just prior to or immediately after blooming, dry quickly at 90°F or more, and store in an airtight container.

Propagating

Divide in early spring, take stem cuttings in spring or summer, or allow to self-seed.

Mentha

Mint, Pennyroyal, Pudding grass

Type HP
Zone 3–9: M. x *piperita*;
5–9: M. x *gentilis*,
M. *suaveolens*; 7–9:
M. *requienii*
Flowering Season Summer

Spreading perennials usually grown for their aromatic leaves, but sometimes also for ornament. Small pink, white, or purple flowers grow in terminal spikes; plants are 18"–36". Best suited to the herb garden where their invasiveness is less troublesome.

Germinating

Requirements Propagation most successful by division or cuttings.

Planting Seedlings Outdoors

Time Spring or autumn.
Spacing Small species: 8"–10". Medium species: 12"–15". Large species: 24".
Light Full sun or part shade.
Soil Moist, well-drained, with a pH level of 6.5–8.0. Amend with compost (do not use manure, which may cause rust).

Caring for Plants

Easy. Pinch back tips of young plants to increase leaf production. Divide and replant to a new location every 3–4 years to maintain vigor. To prevent mint from overtaking your garden, plant roots in a well-drained tub, either above or below ground, cutting back stray growth to prevent rooting. Mint leaves can be dried for use in winter, but retain a more appealing flavor if chopped and frozen (wash and dry thoroughly before hand). Or pot up M. x *rotundifolia* in early autumn to grow indoors, give plants 5 hours of sunlight a day, feed lightly once a month, do not overwater, and keep leggy growth in check.

CHARLES JOSLIN

Mentha cardifola

Propagating

Take cuttings, divide, or plant runners. In fact, mint's natural urge to overrun the planet is so strong that it can be reproduced by almost any method, except, perversely, by seed.

A-Annual P-Perennial B-Biennial HHA-Half-hardy annual HA-Hardy annual HB-Hardy biennial HHP-Half-hardy perennial HP-Hardy perennial HHBb-Half-hardy bulb HBb-Hardy bulb

191

Mentzelia

Blazing star

TYPE HA or HB
ZONE 3–8. Prefers cool, dry climates.
FLOWERING SEASON Early summer

Bushy plants with golden yellow, cup-shaped flowers (fragrant in some species) and prominent, hairy stamens; 18"–48". American natives for the sunny border.

SOWING
INDOORS Start seeds outdoors.
OUTDOORS Zones 3–8: after last frost. Zones 9–10: autumn or very early spring.
DEPTH Just cover.

GERMINATING
TIME 5–21 days.
REQUIREMENTS 55°–60°F.

PLANTING SEEDLINGS OUTDOORS
TIME Set out purchased plants after last frost, when temperatures remain above 40°F.
SPACING 8"–10".
LIGHT Full sun.
SOIL Moist, well-drained, fertile, with a pH level of 5.0–8.0; tolerates dry soil.

CARING FOR PLANTS
Easy. Regular feeding and watering are essential for attractive plants. After first heavy blooming, cut back to 2". Flowers will close on cloudy days. Do not move.

PROPAGATING
May self-seed in the South.

Menyanthes

Bog bean, Buck bean

TYPE HP
ZONE 3–9. Prefers cool temperatures.
FLOWERING SEASON Spring to summer

Genus of perennial bog and water plants grown for their neat, rounded, midgreen foliage and small, white, star-shaped flowers with fringed petals. Useful only in very moist areas.

GERMINATING
REQUIREMENTS Not usually propagated by seed.

PLANTING SEEDLINGS OUTDOORS
TIME Set out purchased plants in spring or autumn.
SPACING 8"–12".
LIGHT Sun or part shade.
SOIL Cool, peaty, acid, wet; plants will even grow in shallow water.

CARING FOR PLANTS
Keep soil very moist at all times and deadhead regularly. Divide when plants become overcrowded; otherwise do not disturb.

PROPAGATING
Divide in spring, with each new section containing 1 growing tip.

A-Annual P-Perennial B-Biennial HHA-Half-hardy annual HA-Hardy annual HB-Hardy biennial HHP-Half-hardy perennial HP-Hardy perennial HHBb-Half-hardy bulb HBb-Hardy bulb

192

Mertensia

**Chiming bells, Languid ladies,
Mountain bluebell,
Northern shorewort, Oysterleaf,
Virginia bluebells, Virginia cowslip**

TYPE HP
ZONE 3–8: *M. paniculata,*
  M. viridis; 4–8: *M. ciliata*;
  5–9: *M. maritima, M. virginica*
FLOWERING SEASON Late spring to
  early summer

American wildflowers grown for their handsome blue-green foliage and enchanting clusters of small, purple-pink, trumpet-shaped flowers; 8"–3' tall. Massed and in full bloom these demure plants are a stunning sight, but they are also lovely when grown singly in a mixed woodland planting or rock garden.

SOWING

INDOORS Start seeds outdoors only.
OUTDOORS As soon as fresh seed is available, usually in summer.
DEPTH Just cover.

GERMINATING

TIME 30–60 days.

Mertensia virginica

REQUIREMENTS Sow seeds sparsely in flats, sink in the ground against a north-facing wall, and cover with glass. Moisten soil occasionally, if necessary. Transplant seedlings to the garden in autumn after 1 full growing season.

PLANTING SEEDLINGS OUTDOORS

TIME Set out purchased plants in early spring or autumn.
SPACING 8"–12".
LIGHT Part to full shade; full sun is acceptable only in Northern zones.
SOIL Moist, fertile, woods soil, with nearly neutral pH.

CARING FOR PLANTS

Plants grown from seed will take at least 3 years to flower. Mulch to keep soil cool and moist. Water regularly in spring, easing off after blooming, and ceasing altogether when plants go dormant in summer; plants will disappear entirely at this point. Do not move.

PROPAGATING

Allow to self-seed, or very carefully divide immediately after flowering.

Mesembryanthemum

(synonymous with *Dorotheanthus*)

**Fig marigold, Hottentot fig,
Ice plant, Livingstone daisy,
Sea fig, Sea marigold**

TYPE HHA or HHP
ZONE A: 3–8; P: 9–10. Prefers
  warm, dry climates.
FLOWERING SEASON Spring
  through late summer, depending
  on species and time of sowing

Very large genus of rarely used succulents. The more attractive species are grown for the cheery mass of blooms that cover plants over a long period. Flowers are daisylike, with numerous fine petals in pink, yellow, white, or red. 4"–12" plants are useful in rock gardens, sunny borders, drystone walls, or as edging.

SOWING

INDOORS 10–12 weeks before last frost.
OUTDOORS After last frost, and at intervals until late May for a longer blooming period.
DEPTH Surface.

GERMINATING

TIME 15–20 days.
REQUIREMENTS Darkness and 65°–75°F.

PLANTING SEEDLINGS OUTDOORS

TIME After last frost.
SPACING Small species: 4"–8". Large species: 6"–12".
LIGHT Full sun.
SOIL Poor, dry, sandy or gritty, and very well-drained.

CARING FOR PLANTS

Water moderately during the growing season, but only sparingly otherwise. Feed with a liquid fertilizer after first flowering.

PROPAGATING

Take cuttings in spring.

A-Annual P-Perennial B-Biennial HHA-Half-hardy annual HA-Hardy annual HB-Hardy biennial HHP-Half-hardy perennial HP-Hardy perennial HHBb-Half-hardy bulb HBb-Hardy bulb

Milium

Bowles' golden grass, Millet grass

> TYPE HP
> ZONE 4–9
> FLOWERING SEASON Late spring to
> summer

Small genus of native North American perennial grasses, only one of which is widely grown for its golden yellow foliage. Leaf blades are narrow and refined; feathery inflorescences are used in dried arrangements. Plants grow to 18". Use as a foil for contrasting colors and textures.

SOWING

INDOORS Sow seed outdoors only.
OUTDOORS Early spring to midspring.
DEPTH Just cover.

GERMINATING

TIME 21 days.
REQUIREMENTS 60°–75°F.

PLANTING SEEDLINGS OUTDOORS

TIME Set out purchased plants in spring.
SPACING 12"–24".
LIGHT Shade.
SOIL Moist, fertile.

CARING FOR PLANTS

Water regularly and feed occasionally.

PROPAGATING

Divide in spring in zones 4–6, autumn in 7–9, or allow to self-seed.

Mimulus

Monkey flower, Monkey musk, Musk

> TYPE HHP or HP, often grown as
> HHA
> ZONE A: 2–10; P: 3–9:
> M. *ringens*; 5–9: M. *lewisii*;
> 6–9: M. *guttatus*, M. x *hybridus*,
> M. *luteus*; 7–9: M. *cardinalis*.
> Prefers the mild climate of the
> California coast.
> FLOWERING SEASON Spring to
> autumn, depending on species

Grown for their irresistible, tubular, lipped, often freckled flowers, these charmers come in every shade of red, orange, yellow, and pink, often multicolored; attractive foliage and neat habit are a bonus. Plants grow from 2" to 36". Perfect edging, border, or rock garden plant where the climate is right.

Mimulus ringens

SOWING

INDOORS Pre-chilled seeds 10–12 weeks before last frost.
OUTDOORS Late winter.
DEPTH Surface.

GERMINATING

TIME 7–21 days.
REQUIREMENTS Place seeds in a plastic bag together with moist growing medium and refrigerate for 3 weeks. Provide light and 70°–75°F thereafter.

PLANTING SEEDLINGS OUTDOORS

TIME After last frost.
SPACING Small species: 6"–9". Medium species: 12"–24". Large species: 24"–36".
LIGHT Afternoon shade in hot climates, full sun where summers are cool.
SOIL Moist, rich, with a pH level of 6.0–7.0.

CARING FOR PLANTS

Easy. Keep soil moist, particularly in hot weather; deadhead regularly. Mulch in winter.

PROPAGATING

Divide or take cuttings in spring.

A-Annual P-Perennial B-Biennial HHA-Half-hardy annual HA-Hardy annual HB-Hardy biennial HHP-Half-hardy perennial HP-Hardy perennial HHBb-Half-hardy bulb HBb-Hardy bulb

194

Mina

See *Quamoclit*

Mirabilis

Beauty-of-the-night, Four-o'clock, Marvel of Peru

> TYPE HHP usually grown as HHA
> ZONE A: 3–7; P: 8–10. Requires warm temperatures, but does not like humid climates.
> FLOWERING SEASON Summer to late autumn

Bushy plants with fragrant, trumpet-shaped, evening-blooming flowers in white, pink, red, or yellow; 2'–4'. Plant near a patio, door, or window to catch the heavenly scent.

SOWING
INDOORS 6–8 weeks before planting out, in peat pots.
OUTDOORS 1 week after last frost, or in autumn where winters are mild.
DEPTH Surface.

GERMINATING
TIME 5–21 days.
REQUIREMENTS Light and 70°F.

PLANTING SEEDLINGS OUTDOORS
TIME After last frost.
SPACING Small species: 6"–9". Medium species: 12"–18". Large species: 24"–36".
LIGHT Full sun to partial shade.
SOIL Average, well-drained, with a pH level of 6.0–7.0. M. *multiflora* is drought tolerant.

CARING FOR PLANTS
Easy. Feed monthly. Blooms more prolifically if watered regularly. Cut back to the ground after flowering.

PROPAGATING
Divide tubers in spring. Self-seeds in mild climates.

Miscanthus

Amur silver grass, Eulalia, Japanese silver grass, Maiden grass, Nepal silver grass, Silver banner grass, Zebra grass

> TYPE HP
> ZONE 5–9
> FLOWERING SEASON Late summer to autumn

The most widely grown ornamental grass, *Miscanthus* comes in many sizes and colors. Most are vigorous and upright, growing from 3' to 9', with handsome, flat leaf blades and very showy, silky inflorescences. Useful in borders or mixed grass plantings.

SOWING
INDOORS Start seeds outdoors.
OUTDOORS After last frost.
DEPTH Surface.

GERMINATING
TIME 14–60 days.
REQUIREMENTS Start species only from seed. Provide light and 60°–75°F.

PLANTING SEEDLINGS OUTDOORS
TIME Set out purchased plants in spring or autumn.
SPACING Small species: 24"–36". Large species: Singly.
LIGHT Full sun or light shade.
SOIL Average, well-drained. *Miscanthus* is drought tolerant, but prefers moist soil that is well drained; some species grow well in wet soil.

CARING FOR PLANTS
Little care required and, with any encouragement, these grasses will become invasive. Cut back hard in late winter. Many species have a tendency to die back in the center and require dividing every 3–5 years to maintain vigor. Warning: Exercise caution when dividing these plants as the physical exertion required can result in serious back injuries.

PROPAGATING
Divide in spring, or also in autumn in the South; rampant self-seeder.

A-Annual P-Perennial B-Biennial HHA-Half-hardy annual HA-Hardy annual HB-Hardy biennial HHP-Half-hardy perennial HP-Hardy perennial HHBb-Half-hardy bulb HBb-Hardy bulb

Mitchella

Partridgeberry, Running box, Squawberry

> TYPE HP
> ZONE 3–9. Prefers cool climates.
> FLOWERING SEASON Early
> summer

Genus of one prostrate evergreen subshrub with attractive, shiny leaves and tiny white flowers followed by showy, bright red berries. An unusual rock garden plant or ground cover.

SOWING

INDOORS Sow seeds *in situ*.
OUTDOORS As soon as ripe seed is available, usually in October.
DEPTH ¼".

GERMINATING

TIME Very slow and irregular.
REQUIREMENTS Sow seeds thinly in flats, sink flats in the ground against a north-facing wall, and cover with glass. Moisten soil occasionally, if necessary. Transplant seedlings the following autumn.

PLANTING SEEDLINGS OUTDOORS

TIME Set out purchased plants in spring or autumn.
SPACING 10"–15".
LIGHT Part to full shade.
SOIL Rich, moist, with a pH level of 4.0–6.0.

CARING FOR PLANTS

Difficult to establish. Apply a complete fertilizer in spring, mulch to keep soil cool and moist, and do not disturb roots.

PROPAGATING

Divide roots in spring (zones 3–6) or autumn (zones 7–9), take cuttings in summer, or root runners.

Mitella

Bishop's-cap, Miterwort

> TYPE HP
> ZONE 3–8: M. *diphylla*;
> 5–7: M. *breweri*
> FLOWERING SEASON Spring or
> summer, depending on species

Small genus of delicate woodland perennials that form neat clumps of heart-shaped leaves; tiny, tubular, greenish white flowers grow along tall, hairy spikes. North American and East Asian natives growing to 12"; used as a woodland ground cover or in rock gardens.

SOWING

INDOORS Sow seeds *in situ*.
OUTDOORS As soon as seed is ripe in summer.
DEPTH ¼".

GERMINATING

REQUIREMENTS Because *Mitella* is so easily propagated by runners, plants are rarely started from seed.

PLANTING SEEDLINGS OUTDOORS

TIME Set out purchased plants in spring or autumn.
SPACING 5"–9".
LIGHT Part to full shade.
SOIL Rich, moist, acid.

CARING FOR PLANTS

Water regularly during dry spells. Roots will not tolerate competition or disturbance.

PROPAGATING

Very carefully divide in early spring, or allow to self-seed.

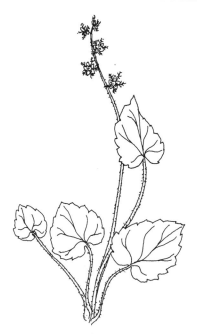

Mitella nuda

A-Annual P-Perennial B-Biennial HHA-Half-hardy annual HA-Hardy annual HB-Hardy biennial HHP-Half-hardy perennial HP-Hardy perennial HHBb-Half-hardy bulb HBb-Hardy bulb

196

Moluccella

**Bells of Ireland, Irish bells,
Molucca balm, Shellflower**

> TYPE HA or HHA
> ZONE 2–10. Happiest in cool
> climates.
> FLOWERING SEASON Late spring to
> early summer

Upright, branching annuals grown for their densely covered spikes of unusual "flowers," which are in fact green, cone-shaped calyxes encircling the tiny, white, true flowers. Plants grow 18"–36" and make an unusual addition to the border or cottage garden.

SOWING

INDOORS 8–10 weeks before planting out, in peat pots.
OUTDOORS Early spring, when soil is cool and a light frost is still possible. Where winters are mild, seeds may also be sown in late summer for autumn blooms.
DEPTH Surface.

GERMINATING

TIME 8–35 days.
REQUIREMENTS Place seeds in a plastic bag together with moist growing medium and refrigerate for 5 days; provide light and 50°–60°F thereafter.

PLANTING SEEDLINGS OUTDOORS

TIME After last frost.
SPACING 12".
LIGHT Sun to part shade.
SOIL Ordinary.

CARING FOR PLANTS

Easy. Water regularly and fertilize monthly. Stake plants and leave roots undisturbed.

PROPAGATING
Self-seeds.

Moluccella laevis

Momordica

Balsam apple, Balsam pear

> TYPE HHP usually grown as
> HHA
> ZONE A: 3–7; P: 8–10. Prefers
> warm climates.
> FLOWERING SEASON All summer

Genus of annual vines growing 8'–10', with deeply lobed leaves and showy white or yellow flowers followed by attractive orange fruit.

SOWING

INDOORS 4–6 weeks before planting out, in peat pots.
OUTDOORS Only where summers are very warm, in early spring.
DEPTH 1/8".

GERMINATING

TIME 14–21 days.
REQUIREMENTS 65°–75°F.

PLANTING SEEDLINGS OUTDOORS

TIME After last frost.
SPACING Small species: 8"–12". Large species: 12"–24".
LIGHT Full sun.
SOIL Rich and moist.

CARING FOR PLANTS

Water well during dry spells and feed occasionally when plants are in fruit. Provide a trellis or other support.

PROPAGATING

Seed only.

A-Annual P-Perennial B-Biennial HHA-Half-hardy annual HA-Hardy annual HB-Hardy biennial HHP-Half-hardy perennial HP-Hardy perennial HHBb-Half-hardy bulb HBb-Hardy bulb

Monarda

Beebalm, Bergamot, Horsemint, Oswego tea

> TYPE HP
> ZONE 4–9
> FLOWERING SEASON Summer

Genus of upright, vigorous, rather coarse, summer-blooming perennials grown for their unique, mop-headed flowers that appear to have stepped out before brushing their hair. Strong 2'–4' stems hold vibrant red, purple, pink, or white blooms. A joy to behold in the summer border or wildflower garden.

SOWING

INDOORS 8–10 weeks before planting out.
OUTDOORS Early spring, when soil is cool and a light frost is still possible, or early autumn.
DEPTH Just cover.

GERMINATING

TIME 10–40 days.
REQUIREMENTS 60°–70°F.

CHARLES JOSLIN

Monarda didyma

PLANTING SEEDLINGS OUTDOORS

TIME Early spring, when soil is cool and a light frost is still possible, or early autumn.
SPACING 18"–24".
LIGHT Part shade; plant in full sun if soil is moist.
SOIL Ordinary, with a pH level of 5.5–7.0.

CARING FOR PLANTS

Easy. Where summers are long and hot, plants will be short-lived and prone to mildew. Mulch plants and water frequently, keeping leaves as dry as possible to minimize the risk of disease. Deadhead regularly to prolong blooming. Cut back stems completely in winter. Prune roots to restrict rampant spreading and divide plants every 3 years in spring or autumn.

PROPAGATING

Divide in spring.

Montbretia

See *Crocosmia*

Moraea

Butterfly iris, Fortnight lily, Natal lily

> TYPE HHBb
> ZONE Divided into 2 categories: summer growers and winter growers. The winter growers are suitable only for zones 9–10, but summer growers can be planted as annuals farther north.
> FLOWERING SEASON Spring, summer, or early autumn, depending on species

Genus of corms bearing flowers that strongly resemble the flag iris. Leaves are short and narrow; flowers are yellow, purple, red, or white, often multicolored, held on tall stems growing 6"–8'.

SOWING

INDOORS Start seeds outdoors.
OUTDOORS Seed: Sow summer growers in spring, winter growers in autumn. Bulb: Plant spring bloomers in autumn, summer bloomers in spring.
DEPTH Seed: ⅛". Large bulb: 3"–4". Small bulb: 2".

GERMINATING

TIME 30–90 days.
REQUIREMENTS 55°–60°F.

PLANTING SEEDLINGS OUTDOORS

SPACING Dwarf species: 3". Medium species: 6"–9". Large species: 12"–24".
LIGHT Full sun.
SOIL Average, well-drained.

CARING FOR PLANTS

Fertilizing is not necessary in average soils. Cut back flower stems partway after blooming. *Summer bloomers:* Water from spring through autumn, tapering off during winter. *Winter bloomers:* Water during winter and early spring, keeping quite dry in summer. Where summers are habitually wet, dig and store both winter and spring bloomers, replanting in early autumn.

PROPAGATING

Plant offsets during the dormant period.

Moraea huttonii

A-Annual P-Perennial B-Biennial HHA-Half-hardy annual HA-Hardy annual HB-Hardy biennial HHP-Half-hardy perennial HP-Hardy perennial HHBb-Half-hardy bulb HBb-Hardy bulb

198

Muscari

Grape hyacinth, Tassel hyacinth

TYPE HBb
ZONE 4–8
FLOWERING SEASON Spring

Small, spring-blooming bulbs with upright, leafless stems bearing dense clusters of tiny, spherical, purple or white flowers. Commonly grown species are 4"–8". Native to the Mediterranean. Plant in masses beneath trees or shrubs or in the rock garden.

SOWING

INDOORS Start seeds outdoors.
OUTDOORS Seed: as soon as seed is ripe. Bulb: autumn.
DEPTH Seed: just cover. Bulb: 3".

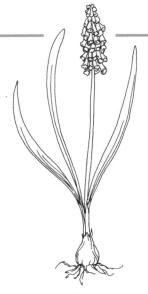

Muscari botryoides

GERMINATING

TIME 42–60 days.
REQUIREMENTS Sow seeds in flats, sink in the ground against a north-facing wall, and cover with glass. Moisten soil from time to time. Remove glass when seeds sprout. Transplant young bulbs to the garden in autumn, after 1 full season of growth.

PLANTING SEEDLINGS OUTDOORS

SPACING 2"–3".
LIGHT Sun or part shade.
SOIL Average, well-drained, with a pH level of 6.0–7.0.

CARING FOR PLANTS

Easy. Water during the growing season if weather is dry. Mulch with well-rotted manure in autumn. Divide plants every 3–4 years.

PROPAGATING

Divide bulblets after foliage has died back in summer, or allow to self-seed.

Myosotis

Forget-me-not

TYPE HA, HP, or HB grown as HA
ZONE 4–8
FLOWERING SEASON Early spring to summer, depending on species

Genus of ever-popular, clump-forming plants prized for their masses of tiny, delicate blue flowers. Foliage and habit are neat; plants grow no more than 8". Use in rock gardens, mixed woodland plantings, or borders; lovely ground cover for a lightly shaded spot.

SOWING

INDOORS 8–10 weeks before planting out.
OUTDOORS Early spring, when soil is cool and a light frost is still possible. Where winters are mild, sow in early autumn. B: mid-summer.
DEPTH Surface.

GERMINATING

TIME 8–30 days.
REQUIREMENTS Darkness and 65°–70°F. Highly susceptible to damping-off; sow in vermiculite and water from below only.

PLANTING SEEDLINGS OUTDOORS

TIME Early spring, when soil is cool and a light frost is still possible, or late autumn.
SPACING 6"–8".
LIGHT Part shade, or sun where soil is moist or summers are cool.
SOIL Moist, rich. Annuals prefer a pH level of 6.0–7.0, perennials prefer 5.5–7.0.

CARING FOR PLANTS

Easy. Water regularly. Remove plants after flowering to avoid self-seeding.

PROPAGATING

Divide in early spring. All are inclined to self-seed quite unabashedly.

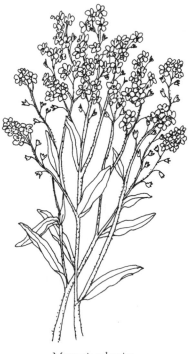

Myosotis sylvatica

A-Annual P-Perennial B-Biennial HHA-Half-hardy annual HA-Hardy annual HB-Hardy biennial HHP-Half-hardy perennial HP-Hardy perennial HHBb-Half-hardy bulb HBb-Hardy bulb

Myrrhis

Anise, Anise fern, Chervil, Myrrh, Sweet chervil, Sweet cicely

TYPE HP
ZONE 3–9
FLOWERING SEASON Summer

Genus of one species of perennial with aromatic, fernlike leaves and wiry stalks of 3'–5' bearing umbels of tiny white flowers. Best used in mixed plantings for textural contrast.

SOWING

INDOORS 8–10 weeks before planting out.
OUTDOORS 3 months before last frost.
DEPTH ⅛".

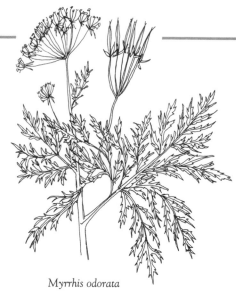

Myrrhis odorata

GERMINATING

TIME 14–42 days.
REQUIREMENTS Freeze seeds for 1 month; provide 55°–65°F thereafter.

PLANTING SEEDLINGS OUTDOORS

TIME Spring or autumn.
SPACING 24".
LIGHT Sun or part shade.
SOIL Fertile, with a pH level of 5.5–6.5. Prepare beds deeply, mixing in plenty of manure.

CARING FOR PLANTS

Prepare beds deeply to accommodate taproot and do not move once established. Allow flowers to set seeds if growing for culinary use, otherwise deadhead to prevent self-seeding.

PROPAGATING

Self-seeds.

Narcissus

Daffodil, Hoop petticoat, Jonquil, Lent lily

TYPE HBb
ZONE 4–8. Performs most successfully in cool climates.
FLOWERING SEASON Spring

Large genus of widely-grown, spring-flowering bulbs. Leaves are usually long and slender, flowers are yellow or white with a ring of petals framing a cup or trumpet; 3"–18" tall. Incomparable when massed in borders, woodland, or the lawn.

SOWING

INDOORS Seeds should be started outdoors.
OUTDOORS Seed: as soon as seed is ripe, usually late summer or autumn. Bulb: late autumn in the South, late summer to early autumn farther north.
DEPTH Seed: just cover. Small bulb: 3"–4". Large bulb: 5"–6".

GERMINATING

TIME 28–56 days.
REQUIREMENTS Sow seeds in flats, sink flats in the ground against a north-facing wall, and cover with glass. Moisten soil occasionally, if necessary. Transplant seedlings in the autumn after 2 years of growth.

PLANTING SEEDLINGS OUTDOORS

TIME Autumn.
SPACING Small species: 4". Large species: 6".
LIGHT Full sun in spring, but will tolerate part shade after flowering.
SOIL Average, with good drainage and a pH level of 6.0–7.5. Add a slow-release, low-nitrogen fertilizer (e.g., bonemeal) to each planting hole.

CARING FOR PLANTS

Easy. Plants grown from seed flower in 3–8 years. Feed once in spring and water during dry spells, discontinue after flowering ceases. Cut stalks to the ground after blooming but before seeds set to maintain a neat appearance and conserve bulbs' energy. Allow foliage to die back naturally before removing.

Narcissus pseudonarcissus

PROPAGATING

Divide in spring, after foliage has died back (about 6 weeks after flowering).

A-Annual P-Perennial B-Biennial HHA-Half-hardy annual HA-Hardy annual HB-Hardy biennial HHP-Half-hardy perennial HP-Hardy perennial HHBb-Half-hardy bulb HBb-Hardy bulb

200

Nelumbo

American lotus, Lotus, Waterlily

> **TYPE** HHP
> **ZONE** 4–10. Will only survive in colder regions if the roots do not freeze.
> **FLOWERING SEASON** Summer

Genus of water plants grown for their exquisitely beautiful and fragrant flowers which resemble delicate artichokes opening to the sun. Flowers are shades of pink or yellow; showy leaves like dinner plates are 1'–3' across.

SOWING

INDOORS Any time.
OUTDOORS Spring.
DEPTH Seed: see "Germinating, Requirements." Tuber: 1".

GERMINATING

TIME 14–30 days.
REQUIREMENTS Chip seed and submerge in hot water (75°–85°F); change water twice a day until seeds germinate. To sow *in situ*, roll each seed in a ball of clay and drop onto the bottom of your pond.

PLANTING SEEDLINGS OUTDOORS

TIME After last spring frost, when temperatures remain above 40°F.
SPACING 36"–48".
LIGHT Full sun or very light shade.
SOIL Grows in still water, 2'–5' deep, at 60°–70°F.

CARING FOR PLANTS

Easy. Feed monthly during the growing season with commercial aquatic fertilizer. Groom plants by regular removal of faded leaves. Protect from winter freeze by covering ponds with boards or canvas, plus a 3" layer of hay. Move container-grown plants to a cool, frost-free location, watering as necessary. Or tubers can be lifted and stored over winter in damp sand in a frost-free location. Divide container-grown plants every 2–3 years to maintain vigor.

PROPAGATING

Divide tubers in spring. While species may be grown from seed, selected forms must be propagated by division.

Nemesia

> **TYPE** HHA
> **ZONE** 2–10. Prefers a long, cool growing season and will not do well where summers are hot and humid.
> **FLOWERING SEASON** Late spring through summer; the blooming period will be shortened by heat

Genus of African subshrubs with lovely, two-lipped, tubular flowers of purple, white, yellow, red, or orange with conspicuously blotched throats. Plants grow 8"–24" and are suitable for edging, containers, rock gardens, borders.

SOWING

INDOORS 8–10 weeks before last frost where summers are hot; 4–6 weeks before last frost and every 6 weeks thereafter where summers are cool.
OUTDOORS After last frost, but only where summers are not too hot; in autumn in western zones 9–10.
DEPTH Surface.

GERMINATING

TIME 5–21 days.
REQUIREMENTS 55°–70°F. Seeds are very susceptible to damping-off; sow in vermiculite and water only from below.

PLANTING SEEDLINGS OUTDOORS

TIME After last frost.
SPACING 6"–12".
LIGHT Afternoon shade in hot climates will prolong plants' lives. In full sun, soil must be kept moist.
SOIL Rich, moist, well-drained.

CARING FOR PLANTS

Easy. Pinch tips of young plants to increase bushiness; feed and water regularly.

PROPAGATING

Seed only.

A-Annual P-Perennial B-Biennial HHA-Half-hardy annual HA-Hardy annual HB-Hardy biennial HHP-Half-hardy perennial HP-Hardy perennial HHBb-Half-hardy bulb HBb-Hardy bulb

201

Nemophila

Baby-blue-eyes, Five-spot

TYPE HA
ZONE 2–9. Only successful where summers are cool and nighttime temperatures remain below 65°F.
FLOWERING SEASON Plants sown in autumn in southern states will bloom in late winter; in northern climates, *Nemophila* will bloom from July to frost

Genus of diminutive annuals of neat habit bearing delightful, cup-shaped flowers with intricate markings: white petals delicately veined and dotted with blue at the tips; blue with white centers and prominent anthers with conspicuous dark stamens. These 6"–12" plants exude personality. Use in rock gardens, containers, or borders, where they make a fine edging.

SOWING

INDOORS 6–8 weeks before planting out, in peat pots.
OUTDOORS Early spring, when soil is cool and a light frost is still possible, or late autumn where winters are mild.
DEPTH Just cover.

Nemophila menziesii

GERMINATING

TIME 7–21 days.
REQUIREMENTS Easy. 55°F.

PLANTING SEEDLINGS OUTDOORS

TIME After last frost.
SPACING Small species: 4"–8". Large species: 12"–15".
LIGHT Full sun or part shade, with afternoon shade where summers are hot.
SOIL Cool, moist, light, well-drained, with a pH level of 5.0–8.0.

CARING FOR PLANTS

Water regularly and mulch to keep soil cool. Plants may be killed by excessive heat or humidity. Do not transplant.

PROPAGATING

Self-seeds freely in its native habitat.

Nepeta

Catmint, Catnip

TYPE HP
ZONE 3–9
FLOWERING SEASON Late spring to late summer

Genus of bushy perennials with a light, airy appearance and masses of tiny purple, blue, white, or yellow flowers; 6"–36". Small species make an excellent edging, taller species add lightness to the border.

SOWING

INDOORS 8–10 weeks before planting out.
OUTDOORS Early spring, when soil is cool and light frost is still possible, or late autumn.
DEPTH Just cover.

GERMINATING

TIME 7–21 days.
REQUIREMENTS Easy. 60°–70°F.

PLANTING SEEDLINGS OUTDOORS

TIME Early spring, when soil is cool and a light frost is still possible, or late autumn.
SPACING Small species: 10"–15". Large species: 18"–24".
LIGHT Full sun or part shade.
SOIL Light, sandy, with a pH level of 5.5–7.0. Drought tolerant.

CARING FOR PLANTS

Easy. Shear after flowering to encourage a light continuous blooming until frost. Divide every 3–4 years. If planting *N. cataria*, be prepared for invasion by troops of neighborhood cats, who love to roll in this feline narcotic and may inadvertently damage nearby plants. Dry leaves and flowers for several days, store in an airtight container, and surprise your feline friends this winter with an unexpected supply of catnip.

PROPAGATING

Divide in early spring, or take cuttings after flowering.

CHARLES JOSLIN

Nepeta cataria

Nerine

Guernsey lily

TYPE HHBb
ZONE 8–10
FLOWERING SEASON Summer to autumn

South African bulbs grown for their late-season blooms resembling clusters of miniature lilies growing on stiff wands 12"–24" tall. Pink, red, or white flowers usually bloom before leaves appear. Most effective massed behind a low edging that hides their gawky, naked legs.

Nerine sarniensis

SOWING

INDOORS Autumn, as soon as seed is ripe.
OUTDOORS Seed: as soon as fresh seed is available. Bulb: early autumn.
DEPTH Seed: surface. Bulb: 4"–6".

GERMINATING

TIME 7–21 days.
REQUIREMENTS 65°–70°F. Be particularly careful not to overwater.

PLANTING SEEDLINGS OUTDOORS

TIME After last frost.
SPACING 5"–8".
LIGHT Full sun or very light shade.
SOIL Moist, well-drained.

CARING FOR PLANTS

Difficult. Plants grown from seed will flower in 4–5 years. Water during early growing period, stopping when plants begin to bloom; resume watering after flowering and continue until leaves die down, tapering off gradually. Flowering is improved when plants are somewhat crowded.

PROPAGATING

Divide bulbs in autumn, after leaves have died back.

Nicandra

Apple of Peru, Shoo-fly plant

TYPE HA or HHP grown as HHA
ZONE Prefers warm climates
FLOWERING SEASON Summer to autumn

Genus of upright, branching, herbaceous plants, only one of which is commonly grown. Plants grow rapidly to 3'–4'; flowers are violet bells with white throats, blooming for just one day, followed by papery, everlasting seed cases. Use in the border or cottage garden.

SOWING

INDOORS 6–8 weeks before planting out.
OUTDOORS Early spring, when soil is cool and a light frost is still possible, or late autumn.
DEPTH Just cover.

GERMINATING

TIME 15–20 days.
REQUIREMENTS 60°–75°F.

PLANTING SEEDLINGS OUTDOORS

TIME 2–3 weeks before last frost.
SPACING 24"–48".
LIGHT Full sun or part shade.
SOIL Rich, well-drained.

CARING FOR PLANTS

Feed monthly during the growing season.

PROPAGATING

Seed only.

A-Annual P-Perennial B-Biennial HHA-Half-hardy annual HA-Hardy annual HB-Hardy biennial HHP-Half-hardy perennial HP-Hardy perennial HHBb-Half-hardy bulb HBb-Hardy bulb

Nicotiana

Flowering tobacco, Tobacco

> **TYPE** HHA or HHP, usually grown as HHA
> **ZONE** A: 2–10; P: 9–10. Prefers warm temperatures.
> **FLOWERING SEASON** Summer

Old-fashioned, erect plants prized for their cheerful, brightly colored, trumpet-shaped flowers growing in a disorganized mass. Flowers are white, pink, red, green, or yellow, and seldom as fragrant as described in the literature; leaves are rather coarse and vary in size. Dependable in the border; very much at home in cottage gardens.

SOWING

INDOORS 6–8 weeks before last frost.
OUTDOORS After last frost.
DEPTH Surface.

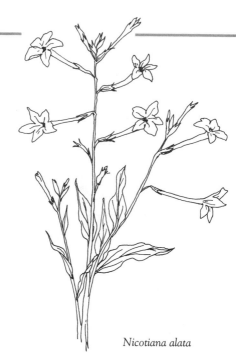

Nicotiana alata

GERMINATING

TIME 10–20 days.
REQUIREMENTS Easy. Light and 70°–75°F.

PLANTING SEEDLINGS OUTDOORS

TIME After last frost.
SPACING Small species: 12". Large species: 18"–24".
LIGHT Light shade or full sun, with shade from hot afternoon sun.
SOIL Tolerant of a wide range of soils, but prefers one that is slightly acid.

CARING FOR PLANTS

Easy. Water during hot, dry spells. Deadhead regularly to maintain a neat appearance and encourage further blooming. Stake in windy sites.

PROPAGATING

Self-seeds.

Nierembergia

Cupflower, Whitecup

> **TYPE** HHP usually grown as HHA
> **ZONE** A: 2–6; P: 7–10. Prefers warm temperatures.
> **FLOWERING SEASON** Summer

Pretty and dainty mat-forming plants grown for the multitude of open, bell-shaped flowers that blanket them all summer. Leaves are small, oval or feathery, neat in appearance; flowers may be white or purple with yellow centers; plants grow from 2" to 12". Excellent container, rock garden, or edging plants.

SOWING

INDOORS 8–10 weeks before planting out.
OUTDOORS Early spring or early autumn.
DEPTH Just cover.

GERMINATING

TIME 15–30 days.
REQUIREMENTS 70°–75°F.

PLANTING SEEDLINGS OUTDOORS

TIME 2–3 weeks before last frost, or early autumn.
SPACING 6"–8".
LIGHT Full sun; part shade where summers are hot.
SOIL Moist, rich, well-drained.

CARING FOR PLANTS

Keep soil moist, especially where summers are hot. Top-dress with well-rotted cow manure in spring. Deadhead regularly for more abundant flowering; cut back in autumn to maintain a tidy appearance.

PROPAGATING

Divide in spring, or take cuttings in autumn.

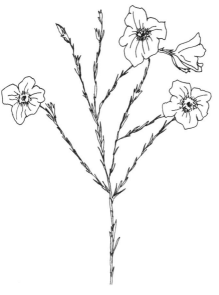

Nierembergia gracilis

Nigella

**Black cumin, Devil-in-a-bush,
Fennel flower, Love-in-a-mist**

> **TYPE** HHA or HA
> **ZONE** 2–10. Performs most
>   successfully in cool climates.
> **FLOWERING SEASON** Summer

Annuals grown for their feathery foliage
and blue, white, or pink flowers. Blooms are
like the layered tulle of a ballerina's skirt,
adorned with very showy stamens; flowers
are often followed by attractive seed pods.
Plants are 6"–24" tall, grown in the border.

SOWING

INDOORS 6–8 weeks before planting out, in
  peat pots; however, sowing *in situ* is usually more successful.
OUTDOORS Early spring, when soil is cool
  and a light frost is still possible, or autumn where winters are mild. Sow every
  4 weeks for the next 3 months for continuous blooms.
DEPTH Just cover.

GERMINATING

TIME 8–15 days.
REQUIREMENTS 65°–70°F.

PLANTING SEEDLINGS OUTDOORS

TIME After last spring frost, or early au-
  tumn.
SPACING 8"–12".
LIGHT Full sun.
SOIL Ordinary, well-drained, with a pH
  level of 6.0–7.0; tolerant of dry soil.

CARING FOR PLANTS

Easy. Fertilize and deadhead regularly. Water plants when the soil is dry. Do not disturb. To use seeds in cooking, detach brown
pods from plants, dry in a shady place, then
rub gently to release seeds. Dry completely
before storing in an airtight jar.

PROPAGATING

Self-seeds.

Nigella damascena

Nolana

Chilean bellflower

> **TYPE** HHP usually grown as
>   HHA
> **ZONE** A: 2–8; P: 9–10
> **FLOWERING SEASON** Summer

Prostrate, heat-tolerant annuals grown for
their ruffle-edged, trumpet-shaped flowers
of purple, with yellow centers outlined in
white. These 3"-tall plants are native to
China and Peru. Excellent edging, container, or rock garden plants.

SOWING

INDOORS 4–6 weeks before planting out, in
  peat pots.
OUTDOORS After last frost.
DEPTH Just cover.

GERMINATING

TIME 7–30 days.
REQUIREMENTS 60°–70°F.

PLANTING SEEDLINGS OUTDOORS

TIME After last frost.
SPACING 6"–8".
LIGHT Full sun.
SOIL Poor, dry, sandy or gravelly. Plants will
  become sprawling in moist soil.

CARING FOR PLANTS

Flowers refuse to open on cool, grey days.
Prolonged hot weather weakens plants.
Difficult to transplant.

PROPAGATING

Seed only.

A-Annual P-Perennial B-Biennial HHA-Half-hardy annual HA-Hardy annual HB-Hardy biennial HHP-Half-hardy perennial HP-Hardy perennial HHBb-Half-hardy bulb HBb-Hardy bulb

205

Nomocharis

Genus of summer-blooming bulbs with showy, nodding, somewhat flat, lily-like flowers of white, pink, or purple, often spotted and frilled. Flowers are held on slim, erect stalks of 1'–3'. Unusual border plants.

SOWING

INDOORS 10–12 weeks before planting out, in peat pots.
OUTDOORS Seed: autumn. Bulb: spring.
DEPTH Seed: just cover. Bulb: 3"–4".

GERMINATING

TIME 30–180 days.
REQUIREMENTS Difficult. *Outdoor sowing:* Sow seeds in flats, sink in the ground against a north-facing wall, and cover with glass. Moisten soil occasionally, if necessary. Transplant seedlings to the garden when they reach 3".

PLANTING SEEDLINGS OUTDOORS

TIME After last frost.
SPACING Small species: 5"–6". Large species: 12"–16".
LIGHT Sun or part shade.
SOIL Performs best in soil that is deep, cool, moist, well drained, and acid.

CARING FOR PLANTS

Difficult. Keep soil moist but not wet in summer; mulch in spring. Do not disturb bulbs.

PROPAGATING

Seed only; division of these fragile bulbs is seldom successful.

Nomocharis pardanthina

Ocimum

Basil

Genus of herbs grown both for culinary use and for their ornamental foliage. Plants are upright and branching, 16"–24" tall, with midgreen, deep plum, or blue-green leaves. Useful in the border as well as the herb garden.

SOWING

INDOORS 4–6 weeks before planting out.
OUTDOORS Start seeds outdoors only where summers are long, in early spring and again in midsummer.
DEPTH Surface.

GERMINATING

TIME 5–42 days.
REQUIREMENTS Easy. Light and 60°–70°F.

PLANTING SEEDLINGS OUTDOORS

TIME In spring, when temperatures remain above 65°F.
SPACING 10"–12".
LIGHT Sun.
SOIL Rich, well-drained, with a pH level of 5.5–6.5.

CARING FOR PLANTS

Easy. Pinch back tips when plants are 5"–6" tall to encourage bushiness. Water regularly. In midsummer, cut plant back by one-half and apply fertilizer. Harvest leaves for culinary use just before flowering, then either dry leaves in a dark place or freeze immediately. Plants can be lifted in autumn, potted up, and brought inside for winter use. Give plants 5 hours of sunlight a day and a light monthly feeding.

PROPAGATING

Some species may be propagated by cuttings, but seed is the most common method.

CHARLES JOSLIN

Ocimum basilicum

A-Annual P-Perennial B-Biennial HHA-Half-hardy annual HA-Hardy annual HB-Hardy biennial HHP-Half-hardy perennial HP-Hardy perennial HHBb-Half-hardy bulb HBb-Hardy bulb

206

Oenothera

**Desert evening primrose,
Evening primrose,
Missouri evening primrose,
Sundrops**

TYPE HA, HB, or HP, often
grown as A
ZONE 4–9. Happiest in warm
climates, and quite tolerant of
high heat combined with high
humidity.
FLOWERING SEASON Late spring to
summer, depending on species

Large genus of annuals, biennials, and perennials of varying habit grown for their
attractive, profuse — though short-lived —
flowers, most of which are cup-shaped, pink,
yellow, or white; some are night bloomers.
These North American natives, growing
from 6" to 36", are most effective when
massed in the border.

SOWING

INDOORS 8–10 weeks before last frost, in
peat pots.
OUTDOORS Early spring; seeds also may be
sown in autumn where winters are mild.
DEPTH Just cover.

GERMINATING

TIME 5–30 days.
REQUIREMENTS Darkness and 65°–70°F.

PLANTING SEEDLINGS OUTDOORS

TIME After last frost.
SPACING Small species: 5"–9". Medium spe-
cies: 12"–18". Large species: 18"–24".
LIGHT Full sun or light shade.
SOIL Light, well-drained, rather sandy, with
a pH level of 5.5–7.0; tolerates dry soil.
Excess fertility results in luxuriant foli-
age but few blooms.

Oenothera tetragona

CARING FOR PLANTS

Easy. Top-dress with cow manure in spring,
water during dry spells, and prune after
flowering to keep plants looking neat. Hot
weather may reduce blooming temporarily.

PROPAGATING

Divide in spring in zones 4–6, in autumn
in zones 7–9. Take cuttings in spring. Self-
seeds to the point of invasiveness.

Omphalodes

**Blue-eyed Mary,
Creeping forget-me-not, Navelwort**

TYPE HA or HP
ZONE A: 1–10; P: 5–9. Prefers
cool temperatures.
FLOWERING SEASON Midspring to
summer, depending on species

Annuals and perennials with pretty, delicate, cup-shaped flowers of blue or white.
Some, resembling forget-me-nots, are borne
on short stalks close to compact foliage;
others grow in airy masses along wiry 12"
stems; leaves may be green or greyish. Use
for edging or in rock gardens.

SOWING

INDOORS 10–12 weeks before planting out.
OUTDOORS Where winters are mild, sow
seeds in autumn for early spring blooms;
elsewhere, sow after last frost.
DEPTH ⅛".

GERMINATING

TIME 14–42 days.
REQUIREMENTS 65°–75°F.

Omphalodes verna

PLANTING SEEDLINGS OUTDOORS

TIME After last frost.
SPACING 6"–10".
LIGHT Part to full shade.
SOIL Cool, moist, well-drained soil, peaty,
and slightly alkaline.

CARING FOR PLANTS

Top-dress with well-rotted manure in
spring, mulch to keep soil cool, and water
well during dry spells. Where summers are
hot, cut plants back hard after blooming.

PROPAGATING

Divide perennials in spring (zones 5–6) or
autumn (zones 7–8). Both annuals and perennials self-seed.

A-Annual P-Perennial B-Biennial HHA-Half-hardy annual HA-Hardy annual HB-Hardy biennial HHP-Half-hardy perennial HP-Hardy perennial HHBb-Half-hardy bulb HBb-Hardy bulb

207

Onosma

Golden drop

Unusual plants grown for the clusters of pendulous, tubular flowers clasped tightly by long, green calyxes. Flowers may be pink, white, or yellow; plants grow 6"–18" tall. Use in borders and rock gardens.

SOWING

INDOORS 10–12 weeks before planting out.
OUTDOORS Autumn.
DEPTH Just cover.

Onosma albo-roseum

GERMINATING

TIME 30–60 days.
REQUIREMENTS 50°F.

PLANTING SEEDLINGS OUTDOORS

TIME After last frost.
SPACING Small species: 6". Large species: 12"–18".
LIGHT Full sun.
SOIL Poor, dry, gritty, very well drained, especially in winter.

CARING FOR PLANTS

Apply a top-dressing of well-rotted cow manure in spring. Keep roots cool and moist by mulching lightly with rock chips; mulch again with organic matter after the first hard frost to minimize the chance of winter rot. Plants are short-lived and require renewal every few years. Do not move.

PROPAGATING

Take cuttings in summer.

Ophiopogon

Jaburan, Lilyturf, Mondo grass, Snakesbeard

TYPE HP
ZONE 7–10
FLOWERING SEASON Midsummer

Small genus of diminutive, grassy, evergreen perennials growing 6"–12". Leaves are narrow and flat, dark green or deepest purple; short spikes of tiny blue or white flowers are followed by deep blue-black berries. Useful edging or ground cover; "black" variety is stunning in combination with plants of contrasting color.

SOWING

INDOORS 6–8 weeks before planting out.
OUTDOORS Autumn.
DEPTH ¼".

GERMINATING

TIME 30–42 days.
REQUIREMENTS Soak seeds for 24 hours in warm water, then sow and place flats where the temperature will be a constant 65°–70°F.

PLANTING SEEDLINGS OUTDOORS

TIME After last frost.
SPACING Small species: 4"–6". Large species: 12".
LIGHT Full sun to full shade; at least part shade is desirable where summers are very hot.
SOIL Any, even very dry.

CARING FOR PLANTS

Easy. Tends to look rather scruffy in winter in the North, but a radical haircut in early spring will greatly improve appearances. Divide every 4–5 years.

PROPAGATING

Divide in early spring (early autumn in the South).

Orchis

Gandergoose, Green-veined orchid

TYPE HBb
ZONE 5–8: *O. fuchsii,*
 O. maculata, O. majalis;
 6–8: *O. elata;* 7–8: *O. foliosa.*
 Prefers warm temperatures.
FLOWERING SEASON **Late spring to
 summer, depending on species**

Genus of orchids native to woods and
swamps. Flowers, growing in terminal
spikes, are small, intricate, lipped, purple,
pink, or white, often spotted. Plants grow
to 1' or 2'.

SOWING

INDOORS Any time.
OUTDOORS Seed: start seeds indoors. Roots:
 early April.
DEPTH Seed: surface. Roots: 3"–4".

GERMINATING

TIME 90–375 days.
REQUIREMENTS Light and 65°–75°F.

PLANTING SEEDLINGS OUTDOORS

TIME After last frost.
SPACING 4"–6".
LIGHT Full sun to light shade.
SOIL Rich, peaty, slightly acid.

CARING FOR PLANTS

Do not allow soil to dry out in summer and
do not disturb plants. Beyond this, each
species has its own specific requirements
and is unlikely to thrive if these are not met.
Serious growers should consult texts devoted to orchid care.

PROPAGATING

Divide in late autumn; mark locations of
plants to be divided before they die back in
summer.

Orchis spectabilis

Origanum

Annual marjoram, Marjoram,
Pot marjoram, Sweet marjoram

TYPE **HP or HHP grown as HHA**
ZONE A: 2–9; P:
 4–9: *O. rotundifolium;*
 5–9: *O. amanum, O. laevigatum,*
 O. pulchellum;
 6–9: *O. libanoticum;*
 7–9: *O. dictamnus.* **Prefers warm
 temperatures.**
FLOWERING SEASON **Summer**

Genus of herbs, some grown for culinary
use, others for foliage and flowers. Ornamental species bear masses of pale pink or
white tubular flowers surrounded by showy
bracts, or clouds of tiny tubular flowers of
deep pink held on wiry stems; 6"–18" tall.
Used in rock and herb gardens.

SOWING

INDOORS 6–8 weeks before planting out.
OUTDOORS When spring temperatures re-
 main above 45°F.
DEPTH Just cover.

GERMINATING

TIME 10 days.
REQUIREMENTS Easy. 55°–65°F.

PLANTING SEEDLINGS OUTDOORS

TIME After last frost.
SPACING Small species: 6"–8". Large spe-
 cies: 12"–15".
LIGHT Full sun.
SOIL Very well-drained, with a pH level of
 6.0–8.0; tolerant of dry, rocky soil.

CARING FOR PLANTS

Easy. In spring, pinch back young plants to
encourage branching and feed with an all-
purpose fertilizer. Harvest leaves for culinary use by cutting back stems just before
blooming. Drying the leaves (in a warm,
dark place) improves their flavor.

PROPAGATING

Divide in spring (early autumn in zones 8–
9) or take cuttings in spring.

A-Annual P-Perennial B-Biennial HHA-Half-hardy annual HA-Hardy annual HB-Hardy biennial HHP-Half-hardy perennial HP-Hardy perennial HHBb-Half-hardy bulb HBb-Hardy bulb

209

Ornithogalum

Chincherinchee, Star of Bethlehem

Type HHBb or HBb
Zone 5–9: *O. nutans, O. umbellatum;* 7–10: *O. saundersiae, O. thyrsoides;* 8–10: *O. arabicum*
Flowering Season Spring or summer, depending on species

Genus of bulbs bearing white, star-shaped flowers in terminal spikes on stiff, leafless stalks. 4"–24" tall. Mass along a path or mix with other spring-flowering bulbs; tall species make an unusual addition to the border.

Sowing
Indoors See "Germinating, Requirements."
Outdoors Seed: see "Germinating, Requirements." Bulb: autumn for spring-flowering species; late spring for summer bloomers.

Depth Seed: just cover. Bulb: 3" in warm climates, 6" where winters are cold.

Germinating
Time 30–180 days.
Requirements *Autumn sowing:* Sow seeds in flats, sink flats in the ground against a north-facing wall, and cover with glass. Moisten soil occasionally, if necessary. Bring flats indoors in spring to 55°–60°F. *Spring sowing:* Sow seeds in flats, seal loosely in plastic bags, and refrigerate. After 2–3 weeks, remove flats and sink in the ground in a shady location, covering with glass. Transplant seedlings as they appear.

Planting Seedlings Outdoors
Spacing 4"–6".
Light Full sun to full shade.
Soil Prefers rich, well-drained.

Ornithogalum arabicum

Caring for Plants
Flowers from seed in 4 years. Top-dress with well-rotted manure in April and apply a weak fertilizer periodically throughout the summer. Divide frequently. Some species may be invasive. Tender species may be lifted, stored over winter in a dry, frost-free location, and replanted in the spring.

Propagating
Plant offsets in autumn, or allow to self-seed.

Osteospermum

See *Dimorphotheca*

Oxalis

Shamrock, Sorrel

Type HBb, HP, or HHP, grown as A in the North
Zone A: 3–6; P: 6–8: *O. acetosella, O. violacea;* 7–9: *O. adenophylla, O. laciniata, O. tetraphylla;* 8–10: *O. bowiei, O. braziliensis, O. deppei, O. regnellii, O. rubra;* 9–10: *O. lasiandra, O. pes-caprae, O. purpurea;* 10: *O. corymbosa*
Flowering Season Late spring or summer, depending on species

Large genus of plants grown for their neat, attractive foliage and pretty pink or white, cup-shaped flowers that remain tightly furled until opening; 2"–12" tall. Plant near pathways where their subtlety will not be lost, or in rock gardens.

Sowing
Indoors As soon as fresh seed is available.
Outdoors Seed: as soon as fresh seed is available, usually late summer to autumn. Root: autumn.
Depth Seed: just cover. Root: 1"–2".

Germinating
Time 14–60 days.
Requirements 55°–70°F.

Planting Seedlings Outdoors
Time After last frost, when temperatures remain above 40°F.
Spacing Small species: 4"–6". Large species: 12"–15".
Light Most species require sun, but *O. acetosella* prefers dappled shade.
Soil Average, well-drained, with a pH level of 4.0–5.0.

Oxalis rosea

Caring for Plants
Water only during extremely dry weather. North of zone 7, lift tubers before first frost and store over winter in vermiculite.

Propagating
Divide tubers in autumn (spring in zone 6).

Oxypetalum

(synonymous with *Tweedia*)

Southern star, Star of the Argentine

> TYPE HHP usually grown as
> HHA
> ZONE A: 2–8; P: 9–10. Prefers
> cool temperatures.
> FLOWERING SEASON Summer
> through early autumn

Genus of climbing plants, only one of which is widely grown. A dense curtain of mid-green leaves provides a pleasing backdrop for sprays of pale blue, star-shaped flowers. Grows to 3'.

SOWING

INDOORS 6–8 weeks before planting out.
OUTDOORS After last frost.
DEPTH ¼".

GERMINATING

TIME 10–15 days.
REQUIREMENTS Easy. 70°F.

PLANTING SEEDLINGS OUTDOORS

TIME Transplant seedlings in spring when temperatures remain above 40°F.
SPACING 6"–8".
LIGHT Full sun.
SOIL Prefers a rich, well-drained loam; tolerates poor, dry soil.

CARING FOR PLANTS

Easy. Pinch back young plants to encourage bushy growth. *Oxypetalum* is highly susceptible to whitefly.

PROPAGATING

Take cuttings in spring.

Paeonia

Peony

> TYPE HP
> ZONE 2–9: *P. anomala*,
>   *P. officinalis*; 4–8: *P. lactiflora*,
>   *P. suffruticosa*; 4–9: *P. brownii*,
>   *P. daurica*;
>   5–8: *P. mlokosewitschii*,
>   *P. tenuifolia*; 6–8: *P. emodi*,
>   *P. peregrina*, *P. veitchii*
> FLOWERING SEASON Spring

Shrubby perennials of 18"–36" grown for their large and exquisitely beautiful flowers. Blooms are single or extravagantly double in white, yellow, red, purple, and every shade of pink; foliage is clean and very attractive. Often grown as hedging or in beds of their own, but also attractive in mixed borders.

SOWING

INDOORS Pre-chilled seeds 8–10 weeks before planting out.
OUTDOORS Seed: early spring, when soil is cool and a light frost is still possible. Roots: autumn.
DEPTH Seed: surface. Roots: plant eyes 1½" below surface.

GERMINATING

TIME 30–365 days.
REQUIREMENTS Place seeds in a plastic bag together with moist growing medium and refrigerate for 2–3 weeks. Provide light and 50°–60°F thereafter.

PLANTING SEEDLINGS OUTDOORS

TIME After last frost.
SPACING 24"–36".
LIGHT Full sun or part shade; prefers afternoon shade in zones 7–9.
SOIL Moist, well-drained, fertile, with a pH level of 5.5–7.0. Prepare planting holes to a depth of 18" and backfill with compost and good loam.

CARING FOR PLANTS

Fertilize in early spring when new shoots are about 12" and again lightly after blooming. Do not feed with manure. Water regularly. Deadhead after blooming and cut plants back to ground level in autumn. As growth is retarded for up to 3 years after moving, divide or move plants no more than every 10 years.

Paeonia lactiflora

PROPAGATING

Careful division of roots in early spring (zones 2–6) or autumn (zones 7–9). Each new root must contain at least 2 buds.

A-Annual P-Perennial B-Biennial HHA-Half-hardy annual HA-Hardy annual HB-Hardy biennial HHP-Half-hardy perennial HP-Hardy perennial HHBb-Half-hardy bulb HBb-Hardy bulb

211

Panicum

**Broom corn millet, Panic grass,
Switch grass**

> **TYPE** HA, HHA, or HP
> **ZONE** 4–10. Prefers warm
> temperatures.
> **FLOWERING SEASON** Summer

Ornamental grasses of erect habit with leaves that are flat, 8"–24" long; flower stems are 2'–6', bearing either silken tassels or tiny, airy inflorescences in summer. Use in borders or displays of mixed grasses.

SOWING

INDOORS Start seeds outdoors only.
OUTDOORS After last frost.
DEPTH ⅛".

GERMINATING

TIME 21 days.
REQUIREMENTS Easy. 60°–75°F.

PLANTING SEEDLINGS OUTDOORS

TIME Set out purchased plants in spring or autumn.
SPACING Small species: 12". Large species: 48".
LIGHT Sun or light shade.
SOIL Moist soil if sited in sun; will tolerate dry soil in shade.

CARING FOR PLANTS

Divide every 2–3 years. This is the grass from which brooms are made. To make your own broom, bend stalks about 24" from tips and hang for 2 weeks with tips pointing downward. Cut broom at the bend and fasten securely.

PROPAGATING

Divide perennials in spring in the North, in autumn south of zone 6, or allow to self-seed. Propagate annuals by seed.

Papaver (Annual)

**Corn poppy, Flanders poppy, Poppy,
Shirley poppy, Tulip poppy**

> **TYPE** HA or HHA
> **ZONE** 1–10. Flowers most
> successfully where temperatures
> are cool.
> **FLOWERING SEASON** Spring to
> summer

Genus of annuals grown for their large, delicate, cup-shaped flowers with papery petals in every color but blue. Flowers are held singly on 4"–36" leafless stems; foliage is lobed or toothed. The perfect plant for any sunny location.

SOWING

INDOORS 6–8 weeks before last frost, in peat pots. Best results come from seeds started *in situ*.
OUTDOORS In zones 3–7, in early spring, when soil is cool and a light frost is still possible, or late autumn. Where summers are cool, 3 spring plantings made 6 weeks apart will prolong the blooming season. In zones 8–10, sow only in autumn.
DEPTH Just cover.

GERMINATING

TIME 20 days.
REQUIREMENTS Easy. Darkness and 70°–75°F.

PLANTING SEEDLINGS OUTDOORS

TIME After last frost.
SPACING Small species: 6"–8". Large species: 8"–12".
LIGHT Full sun; *P. somniferum* will stand shade.
SOIL Moist, well-drained, not fertile; prefers a pH level of 6.0–7.0.

CARING FOR PLANTS

Easy. Deadhead frequently and remove plants altogether after flowering to avoid self-seeding. Do not move.

PROPAGATING

Self-seeds freely.

A-Annual P-Perennial B-Biennial HHA-Half-hardy annual HA-Hardy annual HB-Hardy biennial HHP-Half-hardy perennial HP-Hardy perennial HHBb-Half-hardy bulb HBb-Hardy bulb

Papaver (Perennial)

Icelandic poppy, Oriental poppy, Poppy

Genus of biennials, and perennials grown for their large, delicate, cup-shaped flowers with papery petals in every color but blue. Flowers are held singly on 4"–36" leafless stems; foliage is lobed or toothed. The perfect plant for any sunny location.

SOWING

INDOORS 6–8 weeks before last frost, in peat pots. Starting plants *in situ* recommended.

OUTDOORS P: Early spring, when soil is cool and a light frost is still possible, or late autumn. B: August.
DEPTH Surface.

Papaver orientale

GERMINATING

TIME 10–30 days.
REQUIREMENTS 55°F.

PLANTING SEEDLINGS OUTDOORS

TIME After last frost.
SPACING Small species: 9"–12". Large species: 18"–24".
LIGHT Full sun.
SOIL Well-drained, rather poor, with a pH level of 5.5–7.0. Prepare planting hole to 18", adding a layer of gravel and backfilling with half soil and half compost (do not use manure).

CARING FOR PLANTS

Water regularly during dry spells, but do not fertilize. Disbud after blooming to prevent self-seeding. Stake plants in windy sites. Mulch in winter with compost, digging in carefully in spring. Poppies do not like to be disturbed and should be moved with great care only when dormant.

PROPAGATING

Take root cuttings in autumn. Some may self-seed, but often revert to a less desirable color.

Paradisea

Paradise lily, St. Bruno's lily

Genus of one perennial with grey-green, grassy foliage and slim 2' tall stems bearing racemes of fragrant, white, funnel-shaped flowers. Lovely in a mixed planting at the woodland's edge.

SOWING

INDOORS See "Germinating, Requirements."
OUTDOORS Seed: see "Germinating, Requirements." Roots: spring or autumn.
DEPTH Seed: just cover. Roots: 3".

GERMINATING

TIME 30–180 days.
REQUIREMENTS *Autumn sowing:* Sow seeds in flats, sink these in the ground against a north-facing wall, and cover with glass. Moisten soil occasionally, if necessary. Bring flats indoors in spring to 50°F. *Spring sowing:* Sow seeds in flats, secure in plastic bags, and refrigerate. After 2–3 weeks remove flats and sink in the ground in a shady location, covering with glass. Transplant seedlings as they appear.

PLANTING SEEDLINGS OUTDOORS

TIME After last frost.
SPACING 12".
LIGHT Sun or part shade.
SOIL Prefers deep, rich, well-drained.

CARING FOR PLANTS

Easy. Plants grown from seed will flower in 2–3 years. Fertilize in spring, mulch well in autumn, and keep well watered. Plants rest without blooming for 1 year after division.

PROPAGATING

Divide in spring (autumn in zones 7 and 8). Division may lessen blooming for 1 year.

A-Annual P-Perennial B-Biennial HHA-Half-hardy annual HA-Hardy annual HB-Hardy biennial HHP-Half-hardy perennial HP-Hardy perennial HHBb-Half-hardy bulb HBb-Hardy bulb

213

Pardancanda

TYPE HP
ZONE 5–10. Requires hot summer temperatures.
FLOWERING SEASON Summer

Cheerful, understated plants with smallish, freckled, brightly colored, saucer-shaped blooms in many colors growing on 2'–3' stems above long, sword-shaped leaves. Place in the border where unassuming blooms will not be overlooked.

SOWING

INDOORS Pre-chilled seeds 8–10 weeks before planting out.
OUTDOORS Early spring or early autumn.
DEPTH Seed: just cover. Roots: 2"–3".

GERMINATING

TIME 15 days
REQUIREMENTS Easy. Place seeds in a plastic bag together with moist growing medium and refrigerate for 7 days. Place in a warm location (70°–85°F) after chilling.

PLANTING SEEDLINGS OUTDOORS

TIME Early spring, when soil is cool and a light frost is still possible, or late autumn.
SPACING 12".
LIGHT Full sun.
SOIL Tolerates most soils, but prefers moist conditions.

CARING FOR PLANTS

Easy. Water during dry spells and cut plants back to ground level in autumn. Provide a light winter mulch north of zone 7.

PROPAGATING

Divide in spring.

Parnassia

Grass of Parnassus

TYPE HP
ZONE 3–5: P. grandifolia; 3–9: P. palustris
FLOWERING SEASON Summer

Summer-blooming perennials of great charm with white, saucer-shaped flowers like eager, upturned faces. Flowers are borne singly on sturdy stems of 8" to 18"; leaves are heart-shaped. Lovely in combination with low-growing foliar plants in a moist garden.

SOWING

INDOORS Start seeds outdoors only.
OUTDOORS As soon as seed is ripe, usually in late summer.
DEPTH Surface.

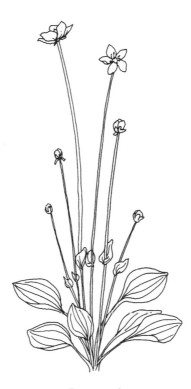

Parnassia glauca

GERMINATING

TIME 30–180 days.
REQUIREMENTS Easy. Sow seeds in flats, sink flats in the ground against a north-facing wall, and cover with glass. Moisten soil occasionally, if necessary. Transplant seedlings to peat pots when 5 true leaves have formed. Place pots on trays in light shade and keep constantly moist, watering from below. Transplant to the garden in autumn.

PLANTING SEEDLINGS OUTDOORS

TIME Set out purchased plants in autumn.
SPACING 6"–8".
LIGHT Full sun or light shade.
SOIL Rich, swampy, with a pH level of 6.0–7.0. Plants are more tolerant of dry soil when sited in light shade.

CARING FOR PLANTS

Mulch in spring and keep soil constantly moist. Divide every 3 years after flowering.

PROPAGATING

Divide after flowering.

A-Annual P-Perennial B-Biennial HHA-Half-hardy annual HA-Hardy annual HB-Hardy biennial HHP-Half-hardy perennial HP-Hardy perennial HHBb-Half-hardy bulb HBb-Hardy bulb

214

Parochetus

Shamrock pea

TYPE HP or HHP
ZONE 6–9. Can be grown north of zone 6 if plants are dug in autumn and overwintered indoors.
FLOWERING SEASON Summer through autumn

Genus of low-growing (1"–2"), trailing perennials with bright green, cloverlike foliage and intense blue, pealike flowers. Useful in rock gardens and containers.

SOWING
INDOORS 6–8 weeks before planting out.
OUTDOORS Start seeds indoors.
DEPTH Just cover.

GERMINATING
TIME 30–90 days.
REQUIREMENTS Soak seeds for 24 hours in warm water; provide 50°F thereafter.

PLANTING SEEDLINGS OUTDOORS
TIME Spring or autumn.
SPACING 12"–18".
LIGHT Sun or light shade.
SOIL Moist, gritty, poor, well-drained; rich soil will produce lush foliage with few flowers.

CARING FOR PLANTS
Water during dry periods.

PROPAGATING
Take cuttings, or divide in early spring or autumn.

Passiflora

Granadilla, Maypop, Passion flower

TYPE HHP or HP
ZONE 9–10; 6–10: *P. lutea*; 7–10: *P. incarnata, P. mollissima*; 8–10: *P. caerulea, P. x colvillii*
FLOWERING SEASON Late summer to early autumn

Genus of vines grown for their large, exotic, and intricate flowers, most often in combinations of white and purple, less frequently red; some have ornamental, egg-shaped fruit. Vines grow from 15'–30'.

SOWING
INDOORS 8 weeks before last frost.
OUTDOORS After last frost.
DEPTH ¼".

GERMINATING
TIME 30–365 days.
REQUIREMENTS Difficult. Use only fresh seed. Soak for 12 hours in warm water, sow in flats, and keep at 80°F.

PLANTING SEEDLINGS OUTDOORS
TIME After last frost, when temperatures remain above 45°F.
SPACING 24"–36".
LIGHT Sun or part shade.
SOIL Deep, moist, well-drained, moderately rich, with a pH level of 6.0–8.0. Soil that is too rich will produce abundant leaves with few flowers.

CARING FOR PLANTS
Easy. Water regularly and provide a good mulch. Prune 3-year-old vines in autumn or early spring, removing dead branches and cutting back side shoots to 6". A trellis or other support will be necessary.

PROPAGATING
Take cuttings in spring or summer.

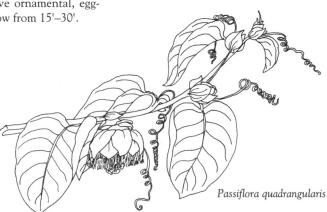
Passiflora quadrangularis

Patrinia

Clump-forming perennials, 8"–24" tall, grown for the airy clusters of tiny white or golden-yellow flowers that cover them in summer. Lacy plants for the rock garden, border, or cutting bed.

SOWING

INDOORS 8–10 weeks before planting out.
OUTDOORS Early spring, when soil is cool and a light frost is still possible, or late autumn.
DEPTH Just cover.

GERMINATING

TIME 10 days.
REQUIREMENTS 60°–65°F.

PLANTING SEEDLINGS OUTDOORS

TIME Early spring, when soil is cool and a light frost is still possible, or late autumn.
SPACING Small species: 6"–12". Large species:12"–18".
LIGHT Full sun to light shade, with afternoon shade where summers are hot.
SOIL Light, rich, moist.

CARING FOR PLANTS

Easy. Keep soil moist.

PROPAGATING

Divide in autumn (spring in zones 5 and 6) or allow to self-seed.

Pelargonium

Geranium

Genus of widely grown plants prized for their long-blooming, brightly colored flowers borne in umbels on short, sturdy stalks; flowers are white, red, orange, or shades of pink. Handsome leaves are round, sometimes lobed; plants grow 6"–36", or much taller in warm climates. Excellent container plant or massed in a display bed.

SOWING

INDOORS 8–10 weeks before last frost.
OUTDOORS After all danger of frost, in zones 9–10 only.
DEPTH Just cover.

CHARLES JOSLIN

Pelargonium graveolens

GERMINATING

TIME 3–21 days.
REQUIREMENTS 70°–75°F. Provide seedlings with plenty of light as soon as germination has begun. Pinch out young plants to establish a compact form.

PLANTING SEEDLINGS OUTDOORS

TIME 1 week after last frost.
SPACING 12"–18".
LIGHT Full sun; light shade is acceptable where summers are very hot. Variegated species must be shaded from direct sunlight.
SOIL Prefers a rich, moist soil with a pH level of 6.0–7.0; performs adequately in average soil with good drainage.

CARING FOR PLANTS

Easy and satisfying, given regular attention. Apply liquid fertilizer monthly, water when soil becomes dry, and deadhead regularly to produce an enviable display. Lift plants before the first frost and overwinter indoors, withholding water. To grow indoors in the winter, give plants 4 hours of sunlight a day, just enough water to keep the soil barely moist, and feed very lightly twice a month.

PROPAGATING

Take cuttings with 5 leaves, remove the bottom 3 leaves, and plant in a small pot. Cover loosely with a plastic bag and fasten securely. Remove bag when roots have begun to grow.

Pennisetum

Feathertop, Fountain grass

TYPE HHA, HHP, or HP
ZONE A: 1–10; P: 5–9:
  P. alopecuroides;
  6–9: *P. incomptum;*
  7–9: *P. orientale;* 8–10: *P. set–*
  aceum. Grows most successfully
  in warm climates.
FLOWERING SEASON Late summer
  to early autumn

Popular ornamental grasses with flat, narrow leaf blades that are sometimes attractively colored, and numerous 2'–4' spikes of soft, fuzzy flowers in late summer. These grasses bring a feel of the wide open spaces to the suburban garden.

SOWING
INDOORS 6–8 weeks before last frost.
OUTDOORS Early spring to midspring.
DEPTH Just cover.

GERMINATING
TIME 15–20 days.
REQUIREMENTS 70°F.

PLANTING SEEDLINGS OUTDOORS
TIME After last frost.
SPACING 18"–30".
LIGHT Full sun.
SOIL Moist, fertile, well-drained.

CARING FOR PLANTS
For best results, water regularly. Provide winter mulch in colder zones. After last frost, cut plants back to ground level.

PROPAGATING
Divide in spring.

Pennisetum setaceum

Penstemon

Beard-tongue

TYPE HHA, HHP, or HP
ZONE A: 1–10; P: 3–9:
  P. barbatus, P. digitalis,
  P. hirsutus, P. ovatus,
  P. serrulatus; 4–10: *P. smallii;*
  5–9: *P. alpinus, P. palmeri,*
  P. pinifolius; 8–10: *P. campan-*
  ulatus, P. spectabilis;
  9–10: *P. gloxiniodes.* Prefers
  cool temperatures.
FLOWERING SEASON Summer

North American natives of somewhat coarse texture, but nevertheless attractive in the sunny border. Leaves grow sparsely along erect, 12"–36" stems topped by loose clusters of tubular, lipped flowers of blue, purple, white, pink, or yellow.

SOWING
INDOORS 8–10 weeks before last frost.
OUTDOORS Spring or autumn.
DEPTH Surface.

GERMINATING
TIME 18–36 days.
REQUIREMENTS Light and 55°–65°F.

Penstemon hirsutus

PLANTING SEEDLINGS OUTDOORS
TIME After last frost.
SPACING Small species: 12"–18". Large species: 20"–30".
LIGHT Sun in cool climates, afternoon shade where summers are hot.
SOIL Fertile, well-drained, with a pH level of 5.5–7.0.

CARING FOR PLANTS
Easy, in ideal conditions. Water regularly in summer and deadhead frequently. Cut plants to ground in autumn and mulch well. Plants will bloom most profusely when grown in full sun but will die out quite quickly, in 1 or 2 years.

PROPAGATING
Take stem cuttings in spring or autumn.

A-Annual P-Perennial B-Biennial HHA-Half-hardy annual HA-Hardy annual HB-Hardy biennial HHP-Half-hardy perennial HP-Hardy perennial HHBb-Half-hardy bulb HBb-Hardy bulb

Perilla

Beefsteak plant, False coleus

TYPE HHA
ZONE 3–10. Prefers warm temperatures.
FLOWERING SEASON Summer

Genus of bushy annuals growing to 2', one of which is grown for its bronze foliage; tiny white tubular flowers are borne on stalks in summer. Use as a foil for plants of contrasting leaf color.

SOWING
INDOORS 10–12 weeks before last frost, in peat pots.
OUTDOORS After last frost.
DEPTH Surface.

GERMINATING
TIME 15–30 days.
REQUIREMENTS Light and 65°–75°F.

PLANTING SEEDLINGS OUTDOORS
TIME After last frost.
SPACING 12"–15".
LIGHT Sun or light shade.
SOIL Slightly dry, well-drained.

CARING FOR PLANTS
Easy. Pinch out tips when plants reach 6". Move only with great care.

PROPAGATING
Take cuttings; self-seeds in warm climates and may become invasive.

Perovskia

Azure sage, Russian sage

TYPE HP
ZONE 3–9
FLOWERING SEASON Late summer

Genus of perennials and subshrubs with fragrant, deeply toothed, silver or grey-green foliage. In bloom, plants are a 3'–4' cloud of silver with slender, flowering spikes delicately etched in purple or blue. Adds a light touch to the border.

GERMINATING
REQUIREMENTS Seed is rarely available.

PLANTING SEEDLINGS OUTDOORS
TIME Set out purchased plants in early spring or autumn.
SPACING 24"–36".
LIGHT Full sun.
SOIL Ordinary, dry, well-drained; must have excellent drainage where winters are wet.

CARING FOR PLANTS
Easy. Cutting plants back to ground level in spring will improve blooming.

PROPAGATING
Take cuttings in spring or summer, plant in flats or individual pots, and cover with glass.

Persicaria

See Polygonum

Petrorhagia

See Tunica

A-Annual P-Perennial B-Biennial HHA-Half-hardy annual HA-Hardy annual HB-Hardy biennial HHP-Half-hardy perennial HP-Hardy perennial HHBb-Half-hardy bulb HBb-Hardy bulb

Petroselinum

Parsley

TYPE HP usually grown as HA
ZONE 4–9
FLOWERING SEASON Parsley will bloom in the early spring of its second year

Genus of herbs grown for their strongly flavored leaves. 6"–18" plants have dark green, deeply toothed, and often curly leaves used extensively in cooking. Strictly for the herb garden.

SOWING
INDOORS Late winter, in peat pots.
OUTDOORS Early spring, when soil is cool and a light frost is still possible, or early autumn.
DEPTH ¼".

GERMINATING
TIME 21–42 days.
REQUIREMENTS Soak seeds in warm water for 24 hours; provide darkness and 70°F thereafter.

PLANTING SEEDLINGS OUTDOORS
TIME Just before last frost.
SPACING 6"–12".
LIGHT Full sun to light shade.
SOIL Rich, well-drained, with a pH level of 5.5–6.5. Amend with compost or manure at planting time.

CARING FOR PLANTS
Easy. Allow free air circulation around plants. Feed with 5–10–5 when stalks are 4"–6", and again 1 month later; a top-dressing of compost will give flagging plants a lift in midseason. Harvest leaves at any time; wash and thoroughly dry before freezing. To grow indoors in winter: Carefully dig and pot up plants in late summer, providing 5 hours sunlight a day, a warm situation (70°F), and constantly moist soil. Curly parsley is best for eating raw, while flat parsley is better for cooking.

PROPAGATING
Seed only.

Petunia

TYPE HHA
ZONE 1–10. Prefers warm temperature.
FLOWERING SEASON Late spring to frost

One of the most widely grown annuals, valued for the abundance of brightly colored trumpet-shaped flowers borne tirelessly over a very long period. The habit is somewhat procumbent with stems growing 12"–18"; flowers are white, red, purple, yellow, often bicolored. Provides strong color in containers, borders, or edging.

SOWING
INDOORS 8–10 weeks before planting out.
OUTDOORS After last frost. Fancy cultivars and hybrids should be started indoors only.
DEPTH Surface.

GERMINATING
TIME 7–21 days.
REQUIREMENTS Light and 70°–80°F.

PLANTING SEEDLINGS OUTDOORS
TIME After last frost.
SPACING 7"–10".
LIGHT Full sun or very light shade.
SOIL Moist, well-drained, with plenty of organic matter added. Prefers a pH level of 6.0–7.5.

CARING FOR PLANTS
Easy. Pinch back young plants to make bushier. Feed only after plants have become established outdoors, then once again 4 weeks later. Water and deadhead regularly, cutting back any straggly growth. Plants may be cut back by one-half at summer's end to encourage new growth.

Petunia × hybrida

PROPAGATING
Self-seeds, but resulting plants usually revert to white.

A-Annual P-Perennial B-Biennial HHA-Half-hardy annual HA-Hardy annual HB-Hardy biennial HHP-Half-hardy perennial HP-Hardy perennial HHBb-Half-hardy bulb HBb-Hardy bulb

219

Peucedanum

See *Anethum*

Phacelia

California bluebell, Wild heliotrope

> TYPE HA
> ZONE 3–10. Grows most success-
> fully where temperatures are
> cool.
> FLOWERING SEASON Summer

Bushy annuals, 1'–2' tall; leaves are often toothed, heart-shaped, and covered in up-turned, bell-shaped flowers of deepest blue or lavender. Use in containers or borders, or as an unusual annual ground cover.

SOWING

INDOORS Sow seeds of *P. campanularia* in March. All other species should be started *in situ*.

Phacelia divaricata

OUTDOORS Early spring, when soil is cool and a light frost is still possible. Where winters are mild, in late summer or early autumn.
DEPTH ¼".

GERMINATING

TIME 12–30 days.
REQUIREMENTS Darkness and 55°–65°F.

PLANTING SEEDLINGS OUTDOORS

TIME After last frost.
SPACING Small species: 4"–8". Large species: 9"–12".
LIGHT Full sun.
SOIL Ordinary, well-drained, with a pH level of 6.5–7.0; tolerates dry soil.

CARING FOR PLANTS

Pinch back young plants to encourage a bushy habit. Continuous hot weather will cause plants to stop blooming. Do not transplant.

PROPAGATING

Self-seeds.

Phalaris

Canary grass, Gardener's garters, Ribbon grass

> TYPE HA or HP
> ZONE A: 3–10; P: 4–9. Prefers
> warm temperatures.
> FLOWERING SEASON Summer

Genus of ornamental grasses grown for their flat, broad, attractively striped green and white leaves; 18"–36" tall. Flowers are somewhat skimpy, borne on very tall stalks. Use with caution as a ground cover for difficult sites; attractive near water.

SOWING

INDOORS Sow seed outdoors only.
OUTDOORS Early to midspring, or before first frost in autumn.
DEPTH Just cover.

GERMINATING

TIME 21 days.
REQUIREMENTS 60°–75°F.

PLANTING SEEDLINGS OUTDOORS

TIME Set out purchased plants in spring or autumn.
SPACING 12"–24".
LIGHT Will grow in light shade, but flowers best in full sun.
SOIL Moist, rich soil produces large, spreading plants; dry soil produces smaller, less invasive plants.

CARING FOR PLANTS

Cut back perennials in spring. Water regularly to encourage more rampant growth; hold back water and/or dig up and discard clumps to restrict growth. Divide every 5 years.

PROPAGATING

Divide creeping root stock of perennials in spring. Allow annuals to self-seed.

Phalaris arundinacea

Phaseolus

(synonymous with *Vigna*)

**Corkscrew vine,
Scarlet runner bean, Snail flower,
White Dutch runner bean**

> **TYPE** HHA, HA, or HHP
> **ZONE** A: 1–10; P: 9–10
> **FLOWERING SEASON** Summer

Fast-growing, mainly twining plants, 2'–6' tall, bearing papery blooms of red or white; one species has purple, white, or yellow snail-shaped flowers resembling a cluster of 1930s cocktail hats; long, flat seed pods follow.

SOWING

INDOORS 4–6 weeks before planting out, in peat pots.
OUTDOORS 2 weeks after last frost.
DEPTH 1".

GERMINATING

TIME 4–5 days.
REQUIREMENTS Dust seeds with pea or bean inoculant; plant with the eye facing downward. Provide 60°–70°F.

PLANTING SEEDLINGS OUTDOORS

TIME In spring, when temperatures remain above 55°F.
SPACING 6"–8".
LIGHT Sun.
SOIL Moist, rich, well-drained.

CARING FOR PLANTS

Easy. Provide a trellis for support, water regularly, then sit back and watch them grow. Pick beans for eating when about 4" long, before they become tough.

PROPAGATING

Take cuttings in early spring.

Phaseolus coccineus

Phlomis

Jerusalem sage

> **TYPE** HP
> **ZONE** 3–9: *P. tuberosa*; 5–9: *P. russeliana*. Does not do well in hot, humid climates.
> **FLOWERING SEASON** Spring to summer

Eye-catching perennials of unusual construction with widely spaced pairs of leaves cushioning clusters of flowers along stiff, upright stems of 18"–36"; flowers may be purple, yellow, or white. Grow as a specimen or at the back of a spacious border.

SOWING

INDOORS 8–10 weeks before planting out.
OUTDOORS Spring.
DEPTH Just cover.

GERMINATING

TIME 14–42 days.
REQUIREMENTS 60°F.

PLANTING SEEDLINGS OUTDOORS

TIME After last frost.
SPACING 24".
LIGHT Sun to light shade.
SOIL Light, sandy, infertile.

CARING FOR PLANTS

Easy. Water during dry spells. Lightly prune flowering branches in winter. Divide every 3 years to maintain vigor.

PROPAGATING

Take cuttings in summer or autumn. Divide in spring (zones 3–6) or early autumn (zones 7–10).

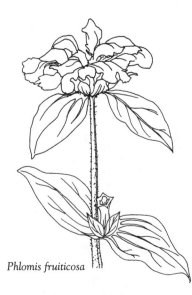

Phlomis fruiticosa

A-Annual **P**-Perennial **B**-Biennial **HHA**-Half-hardy annual **HA**-Hardy annual **HB**-Hardy biennial **HHP**-Half-hardy perennial **HP**-Hardy perennial **HHBb**-Half-hardy bulb **HBb**-Hardy bulb

Phlox (Annual)

(includes *P. drummondii*)

Annual phlox, Drummond phlox, Texas pride

TYPE HA or HHA
ZONE 2–10
FLOWERING SEASON Late spring to summer

Upright, fast-growing, cheerful plants with masses of flat, red, pink, purple, or white flowers; petals are sometimes fringed. 6" plants are useful for containers or edging.

SOWING

INDOORS 6–8 weeks before planting out, in peat pots.
OUTDOORS Early spring, when soil is cool and a light frost is still possible. Where winters are mild, sow between late summer and late autumn.
DEPTH Just cover.

GERMINATING

TIME 10–21 days.
REQUIREMENTS Darkness and 55°–65°F.

PLANTING SEEDLINGS OUTDOORS

TIME 2–3 weeks before last frost.
SPACING Dwarf species: 4"–6". Large or spreading species: 12"–18".
LIGHT Full sun or light shade.
SOIL Rich, moist, well-drained, with a pH level of 6.5–7.0.

CARING FOR PLANTS

Pinch back young plants to establish a bushy habit. Water regularly and feed once in midsummer. Deadhead frequently to extend the blooming period. Flagging plants may be rejuvenated by cutting back to 2", although excessive heat may weaken them beyond repair. Dislikes transplanting.

PROPAGATING

Seed only.

Phlox (Perennial)

Moss pink, Perennial phlox

TYPE HP
ZONE 3–9: *P. glaberrima*,
  P. x lilacina, P. ovata,
  P. paniculata, P. stolonifera,
  P. subulata; 4–8: *P. bifida,*
  P. maculata; 4–9: *P. carolina,*
  P. divaricata, P. pilosa;
  5–7: *P. douglasii;*
  5–9: *P. adsurgens, P. x procumbens;* 6–9: *P. nivalis;*
  7–9: *P. mesoleuca*
FLOWERING SEASON Spring to early autumn, depending on species

Large genus of plants grown for their show-stopping floral display. Spring bloomers are mainly prostrate and evergreen, covered in star-shaped flowers of pink, purple, white, or blue; summer bloomers bear thick clusters of brightly colored flowers on tall, erect stems. Uses are endless: borders, edging, rock gardens, or ground cover, in formal, woodland, or wildflower gardens.

SOWING

INDOORS Start seeds outdoors only.
OUTDOORS Autumn.
DEPTH Just cover.

GERMINATING

TIME 25–50 days.
REQUIREMENTS Sow seeds in flats, sink in the ground against a north-facing wall, and cover with glass. Moisten soil occasionally, if necessary. Transplant seedlings in spring or autumn.

PLANTING SEEDLINGS OUTDOORS

TIME Spring or autumn.
SPACING Small species: 6"–8". Medium species: 10"–15". Large species: 24".

LIGHT Full sun or part shade.
SOIL Moist, well-drained, fertile, enriched with organic matter (wood ash is ideal). Prefers a pH level between 6.5 and 7.5.

CARING FOR PLANTS

Deadhead regularly and cut back severely after flowering to keep plants looking neat. Phlox are highly prone to mold in warm, damp weather; to minimize the risk, site where air circulation is unrestricted (do not plant near walls), thin plants in spring by cutting back all but 3–4 stalks, and avoid wetting leaves when watering. Pull up self-seeded plants as these do not retain the parent flower's color.

PROPAGATING

Divide in spring in the North, in autumn south of zone 6. Take cuttings in early spring.

Phlox subulata

A-Annual P-Perennial B-Biennial HHA-Half-hardy annual HA-Hardy annual HB-Hardy biennial HHP-Half-hardy perennial HP-Hardy perennial HHBb-Half-hardy bulb HBb-Hardy bulb

222

Phormium

**Flax lily, Mountain flax,
New Zealand flax**

Type HHP
Zone 8–10
Flowering Season Summer

Evergreen perennials resembling yucca with stiff, sword-shaped leaves, some with red, yellow, or white stripes. These 3'–10' giants must be positioned with care, but make a stunning specimen or mass planting; the strongly architectural form should be exploited.

SOWING
Indoors 10–12 weeks before planting out.
Outdoors February.
Depth Just cover.

GERMINATING
Time 30–180 days.
Requirements 60°–65°F.

PLANTING SEEDLINGS OUTDOORS
Time Late spring.
Spacing Small species: 12". Medium species: 18"–24". Large species: 24"–36", or singly.
Light Full sun or part shade.
Soil Sandy, moist, fertile.

CARING FOR PLANTS
Easy. Water well during dry spells and divide every 3–4 years.

PROPAGATING
Divide in spring.

Phormium tenax

Phuopsis

(synonymous with *Crucianella*)

Crosswort

Type HP sometimes grown as
  HA
Zone 6–9. Not tolerant of high
  heat and humidity.
Flowering Season Summer

Genus of one species of mat-forming perennial, with narrow leaves growing in whorls along thin stalks topped with round clusters of tiny, pink, tubular flowers; 12" tall. Allow plants to cascade over walls, rock gardens, or the front of the border.

Phuopsis stylosa

SOWING
Indoors Start seeds outdoors.
Outdoors Autumn.
Depth Surface.

GERMINATING
Time 30–40 days.
Requirements Easy. Light and 50°–60°F.

PLANTING SEEDLINGS OUTDOORS
Time Set out purchased plants in spring or autumn.
Spacing 18"–24".
Light Sun or part shade.
Soil Dry.

CARING FOR PLANTS
Plants spread rapidly and, given the opportunity, will appropiate your entire garden.

PROPAGATING
Divide in spring, or take cuttings in summer.

Phygelius

Cape fuchsia

TYPE HP or HHP
ZONE 5–9
FLOWERING SEASON Summer

South African subshrubs, 3'–5' tall, grown for their panicles of drooping, trumpet-shaped flowers of white, red, yellow, or pink. Use in the border or in mixed shrub plantings.

SOWING

INDOORS 6–8 weeks before planting out.
OUTDOORS Spring or summer.
DEPTH Just cover.

Phygelius capensis

GERMINATING

TIME 10–14 days.
REQUIREMENTS 70°–75°F.

PLANTING SEEDLINGS OUTDOORS

TIME After last frost.
SPACING 24"–36".
LIGHT Full sun, with afternoon shade where summers are hot and humid.
SOIL Light, well-drained, with abundant moisture during the growing season.

CARING FOR PLANTS

Water when the ground becomes dry. Prune occasionally to maintain a compact size, and cut back to ground level in spring. In colder areas, plant against a south wall and mulch well in autumn.

PROPAGATING

Divide in autumn (spring in zones 5–6) or take cuttings in late summer.

Physalis

Cape gooseberry, Chinese lanterns, Husk tomato, Winter cherry

TYPE HP
ZONE 3–9
FLOWERING SEASON Summer to
    early autumn

Spreading perennials with inconspicuous flowers but very showy orange seed cases resembling paper lanterns that are often used in dried flower arrangements. Plants are 1'–4' tall. Grow in the border or cutting bed.

SOWING

INDOORS Early spring.
OUTDOORS Spring or summer.
DEPTH Surface.

GERMINATING

TIME 15–30 days.
REQUIREMENTS Difficult. Light and 70°–75°F.

PLANTING SEEDLINGS OUTDOORS

TIME After last frost.
SPACING Small species: 10"–15". Large species: 24"–36".
LIGHT Full sun or part shade.
SOIL Average, well-drained. Plants tend to become weedy in very rich soil.

CARING FOR PLANTS

Easy. Water regularly; cut stems to the ground in autumn.

PROPAGATING

Divide in early spring.

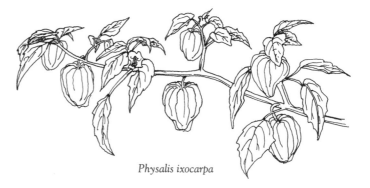

Physalis ixocarpa

A-Annual P-Perennial B-Biennial HHA-Half-hardy annual HA-Hardy annual HB-Hardy biennial HHP-Half-hardy perennial HP-Hardy perennial HHBb-Half-hardy bulb HBb-Hardy bulb

Physostegia

(synonymous with *Dracocephalum*)

False dragonhead, Obedient plant

> TYPE HP
> ZONE 3–9
> FLOWERING SEASON Midsummer
>   to early autumn

Stiff, rather coarse perennials bearing 1'–4' spikes of tubular, pink, white, or purple flowers generally growing on opposite sides of the stem, giving plants a rather flat appearance. Used in borders and wildflower gardens.

SOWING

INDOORS 8–10 weeks before planting out.
OUTDOORS Early spring or early autumn.
DEPTH Just cover.

GERMINATING

TIME 15–30 days.
REQUIREMENTS 60°–75°F.

PLANTING SEEDLINGS OUTDOORS

TIME Early spring, when soil is cool and a light frost is still possible, or early autumn.
SPACING Small species: 12"–18". Large species: 24".
LIGHT Full sun where soil is moist, part shade in drier soil.
SOIL Prefers cool, light, moist, slightly acid (pH 5.0–7.0). Grow in dry soil to reduce rampant spreading.

CARING FOR PLANTS

Easy. Mulch plants and water regularly. Stake tall species. Prune roots to control spreading. Cut back to ground level in autumn.

PROPAGATING

Divide in spring.

Phyteuma

Rampion

> TYPE HP
> ZONE 5–8
> FLOWERING SEASON Summer

Genus of tufted or rosette-forming alpine perennials bearing white, purple, or blue flowers either in spikes or on round heads like small barbed sputniks; 2"–36" tall. Useful in rock gardens and drystone walls.

SOWING

INDOORS See "Germinating, Requirements."
OUTDOORS See "Germinating, Requirements."
DEPTH Just cover.

GERMINATING

TIME 30–90 days.
REQUIREMENTS *Autumn sowing:* Sow seeds in flats, sink flats in ground against a north-facing wall, and cover with glass. Moisten soil occasionally. Bring flats indoors in spring to 60°–70°F. *Spring sowing:* Sow seeds in flats of moistened medium, secure in a plastic bag, and refrigerate for 2–3 weeks. Sink flats in the ground in a shady location, covering with glass. Transplant seedlings as they appear.

PLANTING SEEDLINGS OUTDOORS

TIME After last frost.
SPACING Small species: 8"–12". Large species: 18".
LIGHT Sun, or light shade where summers are very hot.
SOIL Light, fertile, limy, gritty or sandy.

CARING FOR PLANTS

Keep plants well watered during dry weather. Do not disturb roots.

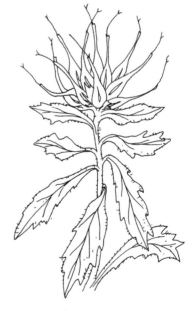

Phyteuma comosum

PROPAGATING

Divide in spring in zones 5–6, in autumn in zones 7–8.

A-Annual P-Perennial B-Biennial HHA-Half-hardy annual HA-Hardy annual HB-Hardy biennial HHP-Half-hardy perennial HP-Hardy perennial HHBb-Half-hardy bulb HBb-Hardy bulb

225

Pimpinella

Anise, Aniseed

TYPE HA
ZONE 4–9
FLOWERING SEASON Summer

Annual herbs, 18"–36" tall, grown for culinary use. Basal foliage is pear-shaped and toothed, while upper leaves are feathery; tiny white flowers, borne in umbels, are similar to Queen Anne's lace. Usefulness is restricted to the herb garden.

SOWING

INDOORS 8–10 weeks before last frost, in peat pots.
OUTDOORS After last frost.
DEPTH ¼".

GERMINATING

TIME 20–28 days.
REQUIREMENTS 70°F.

PLANTING SEEDLINGS OUTDOORS

TIME After last frost.
SPACING 4"–12"; plants grown close together will provide support for each other.
LIGHT Full sun.
SOIL Ordinary, well-drained, with a pH level of 5.5–6.5.

CARING FOR PLANTS

Water regularly during dry spells and provide support for lanky growth. Do not move. When seeds start turning grey and come away from seed heads easily, they are ready to harvest. Wash and dry seeds thoroughly before storing in an airtight container.

PROPAGATING

Seed only.

Pinguicula

Butterwort

TYPE HHP
ZONE 3–8: *P. vulgaris*;
  7–9: *P. grandiflora*. **Prefers cool temperatures.**
FLOWERING SEASON **Spring to summer**

Genus of small, rosette-forming, carnivorous plants, 5"–8",with sticky, oval, basal leaves and slender stalks bearing lipped, funnel-shaped flowers of purple, white, or yellow. Grow in moist rock gardens.

SOWING

INDOORS 8–10 weeks before planting out.
OUTDOORS Autumn.
DEPTH Surface.

GERMINATING

TIME 30–130 days.
REQUIREMENTS Light and 55°–60°F.

PLANTING SEEDLINGS OUTDOORS

TIME When spring temperatures remain above 45°F.
SPACING 2"–4".
LIGHT Full sun.
SOIL Prefers moist, neutral, or slightly acid.

CARING FOR PLANTS

Top-dress with leaf mold in early spring. Water well during dry spells.

PROPAGATING

Plant offsets, or root single leaves anchored to moist sand.

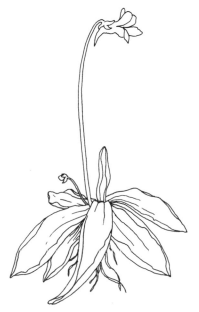

Pinguicula vulgaris

Platycodon

Balloon flower, Bellflower

> **Type** HP
> **Zone** 3–9
> **Flowering Season** Summer

One species of erect perennial grown for its white, purple, or blue flowers growing along arching, 1'–3' stems. New flowers are completely round, but suddenly open into wide-mouthed, upturned bells. Lovely in the summer border.

Sowing

Indoors 6–8 weeks before planting out, in peat pots.
Outdoors Spring or summer.
Depth Surface.

Platycodon grandiflorus

Germinating

Time 15–30 days.
Requirements Light and 70°F. Seedlings are extremely fragile.

Planting Seedlings Outdoors

Time Late spring.
Spacing Small species: 9"–12". Large species:12"–18".
Light Full sun or light shade.
Soil Prefers rich, moist, well-drained.

Caring for Plants

Easy. Water and deadhead frequently to prolong the blooming period. Feed lightly from time to time. Stake tall species. *Platycodon* is very fragile and must be handled with care; mark locations to avoid damage before plants emerge in late spring. Plants are slow to recover after division.

Propagating

Take cuttings in summer, or divide in spring (autumn in zones 7–9), taking care not to damage the taproot.

Platystemon

Creamcups

> **Type** HA or HHA
> **Zone** Prefers temperate Western climates
> **Flowering Season** Summer

Genus of one species of annual native to the western United States. Sunny yellow, saucer-shaped flowers are held individually on wiry 12" stems above dull green, lance-shaped leaves. Use in the border or for edging.

Sowing

Indoors Start outdoors only.
Outdoors Early spring, when soil is cool and a light frost is still possible, or late autumn.
Depth Just cover.

Germinating

Time 14–30 days.
Requirements 55°–65°F.

Planting Seedlings Outdoors

Time Set out purchased plants after last spring frost.
Spacing 4"–8".
Light Full sun.
Soil Prefers a sandy loam; will tolerate dry soil.

Caring for Plants

Top-dress with well-rotted manure in spring. Water regularly.

Propagating

Self-seeds.

A-Annual P-Perennial B-Biennial HHA-Half-hardy annual HA-Hardy annual HB-Hardy biennial HHP-Half-hardy perennial HP-Hardy perennial HHBb-Half-hardy bulb HBb-Hardy bulb

Podophyllum

Himalayan mayapple, Mandrake, Mayapple

> TYPE HP
> ZONE 3–9: *P. peltatum*; 5–8: *P. hexandrum*
> FLOWERING SEASON Spring

Serene, secretive wildflowers grown for their large, flat, lobed leaves growing in pairs above long, slender stems; shy, white, cup-shaped flowers peek out from beneath leaves in spring. Beautiful woodland ground cover.

SOWING

INDOORS Start seeds outdoors.
OUTDOORS As soon as ripe seed is available, usually July to September.
DEPTH Seed: just cover. Rhizome: 1".

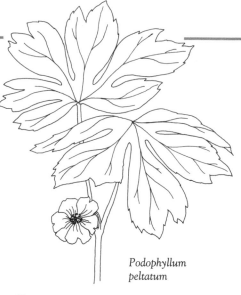

Podophyllum peltatum

GERMINATING

TIME 30–180 days.
REQUIREMENTS Difficult. Sow seeds in flats, plunge these to the rim against a north-facing wall, and cover with glass. Moisten soil, as necessary. Transplant to individual pots after 1 growing season, to the garden after 2.

PLANTING SEEDLINGS OUTDOORS

TIME Set out purchased plants in spring or autumn.
SPACING 12"–15".
LIGHT Light to full shade.
SOIL Rich, moist, with a pH level of 4.0–7.0.

CARING FOR PLANTS

Easy. Mulch in spring with wood chips and again in autumn with leaf mold; keep the soil constantly moist. Some species die back completely after flowering. Mayapples will quickly fill as much space as they are given.

PROPAGATING

Divide after blooming, or allow to self-seed.

Polemonium

Jacob's ladder

> TYPE HP
> ZONE 3–8: *P. caeruleum, P. pauciflorum, P. pulcherrimum, P. reptans*; 4–8: *P. foliosissimum*; 5–8: *P. carneum*
> FLOWERING SEASON Late spring to summer

Genus of perennials with pairs of small, narrow leaves that give plants an airy look, and pretty, cup-shaped flowers of blue, white, pink, or yellow; 6"–36" tall. Used in borders and woodland plantings.

SOWING

INDOORS 8–10 weeks before planting out.
OUTDOORS Early spring or early autumn.
DEPTH Just cover.

GERMINATING

TIME 20–25 days.
REQUIREMENTS 70°F.

PLANTING SEEDLINGS OUTDOORS

TIME Early spring, when soil is cool and a light frost is still possible, or early autumn.
SPACING Small species: 9"–12". Large species:18"–24".
LIGHT Part shade; full sun only where summers are cool.
SOIL Cool, moist, rich, well-drained, with a pH level of 5.0–8.0.

CARING FOR PLANTS

Easy. Top-dress with manure or leaf mold in spring. Water plants during dry spells. Cut back stems to the ground after flowering. Divide with extreme care as roots are very fragile. Flowering will be inhibited by hot weather.

PROPAGATING

Allow to self-seed, or divide in spring.

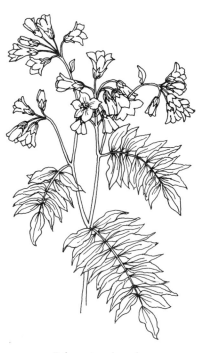

Polemonium boreale

Polianthes

Tuberose

> TYPE HHP often grown as A
> ZONE A: 7–8; P: 9–10
> FLOWERING SEASON Late summer
>   to autumn

Tuberous plants of 8"–48", with grassy foliage and stiff spikes of deeply scented, tubular flowers that are usually white. Grow in borders and containers where their heavenly fragrance will not be missed.

SOWING

OUTDOORS Tuber: when temperatures remain above 60°F.
DEPTH Tuber: 3".

GERMINATING

REQUIREMENTS Extremely difficult, if not impossible. Trying to grow tuberoses from seed can only end in heartbreak and is not recommended.

PLANTING SEEDLINGS OUTDOORS

SPACING 6"–8".
LIGHT Full sun.
SOIL Humus-rich, with a pH level of 6.0–7.5.

CARING FOR PLANTS

Tuberoses are not difficult to grow, but do require time and attention to grow *well*. Water regularly in spring and summer and apply liquid fertilizer every 2 weeks during the growing season. Plants may need staking in windy locations. North of zone 9, lift in autumn and store in a cool, frost-free location, replanting in the spring.

PROPAGATING

Divide tubers in spring.

Polygonatum

Solomon's seal

> TYPE HP
> ZONE 4–9
> FLOWERING SEASON Early summer

Genus of greatly varying perennials, the most widely grown being unassuming but graceful woodland plants with gently arching stems of 2"–48", with paired leaves below which hang small clusters of white, tubular flowers. Effective either massed or in mixed woodland plantings.

SOWING

INDOORS See "Germinating, Requirements."
OUTDOORS See "Germinating, Requirements."
DEPTH Seed: just cover. Roots: 2".

Polygonatum biflorum

GERMINATING

TIME 1–18 months.
REQUIREMENTS *Autumn sowing:* Sow seeds in flats, sink flats in the ground against a north-facing wall, and cover with glass. Moisten soil occasionally, if necessary. Bring indoors in spring to 50°F. *Spring sowing:* Sow seeds in flats, secure in plastic bags, and refrigerate for 2–3 weeks. Remove flats and sink in the ground in a shady location, covering with glass. Transplant seedlings as they emerge.

PLANTING SEEDLINGS OUTDOORS

TIME Spring or autumn.
SPACING 18".
LIGHT Part to full shade.
SOIL Light, moist, with a pH level of 6.0–7.0; tolerates dry soil if grown in full shade.

CARING FOR PLANTS

Easy. Top-dress with manure in early spring and feed periodically throughout the growing season. Cut back to ground level in autumn.

PROPAGATING

Divide in early spring in the North, autumn south of zone 6.

A-Annual P-Perennial B-Biennial HHA-Half-hardy annual HA-Hardy annual HB-Hardy biennial HHP-Half-hardy perennial HP-Hardy perennial HHBb-Half-hardy bulb HBb-Hardy bulb

Polygonum

(synonymous with *Persicaria*)

Bistort, China fleece vine, Himalayan fleece flower, Kiss-me-over-the-garden-gate, Knotweed, Prince's feather, Russian vine, Silver lace vine, Smartweed, Snakeweed

> **TYPE** HA, HP, HHA, or HHP
> **ZONE** A: 3–10; P: 3–9: *P. affine*, *P. bistorta*, *P. cuspidatum*, *P. macrophyllum*; 4–8: *P. vacciniifolium*, *P. virginianum*; 6–9: *P. amplex-icaule*, *P. campanulatum*. Prefers warm temperatures.
> **FLOWERING SEASON** Summer to autumn

Large genus of annuals and perennials, some of which are evergreen, some trailing or climbing, some aquatic. Most bear small white or red flowers in profusion in racemes or spikes and have strong foliage. Use in borders, wildflowers gardens, and bog or water gardens.

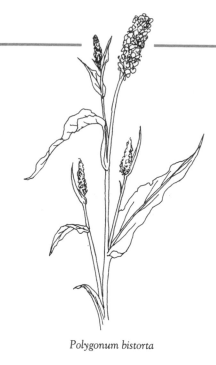

Polygonum bistorta

SOWING

INDOORS 2–3 weeks before last frost.
OUTDOORS After last frost.
DEPTH Just cover.

GERMINATING

TIME 20–60 days.
REQUIREMENTS 70°–75°F.

PLANTING SEEDLINGS OUTDOORS

TIME After last frost.
SPACING Small species: 8"–12". Medium species: 12"–24". Large species: 24"–48".
LIGHT Part shade, or full sun where summers are cool.
SOIL Moist, well-drained, with a pH level of 6.0–7.5.

CARING FOR PLANTS

Water well during the flowering season. Cut back flower stems in autumn. Prune climbers severely in spring to restrict growth and create a more attractive habit. Some species may be invasive.

PROPAGATING

Divide in early spring in zones 3–6, in early autumn elsewhere; or allow to self-seed.

Polypogon

Beard grass, Rabbit-foot grass

> **TYPE** P usually grown as HA
> **ZONE** A: prefers warm climates; P: 8–10
> **FLOWERING SEASON** Summer to autumn

Genus of grasses native to North America with flat leaves and fluffy, ornamental flower spikes. 24" tall.

SOWING

INDOORS Start seed *in situ*.
OUTDOORS Early spring to midspring.
DEPTH Surface.

GERMINATING

TIME 21 days.
REQUIREMENTS Light and 60°–75°F. Seed is seldom available.

PLANTING SEEDLINGS OUTDOORS

TIME Set out purchased plants after last frost.

SPACING 12"–18".
LIGHT Flowers best in full sun, but will grow in light shade.
SOIL Well drained, fertile.

CARING FOR PLANTS

Feed once in spring with organic fertilizer. Protect plants from damaging wind and rain. Discard plants after flowering as the foliage has little ornamental value.

PROPAGATING

Take cuttings.

Porteranthum

See *Gillenia*

A-Annual P-Perennial B-Biennial HHA-Half-hardy annual HA-Hardy annual HB-Hardy biennial HHP-Half-hardy perennial HP-Hardy perennial HHBb-Half-hardy bulb HBb-Hardy bulb

230

Portulaca

**Purslane, Pussley, Rose moss,
Sun moss, Sun plant, Wax pink**

> TYPE HA or HHA
> ZONE 2–10. Thrives where
>   summers are hot.
> FLOWERING SEASON Summer to
>   late autumn

Hard-working annual plants bearing a profusion of brightly colored flowers, even in
extreme heat. Plants are 6"–18" tall with
small, succulent leaves and prominent, cup-
shaped blooms in every shade of red, pink,
yellow, or white. Use in containers and borders; interesting informal ground cover.

SOWING

INDOORS Pre-chilled seeds 6–8 weeks be-
fore planting out, in peat pots.
OUTDOORS After last frost.
DEPTH Surface.

GERMINATING

TIME 7–21 days.
REQUIREMENTS Place seeds in a plastic bag
together with moist growing medium and
refrigerate for 2 weeks; thereafter provide
light and 70°–85°F.

PLANTING SEEDLINGS OUTDOORS

TIME Late spring.
SPACING Small species: 5"–8". Large spe-
cies: 12"–24".
LIGHT Full sun.
SOIL Poor, sandy, with a pH level of 5.5–
7.5.

CARING FOR PLANTS

Easy, requiring almost no care. Do not water excessively and do not transplant. Discard plants after flowering to avoid self-
seeding.

PROPAGATING

Self-seeds, especially in warm climates.

Potentilla

Cinquefoil

> TYPE HP
> ZONE 4–9; 2–8: *P. tridentata*
> FLOWERING SEASON Midspring to
>   autumn, depending on species

Perennial subshrubs of rather messy habit
grown for the bright yellow, pink, red, or
white saucer-shaped flowers that appear
over a long period. Stems are wiry and foliage very fine; plants grow 3"–24". Use in
rock gardens and borders.

SOWING

INDOORS 8–10 weeks before planting out.
OUTDOORS Early spring or early autumn.
DEPTH Just cover.

GERMINATING

TIME 14–30 days.
REQUIREMENTS 65°–70°F.

PLANTING SEEDLINGS OUTDOORS

TIME Early spring, when soil is cool and a
light frost is still possible, or early autumn.
SPACING Small species: 8"–12". Large species: 12"–18".
LIGHT Full sun, with afternoon shade where
summers are very hot.
SOIL Sandy, somewhat poor soil, with a pH
level of 5.0–7.0.

CARING FOR PLANTS

Easy. Apply a light organic dressing in
spring and cut back flowering stems in autumn. Tall species may be planted close together to provide support. Divide every 3
years.

PROPAGATING

Divide in spring in zones 2–6, in autumn
elsewhere; take cuttings in spring or autumn.

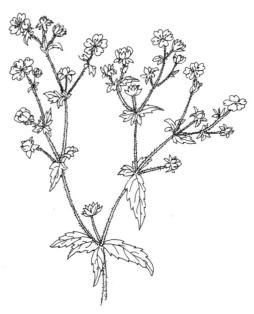

Potentilla astrosanguinea

Poterium

See *Sanguisorba*

A-Annual P-Perennial B-Biennial HHA-Half-hardy annual HA-Hardy annual HB-Hardy biennial HHP-Half-hardy perennial HP-Hardy perennial HHBb-Half-hardy bulb HBb-Hardy bulb

231

Primula

Cowslip, English primrose,
Fairy primrose, German primrose,
Polyanthus, Primrose

TYPE HHP or HP, often grown as
HHA
ZONE 3–8: P. capitata,
P. chungensis, P. denticulata,
P. waltonii; 3–9: P. auricula,
P. x polyantha, P. sieboldii;
5–8: P. alpicola, P. x bullesiana,
P. chionantha, P. japonica,
P. nutans, P. pulverulenta,
P. rosea 'Grandiflora'; 5–9:
P. beesiana, P. florindae,
P. veris, P. vialii, P. vulgaris;
8–10: P. malacoides, P. obconica.
Most primroses are happiest in
cool, humid climates.
FLOWERING SEASON Late winter to
early summer, depending on
species

Very large genus of mainly perennial plants with leaves in basal rosettes and tubular, bell-shaped or flat flowers in a wide array of colors. Plants are usually low-growing (3"–12"), although some reach 30". Variously suited to rock, bog, and woodland gardens, borders or mass displays.

Primula japonica

SOWING

INDOORS Pre-chilled seeds 8–10 weeks before last frost.
OUTDOORS In autumn in zones 8–10 only.
DEPTH Surface.

GERMINATING

TIME 10–40 days.
REQUIREMENTS Difficult. Place seeds in a plastic bag together with moist growing medium and refrigerate for 3 weeks. Then provide light and 60°–65°F.

PLANTING SEEDLINGS OUTDOORS

TIME After last frost.
SPACING Small species: 6"–8". Large species: 12"–18".
LIGHT Full sun in cool climates; elsewhere part shade.
SOIL Cool, moist, humus-rich, with a pH level of 5.5–7.0. Good winter drainage is essential.

CARING FOR PLANTS

Easy. Feed before flowering (do not use manure). When blooming finishes, top-dress with peat moss and remove flowering stems. Mulch well where summers are hot. Plants may be attractive to slugs and snails.

PROPAGATING

Divide after flowers fade in the North, in early autumn in the South.

Prunella

Self heal

TYPE HP
ZONE 6–9
FLOWERING SEASON Spring
through autumn

Long-blooming, evergreen, mat-forming perennials of 6"–12", some of which are weedy. Tiny flowers growing in terminal clusters are hooded, mainly blue or purple, but sometimes pink or white. Grow in rock gardens and borders.

SOWING

INDOORS 8–10 weeks before planting out.
OUTDOORS Early spring, when soil is cool and a light frost is still possible.
DEPTH Just cover.

GERMINATING

TIME 30–60 days.
REQUIREMENTS Easy. 55°–65°F.

Prunella grandiflora

PLANTING SEEDLINGS OUTDOORS

TIME Spring.
SPACING 12"–18".
LIGHT Full sun in cool climates, part shade where summers are hot.
SOIL Fairly tolerant of dry soil when sited in part shade, but must be kept moist during hot weather; prefers a pH level of 6.0–7.5

CARING FOR PLANTS

Easy. Deadhead regularly. Keep soil moist during hot summers. Cut back to ground level after flowering. May be invasive and should not be planted near lawns, where it can become a nuisance.

PROPAGATING

Divide in early spring, or allow to self-seed.

A-Annual P-Perennial B-Biennial HHA-Half-hardy annual HA-Hardy annual HB-Hardy biennial HHP-Half-hardy perennial HP-Hardy perennial HHBb-Half-hardy bulb HBb-Hardy bulb

232

Pulmonaria

Bethlehem sage, Lungwort

Type HP
Zone 3–9
Flowering Season Spring

Genus of woodland plants grown for their tubular, pink or purple flowers and attractive foliage, which is often freckled or deeply blotched with white or silver. Useful woodland plants, where they make an excellent ground cover or edging.

Sowing

Indoors 7–9 weeks before planting out.
Outdoors Early spring.
Depth Just cover.

Germinating

Time 30–42 days.
Requirements Seldom grown from seed as resulting plants are of variable quality. Provide 60°–65°F.

Planting Seedlings Outdoors

Time Autumn.
Spacing Small species: 6"–10". Large species: 12"–18".
Light Part to full shade.
Soil Moist, cool, rich.

Caring for Plants

Easy. In early spring, mulch plants well to keep soil moist and apply a balanced fertilizer. Cut back lightly after flowering. Divide plants every 4–5 years. Will survive a certain amount of neglect, but most abundant blooms and attractive foliage will be found on plants that receive ample food and water.

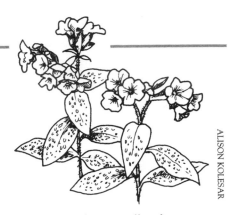

Pulmonaria officinalis

Propagating

Divide in the spring north of zone 7, autumn in the South.

Pulsatilla

Alpine anemone, Pasque flower, Spring anemone

Type HP
Zone 4–8
Flowering Season Spring or early summer, depending on species

Small genus of perennials, some of which are evergreen, with fine, feathery leaves. Bell- or cup-shaped flowers are borne singly on thick, hairy stalks before foliage emerges; flowers are yellow, purple, bronze, white, or red. Plants grow to 12". Suitable for walls and rock gardens.

Sowing

Indoors Sow seed outdoors only.
Outdoors As soon as fresh seed is available, usually in summer.
Depth Just cover.

Pulsatilla vulgaris

Germinating

Time 30–180 days.
Requirements Difficult. Only use fresh seed. Sow seeds in flats, sink flats in the ground against a north-facing wall, and cover with glass. Moisten soil occasionally, if necessary. Bring indoors in spring to 60°–70°F.

Planting Seedlings Outdoors

Time Spring or autumn.
Spacing 8"–12".
Light Full sun; part shade where summers are hot.
Soil Rich, moist, well-drained, and slightly alkaline.

Caring for Plants

Easy. Water regularly during dry spells. Do not disturb established plants.

Propagating

Take cuttings from the tips of shoots. Successful division is difficult because of deep roots.

A-Annual **P**-Perennial **B**-Biennial **HHA**-Half-hardy annual **HA**-Hardy annual **HB**-Hardy biennial **HHP**-Half-hardy perennial **HP**-Hardy perennial **HHBb**-Half-hardy bulb **HBb**-Hardy bulb

Puschkinia

Striped squill

> **TYPE** HBb
> **ZONE** 4–10. Most successful in cool climates.
> **FLOWERING SEASON** Early spring

Genus of dwarf bulbs with erect, strap-shaped leaves curving lengthwise, and 6" spikes of pure white or blue-and-white-striped, star-shaped flowers. Use in rock gardens and borders.

SOWING

INDOORS Start seeds outdoors.
OUTDOORS Seed: autumn. Bulb: autumn.
DEPTH Seed: ⅛". Bulb: 3"–4".

GERMINATING

TIME 30+ days.
REQUIREMENTS Sow seeds in flats, sink these in the ground against a north-facing wall, and cover with glass. Moisten soil occasionally, if necessary. Transplant seedlings as they appear.

PLANTING SEEDLINGS OUTDOORS

SPACING 3"–4".
LIGHT Sun or part shade.
SOIL Moist, well-drained.

CARING FOR PLANTS

Plants grown from seed will bloom in 4 years. Ample moisture is required for successful flowering. Foliage dies back to the ground in summer. Mulch in autumn and do not disturb bulbs.

PROPAGATING

Plant bulblets after foliage dies back in autumn. Allow plenty of recuperation time before dividing again.

Pyrethrum

Feverfew, Painted daisy

> **TYPE** HP, often treated as HHA
> **ZONE** A: 1–10; P: 5–10
> **FLOWERING SEASON** Midspring to summer

Unpretentious plants bearing large, bright, daisylike blossoms of white, red, pink, or purple on erect stems of 4"–36"; some have silver fernlike foliage. For borders, edging, or wildflower gardens.

CHARLES JOSLIN

Pyrethrum cinerariifolium

SOWING

INDOORS 8–10 weeks before planting out.
OUTDOORS Early spring or early autumn.
DEPTH Just cover.

GERMINATING

TIME 20–60 days.
REQUIREMENTS 55°F.

PLANTING SEEDLINGS OUTDOORS

TIME Early spring, when soil is cool and a light frost is still possible, or late autumn.
SPACING Small species: 8"–12". Large species: 18"–24".
LIGHT Full sun.
SOIL Ordinary, well-drained, with a pH level of 6.0–7.5.

CARING FOR PLANTS

Pinch back tips of young plants to induce branching. After flowering, cut back lightly and feed to encourage a second bloom.

PROPAGATING

Divide in spring.

A-Annual P-Perennial B-Biennial **HHA**-Half-hardy annual **HA**-Hardy annual **HB**-Hardy biennial **HHP**-Half-hardy perennial **HP**-Hardy perennial **HHBb**-Half-hardy bulb **HBb**-Hardy bulb

Quamoclit

(synonymous with *Mina* and *Ipomoea quamoclit*)

Cardinal climber, Cypress vine, Scarlet star-glory, Spanish flag, Star ipomoea

TYPE HHP usually treated as
  HHA
ZONE 3–10
FLOWERING SEASON Summer to
  autumn

Genus of vines with interesting foliage that is either deeply lobed or segmented; flowers are tubular, bright orange, scarlet, or yellow. Vines reach 10'–20'.

SOWING
INDOORS 6–8 weeks before planting out, in peat pots.
OUTDOORS 2 weeks after last frost.
DEPTH ⅛"

GERMINATING
TIME 5–21 days.
REQUIREMENTS Chip seeds or soak overnight; provide 65°–70°F thereafter.

PLANTING SEEDLINGS OUTDOORS
TIME When spring temperatures remain above 50°F.
SPACING 18"–36".
LIGHT Sun or part shade.
SOIL Light, sandy.

CARING FOR PLANTS
Provide a trellis for support. Excessive feeding will produce lush foliage but few flowers. Site vines where blooms can be enjoyed in the morning and evening, as flowers close up during the hottest part of the day.

PROPAGATING
Seed only.

Ramonda

Serbian queen

TYPE HP
ZONE 5–8. Performs best in cool, humid climates.
FLOWERING SEASON Spring

Sweet, diminutive, rosette-forming perennials with deeply veined and hairy leaves resembling elephant hide, from which short stalks emerge bearing delicate, flat, open flowers of purple, pink, or white. 4" plants for the rock garden plants.

SOWING
INDOORS Spring.
OUTDOORS Early autumn.
DEPTH Surface.

GERMINATING
TIME 30–60 days.
REQUIREMENTS Difficult. Diffused light and 55°–60°F.

PLANTING SEEDLINGS OUTDOORS
TIME After last spring frost, 1 year after germinating.
SPACING 4"–6".
LIGHT Part shade.
SOIL Sandy, well-drained, moist during the growing season.

CARING FOR PLANTS
Difficult. Plants grown from seed will take 3–4 years to flower. Plant against a north-facing wall. Water during dry spells, keeping water off of leaves.

Ramonda pyrenaica

PROPAGATING
Take leaf cuttings or plant offsets in summer.

Ranunculus

**Bachelor's buttons, Buttercup,
Creeping buttercup,
Greater spearwort, Lesser celandine**

Ranunculus repens

> **TYPE** HP or HHP treated as
> HHA
> **ZONE** 4–9: *R. aconitifolius*,
> *R. lingua*, *R. pyrenaeus*;
> 5–9: *R. acris*, *R. gramineus*,
> *R. montanus*; 7–9: *R. asiaticus*
> **FLOWERING SEASON** Late winter to
> early summer, depending on
> species

Large and varied genus of plants mostly grown for their showy blooms. Flowers are cup-shaped and may be of simple structure or intricately double; colors are rich, intense, and widely assorted. Use in borders and rock gardens, massed or mixed casually with other plants.

SOWING

INDOORS See "Germinating, Requirements."

OUTDOORS See "Germinating, Requirements."

DEPTH Seed: just cover. Roots: 2".

GERMINATING

TIME 15–90 days.

REQUIREMENTS *Autumn sowing:* Sow seeds in flats, sink in the ground against a north-facing wall, and cover with glass. Moisten soil occasionally, if necessary. Bring flats indoors in spring to 50°F. *Spring sowing:* Sow seeds in flats, secure in a plastic bag, and refrigerate for 2–3 weeks. Remove flats and sink in the ground in a shady location, covering with glass. Transplant seedlings as they appear.

PLANTING SEEDLINGS OUTDOORS

TIME After last frost.

SPACING Small species: 4"–6". Medium species: 8"–12". Large species: 24".

LIGHT Full sun if soil is moist, otherwise part shade.

SOIL Moist, well drained. *R. lingua* prefers boggy soil.

CARING FOR PLANTS

Provide a good summer mulch to keep soil moist, and water during dry spells. In areas where plants will not survive outdoors over winter, lift tubers after foliage dies and store in a cool, dry place, replanting in the spring.

PROPAGATING

Divide in spring (zones 4–6) or autumn (zones 7–9).

Rehmannia

Beverly bells, Chinese foxglove

> **TYPE** HHP often treated as HHA
> **ZONE** 8–10
> **FLOWERING SEASON** Late spring to
> summer

Small genus of clump-forming plants bearing racemes of tubular, intricately multicolored, 2-lipped flowers on 1'–6' stems. An interesting addition to the border or naturalistic planting.

SOWING

INDOORS 6–8 weeks before last frost.

OUTDOORS Early spring, when soil is cool and a light frost is still possible, or late autumn.

DEPTH Just cover.

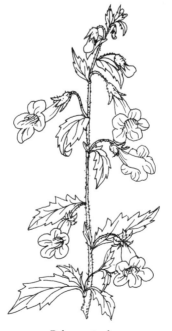

Rehmannia elata

GERMINATING

TIME 15–40 days.

REQUIREMENTS 60°–65°F.

PLANTING SEEDLINGS OUTDOORS

TIME After last frost, when temperatures remain above 40°F.

SPACING Small species: 10"–12". Large species: 18".

LIGHT Sun, with light shade from hot afternoon sun.

SOIL Well-drained, fertile.

CARING FOR PLANTS

Mulch with leaf mold in spring. Water well during dry periods throughout the growing season. Where plants are not hardy, uproot and discard after blooming; provide a good winter mulch for plants left in the ground.

PROPAGATING

Take root cuttings in late winter.

A-Annual P-Perennial B-Biennial HHA-Half-hardy annual HA-Hardy annual HB-Hardy biennial HHP-Half-hardy perennial HP-Hardy perennial HHBb-Half-hardy bulb HBb-Hardy bulb

Reseda

Mignonette

Upright, branching plants grown for their wonderfully fragrant, white or yellow flowers borne in spikes on stems of 1'–3'. Use in containers, borders, and cutting beds.

SOWING

INDOORS 6–8 weeks before last frost, in peat pots.
OUTDOORS Early spring, when soil is cool and a light frost is still possible, and again every 3 weeks until early summer. Sow seeds in late autumn in zones 9–10.
DEPTH Surface.

GERMINATING

TIME 5–21 days.
REQUIREMENTS Light and 70°F.

PLANTING SEEDLINGS OUTDOORS

TIME After last frost.
SPACING Small species: 6"–8". Large species: 10"–12".
LIGHT Part shade, except in very cool regions.
SOIL Rich, with a pH level of 6.0–7.0

CARING FOR PLANTS

Pinch back tips of young plants to encourage branching. Do not move. Blooming will stop in very hot weather.

PROPAGATING

Self-seeds.

JUDY ELIASON

Reseda odorata

Rheum

Rhubarb, Sorrel rhubarb

Exotic-looking perennials grown for culinary or ornamental purposes. Many have enormous, toothed leaves of red or bronze; small white flowers are borne on tall stalks. Grow these 3'–8' giants singly in borders where their color and texture make a good foil, or mass in a bog or waterside garden.

SOWING

INDOORS 8–10 weeks before planting out.
OUTDOORS 1 month before last frost.
DEPTH Seed: ¼". Roots: Plant with buds 1"–2" below surface.

GERMINATING

TIME 21–42 days.
REQUIREMENTS 60°–65°F.

PLANTING SEEDLINGS OUTDOORS

TIME Early spring, when soil is cool and a light frost is still possible, or late autumn.
SPACING Small species: 12"–24". Medium species: 24"–36". Large species: 36"–60". For ornamental use, plant singly except in very large spaces.
LIGHT Sun or light shade.
SOIL Very rich, deep, moist.

CARING FOR PLANTS

Rhubarb grown from seed usually produces plants that, though not desirable for eating, are acceptable for ornamental use. Purchased rootstock should be used for edible rhubarb. Apply a complete fertilizer in spring, then feed every 2 weeks throughout the growing season with a weak fertilizer solution. Mulch well to keep soil cool and moist, and water frequently during dry spells. Cut flower stems to the ground after blooming. If plants are to be eaten, do not cut stalks during their first year; in subsequent years harvest only until late July. Remove flower stems as soon as they appear. Divide when plants show signs of declining.

PROPAGATING

Divide in spring.

Rheum rhabarbarum

Rhodanthe

See *Helipterum*

Rhodochiton

Purple bell vine

TYPE HHP usually treated as HHA
ZONE 6–10. Will bloom only where the growing season is very long.
FLOWERING SEASON Summer through autumn

One species of vigorous, long-blooming climber with handsome, toothed, heart-shaped leaves and masses of drooping, nearly black, tubular flowers, each one umbrellaed by a reddish-purple calyx. Grows to 10'.

SOWING
INDOORS 6–8 weeks before planting out.
OUTDOORS After last frost, in zones 9–10 only.
DEPTH Just cover.

GERMINATING
TIME 12–40 days.
REQUIREMENTS Difficult. 60°–65°F.

PLANTING SEEDLINGS OUTDOORS
TIME 2 weeks after last frost.
SPACING 9"–12".
LIGHT Sun.
SOIL Ordinary.

CARING FOR PLANTS
Provide trellis or canes for support.

PROPAGATING
Take cuttings from spring to summer.

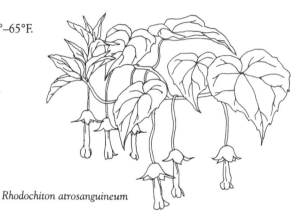

Rhodochiton atrosanguineum

Rhodohypoxis

TYPE HP
ZONE 3–10
FLOWERING SEASON Spring to early summer

Small genus of tufted perennials native to South Africa. Masses of flat, pink, red, or white flowers grow singly on short stems above narrow, lance-shaped leaves. These 2"–4" plants are useful in the rock garden.

SOWING
INDOORS 8–10 weeks before planting out.
OUTDOORS Early spring, when soil is cool and a light frost is still possible.
DEPTH Seed: just cover. Tuber: 1"–2".

GERMINATING
TIME 30–90 days.
REQUIREMENTS 50°F. Plants may not come true from seed.

PLANTING SEEDLINGS OUTDOORS
TIME After last frost.
SPACING 2"–3".
LIGHT Full sun.
SOIL Lime-free and very well-drained, especially in winter.

CARING FOR PLANTS
Feed only occasionally and very lightly. Soil must be fairly dry in winter but moist at all other times. Move only during the growing season.

PROPAGATING
Divide offsets in spring, or allow to self-seed.

Rhodohypoxis baurii

Ricinus

Castor bean plant, Castor oil plant, Palma christi

> TYPE HHP often grown as HHA
> ZONE A: 3–10; P: 8–10. Prefers hot weather.
> FLOWERING SEASON Midsummer

Genus of fast-growing, erect plants valued for their large, deeply lobed, green, bronze, purple, or dark red leaves. Stalks are tipped with clusters of bright red or light green flowers in summer, followed by round, prickly seed pods. 3'–6' tall. Use small groups at the back of the border or mass in a bed of their own.

SOWING

INDOORS 6–8 weeks before planting out, in peat pots.
OUTDOORS Only in zones 8–10, 1 week after last frost.
DEPTH ¼".

GERMINATING

TIME 15–21 days.
REQUIREMENTS Soak seeds in warm water for 24 hours; provide 70°–75° thereafter.

Ricinus communis

PLANTING SEEDLINGS OUTDOORS

TIME 2 weeks after last frost.
SPACING Small species: 24"–36". Large species: 48"–60".
LIGHT Full sun.
SOIL Will grow in almost any soil, but prefers a rich, moist, well-drained loam with a pH level of 6.0–7.0. Rich soil will produce very large plants.

CARING FOR PLANTS

Easy. Feed and water frequently; stake plants if necessary. Likely to become weedy in frost-free climates.

PROPAGATING

Seed only.

Rochea

> TYPE HHP
> ZONE 9–10
> FLOWERING SEASON Spring to autumn

Upright, succulent subshrubs native to South Africa with dull green leaves and umbels of tubular, pink, yellow, red, or white flowers; some species are fragrant. Plants grow to 2'. Use in containers and borders.

SOWING

INDOORS 6–8 weeks before planting out.
OUTDOORS Spring or summer.
DEPTH Surface.

GERMINATING

TIME 14–42 days.
REQUIREMENTS Light and 60°–70°F.

PLANTING SEEDLINGS OUTDOORS

TIME When spring temperatures remain above 50°F.
SPACING 12".
LIGHT Sun.
SOIL Dry, fertile; sandy or coarse.

CARING FOR PLANTS

Pinch back new growth in spring to encourage a bushy habit. Cut back shoots to 1" after flowering. Plants may be brought inside for winter.

PROPAGATING

In spring take 2"–3" cuttings, keep at 55°–60°F, and moisten soil sparingly.

A-Annual P-Perennial B-Biennial HHA-Half-hardy annual HA-Hardy annual HB-Hardy biennial HHP-Half-hardy perennial HP-Hardy perennial HHBb-Half-hardy bulb HBb-Hardy bulb

239

Rodgersia

**Feathered bronze leaf,
Rodgersflower**

> TYPE **HP**
> ZONE **4–9**
> FLOWERING SEASON **Summer**

Small genus of dramatic perennials with very large, compound leaves and tall stalks bearing clusters of small pink or white flowers that resemble enormous astilbes. Plants reach 3'–5' and are most effective massed near water or will add textural interest to the border.

SOWING

INDOORS 6–8 weeks before last frost.
OUTDOORS Autumn.
DEPTH Seed: surface. Rhizome: just below the surface.

GERMINATING

TIME 12–60 days.
REQUIREMENTS Light and 55°–60°F. *Outdoor sowing:* Sow seeds in peat pots, sink these in the ground against a north-facing wall, and cover with glass. Moisten soil occasionally, if necessary. Remove glass when germination begins.

PLANTING SEEDLINGS OUTDOORS

TIME Spring or autumn, after 2 years' growth.
SPACING 24"–36".
LIGHT Full sun; shade from intense sun.
SOIL Rich, moist or even wet.

CARING FOR PLANTS

Difficult. Mulch in spring to keep soil cool and moist, and water freely during dry spells; maintaining very moist soil is essential to succeed with these striking plants. Feed in spring. Leaves may be damaged by winds or strong sun.

PROPAGATING

Divide in spring.

Rodgersia pinnata

Romneya

California tree poppy, Matilija poppy

> TYPE **HHP**
> ZONE **7–10. Not tolerant of high heat combined with high humidity; perfers the California climate.**
> FLOWERING SEASON **Summer to early autumn**

Large, woody plants bearing delicately fragrant, white, poppylike flowers with bright yellow eyes and grey foliage. These natives of southern California and Mexico grow 3'–6'. Use at the back of the border or in combination with shrubs.

SOWING

INDOORS Pre-chilled seeds 6–8 weeks before last frost, in peat pots.
OUTDOORS After last frost.
DEPTH ¼".

Romneya coulteri

GERMINATING

TIME 30 days.
REQUIREMENTS Difficult. 55°–60°F.

PLANTING SEEDLINGS OUTDOORS

TIME After last frost.
SPACING Small species: 24"–36". Large species: 5'–6'.
LIGHT Full sun.
SOIL Average, with very good drainage. Once established, plants are quite drought tolerant.

CARING FOR PLANTS

Difficult. Water only sparingly. Can become invasive; root prune to curtail spreading, but do not otherwise disturb roots.

PROPAGATING

Root suckers. Cut back to 2"–3" after transplanting.

A-Annual P-Perennial B-Biennial HHA-Half-hardy annual HA-Hardy annual HB-Hardy biennial HHP-Half-hardy perennial HP-Hardy perennial HHBb-Half-hardy bulb HBb-Hardy bulb

240

Roscoea

TYPE HP or HHP
ZONE 5–8: *R. purpurea*;
7–10: *R. humeana*;
8–9: *R. cautleoides*. Perform
best where summers are cool
and humid and winters are mild.
FLOWERING SEASON Late spring,
early summer, or autumn,
depending on species

Genus of perennials rarely grown but with loads of personality. Leaves are erect, broad and lance-shaped; flowers are borne on thick stems just above the foliage, each outward-facing bloom hooded, with long lips. A clump of *Roscoea* looks remarkably like a gaggle of old men with flowing beards gathered at the corner to reminisce about the old days. 6"–18" tall. Plant in drifts in rock or shade gardens.

SOWING

INDOORS 8–10 weeks before planting out.
OUTDOORS Autumn or winter.
DEPTH Seed: surface. Roots: 6".

GERMINATING

TIME 30–365 days.
REQUIREMENTS *Indoor sowing*: Place seeds in a plastic bag together with moist growing medium and refrigerate for 2–3 weeks. Provide light and 50°–55°F thereafter. *Outdoor sowing*: Sow seeds in flats, plunge to the rim in a sheltered position, and cover with glass. Remove glass when seeds sprout. Transplant to the garden when seedlings are large enough to handle.

PLANTING SEEDLINGS OUTDOORS

TIME After last frost.
SPACING 6".
LIGHT Full sun or part shade.
SOIL Cool, moist, well-drained, with plenty of organic matter added.

Roscoea purpurea

CARING FOR PLANTS

Mulch to keep soil cool and moist. Water regularly during the growing season.

PROPAGATING

Divide in spring or early summer.

Rosmarinus

Rosemary

TYPE HHP or HP
ZONE 6–9. Prefers dry, mild
winters.
FLOWERING SEASON Late spring to
summer, depending on species

Shrubby perennials grown for culinary use and ornamental appeal. Short, narrow, fragrant, oblong leaves cover the woody stems; small blue flowers are scattered over the entire plant. 3'–6' tall. Attractive hedge where plants are hardy; useful in containers or herb beds.

SOWING

INDOORS Late winter to early spring.
OUTDOORS After last frost.
DEPTH ¼".

GERMINATING

TIME Up to 21 days.
REQUIREMENTS Difficult. Due to extremely slow germination and early growth rate, rosemary is seldom started from seed. If attempted, do not sow in peat. Seeds require 70°F to germinate.

PLANTING SEEDLINGS OUTDOORS

TIME After last frost.
SPACING Small species: 18"–24". Large species: 36"–48".
LIGHT Prefers full sun, but will tolerate part shade.
SOIL Sandy, somewhat poor, with perfect drainage, and a pH level of 6.0–7.5. Plants will not thrive in wet or clay soil.

CARING FOR PLANTS

Easy. Do not fertilize or water. Cut back any frost-damaged branches in spring and prune periodically throughout the year to keep plants looking well-groomed and to restrict their size. Snip leaves for culinary use at any time. Harvest for drying just before flowering; dry leaves in the dark and store in an airtight container. Bring potted plants indoors in winter, either giving 4 hours of sunlight and keeping soil moderately dry in the living room or placing in a cool garage (45°F) with only infrequent watering.

PROPAGATING

Take hardwood cuttings in spring or autumn.

A-Annual P-Perennial B-Biennial HHA-Half-hardy annual HA-Hardy annual HB-Hardy biennial HHP-Half-hardy perennial HP-Hardy perennial HHBb-Half-hardy bulb HBb-Hardy bulb

Rudbeckia

Black-eyed Susan, Coneflower, Gloriosa daisy, Golden-glow

> **Type** HP or P grown as HHA
> **Zone** A: 2–10; P: 3–9: *R. fulgida,*
> *R. laciniata, R. subtomentosa;*
> 6–9: *R. maxima;* 7–9: *R. nitida*
> **Flowering Season** Summer

Widely grown, carefree natives to North America grown for their abundant, yellow or orange, daisylike flowers with prominent brown eyes. Plants are branched and upright, growing from 1' to 6'. Attractive in the border or wildflower garden.

Sowing

Indoors 6–8 weeks before last frost.
Outdoors 2 weeks before last frost.
Depth Surface.

Germinating

Time 5–21 days.
Requirements Easy. Provide light and 70°–75°F. *R. fulgida:* Place seeds in a plastic bag together with moist growing medium and refrigerate for 2 weeks before sowing.

Germinating

Time After last frost.
Spacing Small species: 12"–18". Large species: 24"–36".
Light Full sun, or part shade where summers are very hot.
Soil Tolerant of a wide range of soils, but prefers a well-drained site with a pH level of 6.0–7.0. *R. fulgida* requires heavy soil.

Caring for Plants

Easy. Apply top-dressing of manure annually, water regularly during the summer, and deadhead frequently. Tall species planted in windy locations will require staking. Divide every 3–4 years. Inclined to become invasive.

Rudbeckia hirta

Propagating

Divide in spring north of zone 7, in autumn elsewhere. Take cuttings in spring. Self-seeds.

Ruellia

Wild petunia

> **Type** HP or HHP
> **Zone** 10; 3–9: *R. humilis.*
> Prefers hot, humid climates.
> **Flowering Season** Spring to summer, then intermittently throughout the year

Genus of widely varying woodland perennials and subshrubs, 12"–36" in height, grown for their showy flowers. Some have broad, ornamental leaves of deep green with white veins. Tubular flowers may be small and delicate or large and exotic, fiery red or in a range of purples.

Sowing

Indoors 8–10 weeks before planting out.
Outdoors Spring.
Depth Just cover.

Ruellia formosa

Germinating

Time 30–60 days.
Requirements 65°–75°F. Seed is rarely available.

Planting Seedlings Outdoors

Time Plant out seedlings in spring when the temperatures remain above 60°F.
Spacing 18"–24".
Light Part to full shade.
Soil Moist, well-drained, containing plenty of organic matter.

Caring for Plants

Water regularly and mulch in the spring to keep soil moist.

Propagating

Divide in autumn (in spring north of zone 7) or take cuttings in spring or summer.

A-Annual P-Perennial B-Biennial HHA-Half-hardy annual HA-Hardy annual HB-Hardy biennial HHP-Half-hardy perennial HP-Hardy perennial HHBb-Half-hardy bulb HBb-Hardy bulb

242

Rumex

Sorrel

Perennial herbs grown for culinary use. Leaves are deep green and arrow-shaped; plants are 18"–24" tall.

SOWING

INDOORS 4 weeks before planting out.
OUTDOORS Midspring to late spring, when soil has warmed.
DEPTH ¼".

GERMINATING

TIME 7–10 days.
REQUIREMENTS 65°–70°F.

PLANTING SEEDLINGS OUTDOORS

TIME After last frost.
SPACING Small species: 12". Large species: Singly.
LIGHT Full sun is preferred, but will tolerate part shade.
SOIL Rich, moist, with a pH level of 5.5–6.0.

CARING FOR PLANTS

The only possible reason for growing this most unattractive plant is a passion for sorrel soup. Warning: Sorrel desires a lifetime relationship and divorce can be a long and painful process, the herb being equipped with an impressively tenacious root system and awe-inspiring reproductive capabilities. Bearing that in mind… Feed once in spring. Mulch and frequent watering can help to prevent leaves from becoming bitter in hot, dry weather; or cut back hard when weather becomes hot. Harvest outer leaves frequently to stimulate new growth. *R. acutatus* has the best flavor for cooking. Replace every 3–4 years.

PROPAGATING

Self-seeds rather too efficiently; should that not provide all the plants you need, sorrels can be divided in autumn or early spring.

Sagina

Irish moss, Pearlwort

Cushionlike plants growing just 3"–4", with small, handsome, lance-shaped leaves, deep green or lime green in color, and tiny white flowers. Make fine ground cover, edging, rock, wall, or paving plants.

SOWING

INDOORS 6–8 weeks before last frost.
OUTDOORS Early spring, when soil is cool and a light frost is still possible, or late autumn.
DEPTH Just cover.

GERMINATING

TIME 10–25 days.
REQUIREMENTS Easy. 55°F.

PLANTING SEEDLINGS OUTDOORS

TIME After last frost.
SPACING Small species: 2"–4". Spreading species: 6"–8".
LIGHT Full sun, with some shade where the afternoon sun is very hot.
SOIL Light, rather poor, sandy but moist.

CARING FOR PLANTS

Most species are easy to grow, but need to be renewed periodically. With regular feeding and watering, plants will spread quite happily. Susceptible to aphids and red spider mites.

PROPAGATING

Divide in spring in zones 5 and 6, early autumn in the South.

Salpiglossis

Painted tongue

> TYPE HHA
> ZONE 1–10. Plants prefer cool temperatures.
> FLOWERING SEASON Summer to frost, where summer heat does not kill plants.

Branching annuals 18"–24" tall, with lance-shaped leaves and a profusion of trumpet-shaped blooms, often with dark veins and colored throats; red, orange, pink, and yellow flowers may grow on the same plant. Wonderful for containers, borders, or cut flowers.

Salpiglossis sinuata

SOWING

INDOORS 8–10 weeks before planting out, in peat pots.
OUTDOORS Close to last frost date. Plants need a good start before hot weather sets in.
DEPTH Surface.

GERMINATING

TIME 8–30 days.
REQUIREMENTS Difficult. Darkness and 70°–75°F. If sown outdoors, cover lightly with straw or cheesecloth to prevent seeds being washed away.

PLANTING SEEDLINGS OUTDOORS

TIME 2 weeks before last frost.
SPACING 12"–15"
LIGHT Full sun or light shade.
SOIL Ordinary.

CARING FOR PLANTS

Pinch out young plants to induce branching, and support with twiggy branches pushed into the ground. Mulch in spring, water only during dry spells, and feed occasionally with a weak balanced fertilizer. Deadhead regularly. Do not transplant.

PROPAGATING

Seed only.

Salvia

Meadow clary, Sage

> TYPE HA, HHA, or HHP; often treated as A or B
> ZONE A: 3–10; P: 3–10: *S. officinalis*; 5–9: *S. argentea*, *S. azurea**, *S. x superba*, *S. verticillata*; 6–9: *S. hians***, *S. jurisicii***; 7–9: *S. pratensis*; 8–9: *S. coccinea**, *S. farinacea**, *S. fulgens*, *S. leucantha***, *S. patens*; 8–10: *S. uliginosa*; 9–10: *S. greggii*, *S. guaranitica**. Prefers warm climates.
> FLOWERING SEASON Summer to autumn
>
> *Well suited to hot, humid climates.
> **Intolerant of hot, humid conditions.

Large genus of hard-working annuals and perennials bearing stiff spikes of 2-lipped, tubular flowers of intense purple, violet, red, or pink, or quieter yellows and whites; some species have velvety mauve and grey-green leaves. Stunning in masses, containers, and borders.

SOWING

INDOORS 6–8 weeks before planting out. To grow *S. farinacea* as an annual, start seeds 12 weeks before planting out.
OUTDOORS A or P: 2 weeks after last frost, February or March in zones 9–10. B: early autumn.
DEPTH Surface.

GERMINATING

TIME 4–21 days.
REQUIREMENTS Always start with fresh seed as *Salvia* seeds are very short-lived. Very susceptable to damping-off; sow in vermiculite and water only from below. All species require 65°–75°F. *S. patens* and *S. x superba*: Place seeds in a plastic bag together with moist growing medium and refrigerate for 3 weeks.

PLANTING SEEDLINGS OUTDOORS

TIME Hardy species: after last frost. Half-hardy species: when temperatures remain above 40°F.
SPACING Small species: 6"–9". Medium species: 12"–18". Large species: 20"–30".
LIGHT Full sun, or part shade in very hot climates.
SOIL Rich, moist, well-drained. Annuals prefer a pH level of 6.0–7.5, perennials prefer 5.5–7.0.

CARING FOR PLANTS

Easy. Pinch back tips when plants are 6" tall. Deadhead often, water regularly during dry spells, and do not overfertilize. Tall plants may need staking in windy sites. Cut back perennials in autumn to 1"–2". Divide every 3–4 years. *S. patens* can be lifted and stored over winter in sand in a cool, frost-free place and replanted in the spring. The leaves of *S. officinalis* may be picked at any time to use in cooking. To dry: Cut 6" stalks in late spring and early summer before flowering, hang upside-down in the shade for a week, and store in airtight containers.

PROPAGATING

Divide perennials in autumn (zones 7–10) or spring (zones 3–6) or take softwood cuttings in midsummer. Start annuals and biennials from seed.

A-Annual P-Perennial B-Biennial HHA-Half-hardy annual HA-Hardy annual HB-Hardy biennial HHP-Half-hardy perennial HP-Hardy perennial HHBb-Half-hardy bulb HBb-Hardy bulb

244

Sandersonia

Chinese-lantern lily, Christmas bells

> TYPE HHP often grown as A
> ZONE P: 9–10; A: 5–8
> FLOWERING SEASON Summer

Climbing plants native to South Africa, with a sparse scattering of lance-shaped leaves and whimsical orange lanterns nodding on thin stalks. 2' tall. Provide a sheltered site in the border.

SOWING

INDOORS 8–10 weeks before planting out.
OUTDOORS After last frost.
DEPTH ⅛".

GERMINATING

TIME 30–90 days.
REQUIREMENTS Soak seeds for 24 hours in warm water before planting; provide 75°F thereafter.

PLANTING SEEDLINGS OUTDOORS

TIME After last frost.
SPACING 10"–12".
LIGHT Sun.
SOIL Well-drained, sandy loam amended with well-rotted manure.

CARING FOR PLANTS

Plants grown from seed will bloom in 3 years. Flowering stems may require staking. Plants die back to the ground after flowering. North of zone 9, lift in autumn and store in a cool, frost-free location; *Sandersonias* may survive northern winters if planted deeply against a south-facing wall.

Sandersonia aurantiaca

PROPAGATING

Divide in spring, or allow to self-seed.

Sanguinaria

Bloodroot, Indian plant, Tatterwort, Woods poppy

> TYPE HP
> ZONE 3–9
> FLOWERING SEASON Spring

Genus of one species of perennial native to North America. Bright white flowers, either flat or double, are borne singly on sturdy stalks above grey-green, deeply lobed leaves. A curiously refreshing plant for shady borders or woodland plantings.

SOWING

INDOORS 8–10 weeks before planting out, in peat pots.
OUTDOORS Autumn.
DEPTH Just cover.

Sanguinaria canadensis

GERMINATING

TIME 30–90 days.
REQUIREMENTS 50°–55°F. *Outdoor sowing:* Sow seeds sparsely in containers, sink in the ground against a north-facing wall, and cover with glass. Moisten soil occasionally, if necessary. Remove glass when germination begins.

PLANTING SEEDLINGS OUTDOORS

TIME Late August to September.
SPACING 10"–12".
LIGHT Full sun in early spring, but will tolerate part shade thereafter. Afternoon shade is beneficial where summers are very hot.
SOIL Not fussy, but is happiest in deep, cool soil with a pH level of 5.0–7.0, with plenty of organic matter added.

CARING FOR PLANTS

Easy. Water well during dry spells. Top-dress with well-rotted manure in late winter. Plants die back to the ground after flowering; mark locations to avoid unintentional disturbance. Do not move.

PROPAGATING

Very carefully divide in late summer after plants have begun to die down.

A-Annual P-Perennial B-Biennial HHA-Half-hardy annual HA-Hardy annual HB-Hardy biennial HHP-Half-hardy perennial HP-Hardy perennial HHBb-Half-hardy bulb HBb-Hardy bulb

Sanguisorba

(synonymous with *Poterium*)

Burnet, Toper's plant

> TYPE HP
> ZONE 4–9
> FLOWERING SEASON Midsummer

Perennials grown for the fuzzy bottle-brushes of tiny white, red, or pink flowers borne on 4'–6' stems in summer; leaves are light green and lance-shaped. Mass near water or in the border.

SOWING

INDOORS 10–12 weeks before planting out.
OUTDOORS Early spring or late autumn.
DEPTH Surface.

GERMINATING

TIME 30–60 days.
REQUIREMENTS 50°–55°F.

PLANTING SEEDLINGS OUTDOORS

TIME Plant out seedlings in the spring of their second year.
SPACING Small species: 18"–24". Large species: 24"–48".
LIGHT Full sun, with light afternoon shade where summers are hot.
SOIL Ordinary, moist, with a pH level of 6.0–8.0.

CARING FOR PLANTS

Easy. Mulch in spring and keep soil moist in summer. Cut back leaves regularly to encourage new growth. Plants may require staking. Division will be necessary every year if planted in very rich soil. Pick leaves regularly for use in cooking to stimulate new growth. Pot up seedlings to grow indoors, giving 5 hours sunlight a day.

PROPAGATING

Divide roots in spring in the North, in autumn south of zone 6.

Santolina

Holy flax, Lavender cotton

> TYPE HP
> ZONE 6–9
> FLOWERING SEASON Late spring to summer

Low-growing evergreen shrubs often used in the border, drystone walls, around paving stones, or for edging. Foliage is very fine, grey-green or midgreen, and aromatic. Buttons of yellow flowers are massed on wiry stems above the foliage. Plants stay a compact 12"–30".

SOWING

INDOORS Pre-chilled seeds 8–10 weeks before planting out.
OUTDOORS Early spring or early autumn.
DEPTH 1/8".

GERMINATING

TIME 15–20 days.
REQUIREMENTS Place seeds in a plastic bag together with moist growing medium and refrigerate seeds for 2–4 weeks; provide 65°–70°F thereafter.

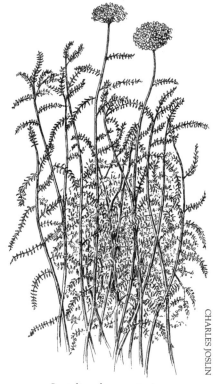

CHARLES JOSLIN

Santolina chamaecyparissus

PLANTING SEEDLINGS OUTDOORS

TIME Early spring, when soil is cool and a light frost is still possible, or late autumn.
SPACING 18"–20".
LIGHT Full sun or part shade.
SOIL Poor, dry soil; must have good drainage.

CARING FOR PLANTS

Very easy, requiring little care. Water only during prolonged dry spells and trim plants to 4"–6" after flowering to keep neat and compact. Some people find the yellow flowers of grey-leaved species unattractive and choose to remove these before blooming. If flowers are desired, deadhead as soon as blooming is finished to avoid that depressing shop-worn look. Plants can be potted up and grown indoors with 5 hours sunlight per day.

PROPAGATING

Take cuttings in late summer or autumn.

A-Annual P-Perennial B-Biennial HHA-Half-hardy annual HA-Hardy annual HB-Hardy biennial HHP-Half-hardy perennial HP-Hardy perennial HHBb-Half-hardy bulb HBb-Hardy bulb

Sanvitalia

Creeping zinnia, Golden stars

> TYPE HA or HHA
> ZONE 3–10. Particularly well suited to hot, dry locations.
> FLOWERING SEASON Summer to early autumn

Prostrate annuals native to North America with neat, oval leaves and yellow or orange flowers resembling small sunflowers with large, deep brown centers. 6" plants make an unusual annual ground cover or container plant.

SOWING

INDOORS 6–8 weeks before planting out, in peat pots.
OUTDOORS In zones 3–8, early spring, before the last frost; in zones 9–10, autumn.
DEPTH Surface.

GERMINATING

TIME 10–21 days.
REQUIREMENTS Light and 70°F.

PLANTING SEEDLINGS OUTDOORS

TIME Late spring.
SPACING 6"–9".
LIGHT Full sun.
SOIL Light, sandy, well-drained; tolerant of dry soil.

CARING FOR PLANTS

Easy. Apply a weak fertilizer periodically and water well during dry spells. Do not move.

PROPAGATING

Seed only.

Sanvitalia procumbens

Saponaria (Annual)

Cow herb, Soapwort

> TYPE HA
> ZONE 3–10
> FLOWERING SEASON Summer; plants will also bloom in spring from an autumn sowing

Mat-forming and tufted plants with narrow, lance-shaped leaves smothered in small, flat, pink, white, or red flowers. 6"–36" tall. Grown in rock gardens and borders.

SOWING

INDOORS Pre-chilled seeds 4–6 weeks before last frost.
OUTDOORS After last frost. Where winters are mild, seeds may be sown again in early autumn for spring blooms.
DEPTH Surface.

GERMINATING

TIME 10–21 days.
REQUIREMENTS Easy. Place seeds in a plastic bag together with moist growing medium and refrigerate for 3 weeks; provide light and 70°F thereafter.

PLANTING SEEDLINGS OUTDOORS

TIME After last frost.
SPACING 9"–10".
LIGHT Sun.
SOIL Ordinary, well-drained.

CARING FOR PLANTS

Easy. Water well during dry spells and feed occasionally throughout the growing season.

PROPAGATING

Seed.

A-Annual P-Perennial B-Biennial HHA-Half-hardy annual HA-Hardy annual HB-Hardy biennial HHP-Half-hardy perennial HP-Hardy perennial HHBb-Half-hardy bulb HBb-Hardy bulb

247

Saponaria (Perennial)

Bouncing bet, Rock soapwort

> TYPE HP
> ZONE 3–9; 6–8: *S.* x *lempergii*
> FLOWERING SEASON Late spring to
> early summer

Mat-forming and tufted plants with narrow, lance-shaped leaves smothered in small, flat, pink, white, or red flowers. 6"–36" tall. Grown in rock gardens and borders.

SOWING

INDOORS 8–10 weeks before planting out, in peat pots.
OUTDOORS Early spring or early autumn.
DEPTH Surface.

GERMINATING

TIME 10–21 days.
REQUIREMENTS Place seeds in a plastic bag together with moist growing medium and refrigerate for 3 weeks; provide light and 70°F thereafter.

Saponaria officianalis

PLANTING SEEDLINGS OUTDOORS

TIME Early spring, when soil is cool and a light frost is still possible, or late autumn.
SPACING Small species: 4"–8". Large species: 10"–15".
LIGHT Full sun or light shade.
SOIL Inclined to become invasive in rich, moist soil, but performs well in dry, rocky soil where its growth will be curtailed.

CARING FOR PLANTS

Easy. Seed-grown plants may vary enormously. Water only during very dry spells and do not overfeed. Cut back after blooming to keep plants compact and encourage further blooming. Do not move.

PROPAGATING

Divide in early spring in zones 3–6, in autumn elsewhere. Take softwood cuttings in early summer, or allow to self-seed.

Sarracenia

**Indian-cup, Pitcher plant,
Side-saddle flower, Trumpetleaf**

> TYPE HP
> ZONE 3–10: *S. purpurea;*
> 7–10: *S. flava*
> FLOWERING SEASON Late spring

Genus of insectivorous plants native to North America. Flowers may be an eerie green or purple, with veined and hooded pitchers growing 6" to 4' long, or complicated structures with drooping yellow petals. A curiosity to try in a damp spot.

SOWING

INDOORS Pre-chilled seeds 8–10 weeks before planting out.
OUTDOORS Spring, in zones 9–10 only.
DEPTH Surface.

GERMINATING

TIME 30–90 days.
REQUIREMENTS Difficult. Place moistened seeds in refrigerator (*without* growing medium) for 7 days, then sow on a damp paper towel in a dish, covering with clear plastic. Keep constantly moist at 65°–75°F. Prick out seedlings to individual pots as they germinate.

PLANTING SEEDLINGS OUTDOORS

TIME Spring, when temperatures remain above 40°F.
SPACING 12"–18".
LIGHT Sun or shade, but plants will not develop good color in strong sun.
SOIL Moist or even wet, neutral or slightly acid.

CARING FOR PLANTS

Difficult unless precise cultural requirements are met. Plants grown from seed will flower in 3–5 years. Plant high to keep crowns dry, but provide plenty of water in summer. Although it is tempting to put on

Sarracenia purpurea

a mealtime show with these carnivorous plants, feeding them insects or meat is extremely bad for their health and may cause rapid deterioration.

PROPAGATING

Divide in spring north of zone 7, in autumn elsewhere.

A-Annual P-Perennial B-Biennial HHA-Half-hardy annual HA-Hardy annual HB-Hardy biennial HHP-Half-hardy perennial HP-Hardy perennial HHBb-Half-hardy bulb HBb-Hardy bulb

Satureja (Annual)

Summer savory

TYPE HA
ZONE 3–10
FLOWERING SEASON Midsummer
to autumn

Annual herbs grown primarily for the culinary use of their aromatic leaves. Upright plants, 6"–36" tall, usually bearing narrow, oblong, grey-green leaves; flowers are small, tubular, 2-lipped, purple or white. Grown in herb and rock gardens.

SOWING
INDOORS 4 weeks before planting out, in peat pots.
OUTDOORS Early spring, then every 3–4 weeks for a continuous supply of leaves.
DEPTH Surface.

GERMINATING
TIME 10–21 days.
REQUIREMENTS Light and 60°–70°F.

PLANTING SEEDLINGS OUTDOORS
TIME After last frost.
SPACING 6"–8". Plants grown close together will provide support for each other.
LIGHT Full sun.
SOIL Light, rich, and well-drained.

CARING FOR PLANTS
Do not move. Cut leaves for immediate culinary use at any time. For drying, harvest in summer before flowering begins and again in autumn, when plants can be cut to the ground. Hang stalks upside-down in a paper bag to dry; remove leaves and store in an airtight container. Dig plants very carefully to pot up and grow indoors for winter. They require 5 hours sunlight a day, a weak monthly feeding, and soil that is allowed to dry out between watering.

PROPAGATING
Seed only.

Satureja (Perennial)

Winter savory

TYPE HP
ZONE 6–9
FLOWERING SEASON June

Genus of perennials and subshrubs grown primarily for the culinary use of their aromatic leaves. Upright plants, 6"–36" tall, usually bearing narrow, oblong, grey-green leaves; flowers are small, tubular, 2-lipped, purple or white. Grown in herb and rock gardens.

SOWING
INDOORS 6–8 weeks before planting out.
OUTDOORS Late spring, although propagation by division is more usual.
DEPTH Surface.

GERMINATING
TIME 20 days.
REQUIREMENTS Light and 60°–70°F.

PLANTING SEEDLINGS OUTDOORS
TIME After last frost.
SPACING 10"–12".
LIGHT Full sun.
SOIL Ordinary, well-drained, with a pH level of 6.5–7.5.

CARING FOR PLANTS
Pinch back young plants to induce bushy growth. Cut out deadwood regularly. Mulch after the ground freezes. Divide every 2–3 years to maintain vigor. Harvest fresh leaves for cooking at any time. For drying, cut stems before plants bloom, using only the tender tips of shoots. Hang stems upside-down in a paper bag to dry; strip leaves from stalks and store in an airtight container. To grow indoors, cut back plants by one-half in late summer, pot up, and allow to rest outdoors for 2–3 weeks. Bring indoors to 5 hours sunlight a day; allow soil to dry between waterings and feed weakly once a month.

PROPAGATING
Divide in spring or autumn, or take stem cuttings in spring.

A-Annual P-Perennial B-Biennial HHA-Half-hardy annual HA-Hardy annual HB-Hardy biennial HHP-Half-hardy perennial HP-Hardy perennial HHBb-Half-hardy bulb HBb-Hardy bulb

249

Saxifraga

London pride, Rockfoil, Saxifrage, St. Patrick's cabbage, Strawberry geranium

TYPE HP
ZONE 3–8: *S. cotyledon;*
4–9: *S. hypnoides;* 5–9:
S. cortusifolia; 6–9: *S. x urbium;*
6–10: *S. stolonifera;*
7–9: *S. oppositifolia, S. umbrosa.*
Will thrive only in cool climates.
FLOWERING SEASON Late spring to autumn, depending on species

Very large genus of widely varying plants, though most in common cultivation are low-growing (under 12"), rosette-forming, with small pink, red, or white flowers. Use in rock gardens and containers.

SOWING

INDOORS See "Germinating, Requirements."
OUTDOORS See "Germinating, Requirements."
DEPTH Just cover.

GERMINATING

TIME 15–60 days.
REQUIREMENTS *Autumn sowing:* Sow seeds in flats, sink flats in ground against a north-facing wall, and cover with glass. Moisten soil occasionally, if necessary. Bring indoors in spring to 65°–75°F. *Spring sowing:* Sow seeds in moistened medium, place in a plastic bag, and refrigerate. After 2–3 weeks remove containers and sink in the ground in a shady location, covering with glass. Transplant seedlings as they emerge.

PLANTING SEEDLINGS OUTDOORS

TIME After last frost.
SPACING Small species: 4"–6". Medium species: 8"–12". Large species: 12"–18".
LIGHT Part to full shade; must have protection from the midday sun, even in mild climates.
SOIL Cool, moist, sandy or gritty, with a little lime added. Must be very well drained in winter.

Saxifraga stellaris

CARING FOR PLANTS

Most *Saxifragas* are easy to grow if given the precise conditions they require. Soil must be kept moist in summer, otherwise little care is required.

PROPAGATING

Root runners separated from the parent plant. Some species self-seed.

Scabiosa

Mourning-bride, Pincushion flower, Scabious, Sweet scabious

TYPE HA, HHA, HB, or HP
ZONE A: 3–10; P: 3–9: *S. caucasica;* 4–8: *S. alpina;* 5–9: *S. graminifolia, S. ochroleuca;* 9–10: *S. africana*
FLOWERING SEASON Summer to early autumn

Large genus of plants, most of which are grown for their domed, lace-edged flowers of purple, blue, red, white, or yellow borne singly on long, wiry stems. Plants are often tufted or mat-forming, 6"–24" tall. For borders and cutting beds.

SOWING

INDOORS A: 4–5 weeks before last frost. P: 8–10 weeks before planting out.

Scabiosa atropurpurea

OUTDOORS A: after last frost in zones 3–7; autumn in zones 8–10. P: early spring; seeds can also be sown in early autumn where winters are mild.
DEPTH Just cover.

GERMINATING

TIME 10–15 days.
REQUIREMENTS 70°–75°F.

PLANTING SEEDLINGS OUTDOORS

TIME A: after last frost. P: early spring, when soil is cool and a light frost is still possible, or late autumn.
SPACING A: 8"–12". P: 12"–18".
LIGHT Full sun.
SOIL Moist, humus-rich, well-drained, with a pH level of 7.0–8.0.

CARING FOR PLANTS

Easy. Deadhead regularly. In windy locations, support with twiggy branches pushed into the ground when plants are young. Cut back to ground level in autumn. Divide perennials occasionally to maintain vigor.

PROPAGATING

Propagate annuals by seed only. Take cuttings of perennials in summer, or divide in early spring.

A-Annual P-Perennial B-Biennial HHA-Half-hardy annual HA-Hardy annual HB-Hardy biennial HHP-Half-hardy perennial HP-Hardy perennial HHBb-Half-hardy bulb HBb-Hardy bulb

Schizanthus

Butterfly flower, Fringe flower, Poor man's orchid

> TYPE HHA
> ZONE 1–10. Performs most successfully where summers are cool, with nighttime temperatures below 65°F.
> FLOWERING SEASON In spring from an autumn sowing, or summer through autumn from a spring sowing

Bushy annuals native to Chile with delicately cut foliage and masses of small but showy, orchidlike flowers in every shade of red, pink, purple, and yellow; many are multicolored. 12"–48" tall. Attractive edging, border, or container plants.

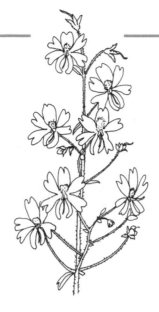

Schizanthus Pinnatus

SOWING

INDOORS 8–10 weeks before last frost.
OUTDOORS Start seeds outdoors only in zones 9–10, where they may be sown in early spring at 2-week intervals for 6 weeks, or in autumn.
DEPTH ⅛"

GERMINATING

TIME 7–20 days.
REQUIREMENTS Darkness and 60°–75°F.

PLANTING SEEDLINGS OUTDOORS

TIME 2 weeks after last frost, when temperatures remain above 40°F.
SPACING Small species: 9"–12". Medium species: 12"–18". Large species: 24"–36".
LIGHT Sun.
SOIL Rich, moist loam with a pH level of 6.0–7.0.

CARING FOR PLANTS

Difficult. Pinch back tips when plants are 3" and again at 6". Provide extra support with twiggy branches pushed into the ground when plants are young. Water frequently, keeping flowers and leaves as dry as possible.

PROPAGATING

Seed only.

Schizostylis

Crimson flag, Kaffir lily

> TYPE HP
> ZONE 8–10. Flowers most profusely where summers are damp.
> FLOWERING SEASON Late summer to autumn

South African natives grown for their spikes of pink or red cup-shaped flowers; foliage is grassy. Plants grow to 24" and are used in cutting beds and borders.

SOWING

INDOORS 8–10 weeks before planting out.
OUTDOORS Seed: early spring, when soil is cool and a light frost is still possible. Tuber: spring.
DEPTH Seed: just cover. Tuber: 2".

GERMINATING

TIME 30–90 days.
REQUIREMENTS 55°–60°F.

PLANTING SEEDLINGS OUTDOORS

TIME After last frost.
SPACING 9"–12".
LIGHT Full sun or part shade.
SOIL Moist, rich, well-drained, acid or neutral.

CARING FOR PLANTS

Mulch in spring to keep soil cool and moist, and water frequently during dry spells. Feed in spring and once or twice more during the growing season. Mulch the first winter to protect newly planted tubers. Divide when plants show signs of deteriorating, about once every 2–4 years. Shelter from damaging winds.

PROPAGATING

Divide in early spring, leaving 3–5 eyes per section.

Schizostylis coccinea

A-Annual P-Perennial B-Biennial HHA-Half-hardy annual HA-Hardy annual HB-Hardy biennial HHP-Half-hardy perennial HP-Hardy perennial HHBb-Half-hardy bulb HBb-Hardy bulb

251

Scilla

Bluebell, Blue squill, Cuban lily, Hyacinth-of-Peru, Spanish bluebell, Squill

TYPE HBb
ZONE 4–8: *S. bifolia, S. hispanica, S. nutans, S. siberica;* 4–10: *S. campanulata;* 5–8: *S. non-scripta, S. pratensis, S. tubergeniana;* 8–10: *S. peruviana*
FLOWERING SEASON Spring to early summer

Scilla hispanica

Perennial bulbs with narrow, grasslike leaves and spikes of mainly tubular, blue, purple, or white flowers; usually 6"–12" tall, rarely up to 36". For greatest impact plant in masses.

SOWING

INDOORS See "Germinating, Requirements."
OUTDOORS Seed: see "Germinating, Requirements." Bulb: autumn.
DEPTH Seed: just cover. Small bulb: 3"–4". Large bulb: 4"–5".

GERMINATING

TIME 30–180 days.
REQUIREMENTS Easy. *Autumn sowing:* Sow seeds in flats, sink in the ground against a north-facing wall, and cover with glass. Moisten soil occasionally, if necessary. Bring flats indoors in spring to 50°F. *Spring sowing:* Sow seeds in moistened medium, secure in a plastic bag, and refrigerate for 2–3 weeks. Remove flats and sink in the ground in a shady location, covering with glass. Transplant seedlings as they appear.

PLANTING SEEDLINGS OUTDOORS

SPACING 3"–5".
LIGHT Most *Scillas* grow well in sun or part shade, with exceptions. Full sun only: *S. peruviana, S. pratensis.* Full shade only: *S. non-scripta, S. siberica.*
SOIL Rich, well-drained loam with a pH level of 6.0–7.0.

CARING FOR PLANTS

Easy. Plants take 4–5 years to bloom from seed. Water regularly until blooming ends, then allow bulbs to dry out. Apply a complete fertilizer in early spring or top-dress with manure in autumn. *Scilla* spread rapidly and may require division every 3 years. Apart from dividing, do not disturb.

PROPAGATING

Plant offsets in autumn.

Scutellaria

Helmet flower, Skullcap

TYPE HP
ZONE 3–8: *S. incana;* 5–8: *S. alpina, S. orientalis;* 6–8: *S. baicalensis, S. indica, S. scordiifolia*
FLOWERING SEASON Summer

Large genus of perennials, the most popular of which are low and spreading, bearing yellow, red, purple, blue, or white tubular flowers that are lipped and hooded. Plants are 4"–36" tall and grown in the border or rock garden.

SOWING

INDOORS Start seeds outdoors only.
OUTDOORS Autumn, when seed is fresh.
DEPTH Just cover.

GERMINATING

TIME 14–180 days.
REQUIREMENTS Sow seeds in flats, sink these in the ground against a north-facing wall, and cover with glass. Moisten the soil occasionally, if necessary. Transplant to the garden after 2 full growing seasons.

PLANTING SEEDLINGS OUTDOORS

TIME Autumn.
SPACING Small species: 8"–12". Large species: 18"–24".
LIGHT Full sun or part shade.
SOIL Moist, well-drained, with a pH level of 6.0–7.0.

CARING FOR PLANTS

Pinch back tips of young plants to encourage bushiness. Mulch well in spring and do not allow soil to dry out. Divide when plants become overgrown.

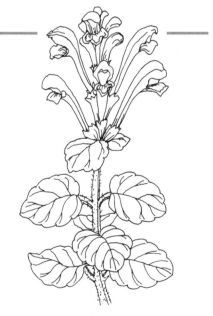

Scutellaria indica

PROPAGATING

Divide in early spring, or take softwood cuttings in summer.

A-Annual P-Perennial B-Biennial HHA-Half-hardy annual HA-Hardy annual HB-Hardy biennial HHP-Half-hardy perennial HP-Hardy perennial HHBb-Half-hardy bulb HBb-Hardy bulb

252

Sedum

**Gold moss, Ice plant,
October daphne, Orpine, Stonecrop,
Wall pepper, Worm grass**

> TYPE HP
> ZONE 3–9: *S. acre, S. album,*
> *S.* x '*Autumn Joy*',
> *S. ellacombianum,*
> *S. kamtschaticum,*
> *S. middendorfianum, S. roseum,*
> *S. spurium, S. telephium;*
> 4–9: *S. aizoon, S. alboroseum,*
> *S. maximum, S. spectabile;*
> 5–9: *S. cauticolum,*
> *S. spathulifolium;* 6–9: *S. sieboldii*
> FLOWERING SEASON **Early summer**
> **to early autumn, depending on**
> **species**

Very large genus of mainly perennial succulents, often trailing, with terminal clusters of small, star-shaped flowers of yellow, pink, or white; 2"–24". Use in containers or drystone walls, rock gardens, between paving, as edging, or in the border.

Sedum telephium

SOWING

INDOORS See "Germinating, Requirements."
OUTDOORS See "Germinating, Requirements."
DEPTH Surface.

GERMINATING

TIME 5–30 days.
REQUIREMENTS *Autumn sowing:* Sow seeds in flats, plunge these to the rim against a north-facing wall, and cover with glass. Moisten the soil occasionally, if necessary. Bring indoors in spring to 60°–65°F. *Spring sowing:* Sow seeds in containers, place in a plastic bag, and refrigerate for 2–3 weeks. Sink containers in the ground in a shady location, covering with glass. Transplant seedlings as they emerge.

PLANTING SEEDLINGS OUTDOORS

TIME After last frost.
SPACING Small species: 6"–8". Medium species: 12"–18". Large species: 24".
LIGHT Full sun.
SOIL Average, well-drained, with a pH level of 5.5–7.0. *S. maximum* requires moist soil, especially in hot climates.

CARING FOR PLANTS

Easy. Overwatering may cause fungal disease. Cut back to ground level in autumn. Be very frugal with fertilizer.

PROPAGATING

Divide in spring in zones 3–6, autumn in zones 7–9, or take cuttings in summer.

Sempervivum

**Hen-and-chickens, Houseleek,
Live-forever, St. Patrick's cabbage**

> TYPE HP or HHP
> ZONE 5–9. **Does not thrive on the**
> **Gulf Coast.**
> FLOWERING SEASON **Early summer**
> **to midsummer**

Genus of mainly low-growing, rosette-forming, evergreen succulents of 4"–12" bearing small, star-shaped flowers of white, yellow, pink, or purple. Useful around paving, in drystone walls, containers, rock gardens, and borders.

SOWING

INDOORS Spring or autumn.
OUTDOORS Spring.
DEPTH Surface.

GERMINATING

TIME 14–42 days.
REQUIREMENTS 70°–80°F.

PLANTING SEEDLINGS OUTDOORS

TIME After last frost.
SPACING Small species: 6"–8". Large species: 12".
LIGHT Full sun.
SOIL Poor, dry.

CARING FOR PLANTS

Water and feed only sparingly. Remove flower heads after blooming to improve appearance.

PROPAGATING

Plant detached offsets. Cannot be relied upon to come true from seed.

Sempervivum arachnoideum

A-Annual P-Perennial B-Biennial HHA-Half-hardy annual HA-Hardy annual HB-Hardy biennial HHP-Half-hardy perennial HP-Hardy perennial HHBb-Half-hardy bulb HBb-Hardy bulb

Senecio

(synonymous with *Cineraria*)

Cineraria, Dusty-miller, Groundsel, Ragwort

> TYPE HHA or HHP
> ZONE A: 3–8; P: 9–10;
> S. x *hybridus* will grow well only on the California Coast
> FLOWERING SEASON At any time of year from early spring through late winter, depending on species

Immense genus of greatly varying annuals, perennials, and subshrubs having in common their daisylike flowers, which are most often yellow. Many species are grown for their attractive grey foliage. Small species (12") make useful edging and rock garden plants, while taller species (up to 36") are grown in borders and wildflower gardens.

SOWING

INDOORS 6–8 weeks before planting out, in autumn in zones 9–10.
OUTDOORS Early spring, when soil is cool and a light frost is still possible, or late autumn.
DEPTH Surface.

GERMINATING

TIME 10–21 days.
REQUIREMENTS Light and 65°–75°F. Highly susceptible to damping-off; sow in vermiculite and water only from below. Do not start S. x *hybridus* from seed.

PLANTING SEEDLINGS OUTDOORS

TIME After last frost, autumn in zones 9–10.
SPACING Small species: 6". Medium species: 10"–12". Large species: 18"–24".
LIGHT Most species require full sun, but some will grow in part shade; S. *petasitis* thrives in full shade.
SOIL Average, well-drained.

CARING FOR PLANTS

Generally easy. Water during very dry spells. Severely cut back perennials in spring. Some people find the yellow flowers of grey-leaved species unattractive and choose to remove these before blooming.

PROPAGATING

Sow seeds for annuals. Divide perennials in spring.

Sesamum

Benne, Sesame

> TYPE HHA
> ZONE 7–10
> FLOWERING SEASON All summer

Erect, annual herbs native to Africa and Asia, 1'–3' tall, with pairs of leaves scattered along stems and pretty, tubular flowers of pink, violet, or white. Use limited to the herb garden.

SOWING

INDOORS 8 weeks before planting out.
OUTDOORS Late spring, when nighttime temperatures remain above 60°F.
DEPTH ¼".

GERMINATING

TIME 5–7 days.
REQUIREMENTS 70°–85°F.

PLANTING SEEDLINGS OUTDOORS

TIME In spring, when nighttime temperatures remain above 60°F.
SPACING 8"–12".
LIGHT Full sun.
SOIL Any that is well drained.

CARING FOR PLANTS

Do not move plants. To harvest seeds, cut stalks to the ground when the uppermost seed pods have turned green and lower pods have not yet opened. Dry flower heads in a paper bag, remove seeds, and store in an airtight container.

PROPAGATING

Seed only.

A-Annual P-Perennial B-Biennial HHA-Half-hardy annual HA-Hardy annual HB-Hardy biennial HHP-Half-hardy perennial HP-Hardy perennial HHBb-Half-hardy bulb HBb-Hardy bulb

254

Setaria

**Foxtail grass, Foxtail millet,
Plains bristle grass,
Yellow bristle grass**

TYPE HA or HHA
ZONE Prefers warm climates
FLOWERING SEASON Summer

Annual grasses with flat, green, 12"-long leaves and dense, 5' spikes of brown, black, yellow, or red flowers. Use in naturalistic gardens and mixed grass plantings.

SOWING

INDOORS Start seeds outdoors only.
OUTDOORS After last frost.
DEPTH Surface.

GERMINATING

TIME 10–21 days.
REQUIREMENTS 70°F.

PLANTING SEEDLINGS OUTDOORS

TIME Set out purchased plants after last frost.
SPACING Small species: 12". Large species: 24"–36".
LIGHT Sun or light shade.
SOIL Light, fertile, moist, and well-drained.

CARING FOR PLANTS

Do not allow soil to dry out.

PROPAGATING

Self-seeds.

Setcreasea

TYPE HHP
ZONE 9–10
FLOWERING SEASON Spring to autumn

Native to Mexico and the southern United States, these neat, trailing plants are grown for their fleshy, oblong, green or purple leaves; white or purple 3-petalled flowers are attractive but of secondary interest. Use in containers or borders with plants of contrasting color or texture.

SOWING

INDOORS Start seed outdoors.
OUTDOORS When seed is ripe, in autumn.
DEPTH Just cover.

GERMINATING

TIME 30–40 days.
REQUIREMENTS 70°F. Propagation is most often by cuttings due to the ease and success of this method.

PLANTING SEEDLINGS OUTDOORS

TIME In spring, when the temperatures remain above 50°F.
SPACING 12"–18".
LIGHT Sun.
SOIL Dry, coarse.

CARING FOR PLANTS

Allow soil to become quite dry before watering. Cut back ruthlessly when plants become straggly.

PROPAGATING

Take cuttings.

A-Annual P-Perennial B-Biennial HHA-Half-hardy annual HA-Hardy annual HB-Hardy biennial HHP-Half-hardy perennial HP-Hardy perennial HHBb-Half-hardy bulb HBb-Hardy bulb

255

Shortia

**Fringe-bell, Fringed galax,
Nippon bells, Oconee bells**

> **TYPE** HP
> **ZONE** 4–8. Performs best in cool climates.
> **FLOWERING SEASON** Spring

Genus of creeping evergreen perennials native to North America. Unusual, fringed, pink, tubular flowers grow singly on stems above attractive, rounded leaves. Grown in rock gardens and cool woodlands.

SOWING

INDOORS As soon as fresh seed is available.
OUTDOORS As soon as seed is ripe, in late summer.
DEPTH Surface.

GERMINATING

TIME 30–60 days.
REQUIREMENTS Difficult; use only very fresh seed. Place seeds in a plastic bag together with moist growing medium and refrigerate for 3 weeks. Provide a constant 60°–65°F thereafter.

PLANTING SEEDLINGS OUTDOORS

TIME After last frost.
SPACING 10"–12".
LIGHT Part to full shade.
SOIL Cool, very moist, acid; amend with leaf mold.

CARING FOR PLANTS

Difficult. Mulch with leaf mold or compost to keep soil cool and moist, and water regularly during dry weather. Do not disturb.

Shortia galacifolia

PROPAGATING

Divide in early spring, or take cuttings in early summer.

Sidalcea

**Checkerbloom, False mallow,
Miniature hollyhock, Prairie mallow**

> **TYPE** HP
> **ZONE** 5–9
> **FLOWERING SEASON** Early to late summer

Small genus of perennials bearing pink, purple, or white hollyhocklike flowers along tall (2'–8'), erect stems; leaves are lobed or deeply cut. Native to western North America. Grown in the border.

SOWING

INDOORS 6–8 weeks before last frost.
OUTDOORS Early spring.
DEPTH ⅛".

GERMINATING

TIME 14–42 days.
REQUIREMENTS Easy. 50°F.

PLANTING SEEDLINGS OUTDOORS

TIME After last frost.
SPACING Small species: 9"–12". Large species: 18".
LIGHT Full sun.
SOIL Ordinary; enrich with manure.

CARING FOR PLANTS

Easy. Water when the weather is dry. Cut plants back severely after flowering to encourage a second bloom, and again in late autumn. Stake tall cultivars. Divide every 2–3 years.

PROPAGATING

Divide in autumn (spring in zones 5–6).

Sidalcea malviflora

A-Annual P-Perennial B-Biennial HHA-Half-hardy annual HA-Hardy annual HB-Hardy biennial HHP-Half-hardy perennial HP-Hardy perennial HHBb-Half-hardy bulb HBb-Hardy bulb

Silene

Catchfly, Campion, Fire pink, Maiden's-tears, Moss campion, None-so-pretty, Rose-of-heaven, Sweet William catchfly, Wild pink

> TYPE HA or HP
> ZONE A: 3–9; P: 3–9: *S. virginica;* 4–9: *S. schafta, S. vulgaris;* 5–8: *S. alpestris, S. caroliniana.* Prefers warm temperatures.
> FLOWERING SEASON Spring to early summer or summer to early autumn, depending on species and sowing time

Genus of annual and perennial plants, some of which are evergreen, grown for the masses of small red, pink, or white flowers borne singly or in clusters over a long period. 2"–24" plants are useful as edging or in the border.

SOWING

INDOORS 8–10 weeks before planting out.
OUTDOORS Early spring, when soil is cool and a light frost is still possible. For spring flowering, sow annuals in late autumn.
DEPTH Just cover.

Silene virginica

GERMINATING

TIME 5–20 days.
REQUIREMENTS 70°F.

PLANTING SEEDLINGS OUTDOORS

TIME Early spring, when soil is cool and a light frost is still possible, or early autumn.
SPACING Small species: 6"–8". Medium species: 12". Large species: 18".
LIGHT Full sun or part shade.
SOIL Well-drained, humus-rich, with a pH level of 5.0–7.0.

CARING FOR PLANTS

Easy. Water frequently and feed occasionally. Discard annuals after flowering. Do not disturb established plants.

PROPAGATING

Sow seeds for annuals. Take softwood cuttings of perennials in spring.

Silphium

Compass plant, Cup plant, Indian cup, Pilotweed, Rosinweed

> TYPE HP
> ZONE 3–9. Prefers warm, dry climates.
> FLOWERING SEASON July to September

Very tall perennials native to the eastern United States, with large, coarse leaves and cheerful, yellow, sunflowerlike blooms. These towering 5'–12' plants need plenty of space at the back of the border, near a pond, or among tall shrubs.

SOWING

INDOORS Best to start seeds outdoors.
OUTDOORS As soon as fresh seed is available, in autumn.
DEPTH ½".

GERMINATING

TIME 21 days.
REQUIREMENTS Chip seeds before sowing. Sow seeds in flats, sink in the ground against a north-facing wall, and cover with glass. Moisten soil occasionally, if necessary. Bring flats indoors in late winter to a cool location.

PLANTING SEEDLINGS OUTDOORS

TIME Set out purchased plants in spring or autumn.
SPACING 3'–5'.
LIGHT Sun to light shade.
SOIL Will grow in most soils, but prefers moist, well-drained, with a pH level of 5.0–7.0.

CARING FOR PLANTS

Apply low-nitrogen fertilizer in spring. Divide every 2–3 years. Plants may require staking.

PROPAGATING

Divide in spring in the North, or early autumn south of zone 6.

A-Annual P-Perennial B-Biennial HHA-Half-hardy annual HA-Hardy annual HB-Hardy biennial HHP-Half-hardy perennial HP-Hardy perennial HHBb-Half-hardy bulb HBb-Hardy bulb

Silybum

**Holy thistle, Lady's thistle,
Milk thistle, Our Lady's milk thistle**

TYPE HA or HB
ZONE 1–10. Prefers cool weather.
FLOWERING SEASON Summer

Coarse plants with purple, thistlelike flowers borne singly on erect stems and spiny, marbled basal leaves; 4' tall. Use in naturalistic plantings or for textural contrast in the border.

SOWING

INDOORS 8 weeks before planting out.
OUTDOORS A: after last frost. B: early summer.
DEPTH ⅛".

Silybum marianum

GERMINATING

TIME 14–21 days.
REQUIREMENTS Easy. 55°–60°F.

PLANTING SEEDLINGS OUTDOORS

TIME A: after last frost. B: late summer to early autumn.
SPACING 24".
LIGHT Full sun or light shade.
SOIL Tolerates wet or dry soil; will produce only lush foliage in fertile soil.

CARING FOR PLANTS

Easy. To grow as a perennial foliage plant, remove flower buds before they open. Leaves are attractive to slugs.

PROPAGATING

Self-seeds most efficiently and may become weedy.

Sisyrinchium

Blue-eyed grass

TYPE HP or HHP
ZONE 3–9: *S. angustifolium;*
  5–9: *S. douglasii, S. mucronatum;*
  7–10: *S. striatum;*
  8–10: *S. bellum, S. californicum*
FLOWERING SEASON Spring to summer

Tufted, clump-forming perennials with stiff, grassy leaves and small yellow, white, purple, or blue star-shaped flowers growing along tall, upright, 12"–36" stems. Native to North America. Grow in rock gardens and borders.

SOWING

INDOORS See "Germinating, Requirements."
OUTDOORS See "Germinating, Requirements."
DEPTH ⅛".

GERMINATING

TIME 30–180 days.
REQUIREMENTS *Autumn sowing:* Sow seeds in flats, sink in the ground against a north-facing wall, and cover with glass. Moisten soil occasionally, if necessary. Bring flats indoors in spring to 50°F. *Spring sowing:* Sow seeds in containers, place in a plastic bag, and refrigerate for 2–3 weeks. Then plunge containers in the ground in a shady location and cover with glass. Transplant seedlings as they appear.

PLANTING SEEDLINGS OUTDOORS

TIME After last spring frost, or in autumn.
SPACING Small species: 4"–6". Large species: 12"–15".
LIGHT Prefers full sun but will tolerate part shade.
SOIL Grows quite well in most situations, but performs best in moist, fertile soil with a pH level of 5.0–6.0.

CARING FOR PLANTS

Do not allow soil to dry out during the growing season. Cut back flowering stems to the

Sisyrinchium angustifolium

ground after blooming. Do not despair if plants disappear in summer; this is normal and they will reappear the following spring. May become invasive if made too comfortable.

PROPAGATING

Divide in spring in zones 3–6 or in autumn in the South. Will self-seed.

Smilacina

**False Solomon's seal,
False spikenard**

> **Type** HP
> **Zone** 3–9
> **Flowering Season** Early summer

Graceful woodland plants native to North America. Pairs of handsome, light green leaves are borne along arching stems, topped with feathery clusters of tiny, white or pink flowers, each cluster resembling a miniature spruce tree. 12"–36" tall. Excellent woodland plants.

Sowing

Indoors Start seed outdoors only.
Outdoors As soon as ripe seed is available, in early autumn.
Depth Just cover.

Germinating

Time 30–180 days.
Requirements Sow seeds thinly in flats, sink these in the ground against a north-facing wall, and cover with glass. Moisten soil occasionally, if necessary. Leave for 1 full growing season before transplanting to the garden.

Planting Seedlings Outdoors

Time Set out purchased plants in spring or autumn.
Spacing 18"–24".
Light Part to full shade.
Soil Moist, rich, acid, with a pH level of 5.0–6.0.

Caring for Plants

Easy. Mulch with leaf mold and apply a complete fertilizer in early spring. Cut plants back to the ground in late autumn, or dig in autumn, leave in a cool, dark location until early spring, then bring into a warm room to force blooms.

Smilacina racemosa

Propagating

Divide in spring or autumn.

Soldanella

**Alpine snowbell, Dwarf snowbell,
Mountain tassel**

> **Type** HP
> **Zone** 6–8. Likes a cool, humid growing season.
> **Flowering Season** Late spring to early summer

Dainty alpine perennials forming clumps of heart-shaped leaves with nodding, fringed, bell-shaped flowers of purple, blue, or white held singly above. Very pretty plants of 6"–15" grown in the rock garden.

Sowing

Indoors As soon as fresh seed is available.
Outdoors As soon as fresh seed is available.
Depth Surface.

Germinating

Time 30–180 days.
Requirements Difficult. *Indoor sowing:* Place seeds in a plastic bag together with moist growing medium and refrigerate for 4 weeks. Provide light and 55°–60°F thereafter. *Outdoor sowing:* Sow seeds in flats, sink in the ground in a sheltered location, and cover with glass. Remove glass when seeds sprout. Transplant seedlings when they are large enough to handle.

Planting Seedlings Outdoors

Time After last frost.
Spacing 4"–6".
Light Sun, with light shade during the hottest part of the day.
Soil Very moist, with perfect drainage. Also peaty and slightly acid.

Caring for Plants

Difficult. Frequent watering is seldom necessary as *Soldanella* should never be planted where soil is likely to dry out. Surround plants with grit to improve winter drainage and discourage slugs. Protect flower buds from frost by covering crowns with a cloche or straw.

Propagating

Divide after flowering.

Soldanella alpina

A-Annual P-Perennial B-Biennial HHA-Half-hardy annual HA-Hardy annual HB-Hardy biennial HHP-Half-hardy perennial HP-Hardy perennial HHBb-Half-hardy bulb HBb-Hardy bulb

259

Solidago

Golden rod

Large genus of erect perennials with terminal sprays or spikes of tiny yellow flowers. Species are from 6" to 8' tall, with most growing from 2' to 4'. Use in borders, rock, or wildflower gardens. Native to North America.

SOWING

INDOORS 6–8 weeks before planting out.
OUTDOORS Early spring, when soil is cool and a light frost is still possible, or late autumn.
DEPTH Just cover.

GERMINATING

TIME 14–42 days.
REQUIREMENTS Easy. 50°F.

PLANTING SEEDLINGS OUTDOORS

TIME Early spring, when soil is cool and a light frost is still possible, or late autumn.
SPACING Small species: 12". Large species: 24"–36".
LIGHT Sun or part shade.
SOIL Moist, well-drained, with a pH level of 5.0–7.0. Very rich soil produces lush foliage but few flowers.

CARING FOR PLANTS

Easy. Deadhead after flowering to prevent unwanted self-seeding and cut back completely in autumn. Staking may be necessary in windy locations. Divide plants every 3–4 years to maintain vigor.

PROPAGATING

Divide in spring (autumn in zones 7–9), or allow to self-seed.

Solidago canadensis

Sparaxis

Harlequin flower, Wandflower

Small genus of South African corms with erect, narrow, lance-shaped leaves and spikes bearing shallow, trumpet-shaped flowers of red, orange, purple, pink, or white, often with yellow centers; 12"–24" tall. Mass in the rock garden or under shrubs, or mix with other spring bulbs; pretty in containers.

SOWING

INDOORS 8–10 weeks before planting out.
OUTDOORS Seed: early spring or early autumn. Bulb: Plant in spring for summer blooms in zones 3–8. Plant in autumn for spring flowering in zones 9–10.
DEPTH Seed: just cover. Bulb: 3".

Sparaxis tricolor

GERMINATING

TIME 30–90 days.
REQUIREMENTS 50°–55°F.

PLANTING SEEDLINGS OUTDOORS

TIME Zones 3–8: after last frost. Zones 9–10: early autumn.
SPACING 4".
LIGHT Sun.
SOIL Somewhat dry, neutral or alkaline. Place a little sand under each bulb at planting.

CARING FOR PLANTS

Easy. Top-dress with cow manure in spring, then water and feed regularly throughout the growing season. Plants may require staking. North of zone 9, lift bulbs after the first frost in autumn and store in a cool, frost-free place until spring. *Sparaxis* are short-lived in the Southeast.

PROPAGATING

Plant offsets. Self-seeding may occur.

Sphaeralcea

**Desert hollyhock, Desert mallow,
Globe mallow, Prairie mallow**

> TYPE HHP
> ZONE 7–9. Prefers warm, dry
>   climates.
> FLOWERING SEASON Summer

Branching subshrubs of 18"–6' with lobed
leaves and mainly hollyhocklike flowers of
red, purple, or orange growing in leaf axils.
Use in the border.

SOWING

INDOORS Start seeds outdoors only.
OUTDOORS In autumn, as soon as seeds
    are ripe.
DEPTH ¼".

GERMINATING

TIME 14–21 days.
REQUIREMENTS Easy. 65°–70°F.

PLANTING SEEDLINGS OUTDOORS

TIME Set out purchased plants in spring or
    autumn.
SPACING Small species: 6"–9". Medium spe-
    cies: 12"–24". Large species: 30"–36".
LIGHT Sun.
SOIL Poor, sandy, with a pH level of 5.0–
    8.0.

CARING FOR PLANTS

Grows admirably in dry soil, but you can
produce very large plants by watering regularly. Do not disturb.

PROPAGATING

Divide in autumn, take softwood cuttings
in summer, or allow to self-seed.

Sprekelia

**Aztec lily, Jacobean lily,
Mexican fire lily, St. James' lily**

> TYPE HHBb, often grown as A
> ZONE A: 3–8; P: 9–10
> FLOWERING SEASON Late spring to
>   early summer

Genus of Mexican bulbs grown for their
exotic, deep red, orchidlike flowers; leaves
are narrow and lance-shaped. Low-growing
plants of 6"–12" massed in a sunny border
or grown in containers.

SOWING

INDOORS Early spring.
OUTDOORS Seed: start indoors only. Bulb:
    2–3 weeks after last frost in zones 3–8;
    autumn in zones 9–10.
DEPTH Seed: just cover. Bulb: 4"–6".

GERMINATING

TIME 21–120 days.
REQUIREMENTS Rarely grown from seed and
    few details are available. Information
    given here should be used as a general
    guideline. Provide 65°–70°F. Grow in
    pots for 1 to 2 years before planting out.

PLANTING SEEDLINGS OUTDOORS

TIME 2–3 weeks after last frost in zones 3–
    8, autumn in zones 9–10.
SPACING 8"–12".
LIGHT Full sun or part shade.
SOIL Fertile, well-drained.

CARING FOR PLANTS

Easy. Plants grown from seed will not bloom
for 7–8 years. Water frequently and apply
liquid fertilizer every 2 weeks during the
growing season. North of zone 9, lift bulbs
before the first frost and store in vermiculite in a frost-free place over winter.

PROPAGATING

Plant bulblets after flowering.

Sprekelia formosissima

Stachys

Betony, Bishop's wort, Donkey's ears, Lamb's ears, Lamb's tongue, Woundwort

> TYPE HP or HHP
> ZONE 3–9: *S. grandiflora*;
> 4–7: *S. nivea*; 4–9:
> *S. byzantina* (will not tolerate hot, humid summers),
> *S. officinalis*, *S. macrantha*;
> 9–10: *S. coccinea* (will not tolerate hot, humid summers).
> Dislikes wet winters.
> FLOWERING SEASON Spring to summer

Large genus of mainly spreading perennials and subshrubs, some grown for their fuzzy, oblong, silver leaves, others for their dense spikes of small, purple, lipped and hooded flowers and crinkled, heart-shaped leaves; 6"–36" tall. Useful ground cover, edging, or border plants; silver species brighten up a humdrum planting.

SOWING

INDOORS 8–10 weeks before planting out.
OUTDOORS Early spring or early autumn.
DEPTH Just cover.

GERMINATING

TIME 15–30 days.
REQUIREMENTS 70°F.

PLANTING SEEDLINGS OUTDOORS

TIME Hardy species: early spring, when soil is cool and a light frost still possible, or late autumn. Half-hardy species: 2–3 weeks after last frost.
SPACING Small species: 8"–12". Medium species: 12"–18". Large species: 18"–24".
LIGHT Full sun to part shade.
SOIL Will tolerate dry conditions, but performs best in rich, well-drained soil.

CARING FOR PLANTS

Easy. Remove flowers after blooming to keep plants looking neat; some people prefer to remove the stems of woolly-leaved species *before* flowering, as the blooms are rather unwieldy and inelegant. Divide every 3–4 years.

Stachys lanata

PROPAGATING

Divide in spring in the North, in autumn south of zone 6.

Statice

See *Limonium*

Stenanthium

Featherbells, Featherfleece

> TYPE HBb
> ZONE 7–10
> FLOWERING SEASON Late summer

Genus of little-known bulbs with narrow, grasslike leaves 12" long, and 2'–5' spikes bearing feathery panicles of tiny white flowers. North American wildflowers for naturalistic gardens and pondsides.

SOWING

INDOORS Spring.
OUTDOORS Seed: autumn. Bulb: early spring.
DEPTH Seed: just cover. Bulb: 3"–5".

GERMINATING

REQUIREMENTS Seldom grown from seed and little literature exists. Information given here can be used as a general guideline, but some experimentation may be necessary. *Outdoor sowing:* Sow seeds in flats, sink in the ground against a north-facing wall, and cover with glass. Remove when germination begins. *Indoor sowing:* Provide a nighttime temperature of 55°F. Grow for 1 year before potting up, then 2 more years before planting out.

PLANTING SEEDLINGS OUTDOORS

TIME After last frost.
SPACING 12"–24".
LIGHT Sun or part shade.
SOIL Moist, acid, and well-drained.

CARING FOR PLANTS

Mulch in spring with compost and keep the soil fairly moist throughout the growing season. Do not disturb.

PROPAGATING

Divide in autumn.

A-Annual P-Perennial B-Biennial HHA-Half-hardy annual HA-Hardy annual HB-Hardy biennial HHP-Half-hardy perennial HP-Hardy perennial HHBb-Half-hardy bulb HBb-Hardy bulb

262

Sternbergia

**Winter daffodil,
Yellow autumn crocus**

> TYPE HBb
> ZONE 6–10
> FLOWERING SEASON Autumn

Small, crocuslike bulbs with grassy foliage and sometimes fragrant, bright yellow or white flowers; 6" tall. Use in rock gardens or as edging.

SOWING

INDOORS Start seed outdoors.
OUTDOORS Seed: late summer. Bulb: late summer through autumn.
DEPTH Seed: just cover. Bulb: 4".

GERMINATING

REQUIREMENTS Little data exists on growing this charming bulb from seed as it is so easily increased by division. Information given here should be used as a general guideline for the adventurous. Bulb seeds usually require 60°–65°F for germination.

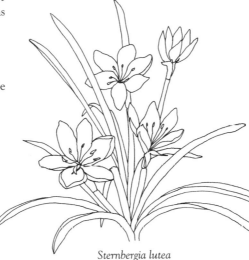

Sternbergia lutea

PLANTING SEEDLINGS OUTDOORS

TIME Late summer, after 1 full growing season.
SPACING 4"–6".
LIGHT Sun or light shade.
SOIL Fertile, well-drained; should be dry in summer when bulbs are resting.

CARING FOR PLANTS

Water regularly during the growing season, tapering off in summer. Allow leaves to wither naturally before removing. Leave plants undisturbed for 3–4 years after planting, then divide only rarely.

PROPAGATING

Plant bulblets in autumn (spring in zone 6).

Stipa

**Feather grass, Needlegrass,
Spear grass**

> TYPE HP
> ZONE 5–9
> FLOWERING SEASON Summer

Ornamental perennial grasses with very showy, feathery flowers on thick, stiff stems of 1'–8'. Small species are grown in borders and mixed grass plantings; tall species make a dramatic specimen.

SOWING

INDOORS 6–8 weeks before planting out.
OUTDOORS Early spring to midspring.
DEPTH ⅛".

GERMINATING

TIME 21–30 days.
REQUIREMENTS Easy. 70°F.

PLANTING SEEDLINGS OUTDOORS

TIME 2 weeks after last frost.
SPACING Small species: 12"–15". Medium species: 18"–24". Large species: 36"–48".
LIGHT Full sun.
SOIL Fertile, well-drained.

CARING FOR PLANTS

Easy. Young plants require plenty of water to become established. Cut back to ground level in early spring. To restrict spreading, divide or remove side growth periodically.

PROPAGATING

Divide in spring.

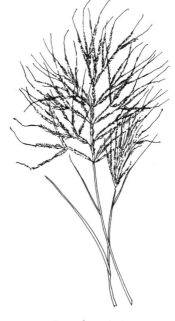

Stipa elegantissima

A-Annual P-Perennial B-Biennial HHA-Half-hardy annual HA-Hardy annual HB-Hardy biennial HHP-Half-hardy perennial HP-Hardy perennial HHBb-Half-hardy bulb HBb-Hardy bulb

Stokesia

Stokes' aster

TYPE HP
ZONE 6–10
FLOWERING SEASON Summer

One species of perennial native to North America grown for its showy, heavily fringed flowers of purple, blue, white, or pink. 1'–2'-tall plants are used near the front of the border.

SOWING

INDOORS 8–10 weeks before planting out.
OUTDOORS Early spring or early autumn.
DEPTH Just cover.

Stokesia laevis

GERMINATING

TIME 20–30 days.
REQUIREMENTS 70°F.

PLANTING SEEDLINGS OUTDOORS

TIME Early spring, when soil is cool and a light frost is still possible, or early autumn.
SPACING Small species: 10"–12". Large species: 18".
LIGHT Full sun or part shade.
SOIL Rich, very well-drained. Will not survive where the ground is wet.

CARING FOR PLANTS

Easy. Cut plants back to the ground in autumn.

PROPAGATING

Divide in early spring.

Symphytum

Blackwort, Comfrey, Knit-bone

TYPE HP
ZONE 4–9
FLOWERING SEASON Late spring through first frost

Small genus of rather coarse perennials, the more attractive species grown for their handsome variegated foliage and clusters of small, nodding, blue, pink, purple, yellow, or white bell-shaped flowers; 1'–4' tall. Often grown in the wildflower garden, but also useful in borders and in front of dark green shrubs.

SOWING

DEPTH Root: 3"–6".

GERMINATING

REQUIREMENTS Growing from seed is not recommended.

PLANTING SEEDLINGS OUTDOORS

TIME Set out purchased plants in autumn or early spring.
SPACING Allow this giant herb plenty of room, at least 36"–48".
LIGHT Prefers full sun, but will grow quite well and remain considerably smaller in shade.
SOIL Moist, rich, with a pH level of 6.5–7.5.

CARING FOR PLANTS

Easy, requiring little attention. Water regularly and remove dead leaves in autumn. Divide occasionally to alleviate crowding. Allow plants to grow for 3 years before harvesting leaves, then cut leaves that are 12"–18" tall just before flowering. Cut off flowering stems before blooming to stimulate further foliar production.

Symphytum officinale

PROPAGATING

Divide or take root cuttings in spring or autumn.

A-Annual P-Perennial B-Biennial HHA-Half-hardy annual HA-Hardy annual HB-Hardy biennial HHP-Half-hardy perennial HP-Hardy perennial HHBb-Half-hardy bulb HBb-Hardy bulb

264

Synthyris

Type HP
Zone 6–9; 2–9: *S. missurica*. At home on the Pacific Coast and will not thrive in hot, dry locations.
Flowering Season Early spring, sometimes repeating in autumn

Low-growing, spreading perennials grown in rock gardens, native to Europe and the western United States. 3"–12" spikes bear small blue, purple, pink, or white flowers; heart-shaped leaves have pinked edges.

Germinating

Requirements Propagate plants by division only.

Planting Seedlings Outdoors

Time Set out purchased plants in spring or autumn.
Spacing 4"–6".
Light Part to full shade; shade from the hot afternoon sun is essential.
Soil Rich, gritty, acid, moist or even wet; amend with organic matter.

Caring for Plants

Difficult. Keep soil moist at all times.

Propagating

Divide after blooming in spring.

Tagetes

African marigold, American marigold, Aztec marigold, Dwarf marigold, French marigold, Mexican marigold, Marigold, Signet marigold

Type HA or HHA
Zone 1–10. Flowers best in warm climates.
Flowering Season Summer through frost

Hard-working and popular annuals of upright habit grown for their abundant yellow or orange flowers borne singly on sturdy stems. Neat, attractive foliage is bushy and finely toothed; plants are 6"–36" tall. Suited to containers, edging, borders, or display beds.

Sowing

Indoors 6–8 weeks before last frost.
Outdoors 2 weeks before last frost.
Depth Just cover.

Tagetes patula

Germinating

Time 4–14 days.
Requirements Easy. 70°F–75°F. Seedlings are somewhat susceptible to damping-off; sow in vermiculite and water only from below as a precaution.

Planting Seedlings Outdoors

Time After last frost.
Spacing Dwarf species: 6". Medium species: 12"–15". Large species: 18"–24".
Light Full sun, with afternoon shade where summers are very hot.
Soil Prefers good soil with a pH level of 6.0–7.0, enriched with organic matter, but will withstand quite dry soil.

Caring for Plants

Easy. Feed during the early growth period and water regularly. Pinch back tall species once or twice when young to give plants a more stable framework and avoid that trampled look in midsummer. If slugs devour young seedlings, replace with more mature plants, which are more resilient. Deadhead to prolong blooming.

Propagating

Seed.

A-Annual P-Perennial B-Biennial HHA-Half-hardy annual HA-Hardy annual HB-Hardy biennial HHP-Half-hardy perennial HP-Hardy perennial HHBb-Half-hardy bulb HBb-Hardy bulb

265

Tecophilaea

Chilean crocus

> TYPE HBb
> ZONE 8–10
> FLOWERING SEASON Early spring

Small genus of diminutive bulbs native to Chile. Flowers are funnel-shaped, blue, sometimes with a white throat; leaves are sparse, erect, and lance-shaped. Rock garden plants of 3"–6".

SOWING

INDOORS Sow seeds outdoors only.
OUTDOORS Seed: autumn. Corm: late summer through autumn.
DEPTH Seed: just cover. Corm: 3"–5".

GERMINATING

TIME 30–365 days.
REQUIREMENTS Difficult. Sow seeds in individual pots, sink these in the ground outdoors in a sheltered position and cover with glass. Remove glass when germination begins. Do not move seedlings for 2–3 years.

PLANTING SEEDLINGS OUTDOORS

TIME Late summer through autumn.
SPACING 4"–6".
LIGHT Full sun.
SOIL Dry, sandy, lime-free.

CARING FOR PLANTS

Feed lightly in late winter. Water in winter and spring, keeping corms on the dry side from early summer through autumn; these bulbs do not like heavy winter rain. Apply mulch in winter, removing it completely as soon as sprouting begins in spring.

PROPAGATING

Plant offsets in autumn.

Tellima

False alumroot, Fringe cups

> TYPE HP
> ZONE 3–9
> FLOWERING SEASON Summer

Unusual perennials native to western North America bearing tall, delicate spikes of loosely scattered, bell-shaped flowers of white, turning to pink; heart-shaped leaves may be green or bronze. 2' tall. Plants for the wildflower or woodland garden.

SOWING

INDOORS See "Germinating, Requirements."
OUTDOORS See "Germinating, Requirements."
DEPTH Surface.

GERMINATING

TIME 30–90 days.
REQUIREMENTS Always use fresh seed. *Autumn sowing:* Sow seeds in flats, sink in the ground against a north-facing wall, and cover with glass. Moisten soil occasionally, if necessary. Bring flats indoors in spring to 55°–60°F. *Spring sowing:* Sow seeds in flats, place flats in plastic bags, and refrigerate. After 2–3 weeks remove and sink in the ground in a shady location. Cover with glass, removing when seeds sprout.

PLANTING SEEDLINGS OUTDOORS

TIME Autumn.
SPACING 18"–24".
LIGHT Part to full shade.
SOIL Cool, moist, rich.

CARING FOR PLANTS

Easy. Mulch in spring and autumn; water during dry spells. *Tellima* spreads rapidly when happy.

PROPAGATING

Divide in spring (zones 3–6) or early autumn (zones 7–9).

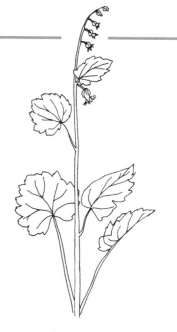

Tellima grandiflora

Teucrium

Germander

> TYPE HP
> ZONE 3–9: *T. canadense;* 4–9:
> *T. chamaedrys, T. pyrenaicum;*
> 5–9: *T. Scorodonia;* 7–9:
> *T. aroanium, T. hircanicum.*
> **Very tolerant of extreme heat.**
> FLOWERING SEASON Summer

Large genus of bushy, branched perennials and subshrubs, 4"–3' tall, with small but showy flowers in clusters or spikes, colored blue, purple, pink, or yellow. Use in rock and wildflower gardens, walls, or borders.

SOWING

INDOORS 6–8 weeks before last frost.
OUTDOORS Early spring, when soil is cool and a light frost is still possible, or late autumn.
DEPTH Surface.

GERMINATING

/TIME 25–30 days.
REQUIREMENTS 70°F.

PLANTING SEEDLINGS OUTDOORS

TIME After last frost.
SPACING 12".
LIGHT Full sun or part shade.
SOIL Prefers ordinary, well-drained soil, but will do quite well even in poor.

CARING FOR PLANTS

Easy. Fertilize periodically and water during dry spells. Cut back stems by up to one-half in spring to maintain size, shape, and vigor.

PROPAGATING

Take cuttings or divide in spring.

Thalictrum

Feathered columbine, Meadow rue

> TYPE HP
> ZONE 3–8: *T. minus;* 5–7:
> *T. kiusianum;* 5–8:
> *T. aquilegifolium, T. delavayi,*
> *T. diffusiflorum, T. rochebrunia-*
> *num;* 5–9: *T. flavum;* 6–9:
> *T. chelidonii.* **Not tolerant of**
> **extreme heat and humidity.**
> FLOWERING SEASON Summer

Perennials with attractive lobed, or toothed foliage and erect stalks crowned with fluffy heads of purple, yellow, white, or pink flowers; 1'–7' tall. Grow at the edge of woodland or near water, in the rock garden, or border, where its fine foliage will contrast with large-leaved plants.

SOWING

INDOORS Seeds should be started outdoors.
OUTDOORS As soon as seed is ripe, in autumn.
DEPTH ⅛".

Thalictrum aquilegifolium

GERMINATING

TIME 15–50 days, or up to 2 years.
REQUIREMENTS Sow seeds in flats, sink in the ground against a north-facing wall, and cover with glass. Moisten soil occasionally, if necessary.

PLANTING SEEDLINGS OUTDOORS

TIME Autumn.
SPACING Small species: 6"–8". Medium species: 12"–18". Large species: 24"–36".
LIGHT Full sun in cool climates, part shade where summers are hot.
SOIL Moist, especially where plants are grown in full sun; a pH level of 5.0–6.0 is preferred.

CARING FOR PLANTS

Easy. Feed once in spring with a weak solution — excessive fertilizing will result in weak growth. Mulch in spring and water well during dry spells. Cut plants back to the ground in late autumn. Very tall species require staking. *Teucrium* is short-lived in hot climates.

PROPAGATING

Divide in early spring.

A-Annual P-Perennial B-Biennial HHA-Half-hardy annual HA-Hardy annual HB-Hardy biennial HHP-Half-hardy perennial HP-Hardy perennial HHBb-Half-hardy bulb HBb-Hardy bulb

267

Thermopsis

Aaron's rod, Carolina lupine, False lupine

> TYPE HP
> ZONE 3–9
> FLOWERING SEASON Late spring to summer

Short-blooming perennials of 1'–5' with strongly horizontal leaves and bright yellow, pealike flowers. These North American natives are used in the shrub or flower border.

SOWING

INDOORS 6–8 weeks before last frost, in peat pots.
OUTDOORS Early spring, when soil is cool and a light frost is still possible, or late autumn.
DEPTH Just cover.

GERMINATING

TIME 15–30 days.
REQUIREMENTS Chip seeds and soak in warm water for 24 hours. Provide 70°F thereafter.

PLANTING SEEDLINGS OUTDOORS

TIME After last frost.
SPACING 18"–24".
LIGHT Full sun; light shade in hot climates.
SOIL Prefers well-drained, gritty, with a pH level of 5.5–7.0, but will grow almost anywhere.

CARING FOR PLANTS

Easy. A long taproot makes these plants highly drought tolerant, but very difficult to move. Staking may be necessary. Removing flower stalks after blooming may prompt a second bloom. Cut plants to ground level in late autumn.

PROPAGATING

Divide in spring; be very careful when digging taproot.

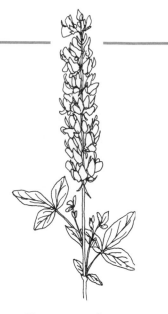

Thermopsis caroliniana

Thunbergia

Black-eyed Susan vine, Clock vine, Orange clock vine, Skyflower, Sky vine

> TYPE HHA
> ZONE 5–10. Most prefer cool summers.
> FLOWERING SEASON Summer to autumn

Climbing plants with attractive foliage and flowers. Blooms may be flat, white, orange, or yellow, sometimes with black centers, or trumpet-shaped and palest blue. Grow against a trellis, in baskets, or in pots, or allow to spill gracefully over a wall.

SOWING

INDOORS 6–8 weeks before planting out, in peat pots.
OUTDOORS Only where winters are very mild, in early spring or late autumn.
DEPTH Just cover.

GERMINATING

TIME 10–21 days.
REQUIREMENTS 65°–75°F.

PLANTING SEEDLINGS OUTDOORS

TIME When nighttime temperatures remain above 50°F.
SPACING 12"–18".
LIGHT Full sun or light shade.
SOIL Moist, fertile, with plenty of organic matter added.

CARING FOR PLANTS

Water well throughout the growth period; prune to keep more compact. Vines can be potted up, grown indoors for the winter, then planted out after the last spring frost. Plants brought through the winter will be much stronger in their second year.

PROPAGATING

Take cuttings in spring.

Thunbergia alata

A-Annual P-Perennial B-Biennial HHA-Half-hardy annual HA-Hardy annual HB-Hardy biennial HHP-Half-hardy perennial HP-Hardy perennial HHBb-Half-hardy bulb HBb-Hardy bulb

268

Thymus

Mother-of-thyme, Thyme

> TYPE HP
> ZONE 5–9
> FLOWERING SEASON Late spring to
>   early summer

Large genus of ground-hugging, strongly aromatic, evergreen plants with neat, tiny leaves and small, pink, purple, or white flowers. Grow in paving, drystone walls, rock gardens, or borders.

SOWING

INDOORS 6–8 weeks before last frost.
OUTDOORS 2–3 weeks before last frost, or late autumn.
DEPTH Surface.

GERMINATING

TIME 15–30 days.
REQUIREMENTS Light and 55°–65°F.

PLANTING SEEDLINGS OUTDOORS

TIME After last frost.
SPACING 8"–12".
LIGHT Sun to part shade.
SOIL Prefers light, well-drained, dry.

CARING FOR PLANTS

Easy. Cut plants back by about one-half after blooming to maintain shape, a tidy appearance, and strong leaf taste. Renew every 3–4 years when plants begin to deteriorate. Pick fresh leaves to use in cooking at any time. To dry, cut stems just before flowering, hang upside-down in a dark place until completely dry, strip leaves from stems, and store in an airtight container. To grow indoors pot up thyme plants in late summer using a sandy soil mix. Give plants 5 hours sunlight a day and allow soil to dry out between waterings.

PROPAGATING

Divide in spring, or take cuttings after flowering.

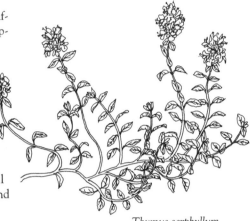

Thymus serphyllum

Tiarella

Foam flower

> TYPE HP
> ZONE 3–8: *T. cordifolia*,
>   *T. wherryi*; 4–7: *T. laciniata*,
>   *T. trifoliata*; 5–8: *T. polyphylla*
> FLOWERING SEASON Late spring to
>   early summer

Charming little woodland plants with heart-shaped leaves that form a neat clump of pale green, and dainty spikes of feathery white flowers; foliage turns red in autumn. These North American natives grow from 1' to 2' tall and are used in the woodland, wildflower, or rock garden.

SOWING

INDOORS See "Germinating, Requirements."
OUTDOORS See "Germinating, Requirements."
DEPTH Surface.

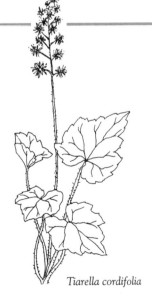

Tiarella cordifolia

GERMINATING

TIME 14–90 days.
REQUIREMENTS *Autumn sowing:* Sow seeds in flats, sink these to the rim outdoors against a north-facing wall, and cover with glass. Moisten soil occasionally, if necessary. Bring indoors in spring to 50°F and transplant to the garden after the last spring frost. *Spring sowing:* Sow seeds in moistened medium, place in a plastic bag, and refrigerate. After 2–3 weeks, sink containers in the ground in a shady location, covering with glass. Remove glass when seeds sprout. Transplant seedlings to the garden in autumn.

PLANTING SEEDLINGS OUTDOORS

TIME Spring or autumn.
SPACING Small species: 6"–8". Medium species: 12". Large species: 18"–24".
LIGHT Part to full shade.
SOIL Cool, rich, moist, well-drained, with a pH level of 5.0–6.0.

CARING FOR PLANTS

Mulch to keep soil cool and moist, and water often during dry spells. Do not disturb plants.

PROPAGATING

Divide in early spring (autumn in zones 7–8).

A-Annual P-Perennial B-Biennial HHA-Half-hardy annual HA-Hardy annual HB-Hardy biennial HHP-Half-hardy perennial HP-Hardy perennial HHBb-Half-hardy bulb HBb-Hardy bulb

Tithonia

Golden flower of the Incas, Mexican sunflower

TYPE HHA
ZONE 3–10. Thrives in warm temperatures.
FLOWERING SEASON Summer to autumn

Genus of annuals native to Central America grown for their bright orange, yellow, or red sunflowerlike blooms; 2'–4' tall. Grow in the border.

SOWING
INDOORS 6–8 weeks before last frost.
OUTDOORS After last frost, only where winters are mild.
DEPTH Surface.

GERMINATING
TIME 5–14 days.
REQUIREMENTS 70°F.

PLANTING SEEDLINGS OUTDOORS
TIME After last frost.
SPACING 24".
LIGHT Full sun.
SOIL Any light soil; quite drought tolerant.

CARING FOR PLANTS
Easy. Stake plants and water only during prolonged dry spells.

PROPAGATING
Seed only.

Tithonia rotundifolia

Torenia

Bluewings, Wishbone flower

TYPE HHA
ZONE 3–10. Happiest in warm, humid climates.
FLOWERING SEASON Summer to early autumn

Genus of annuals native to Asia and Africa grown for their showy, long-blooming, multicolored, tubular flowers which may be any combination of purple, blue, yellow, pink, or white; 12" tall. Useful at the front of the border.

SOWING
INDOORS 6–8 weeks before planting out.
OUTDOORS 1 week after last frost.
DEPTH Surface.

Torenia asiatica

GERMINATING
TIME 7–30 days.
REQUIREMENTS Light and 70°–75°F.

PLANTING SEEDLINGS OUTDOORS
TIME 2 weeks after last frost.
SPACING 6"–8".
LIGHT Sun, only where summers are cool. For more intense flower color, give plants afternoon shade.
SOIL Moist, rich, well-drained, with plenty of organic matter added.

CARING FOR PLANTS
Easy. Pinch back shoots when plants are 3" to establish a bushier habit. Water regularly. *Torenia* can be potted up and brought inside for winter blooming.

PROPAGATING
Take cuttings. Self-seeds in very warm climates.

A-Annual P-Perennial B-Biennial HHA-Half-hardy annual HA-Hardy annual HB-Hardy biennial HHP-Half-hardy perennial HP-Hardy perennial HHBb-Half-hardy bulb HBb-Hardy bulb

Townsendia

TYPE HP
ZONE 3–9
FLOWERING SEASON Spring to
summer

Small genus of very low-growing rock garden perennials with sparse, narrow leaves and asterlike flowers of pink, purple, or white, sometimes with yellow centers; 4"–8" tall. Native to western North America.

SOWING

INDOORS See "Germinating, Requirements."
OUTDOORS See "Germinating, Requirements."
DEPTH Just cover.

GERMINATING

TIME 30–90 days.
REQUIREMENTS *Autumn sowing:* Sow seeds in flats, sink these in the ground against a north-facing wall, and cover with glass. Moisten occasionally, if necessary. Bring flats indoors in spring to 60°F. *Spring sowing:* Sow seeds in containers, secure in plastic bags, and refrigerate for 2–3 weeks. Sink containers in the ground in a shady location, covering with glass. Remove glass when seeds sprout. Transplant seedlings to the garden when they are large enough to handle.

PLANTING SEEDLINGS OUTDOORS

TIME Spring or autumn
SPACING 4"–6".
LIGHT Full sun.
SOIL Moist, gritty, well-drained.

CARING FOR PLANTS

Townsendia will not tolerate winter wetness; surround plants with fine gravel to ensure rapid drainage. Do not disturb once established. Plants are short-lived.

PROPAGATING

Seed only.

Trachelium

(synonymous with *Diosphaera*)

Blue throatwort, Throatwort

TYPE HHP often treated as HHA
ZONE A: 3–7; P: 5–7: T.
asperuloides; 8–10: T.
caeruleum. Prefers warm
weather and dry winters.
FLOWERING SEASON Summer

Small group of annuals native to the Mediterranean, either mat-forming and covered in pale blue pinwheels, or upright, 2'–3' tall, and bearing heads of tiny, fluffy blue flowers. Use in rock gardens, borders, and cutting beds.

SOWING

INDOORS 8–10 weeks before planting out.
OUTDOORS Start seed outdoors in zones 9–10 only, in midwinter.
DEPTH Surface.

GERMINATING

TIME 15–21 days.
REQUIREMENTS Easy. Light and 55°–60°F.

PLANTING SEEDLINGS OUTDOORS

TIME Zones 9–10: early spring or early autumn. North of zone 9: after last frost.
SPACING 12".
LIGHT Full sun to part shade.
SOIL Fertile, slightly limy, fairly moist, but very well-drained.

CARING FOR PLANTS

Easy. Water during dry spells and protect from overhead water in winter.

PROPAGATING

Take cuttings in spring.

A-Annual P-Perennial B-Biennial HHA-Half-hardy annual HA-Hardy annual HB-Hardy biennial HHP-Half-hardy perennial HP-Hardy perennial HHBb-Half-hardy bulb HBb-Hardy bulb

271

Trachymene

(synonymous with *Didiscus*)

Blue lace flower, Laceflower

> TYPE HHP usually treated as HHA
> ZONE 3–8. Prefer cool climates and may not bloom during very hot spells.
> FLOWERING SEASON Summer

Upright, branching plants native to Australia with globes of tiny purple flowers on thick, erect stems; closely resembles *Allium*. 6"–24" tall. Grown in borders and cutting beds.

SOWING
INDOORS 8–10 weeks before last frost, in peat pots.
OUTDOORS After last frost.
DEPTH Just cover.

GERMINATING
TIME 15–30 days.
REQUIREMENTS 70°F and darkness.

PLANTING SEEDLINGS OUTDOORS
TIME After the last spring frost.
SPACING 8"–10".
LIGHT Full sun.
SOIL Average, supplemented with organic matter. Happiest in slightly moist soil, but will tolerate dry conditions.

CARING FOR PLANTS
Easy. Water only moderately. Pinch tips of young plants to encourage bushiness, and support lanky growth with twiggy branches pushed into the soil. Plants will have more blooms when slightly crowded.

PROPAGATING
Seed only.

Tradescantia

Spiderwort, Trinity flower, Wandering Jew

> TYPE HP or HHP
> ZONE 4–9: *T. x andersoniana*, *T. bracteata*, *T. ohiensis*; 6–9: *T. subaspera*; 9–10: *T. albiflora*
> FLOWERING SEASON Summer, with some repeat blooming in autumn

Large genus of perennial plants native to the Americas. Some are grown for their foliage, which may be variegated or an unusual plum color; others are prized for their flat, 3-petalled flowers of purple, white, or blue, despite a disgracefully messy habit. Low species (12") make showy ground covers and container plants; upright species (up to 36") are useful in the woodland or naturalistic garden.

SOWING
INDOORS 6–8 weeks before planting out.
OUTDOORS Early spring, when soil is cool and a light frost is still possible, or late autumn.
DEPTH Just cover.

Tradescantia virginiana

GERMINATING
TIME 10–40 days.
REQUIREMENTS 70°F.

PLANTING SEEDLINGS OUTDOORS
TIME After last frost.
SPACING 12"–18".
LIGHT Full sun where summers are cool and/or soil is moist; plants do better in part shade elsewhere.
SOIL Prefers rich, moist, well-drained soil with a pH level of 5.0–6.0; to curtail spreading of invasive species, plant in poor soil.

CARING FOR PLANTS
Easy, hardy, and trouble-free. Water regularly where spreading of plants is desirable. Cut back after flowering to encourage repeat blooming, and trim straggly growth periodically to maintain a neat appearance (this may entail cutting back the entire plant). Divide every 3 years to maintain vigor.

PROPAGATING
Divide in spring in the North, in autumn south of zone 7, or allow to self-seed.

A-Annual P-Perennial B-Biennial HHA-Half-hardy annual HA-Hardy annual HB-Hardy biennial HHP-Half-hardy perennial HP-Hardy perennial HHBb-Half-hardy bulb HBb-Hardy bulb

272

Tricholaena

Natal grass, Ruby grass

> TYPE HHP usually treated as
>   HHA
> ZONE A: 5–9; P: 9–10
> FLOWERING SEASON Late spring to
>   summer; longer in mild climates

Ornamental grass from South Africa grown for its silky, ruby-colored flowers. Leaves are flat and thin, 8" long.

SOWING
INDOORS 6–8 weeks before planting out.
OUTDOORS Very early spring.
DEPTH Just cover.

GERMINATING
TIME 21 days.
REQUIREMENTS 50°–55°F.

PLANTING SEEDLINGS OUTDOORS
TIME After last frost.
SPACING 12"–18".
LIGHT Full sun.
SOIL Will grow in most soils, but prefers a soil that is light and well drained.

CARING FOR PLANTS
Easy. Shelter from wind and rain, both of which can easily flatten plants. Keep soil moist. Cut back in autumn as plants have little winter interest. Flowers are attractive in arrangements, but will not keep their color when dried.

PROPAGATING
Division is possible but very difficult.

Trichosanthes

Serpent cucumber, Serpent gourd, Snake gourd

> TYPE HHA
> ZONE 9–10
> FLOWERING SEASON Late summer
>   to autumn

Annual vines, the most common species having long, broad leaves, fringed white flowers, and serpentine 2'-long fruits. Vines reach 10'–15'. Grown as a curiosity on a trellis or arbor.

SOWING
INDOORS 6–8 weeks before planting out, in peat pots.
OUTDOORS After temperature has reached 70°F.
DEPTH 1".

GERMINATING
TIME 14–30 days.
REQUIREMENTS 65°–75°F.

PLANTING SEEDLINGS OUTDOORS
TIME In spring when temperatures remain above 60°F.
SPACING 48" or singly.
LIGHT Sun, with shade from the afternoon sun where summers are hot.
SOIL Moist, humus-rich.

CARING FOR PLANTS
Water frequently during the growing season, tapering off when growth stops. Vines require a trellis or other support.

PROPAGATING
Seed only.

A-Annual P-Perennial B-Biennial HHA-Half-hardy annual HA-Hardy annual HB-Hardy biennial HHP-Half-hardy perennial HP-Hardy perennial HHBb-Half-hardy bulb HBb-Hardy bulb

273

Tricyrtis

Toad lily

> TYPE HP or HHP
> ZONE 5–8: *T. formosana,*
> *T. hirta;* 6–9: *T. latifolia;*
> 7–9: *T. flava.* Can be grown as
> an annual north of the recom-
> mended zones.
> FLOWERING SEASON Midsummer
> to early autumn

Small genus of East Asian perennials grown for their pink, red, purple, yellow, or white, usually freckled blossoms. In full bloom the upturned, bell-shaped flowers look as though they've stood in unison, thrown their hands in the air, and yelled, "surprise!", which would be an appropriate gesture as these plants show a reluctance to bloom at all. Mass along the border's edge.

SOWING

INDOORS 6–8 weeks before last frost, in peat pots.
OUTDOORS Early spring, when soil is cool and a light frost is still possible, or late autumn.
DEPTH ⅛".

GERMINATING

TIME 30–90 days.
REQUIREMENTS Difficult. 65°–70°F.

PLANTING SEEDLINGS OUTDOORS

TIME After last frost.
SPACING 4"–6".
LIGHT Part shade; full sun where the growing season is short.
SOIL Moist, rich, peaty, and slightly acid.

CARING FOR PLANTS

Easy. Mulch in spring and water regularly during hot, dry spells. Leaves may be attractive to slugs. North of the recommended zones, dig and store plants in autumn, replanting in spring.

Tricyrtis hirta

PROPAGATING

Divide in the spring.

Trigonella

Bird's-foot, Fenugreek, Greek hay

> TYPE HHA
> ZONE 6–10
> FLOWERING SEASON Midsummer
> through autumn

Annual herb grown for culinary use, grown only in the herb bed. Plants are 1'–2' tall, with compound leaves resembling clover; pealike flowers are small and white.

SOWING

INDOORS Start seeds *in situ.*
OUTDOORS When the soil is very warm — about 60°F.
DEPTH ¼".

GERMINATING

TIME 2–5 days.
REQUIREMENTS 70°–75°F.

PLANTING SEEDLINGS OUTDOORS

TIME Set out purchased plants after the last frost.
SPACING 4".
LIGHT Full sun.
SOIL Rich, well-drained, with a pH level of 6.0–7.0.

CARING FOR PLANTS

Caution: Snails are attracted to tender seedlings. To harvest seeds, cut ripe seed pods and dry in the sun; remove seeds and store in an airtight container.

PROPAGATING

Seed only.

A-Annual P-Perennial B-Biennial HHA-Half-hardy annual HA-Hardy annual HB-Hardy biennial HHP-Half-hardy perennial HP-Hardy perennial HHBb-Half-hardy bulb HBb-Hardy bulb

274

Trillium

Wake-robin

TYPE HP
ZONE 4–9
FLOWERING SEASON **Early spring to early summer**

Stately woodland plants native to North America with three large, flat, pointed leaves growing in horizontal whorls and large, single flowers of white, pink, or red; 6"–18" tall. Plants form dense colonies and are of unrivalled loveliness in the woods.

SOWING

INDOORS Any time that fresh seed is available.
OUTDOORS As soon as fresh seed is available.
DEPTH Seed: surface. Roots: 4"–5".

GERMINATING

TIME 18 months–3 years.
REQUIREMENTS Difficult. Sow seeds in a soil-based medium. *Indoors:* Secure flats in plastic bags and refrigerate for 3 months. Remove containers and leave for 3 months at 60°–70°F. Repeat this cycle once more. *Outdoors:* Sow seeds ¼" deep in flats and sink these in the ground against a north-facing wall; moisten soil periodically, if necessary. Leave outdoors through 2 winters. Bring flats indoors to 60°–70°F and surface-sow seeds individually in peat pots.

PLANTING SEEDLINGS OUTDOORS

TIME Spring or early autumn.
SPACING Small species: 5"–7". Large species: 12".
LIGHT Full to part shade.
SOIL Cool, rich, moist, well-drained, with a pH level of 5.0–6.5.

Trillium erectum

CARING FOR PLANTS

Difficult. Plants grown from seed will bloom in about 5 years. Provide a permanent mulch of leaf mold and water regularly throughout the year. Do not disturb roots.

PROPAGATING

You can carefully divide *Trilliums* in early spring in zones 4–6, or autumn in the South; generally, though, the plants prefer to be left undisturbed.

Tritoma

See *Kniphofia*

Tritonia

(some species may be listed as *Acidanthera, Crocosmia,* or *Ixia*)

Blazing star, Montbretia

TYPE **HBb or HHBb often grown as A**
ZONE A: 3–6; P: 7–10
FLOWERING SEASON **Midsummer**

Genus of South African bulbs with flat, swordlike leaves and arching stems of 6" or 24" bearing spikes of funnel-shaped flowers of red, orange, yellow, pink, or white. Grow in the border.

SOWING

INDOORS 6–8 weeks before planting out.
OUTDOORS Seed: In zones 9–10, sow seeds as soon as ripe in autumn; early spring is preferable in zones 7–8. Corm: autumn in zones 9–10; spring in zones 3–8.
DEPTH Seed: just cover. Corm: 3"–4".

GERMINATING

TIME 30–90 days
REQUIREMENTS Easy. 55°–60°F.

PLANTING SEEDLINGS OUTDOORS

TIME Zones 3–8: after last frost. Zones 9–10: spring or autumn.
SPACING 4"–8".
LIGHT Sun.

SOIL Rich, sandy, well-drained, amended with well-rotted cow manure.

CARING FOR PLANTS

Plants grown from seed take 3 years to flower. During the growing season, feed once and water frequently, tapering off after flowering. Provide a good winter mulch. North of zone 7, lift bulbs in autumn and store in a cool, frost-free place, replanting in spring.

PROPAGATING

Plant offsets at recommended planting time.

A-Annual P-Perennial B-Biennial HHA-Half-hardy annual HA-Hardy annual HB-Hardy biennial HHP-Half-hardy perennial HP-Hardy perennial HHBb-Half-hardy bulb HBb-Hardy bulb

Trollius

Globe flower

TYPE HP
ZONE 3–7: *T. chinensis,*
T. x cultorum, T. ledebourii;
3–8: *T. europaeus;* 5–7:
T. pumilus, T. yunnanensis
FLOWERING SEASON Early spring
to late summer, depending on
species

Perennial plants native to North America. Many-petalled orange and yellow flowers held singly high above the foliage resemble large, elegant buttercups, to which they are closely related; handsome leaves are lobed and deeply cut. Plants grow from 6" to 36". Excellent plants for the rock garden, border, or woodland's edge.

SOWING

INDOORS Start seed outdoors only.
OUTDOORS Late summer, as soon as fresh seed is available, in peat pots.
DEPTH Surface.

GERMINATING

TIME 30–365 days.
REQUIREMENTS Difficult. Due to a very poor germination rate and wide availability of rootstock, *Trollius* is seldom grown from seed. For the determined: Sow seeds in peat pots; stand these in a pan and water from below. Transplant to the garden in autumn.

PLANTING SEEDLING OUTDOORS

SPACING 12"–18".
LIGHT Part to full shade is necessary in hot climates. Where plants are grown in full sun, keep the soil very moist.
SOIL Humus-rich, moist or even boggy, with a pH level of 5.0–7.0.

CARING FOR PLANTS

Easy to grow if correctly situated. Keep plants well watered, deadhead regularly, and do not disturb once they are established. Divide with care no more than once every 4 years.

Trollius europaeus

PROPAGATING

Divide in spring, or early autumn in zones 7–8.

Tropaeolum (Annual)

(includes *T. majus, T. peregrinum*)

Canary-bird flower, Canary creeper, Indian cress, Nasturtium, Scottish flame flower

TYPE HA
ZONE 1–10. Most successful where summers are mild and dry and nighttime temperatures remain below 65°F.
FLOWERING SEASON Summer to autumn

Genus of annuals, some of which are climbers. Leaves are rounded; unusual flowers are trumpet-shaped with long spurs, colored yellow, orange, or deep red. Native to Central and South America. Informal plants for containers, edging, or trellises; often seen sprawling casually across a garden path.

Tropaeolum majus

SOWING

INDOORS Seeds may be started in peat pots 2–4 weeks before last frost, but sowing *in situ* is usually more successful.
OUTDOORS 1 week after last frost.
DEPTH ¼".

GERMINATING

TIME 7–12 days.
REQUIREMENTS Darkness and 65°F.

PLANTING SEEDLINGS OUTDOORS

TIME After last frost.
SPACING Small species: 8"–12". Medium species: 12"–20". Large species: 24"–36".
LIGHT Full sun, with afternoon shade where summers are hot.
SOIL Poor to average, moist, well-drained, slightly acid.

CARING FOR PLANTS

Easy. Water during dry spells and do not fertilize as this will stimulate lush foliar growth but few flowers. Inspect plants regularly for aphids and treat immediately with insecticidal soap. Provide a trellis or other support for climbing species.

PROPAGATING

Take cuttings.

A-Annual P-Perennial B-Biennial HHA-Half-hardy annual HA-Hardy annual HB-Hardy biennial HHP-Half-hardy perennial HP-Hardy perennial HHBb-Half-hardy bulb HBb-Hardy bulb

Tropaeolum (Perennial)

(includes *T. polyphyllum*, *T. speciosum*, *T. tricolorum*, *T. tuberosum*)

Climbing nasturtium, Flame flower, Nasturtium

TYPE HP or HHP
ZONE 7–9. Prefers cool temperatures.
FLOWERING SEASON Summer

Genus of perennials, most of which are climbers. Leaves are midgreen or grey-green, often 5- or 6-lobed. Flowers are red, yellow or orange, unique in appearance, but generally trumpet-shaped with long spurs. Climbers reach 3'–10'; non-climbers are just 3"–4" tall. Use in informal settings.

SOWING
INDOORS 2–3 weeks before last frost.
OUTDOORS 2 weeks before last frost.
DEPTH Just cover.

GERMINATING
TIME Up to 2 years.
REQUIREMENTS 55°–65°F.

PLANTING SEEDLINGS OUTDOORS
TIME 1–2 weeks after last frost.
SPACING 6"–12".
LIGHT Full sun with shaded roots. Roots may be shaded with a rock or flagstone slab.
SOIL Prefers moist, acid.

CARING FOR PLANTS
Difficult. Roots prefer to be shaded and should be lavishly mulched in spring. Keep well watered and do not move established plants.

PROPAGATING
Take cuttings, or divide in spring.

Tulipa

Tulip

TYPE HBb
ZONE 3–8
FLOWERING SEASON Spring

Wildly popular but never tiresome bulbs grown for their lovely, upward-facing, bell- or saucer-shaped flowers held proudly on rigid stems of 4"–24"; blooms come in every imaginable color. There is no place where tulips do not look splendid: massed formally, scattered casually, in containers, rock gardens, and borders.

SOWING
INDOORS See "Germinating, Requirements."
OUTDOORS Seed: see "Germinating, Requirements." Bulb: autumn.
DEPTH Seed: ⅛". Bulb: To prolong the life of bulbs in hot climates, plant 6"–7" deep; elsewhere plant 3"–5".

Tulipa x 'Darwin'

GERMINATING
TIME 60–90 days.
REQUIREMENTS As plants grown from seed won't flower for 4–6 years, this method of propagation is seldom used. *Autumn sowing:* Sow seeds in flats, sink in the ground against a north-facing wall, and cover with glass. Moisten soil periodically, if necessary. Bring indoors in spring to 50°F. *Spring sowing:* Place seeds in a plastic bag together with moist growing medium and refrigerate for 2–3 weeks. Sow seeds in flats, sink in the ground outdoors in a shady location, and cover with glass. Transplant seedlings as they appear.

PLANTING SEEDLINGS OUTDOORS
TIME Autumn.
SPACING Dwarf species: 4". Large species: 6"–10".
LIGHT Full sun to light shade.
SOIL Ordinary, very well-drained, with a pH level of 6.0–7.0. The perfect planting hole consists of a layer of very well-rotted manure topped with ½" soil; place the bulb on top of this and back-fill with soil mixed with 1 teaspoon bonemeal. However, few of us are that virtuous and for us, loosening soil at the bottom of the hole and mixing in bonemeal will suffice.

CARING FOR PLANTS
Store bulbs at no more than 70°F before planting. Water newly planted bulbs immediately, then only during dry spells. Feed lightly in spring. After flowering, do not remove leaves until they are about half dead. Where summers are very hot (zones 8–10), bulbs can be lifted and stored in a cool place (40°–45°F), to be replanted in November or December, or start with new bulbs every year.

PROPAGATING
The only really successful way to increase your stock of tulips is to buy new bulbs; off-sets seldom produce robust or attractive flowers.

Tunica

(synonymous with *Petrorhagia*)

Coat flower, Saxifrage pink, Tunic flower

TYPE HP
ZONE 5–7
FLOWERING SEASON Summer

Spreading, low-growing, 4" plants for the rock garden or border's edge, with very fine, feathery leaves and a profusion of small, flat, pink or purple flowers. Native to the Mediterranean region.

SOWING

INDOORS See "Germinating, Requirements."
OUTDOORS See "Germinating, Requirements."
DEPTH Just cover.

GERMINATING

TIME 14–60 days.
REQUIREMENTS Easy. *Autumn sowing:* Sow seeds in flats, sink in the ground against a north-facing wall, and cover with glass. Moisten soil occasionally, if necessary. Bring flats indoors in spring to 50°F. *Spring sowing:* Sow seeds in flats, place in a plastic bag, and refrigerate for 2–3 weeks. Sink flats in the ground in a shady location, covering with glass. Transplant seedlings as they appear.

PLANTING SEEDLINGS OUTDOORS

TIME Spring or autumn.
SPACING 4"–6".
LIGHT Sun.
SOIL Well-drained, limy.

CARING FOR PLANTS

Easy. No special care is required.

PROPAGATING

Divide in spring, or allow to self-seed.

Tweedia

See *Oxypetalum*

Ursinia

Orange African daisy

TYPE HHA
ZONE 3–9. Perform most successfully where there is a long, cool summer.
FLOWERING SEASON Midsummer to late summer

Annuals from South Africa with narrow, often strongly scented leaves and solitary orange or yellow, daisylike flowers; 1'–2' tall. A cheerful addition to the border.

SOWING

INDOORS 6–8 weeks before planting out.
OUTDOORS After last frost.
DEPTH Just cover.

GERMINATING

TIME 14–30 days.
REQUIREMENTS 55°–60°F.

PLANTING SEEDLINGS OUTDOORS

TIME In spring, when the temperature remain above 40°F.
SPACING 8"–10".
LIGHT Full sun.
SOIL Average or poor, well-drained; *Ursinia* is quite drought tolerant.

CARING FOR PLANTS

Plants may require staking, especially when grown in rich soil. Excessive summer heat may kill plants. *Ursinia* is attractive to aphids.

PROPAGATING

Seed only.

A-Annual P-Perennial B-Biennial HHA-Half-hardy annual HA-Hardy annual HB-Hardy biennial HHP-Half-hardy perennial HP-Hardy perennial HHBb-Half-hardy bulb HBb-Hardy bulb

278

Uvularia

Bellwort, Cowbells, Merry-bells, Wood daffodil

> Type **HP**
> Zone **3–9**
> Flowering Season **Spring**

Genus of perennials native to North America grown for their pretty, yellow, nodding, bell-shaped flowers. Invariably described as elegant, but drooping leaves and flowers give these plants a depressed look that makes one consider the psychological state of the man who named them "Merry-bells." 12"–18" tall. Grown in borders and wildflower gardens.

Sowing

Indoors It is best to start seeds outdoors.
Outdoors As soon as seed is ripe, usually late summer.
Depth Just cover.

Germinating

Time 30–180 days.
Requirements Sow seeds in flats, plunge in the ground against a north-facing wall, and cover with glass. Moisten soil occasionally, if necessary. Remove glass when seedlings appear. Transplant to the garden in summer.

Planting Seedlings Outdoors

Time Summer.
Spacing Small species: 6"–8". Large species: 12".
Light Part to full shade.
Soil Rich, moist, slightly acid, woodland soil with a pH level of 5.0–6.0.

Caring for Plants

Easy. Keep soil cool and moist with a permanent mulch of leaf mold. Water regularly during dry spells. Do not disturb roots.

Propagating

Divide in early spring north of zone 7, or in autumn in the South.

Uvularia sessilifolia

Valeriana

Garden heliotrope, Valerian

> Type **HP**
> Zone **4–9. Not tolerant of high heat and humidity.**
> Flowering Season **Summer**

Genus of perennials native to North America, most of which are grown for their heads of tiny white or pink flowers borne on stiff, branched stems of 6"–36". Use in borders, wildflower, or rock gardens.

Sowing

Indoors 10–12 weeks before planting out.
Outdoors Early spring.
Depth Just cover.

Germinating

Time 21–25 days.
Requirements 70°F.

Planting Seedlings Outdoors

Time After last frost.
Spacing Small species: 6"–12". Tall species: 18"–24".
Light Full sun to part shade.
Soil Prefers rich, moist soil with a pH level of 5.5–7.0, but will grow in almost any.

Caring for Plants

Easy. Plants may require staking. Remove faded blooms to prevent seed formation, and cut back flowering stems altogether in autumn. Divide every 3–4 years when plants begin to die out.

Propagating

Divide in spring (zones 4–6), or autumn (zones 7–9).

Valeriana officinalis

A-Annual P-Perennial B-Biennial HHA-Half-hardy annual HA-Hardy annual HB-Hardy biennial HHP-Half-hardy perennial HP-Hardy perennial HHBb-Half-hardy bulb HBb-Hardy bulb

279

Veltheimia

TYPE HHBb
ZONE 8–10. Can be grown as an annual north of zone 8.
FLOWERING SEASON Early spring

Strange but appealing South African bulbs bearing dense clusters of long, drooping, red or yellow, tubular flowers atop thick, erect stems; leaves are lance-shaped, often with wavy edges; 12"–18" tall. Guaranteed to enliven a dull border.

SOWING

INDOORS 8–10 weeks before planting out.
OUTDOORS Seed: autumn. Bulb: autumn.
DEPTH Seed: just cover. Bulb: Plant with top third of bulb above ground.

Veltheimia viridifolia

GERMINATING

TIME 30–90 days.
REQUIREMENTS 55°–65°F.

PLANTING SEEDLINGS OUTDOORS

TIME When spring temperatures remain above 50°F.
SPACING 12".
LIGHT Will grow in light shade, but flowers develop best colors and maintain a neat habit only in full sun.
SOIL Acid, well-drained.

CARING FOR PLANTS

Easy. Plants grown from seed will bloom in 3 years. Feed with a liquid fertilizer as soon as new growth shows in spring, and again every 2 weeks throughout the growth period. Reduce watering and stop feeding in summer. North of zone 8, lift and pot up bulbs in early autumn. Water very lightly initially, increasing when leaves appear in late winter. Plant out in spring.

PROPAGATING

Plant offsets in spring, or insert leaves in sandy soil in spring or summer.

Venidium

Cape daisy, Monarch of the veldt, Namaqualand daisy

TYPE HHA
ZONE 6–10. Not tolerant of high heat and humidity.
FLOWERING SEASON Summer

Genus of South African annuals with sunflowerlike blooms on restrained, 18"–24" stems, some of which are surprisingly genteel. Flowers are orange or yellow with large black centers; leaves are deeply lobed and silvery in color. Border or cottage garden plants.

SOWING

INDOORS 8–10 weeks before last frost.
OUTDOORS Start seeds outdoors in zones 9–10 only, from midsummer to late winter.
DEPTH ⅛".

GERMINATING

TIME 6–14 days.
REQUIREMENTS 60°–65°F.

PLANTING SEEDLINGS OUTDOORS

TIME After last frost.
SPACING 12".
LIGHT Full sun.
SOIL Prefers light, dry soil.

CARING FOR PLANTS

Fertilize sparingly and keep soil on the dry side. Plants may require staking. *Venidium* is prone to stem rot in the East and performs most satisfactorily in California.

PROPAGATING

Seed only.

A-Annual P-Perennial B-Biennial HHA-Half-hardy annual HA-Hardy annual HB-Hardy biennial HHP-Half-hardy perennial HP-Hardy perennial HHBb-Half-hardy bulb HBb-Hardy bulb

280

Veratrum

False hellebore, Indian poke, White hellebore

> TYPE HP
> ZONE 3–8. Will not perform well where summers are hot and humid.
> FLOWERING SEASON Summer

Genus of North America perennials with very large leaves and stiff, dense spikes of greenish white or brownish purple flowers. At 3'–9', these plants make an extraordinary spectacle in full bloom in a spacious border or near water.

SOWING

INDOORS See "Germinating, Requirements."
OUTDOORS See "Germinating, Requirements."
DEPTH ¼".

GERMINATING

TIME 90–365 days.
REQUIREMENTS Difficult. *Autumn sowing:* Sow seeds in flats, sink these in the ground against a north-facing wall, and cover with glass. Moisten soil from time to time, if necessary. Bring indoors in spring to 55°–60°F. *Spring sowing:* Sow seeds in containers with moistened medium, place in a plastic bag, and refrigerate. After 2–3 weeks, sink containers in the ground in a shady location, covering with glass. Transplant seedlings as they emerge.

PLANTING SEEDLINGS OUTDOORS

TIME After last frost.
SPACING 24".
LIGHT Part to full shade.
SOIL Light, moist or even wet.

CARING FOR PLANTS

Easy. Mulch heavily in spring to keep soil cool and moist. It may be useful to mark the location of plants before they die back to the ground in summer to avoid inadvertent disturbance. Slugs can do considerable damage to leaves. Division is rarely required.

PROPAGATING

Divide in early spring (early autumn in zones 7–8).

Verbascum

Mullein

> TYPE HP, HHP, or HB
> ZONE 5–9: V. chaixii,
>   V. densiflorum, V. nigrum,
>   V. spinosum; 6–9: V. blattaria,
>   V. bombyciferum, V. x hybridum,
>   V. olympicum, V. phoeniceum;
>   8–9: V. dumulosum
> FLOWERING SEASON Summer

Large genus of rather coarse, erect plants, 1'–5' tall, with rosettes of silvery green, downy leaves and usually yellow flowers borne along tall spikes. For borders and cottage gardens.

SOWING

INDOORS 6–8 weeks before planting out.
OUTDOORS Early spring, when soil is cool and a light frost is still possible, or late summer.
DEPTH Just cover.

GERMINATING

TIME 14–30 days.
REQUIREMENTS 55°–60°F.

PLANTING SEEDLINGS OUTDOORS

TIME After last frost or late summer.
SPACING Small species: 12"–18". Large species: 24"–36" or singly.
LIGHT *V. x hybridum* and *V. phoeniceum* will grow in part shade; plant all other species in full sun.
SOIL Ordinary, warm, slightly alkaline; tolerant of dry soil.

CARING FOR PLANTS

Easy. Cut back flower stalks after blooming and provide a good winter mulch. Take care not to damage the taproot when transplanting. Plants are short-lived.

PROPAGATING

Take root cuttings in early spring, or allow to self-seed.

CHARLES JOSLIN

Verbascum thapsus

A-Annual P-Perennial B-Biennial HHA-Half-hardy annual HA-Hardy annual HB-Hardy biennial HHP-Half-hardy perennial HP-Hardy perennial HHBb-Half-hardy bulb HBb-Hardy bulb

Verbena

Vervain

TYPE HP, HHP, or HHA
ZONE A: 1–10; P: 3–10: *V. hastata*; 6–10: *V. canadensis*; 7–10: *V. bonariensis*; 8–10: *V. rigida, V. tenuisecta*. Prefers warm, dry climates.
FLOWERING SEASON Summer to frost

Large genus of rugged plants native to North America, most with stiff stems and clusters of small, flat, brightly colored flowers that bloom over a long period. Foliage is usually dark green, toothed or cut. Plants generally grow from 4"–24", although one species is a towering 5'. Use in containers, borders, rock gardens, or as edging.

SOWING

INDOORS 8–10 weeks before planting out.
OUTDOORS After last frost.
DEPTH Just cover.

GERMINATING

TIME 14–90 days.
REQUIREMENTS Darkness and 65°–75°F. *V. bonariensis* and *V. rigida:* Place seeds in a plastic bag together with moist growing medium, and refrigerate for 2 weeks, then sow.

Verbena canadensis

PLANTING SEEDLINGS OUTDOORS

TIME After last frost, when nighttime temperatures remain above 50°F.
SPACING Small species: 8"–10". Medium species: 12"–18". Large species: 24"–36".
LIGHT Full sun, or light shade where summers are very hot.
SOIL Prefers a well-drained, fertile soil with a pH level of 6.0–7.0; will tolerate dry.

CARING FOR PLANTS

Easy. Feed once or twice in spring. *Verbenas* can withstand drought but will reward you for regular watering. Pinch out tips of young plants and deadhead frequently to ensure maximum blooming. *V. rigida* and *V. tenuisecta* can be lifted in autumn and stored over winter in a frost-free location; replant in the spring.

PROPAGATING

Take cuttings in spring or early autumn.

Veronica

Blackroot, Culver's root, Speedwell

TYPE HP
ZONE 3–10: *V. incana, V. virginica*; 4–7: *V. prostrata*; 4–8: *V. alpina, V. spicata*; 4–9: *V. gentianoides*; 4–10: *V. longifolia, V. grandis, V. teucrium*
FLOWERING SEASON Summer to early autumn

Large genus of mainly upright plants of 4"–48" with lavish spikes of small, intensely blue, purple, or white flowers. Lovely plants for the border, container, or rock garden.

SOWING

INDOORS 8–10 weeks before planting out.
OUTDOORS Early spring or early autumn.
DEPTH Surface.

GERMINATING

TIME 15–90 days.
REQUIREMENTS Light and 60°–70°F.

PLANTING SEEDLINGS OUTDOORS

TIME Early spring, when soil is cool and a light frost is still possible, or late autumn.
SPACING Small species: 6"–12". Spreading species: 12"–18".
LIGHT Full sun, except *V. prostrata*, which will take sun or part shade.
SOIL Well-drained, average, with a pH level of 5.5–7.0. Soil that is too rich produces weak plants.

CARING FOR PLANTS

Easy. Water and deadhead regularly but feed only occasionally. Tall species may need some support. Flowering will be reduced in extreme heat. Cut back to ground level in late autumn.

PROPAGATING

Divide after flowering, or take cuttings in summer.

Veronica longifolia

A-Annual P-Perennial B-Biennial HHA-Half-hardy annual HA-Hardy annual HB-Hardy biennial HHP-Half-hardy perennial HP-Hardy perennial HHBb-Half-hardy bulb HBb-Hardy bulb

282

Vigna

See *Phaseolus*

Viola

(see next entries for *Viola odorata* and *Viola tricolor*)

Horned violet, Pansy, Tufted pansy, Tufted violet

TYPE HP or HHP
ZONE 2–5: *V. labradorica*;
3–8: *V. canadensis, V. pedata, V. pensylvanica*; 3–9: *V. blanda, V. conspersa, V. nuttallii, V. primulifolia*; 4–8: *V. cucullata, V. striata*; 6–9: *V. cornuta, V. nigra*; 7–9: *V. douglasii*; 8–10: *V. hallii*
FLOWERING SEASON May bloom at any time of year, depending on the species and the climate

Very large genus of perennials instantly recognizable by their colored markings, or "faces," that give the flowers a strong personality. Solid or multicolored flowers are every shade of red, purple, yellow, orange, blue, pink, black, and white. 2"–12" tall. Always successful in containers, borders, rock gardens, and edging.

SOWING
INDOORS Pre-chilled seeds 8–10 weeks before planting out.
OUTDOORS Early spring or early autumn.
DEPTH Just cover.

GERMINATING
TIME 10–21 days.
REQUIREMENTS Place seeds in a plastic bag together with moist growing medium and refrigerate for 2 weeks. Then sow and place in a dark location at 65°–75°F.

Viola cornuta

PLANTING SEEDLINGS OUTDOORS
TIME Early spring, when soil is cool and a light frost is still possible, or late autumn.
SPACING 8"–12".
LIGHT Part shade; site violets in full sun only in cool climates.
SOIL Rich, moist, well-drained, with a pH level of 5.5–7.0.

CARING FOR PLANTS
Easy. Mulch to keep soil cool and moist. Feed with liquid seaweed during the early growth stage. Deadhead often to prolong flowering, and cut back drastically after the first heavy bloom to encourage further bud formation.

PROPAGATING
Divide in spring.

Viola odorata

Sweet violet

TYPE HP
ZONE 6–9. Will not perform well where summers are very hot.
FLOWERING SEASON Winter through spring in warm climates, spring to early summer elsewhere.

Dainty perennials with heart-shaped leaves and modest but pretty, scented, purple or white flowers held on slim stems of 4"–8". Plant near a walk or woodland path where their charm will not be lost.

SOWING
INDOORS Sow seeds outdoors only.
OUTDOORS Autumn.
DEPTH Just cover.

GERMINATING
TIME 50 days.
REQUIREMENTS Sow seeds in flats, sink in the ground against a north-facing wall, and cover with glass. Moisten soil occasionally, if necessary. Remove glass when seedlings emerge.

PLANTING SEEDLINGS OUTDOORS
TIME Set out purchased plants after last frost, or autumn where winters are mild.
SPACING 6"–8".

LIGHT Part shade, or full sun where summers are cool.
SOIL Deep, rich, moist, with a pH level of 5.5–7.0. Add well-rotted manure at planting time.

CARING FOR PLANTS
Easy. Mulch to keep soil cool and moist. Water frequently and apply a liquid fertilizer in early spring. Where summers are hot, cut plants back hard after flowering or discard altogether.

PROPAGATING
Divide in early spring.

A-Annual P-Perennial B-Biennial HHA-Half-hardy annual HA-Hardy annual HB-Hardy biennial HHP-Half-hardy perennial HP-Hardy perennial HHBb-Half-hardy bulb HBb-Hardy bulb

283

Viola tricolor

Heart's ease, Johnny jump up, Pansy, Wild pansy

> TYPE HB usually grown as HA
> ZONE 3–10. Will not survive where summers are very hot.
> FLOWERING SEASON Spring

Bright little plants with small purple, yellow, and white faces dancing above a 3"–8" mound of narrow, lance-shaped leaves. Use in containers, rock gardens, borders, or edging, remembering that plants are short-lived.

SOWING

INDOORS 10–12 weeks before planting out.
OUTDOORS Summer in zones 9–10, elsewhere late summer to early autumn.
DEPTH ¼".

GERMINATING

TIME 14 days.
REQUIREMENTS Difficult. Darkness and 65°–75°F.

PLANTING SEEDLINGS OUTDOORS

TIME After last frost.
SPACING 6"–9".
LIGHT Part shade, or full sun where summers are cool.
SOIL Cool, rich, moist, well-drained, with a pH level of 5.5–6.5.

CARING FOR PLANTS

Easy. Feed once or twice while plants are young. Flowering is diminished by excessive heat; mulch in spring to keep soil cool and moist. Remove plants after flowering to prevent self-seeding. These pansies will not survive hot summers and are short-lived even in mild climates. In the North, a thick mulch may bring plants through the winter.

PROPAGATING

Allow to self-seed.

Viscaria

See Lychnis

Watsonia

Bugle lily

> TYPE HBb or HHBb
> ZONE P: 8–10. Grow as an annual north of zone 8.
> FLOWERING SEASON Late summer

South African bulbs with long, sword-shaped leaves and stiff spikes of bright pink, red, or white trumpet-shaped flowers; 1'–6' tall. Grow in the border.

SOWING

INDOORS Midwinter.
OUTDOORS Seed: autumn. Corm: autumn (after last spring frost north of zone 8).
DEPTH Seed: ⅛". Corm: 4".

Watsonia beatricis

GERMINATING

TIME 30–180 days.
REQUIREMENTS 55°–65°F.

PLANTING SEEDLINGS OUTDOORS

TIME After last frost.
SPACING 12".
LIGHT Full sun.
SOIL Moist, well-drained, with manure.

CARING FOR PLANTS

Plants grown from seed will bloom in about 3 years. Feed with liquid manure when buds begin to form and water regularly throughout the blooming period. Stake when plants reach 6" and tie up new growth periodically to avoid damage to stems. North of zone 8, lift corms and store over winter in cool, dry place.

PROPAGATING

Divide cormels in late autumn.

Wisteria

Chinese kidney bean

TYPE HP
ZONE 4–9
FLOWERING SEASON Late spring to
early summer

Much-loved climbing plants with handsome compound leaves and an abundance of long, elegant racemes of purple or white pealike flowers. The perfect climber for any pergola or wall. Grows to 30'.

SOWING

INDOORS 6–8 weeks before last frost.
OUTDOORS Early spring, when soil is cool and a light frost is still possible, or late autumn.
DEPTH 1".

GERMINATING

TIME 30–35 days.
REQUIREMENTS Chip seeds or soak for 24 hours in warm water; provide 55°–65°F thereafter.

PLANTING SEEDLINGS OUTDOORS

TIME After last frost.
SPACING Singly.
LIGHT Full sun or part shade.
SOIL Prefers moist, rich, well-drained soil.

CARING FOR PLANTS

Plants grown from seed take up to 20 years to flower. Mulch in spring and water well during the growing season. Avoid high-nitrogen fertilizers. Prune after flowering and again in winter, cutting back shoots to 2 or 3 buds. Plants seldom flower their first few years after planting; if vines continue not to bloom, prune during the summer to about 6 buds. Root-pruning in autumn is a more drastic and potentially harmful measure, but often induces flowering when nothing else works. Do not move.

PROPAGATING

Take root and hardwood cuttings in spring or summer. Divide in spring.

Xanthisma

**Sleepy daisy, Star of Texas,
Texas star**

TYPE HA
ZONE Prefers cool weather.
FLOWERING SEASON Summer

A cheerful annual native to Texas grown for its wealth of large, bright yellow, daisylike flowers. Plants make a lively display in the border.

SOWING

INDOORS 6–8 weeks before last frost.
OUTDOORS After last frost.
DEPTH Just cover.

GERMINATING

TIME 25–30 days.
REQUIREMENTS 70°–75°F.

PLANTING SEEDLINGS OUTDOORS

TIME After last frost.
SPACING Small species: 6". Medium species: 12". Large species: 18"–24".
LIGHT Sun.
SOIL Light, sandy, well-drained, with a pH level of 6.5–7.0; will tolerate poor, dry soil.

CARING FOR PLANTS

Easy. Plants may require staking.

PROPAGATING

Seed only.

A-Annual P-Perennial B-Biennial HHA-Half-hardy annual HA-Hardy annual HB-Hardy biennial HHP-Half-hardy perennial HP-Hardy perennial HHBb-Half-hardy bulb HBb-Hardy bulb

285

Xeranthemum

Immortelle

TYPE HA
ZONE 2–10. Prefers cool temperatures.
FLOWERING SEASON Midsummer to late summer

Small genus of annuals native to the Mediterranean with silvery leaves and tall, wiry stems bearing solitary, everlasting, daisylike flowers of pink or purple; 24"–36" tall. Grow in the border or cutting bed.

SOWING

INDOORS 2–3 weeks before planting out, in peat pots.
OUTDOORS After last frost, but only where the growing season is long.
DEPTH Just cover.

GERMINATING

TIME 10–15 days.
REQUIREMENTS 70°F.

PLANTING SEEDLINGS OUTDOORS

TIME After last frost.
SPACING 10"–15".
LIGHT Full sun.
SOIL Average; will tolerate dry conditions.

CARING FOR PLANTS

Easy. Support with twiggy branches pushed into the ground when plants are young. To dry for floral arrangements, cut stems when flowers are fully open.

PROPAGATING

Seed.

Xeranthemum annuum

Xerophyllum

Bear grass, Mountain asphodel, Squaw grass, Turkeybeard

TYPE HP
ZONE 6–8: X. *asphodeloides*;
7–9: X. *tenax*
FLOWERING SEASON Early summer

Genus of two species of wildflowers, one native to the eastern United States, the other to the West. Foliage resembles very fine pine needles; tiny, white, star-shaped flowers are borne in terminal clusters on long, wiry stems; 2'–6' tall. Elegant plants for the wildflower or woodland garden.

SOWING

INDOORS Start seeds outdoors only.
OUTDOORS Late summer, as soon as fresh seed is available.
DEPTH ¼".

Xerophyllum asphodeloides

GERMINATING

TIME 30–60 days.
REQUIREMENTS Sow seeds in flats, sink flats in ground against a north-facing wall, and cover with glass. Moisten soil periodically, if necessary. Allow 1 full growing season before transplanting seedlings to the garden.

PLANTING SEEDLINGS OUTDOORS

TIME After last spring frost.
SPACING 12"–24".
LIGHT Sun.
SOIL Dry or wet, rich, well-drained with a pH level of 6.0–8.0.

CARING FOR PLANTS

Difficult. Water regularly and mulch in spring to keep soil cool. Do not move.

PROPAGATING

Divide in spring north of zone 7, in autumn in the South.

A-Annual P-Perennial B-Biennial HHA-Half-hardy annual HA-Hardy annual HB-Hardy biennial HHP-Half-hardy perennial HP-Hardy perennial HHBb-Half-hardy bulb HBb-Hardy bulb

Yucca

**Adam's needle, Soapweed,
Spanish bayonet, Spanish dagger**

TYPE HP or HHP
ZONE 3–10: *Y. glauca*; 4–10:
  Y. baccata, *Y. filamentosa*,
  Y. flaccida; 5–10: *Y. smalliana*,
  Y. whipplei; 7–10: *Y. gloriosa*;
  8–10: *Y. elata*
FLOWERING SEASON Midsummer
  to autumn

Overused evergreen plants with dangerous, sword-shaped leaves and tall, thick, remarkably unattractive stalks bearing small, drooping, white flowers; 1'–10' tall. Strongly architectural form is useful in the border; often grown in containers.

SOWING

INDOORS Late winter to early spring.
OUTDOORS Spring.
DEPTH Just cover.

GERMINATING

TIME 30–365 days.
REQUIREMENTS 65°–75°F. Indoors, grow seedlings for 2–3 years before planting out.

PLANTING SEEDLINGS OUTDOORS

TIME When spring temperatures will remain above 45°F.
SPACING Small species: 18"–24". Medium species: 24"–36". Large species: 48"–60" or singly.
LIGHT Full sun.
SOIL Average to poor, dry or very well-drained; prefers a pH level of 5.5–7.5.

CARING FOR PLANTS

Easy. *Yuccas* require no watering. Plants that are not groomed will gradually take on a derelict look: Remove dead leaves regularly, wearing armor-plated gloves. Plants may not bloom every year.

PROPAGATING

Take root cuttings or plant offsets.

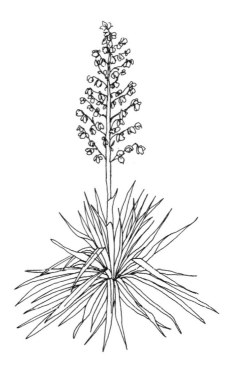

Yucca filamentosa

Zantedeschia

Arum lily, Calla lily, Lily of the Nile

TYPE HHP also grown as HHA
ZONE A: 7–8; P: 9–10
FLOWERING SEASON Early summer

Exotic plants native to South Africa with bold, arrow-shaped leaves and large, elegant, funnel-shaped spathes of white, pink, red, or yellow surrounding a white, yellow, or purple spadix; 12"–36" tall. Lovely plants for borders or containers; some are water plants.

SOWING

INDOORS Early spring.
OUTDOORS Autumn, but only where the growing season is long.
DEPTH Seed: surface. Rhizome: 2".

GERMINATING

TIME 30–90 days.
REQUIREMENTS Soak seeds in warm water for 24 hours, sow, and place in a light location at 70°–80°F.

Zantedeschia aethiopica

PLANTING SEEDLINGS OUTDOORS

TIME In spring, when temperatures remain above 50°F.
SPACING 12"–15".
LIGHT Full sun, or light shade in very hot regions.
SOIL Prefers acid, humus-rich. Add plenty of manure at planting time. Some species grow in water.

CARING FOR PLANTS

The elegance of these plants belies their easy care — plant a few and your friends will be wildly impressed. Feed regularly using a liquid fertilizer and water frequently. In zones 7–8, lift plants in autumn before the first frost and store in a frost-free place over winter.

PROPAGATING

Divide tubers in spring.

Zauschneria

California fuchsia

TYPE HHP
ZONE 8–10. Does not like wet winters and so is seldom successful in Eastern states.
FLOWERING SEASON Summer to early autumn

Genus of 1'–2' perennials, some of which are woody, bearing small, greyish green, lance-shaped leaves and a tangle of bright red, tubular flowers. Grow in the border or rock garden.

SOWING

INDOORS Start seeds outdoors only.
OUTDOORS Spring.
DEPTH Surface.

Zauschneria californica

GERMINATING

TIME 30–60 days.
REQUIREMENTS Light and 60°–65°F.

PLANTING SEEDLINGS OUTDOORS

TIME Set out purchased plants after last frost.
SPACING 14"–18".
LIGHT Sun or part shade.
SOIL Any very well-drained soil with a pH level between 7.0 and 8.0; drought tolerant.

CARING FOR PLANTS

Pinch back tips of young plants to encourage bushy growth and deadhead frequently to make plants look more attractive. Protect from overhead water. May become invasive.

PROPAGATING

Take stem cuttings in autumn, or divide in spring.

Zephyranthes

Atamasco lily, Flowers of the Western wind, Rain lily, Zephyr lily

TYPE HBb or HHBb
ZONE A: 3–8; P: 7–10:
Z. *Atamasco*; 9–10: *Z. candida*,
Z. citrina, *Z. grandiflora*;
10: *Z. rosea*
FLOWERING SEASON Spring, summer, or autumn, depending on species

Genus of small bulbs with grassy leaves and delicate, funnel-shaped flowers of pink, red, yellow, or white held singly on erect stems of 2"–12". Suitable for rock gardens or massed under shrubs.

SOWING

INDOORS Late winter.
OUTDOORS Seed: autumn or spring. Bulb: October to early November in zones 9–10, after last spring frost elsewhere.
DEPTH Seed: just cover. Bulb: 3".

GERMINATING

TIME 4 months.
REQUIREMENTS 60°–75°F.

PLANTING SEEDLINGS OUTDOORS

TIME Autumn in zones 9–10; after last spring frost north of zone 9.
SPACING 3"–6".
LIGHT Sun or part shade.
SOIL Light, rich, moist, well-drained, with a pH level of 6.0–7.0.

CARING FOR PLANTS

Easy. Plants grown from seed will take 3 years to flower. Apply a complete fertilizer in spring and water during dry weather. In colder regions, plant bulbs against a south-facing wall and mulch well in autumn. Where bulbs are grown as annuals, lift in autumn, and store in moist sand over winter.

PROPAGATING

Plant offsets.

A-Annual P-Perennial B-Biennial HHA-Half-hardy annual HA-Hardy annual HB-Hardy biennial HHP-Half-hardy perennial HP-Hardy perennial HHBb-Half-hardy bulb HBb-Hardy bulb

Zinnia

Youth-and-old-age

Type HHA
Zone 2–10. Prefers warm temperatures.
Flowering Season Summer to frost

Genus of plants grown for their intensely colored, extravagantly double blooms held singly on tall stems of 8"–36". Colors range from light pinks and whites to deep reds and oranges. Plants can be used successfully in carefree summer plantings, formal beds, or containers.

Sowing

Indoors 6–8 weeks before planting out; most successful when started *in situ*.
Outdoors After last frost, but only where summers are long.
Depth Just cover.

Germinating

Time 5–24 days.
Requirements 70°–80°F.

Planting Seedlings Outdoors

Time After last frost.
Spacing Dwarf species: 6"–9". Medium species: 10"–12". Large species: 15"–18".
Light Full sun, with some afternoon shade in very hot climates.
Soil Ordinary, well-drained, enriched with manure; prefers a pH level of 6.0–7.0.

Caring for Plants

Easy. When plants are young, pinch tips to stimulate bushy growth. Feed soon after planting out and again when blooming begins. Water regularly, keeping leaves dry, and deadhead frequently to keep plants looking neat. Avoid transplanting.

Propagating

Seed.

A-Annual P-Perennial B-Biennial HHA-Half-hardy annual HA-Hardy annual HB-Hardy biennial HHP-Half-hardy perennial HP-Hardy perennial HHBb-Half-hardy bulb HBb-Hardy bulb

289

USDA Hardiness Zone Map

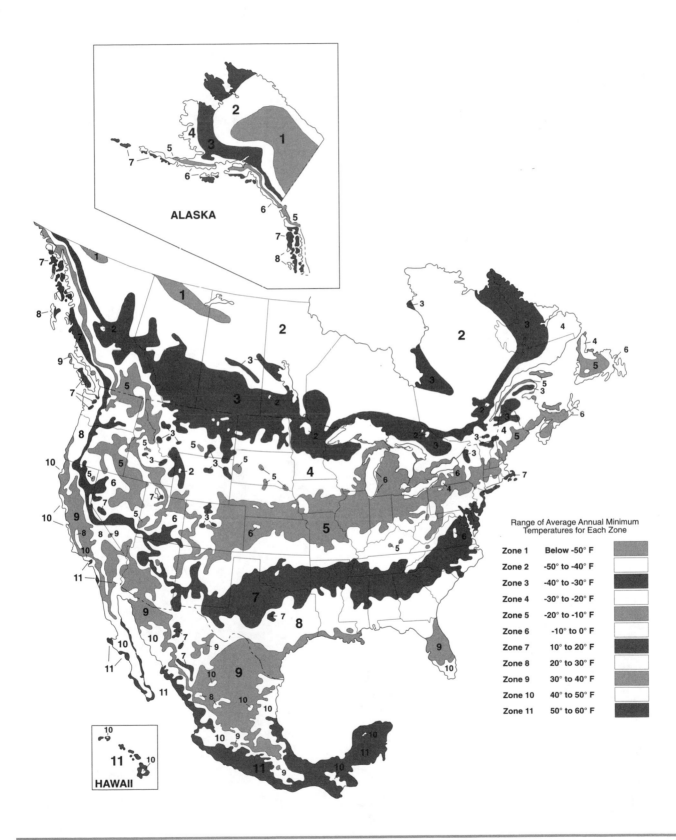

ALASKA

HAWAII

Range of Average Annual Minimum Temperatures for Each Zone		
Zone 1	Below -50° F	
Zone 2	-50° to -40° F	
Zone 3	-40° to -30° F	
Zone 4	-30° to -20° F	
Zone 5	-20° to -10° F	
Zone 6	-10° to 0° F	
Zone 7	10° to 20° F	
Zone 8	20° to 30° F	
Zone 9	30° to 40° F	
Zone 10	40° to 50° F	
Zone 11	50° to 60° F	

Probable First Frost Dates

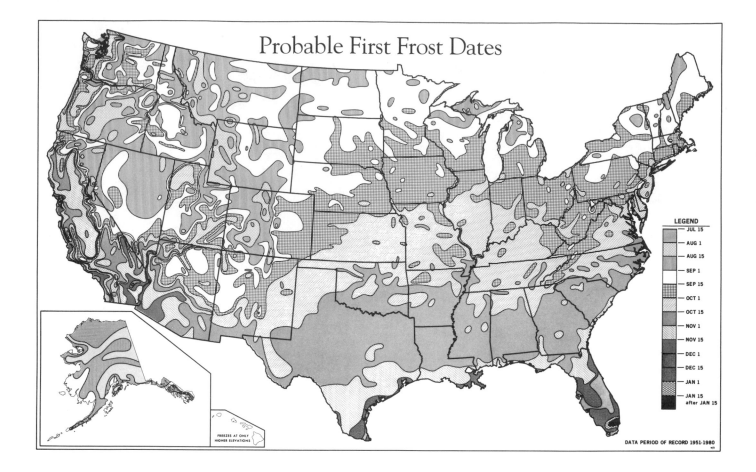

LEGEND

JUL 15
AUG 1
AUG 15
SEP 1
SEP 15
OCT 1
OCT 15
NOV 1
NOV 15
DEC 1
DEC 15
JAN 1
JAN 15
after JAN 15

FREEZES AT ONLY HIGHER ELEVATIONS

DATA PERIOD OF RECORD 1951-1980

Probable Last Frost Dates

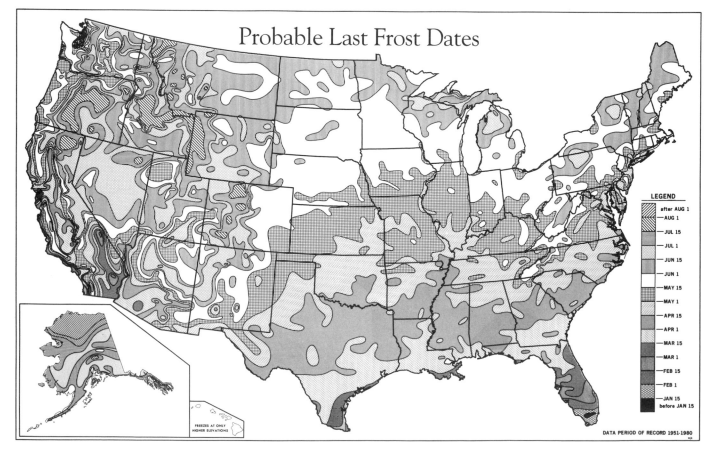

LEGEND

after AUG 1
AUG 1
JUL 15
JUL 1
JUN 15
JUN 1
MAY 15
MAY 1
APR 15
APR 1
MAR 15
MAR 1
FEB 15
FEB 1
JAN 15
before JAN 15

FREEZES AT ONLY HIGHER ELEVATIONS

DATA PERIOD OF RECORD 1951-1980

DIRECTORY OF SEED COMPANIES

WHEN PURCHASING PLANTS by mail it is a good idea to buy from nurseries in your geographic region whenever possible. Their stock will be best suited to your climate and soil type, and consequently more likely to thrive in your own garden.

Restrictions on the import of plant materials from foreign countries may make it necessary to obtain a permit before ordering plants from foreign nurseries; there are seldom restrictions on the import of seeds. To obtain further information on restrictions and permits, Canadian gardeners should contact the Plant Protection Division, Agriculture Canada, Ottawa, ON K1A OC7 Canada before ordering plants from the United States. Americans ordering plants from Canadian or other foreign nurseries should contact the USDA Plant Health Inspection Service, Plant Protection Quarantine, Federal Building Room 632, Hyattsville, MD 20782 (301-436-8645).

Before purchasing live wildflower plants it is recommended that you contact the New England Wild Flower Society, Inc., Garden in the Woods, Hemenway Road, Framingham, MA 01701, whose publication *Nursery Sources: Native Plants and Wildflowers* lists those nurseries that sell only propagated (not wild-collected) plants. Please include a self-addressed stamped envelope (SASE).

S = Seeds   P = Live Plants   B = Bulbs   W = Wildflower seeds and/or plants   H = Herb seeds and/or plants

Abundant Life Seed Foundation
P.O. Box 772
Port Townsend, WA 98368
206-385-5660
S

Aimers Seeds & Bulbs
81 Temperance Street
Aurora, ON L4G 2R1
Canada
905-841-6226
P, S

Alberta Nurseries & Seeds, Ltd.
P.O. Box 20
Bowden, AB TOM OKO
Canada
403-224-3544
(Catalog: $4)
P, S

Alpenglow Gardens
13328 King George Highway
Surrey, BC B3T 2T6
Canada
P

Appalachian Wildflower Nursery
Rt. 1, Box 275A
Reedsville, PA 17084
(Catalog: $2)
P, W

Applewood Seed Company
5380 Vivian Street
Arvada, CO 80002
303-431-6283
S, W

B & D Lilies
330 P Street
Port Townsend, WA 98368
206-385-1738
(Catalog: $3)
B

Bayport Plant Farm
R.R. 1
Rose Bay, NS BOJ 2XO
Canada
902-766-4319
(No shipping to United States)
P

Bay View Gardens
1201 Bay Street
Santa Cruz, CA 95060
408-423-3656
Iris

Bernardo Beach Native Plant Farm
1 Sanchez Road
Veguita, NM 87062
505-345-6248
P, W native to the Southwest

Kurt Bluemel, Inc.
2740 Greene Lane
Baldwin, MD 21013
410-557-7229
(Catalog: $3)
Ornamental grasses, P

Bluestone Perennials, Inc.
7211 Middle Ridge Road
Madison, OH 44057
800-852-5243/216-428-7535
P

Borbeleta Gardens, Inc.
15980 Canby Avenue
Faribault, MN 55021
507-334-2807
(Catalog: $3)
Daylilies, Iris, Lilies

Boughen Nurseries Valley River Ltd.
Box 12
Valley River, MB ROL 2BO
Canada
204-638-7618
P

Breck's
6523 N. Galena Road
Peoria, IL 61656
800-722-9069
B

Burgess Seed and Plant Company
905 Four Seasons Road
Bloomington, IL 61701
309-663-9551
P, S

W. Atlee Burpee Seed Company
Warminster, PA 18974
215-674-9633
B, P, S

D.V. Burrell Seed Growers Company
P.O. Box 150
Rocky Ford, CO 81067
719-254-3318
S

Busse Gardens
5873 Oliver Avenue S.W.
Cokato, MN 55321
612-286-2654
(Catalog: $2)
P, W

California Flora Nursery
P.O. Box 3
Fulton, CA 95439
707-528-8813
P

Canyon Creek Nursery
3527 Dry Creek Road
Oroville, CA 95965
916-533-2166
Unusual California natives, Mediterranean plants

Caprice Farm Nursery
15425 S.W. Pleasant Hill Road
Sherwood, OR 97140
503-625-7241
P

Caprilands Herb Farm
534 Silver Street
Coventry, CT 06238
203-742-7244
H, P, S

Carroll Gardens
P.O. Box 310
444 East Main Street
Westminster, MD 21158
410-848-5422
(Catalog: $3)
H, P

S = Seeds   P = Live Plants   B = Bulbs   W = Wildflower seeds and/or plants   H = Herb seeds and/or plants

Catnip Acres Herb Farm
67 Christian Street
Oxford, CT 06478
203-888-5649
H, P, S

Comstock, Ferre, and Company
263 Main Street
Wethersfield, CT 06109
203-571-6590
(Catalog: $3)
H, S

Connell's Dahlias
10616 Waller Road East
Tacoma, WA 98446
206-531-0292
(Catalog: $2)
B

Cooley's Gardens
P.O. Box 126-GE
Silverton, OR 97381
503-873-5463
(Catalog: $4)
B (Balm-bearded Iris Rhoizomes)

Country Gardens
74 South Road
Pepperell, MA 01463
617-433-6236
P

**Country Wetlands Nursery and
Consulting**
South 75 West 20755 Field Drive
P.O. Box 337
Muskego, WI 53150
414-679-1268
(Catalog: $3)
P, W

The Crownsville Nursery
P.O. Box 797
Crownsville, MD 21032
410-849-3143
(Catalog: $2)
P

Cruickshank's Ltd.
1015 Mount Pleasant Road
Toronto, ON M4P 2M1
Canada
416-488-8292
B, P

The Daffodil Mart
Rt. 3, Box 794
Gloucester, VA 23061
804-693-3966
B

William Dam Seeds
P.O. Box 8400
Dundas, ON L9H 6M1
Canada
905-628-6641
(Catalog: $2)
B, S

De Giorgi Seed Company
6011 N Street
Omaha, NE 68117-1634
402-731-3901
(Catalog: $2)
S

DeGroot, Inc.
P.O. Box 934
Coloma, MI 49038
616-468-6714
B, P

Peter de Jaeger Bulb Company
P.O. Box 2010
1888 Asbury Street
South Hamilton, MA 01982
508-468-4707
B

Dutch Gardens
P.O. Box 200
Adelphia, NJ 07710
908-780-2713
B

Englerth Gardens
Rt. 2
Hopkins, MI 49328
616-793-7196
Daylilies, Hostas

Environmental Concern, Inc.
P.O. Box P
St. Michaels, MD 21663
410-745-9620
P

Farmer Seed and Nursery Company
P.O. Box 129
Faribault, MN 55021
507-334-1623
P, S

Far North Gardens
16785 Harrison, Dept. RD
Livonia, MI 48154
313-522-9040
(Catalog: $2)
Unusual S, W

Ferncliff Gardens
8394 McTaggart Street
Mission, BC V2V 6S6
Canada
604-826-2447
B, P

Four Seasons Nursery
1706 Morrissey Drive
Bloomington, IL 61701
309-663-9551
P, S

Fox Hill Farm
444 W. Michigan Avenue
Parma, MI 49269
517-531-3179
H, P

Frosty Hollow Nursery
Box 53
Langley, WA 98260
206-579-2332
S

Garden Place
6780 Heisley Road
P.O. Box 388
Mentor, OH 44061
216-255-3705
(Catalog: $1)
P

S = Seeds   P = Live Plants   B = Bulbs   W = Wildflower seeds and/or plants   H = Herb seeds and/or plants

Gardens North
34 Helena Street
Ottawa, ON K1Y 3M8
Canada
613-489-0065
(Catalog: $3)
P, S

Gardens of the Blue Ridge
P.O. Box 10
Pineola, NC 28662
704-733-2417
(Catalog: $3)
P, W

D.S. George Nurseries
2491 Penfield Road
Fairport, NY 14450
Clematis

Goodwin Creek Gardens
P.O. Box 83
Williams, OR 97544
503-846-7357
(Catalog: $1)
H, P

Russell Graham
4030 Eagle Crest Road, N.W.
Salem, OR 97304
503-362-1135
B, P, W

Green Horizons
218 Quinlan 571
Kerrville, TX 78028
210-257-5141
S, W

Gurney Seed and Nursery Company
110 Capital
Yankton, SD 57079
605-665-1671
P, S

Harris Seeds
60 Saginaw Drive
P.O. Box 22960
Rochester, NY 14692
716-442-0410
S

H.G. Hastings Company
2350 Cheshire Bridge Road (at Lindbergh)
P.O. Box 115535
Atlanta, GA 30310-5535
404-755-6580
P, S

Hauser's Superior View Farm
Route 1, Box 199
Bayfield, WI 54814
715-779-5404
P

Hazelgrove Gardens
14219 Middle Bench Road, R.R. 1
Oyama, BC VOH 1WO
Canada
P

Herb Gathering, Inc.
5742 Kenwood Avenue
Kansas City, MO 64110
816-523-2653
H, S

High Altitude Gardens
308 South River
P.O. Box 1048
Hailey, ID 83333
208-788-4363
H, W

Hilltop Herb Farm
1 Victorian Place
Cleveland, TX 77327
713-592-5859
H, P

Holbrook Farm and Nursery
115 Lance Road
P.O. Box 368
Fletcher, NC 28732
704-891-7790
P, W

Holland Wildflower Farm
290 O'Neal Lane
Elkins, AR 72727
501-643-2622
(Catalog: $2.50)
S, W

Honeywood Lilies
Box 63
Parkside, SK SOJ 2AO
Canada
B

Hortico, Inc.
723 Robson Road
R.R. 1
Waterdown, ON LOR 2H1
Canada
905-689-6984
(Catalog: $3)
P

J.L. Hudson, Seedsman
P.O. Box 1058
Redwood City, CA 94064
P, S

Jackson & Perkins
1 Rose Lane
Medford, OR 97501-0702
800-872-7673
B, P

Jacobs Ladder Natural Gardens, Inc.
Conshohocken State Road
Box 145
Gladwyne, PA 19035
W

Johnny's Selected Seeds
299 Foss Hill Road
Albion, ME 04910
207-437-9294
S

J.W. Jung Seed Company
335 S. High Street
Randolph, WI 53957
414-326-3121
B, P, S

King's Mums
20303 East Liberty Road
P.O. Box 368
Clements, CA 95227
Chrysanthemums

S = Seeds   P = Live Plants   B = Bulbs   W = Wildflower seeds and/or plants   H = Herb seeds and/or plants

Klehm Nursery
4210 North Duncan Road
Champaign, IL 61821
800-553-3715/312-551-3715
(Catalog: $4)
B, P

Lamb Nurseries
E. 101 Sharp Avenue
Spokane, WA 99202
206-642-4856
(Catalog: $1)
Unusual P

Larner Seeds
P.O. Box 407
Bolinas, CA 94924
415-868-9407
(Catalog: $2)
W

Las Pilitas Nursery
Las Pilitas Road
Santa Margarita, CA 93453
714-951-1648
W

Orol Ledden & Sons
P.O. Box 7
Sewell, NJ 08080-0007
800-783-7333/609-468-1000
B, P, S

Liberty Seed Company
Box 806
New Philadelphia, OH 44663
216-364-1611
S

Lindel Lilies
5510 239th Street
Langley, BC V3A 7N6
Canada
604-534-4729
B

Logee's Greenhouses
141 North Street
Danielson, CT 06239
203-774-8038
(Catalog: $3)
Rare P

Earl May Seed and Nursery Company
208 N. Elm Street
Shenandoah, IA 51603
712-246-1020
B, P, S

McClure & Zimmerman
108 W. Winnebago Street
P.O. Box 368
Friesland, WI 53935
414-326-4220
B

McLaughlin's Seeds
Buttercup's Acre
Mead, WA 99021-0550
509-466-0230
W

McMillen's Iris Gardens
R.R. 1
Norwich, ON N0J 1P0
Canada
519-468-6508
(Catalog: $2)
B, *Iris, Daylilies*

Meadowbrook Herb Garden
Rt. 138
Wyoming, RI 02898
401-539-7603
S

Mellinger's Inc.
South Range Road
Dept. FSTB
North Lima, OH 44452
216-549-9861
P, S

Merry Gardens
P.O. 595
Camden, ME 04843
207-236-9064
(Catalog: $2)
P, H

Michigan Bulb Co.
1950 Waldorf, N.W.
Grand Rapids, MI 49550
616-771-9500
B, P

Milaeger's Gardens
4838 Douglas Avenue
Racine, WI 53402-2498
414-639-2371
(Catalog: $1)
P Perennials

Millar Mountain Nursery
R.R. 3, McLay Road
Duncan, BC V9L 2X1
Canada
604-748-0487
(No shipping to United States; Catalog: $2)
Beardless Irises

Missouri Wildflowers Nursery
9814 Pleasant Hill Road
Jefferson City, MO 65109
314-496-3492
(Catalog: $1)
P, S, W

Grant E. Mitsch Novelty Daffodils
P.O. Box 218
Hubbard, OR 97032
503-651-2742
B

Monashee Perennials
Site 6, Comp. 9, R.R. 7
Vernon, BC V1T 7Z3
Canada
604-542-2592
(Catalog: $2)
Daylilies, Irises, Lilies

Moon Mountain Wildflowers
P.O. Box 725
Carpinteria, CA 93014
805-684-2565
(Catalog: $5)
W

Sandy Mush Herb Nursery
316 Surrett Cove Road
Leicester, NC 28748
704-683-2014
H, P

Native Gardens
5737 Fisher Lane
Greenback, TN 37742
615-856-0220
(Catalog: $2)
P, W

Native Sons
379 West El Campo Road
Arroyo Grande, CA 93420
805-481-5996
W

The Natural Garden
38W443 Hwy. 64
St. Charles, IL 60175
708-584-0150
P, W

Nichols Garden Nursery
1190 N. Pacific Highway
Albany, OR 97321
503-928-9280
Unusual H, P, S, W

Orchid Gardens
2232 139th Avenue N.W.
Andover, MN 55744
(Catalog: $.75)
W *(Midwestern)*

Oregon Bulb Farms
39391 S.E. Lusted Road
Sandy, OR 97055
503-663-3133
B

Park Seed Co.
Cokesbury Road
Greenwood, SC 29647-0001
800-845-3369
B, P, S

Pinetree Garden Seeds
Rt. 100
New Gloucester, ME 04260
207-926-3400
S

Plants of the Southwest
1812 Second Street
Santa Fe, NM 87501
505-983-1548
S, W

Plants of the Wild
P.O. Box 866
Tekoa, WA 99033
509-284-2848
P

Powell's Gardens
9468 U.S. Highway 70 E.
Princeton, NC 27569
919-936-4421
B, P

Prairie Moon Nursery
Rt. 3, Box 163
Winona, MN 55987
507-452-1362
(Catalog: $2)
P, S, W

Prairie Nursery
P.O. Box 306
Westfield, WI 53964
608-296-3679
(Catalog: $3)
P, S, W

Prairie Ridge Nursery
CRM Ecosystems, Inc.
9738 Overland Road
Mount Horeb, WI 53572
608-437-5245
(Catalog: $3)
P, S, W

Prairie Seed Source
P.O. Box 83
North Lake, WI 53064
(Catalog: $1)
S, W

The Primrose Path
R.D. 2, Box 110
Scottsdale, PA 15683
(Catalog: $2)
P, W

Putney Nursery, Inc.
Box 265
Putney, VT 05346
802-387-5577
W

Rainforest Gardens
13139 224 Street, R.R. 2
Maple Ridge, BC V2X 7E7
Canada
604-467-4218
P

Redwood City Seed Company
P.O. Box 361
Redwood City, CA 94064
415-325-7333
S

Richter's
357 Highway 47
Goodwood, ON L0C 1A0
Canada
905-640-6677
(Catalog: $2)
H

Clyde Robin Seed Co.
3670 Enterprise Avenue
Hayward, CA 94545
510-785-0425
W

Rocknoll Nursery
7812 Mad River Road
Hillsboro, OH 45133
513-393-5545
(Catalog: $1)
P

The Rosemary House
120 S. Market Street
Mechanicsburg, PA 17055
717-697-5111
(Catalog: $2)
H

Rowlands
7404 Menaul Blvd. N.E.
Albuquerque, NM 87110
800-447-6177
B, H, P

Savory's, Inc.
5300 Whiting Avenue
Edina, MN 55439-1249
612-941-8755
(Catalog: $2)
Hostas

S = Seeds   P = Live Plants   B = Bulbs   W = Wildflower seeds and/or plants   H = Herb seeds and/or plants

John Scheepers, Inc.
PO Box 700
Bantam, CT 06750
203-567-0838
B

Schreiner's Irises
3624 Quinaby Road, N.E.
Salem, OR 97303
503-393-3232
Irises

Seeds Blum
Idaho City Stage
Boise, ID 83706
208-342-0858
S

Shady Oaks Nursery
112 10th Ave. S.E.
Waseca, MN 56093
507-835-5033
(Catalog: $2.50)
Shade-loving P

Sharp Bros. Seed Co.
P.O. Box 140
Healy, KS 67850
316-398-2231
W

Shepherd's Garden Seeds
30 Irene Street
Torrington, CT 06790
Horticultural advice: 408-335-6910
Orders: 203-482-3638
H, S

Siskiyou Rare Plant Nursery
2825 Cummings Road
Medford, OR 97501
503-772-6846
P, W

Anthony J. Skittone
2271 31st Avenue
San Francisco, CA 94116
415-753-3332
Unusual B, P, S

Smith & Hawken
25 Corte Madera
Mill Valley, CA 94941
415-383-2000
B

Southern Exposure Seed Exchange
P.O. Box 170
Earlysville, VA 22936
804-973-4703
(Catalog: $2)
S

Spring Hill Nurseries
6523 North Galena Road
Peoria, IL 61632
309-689-3849
B, P

Stallings Nursery
910 Encinitas Blvd.
Encinitas, CA 92024
619-753-3079
(Catalog: $3)
P

Stock Seed Farms, Inc.
28008 Mill Road
Murdock, NE 68407
402-867-3771
S, W

Stokes Seeds, Inc.
P.O. Box 548
Buffalo, NY 14240
716-695-6980
S

Sunnybrook Farms Nursery
P.O. Box 6
9448 Mayfield Road
Chesterland, OH 44026
216-729-7232
H, P

Sunnyslope Gardens
8638 Huntington Drive
San Gabriel, CA 91775
818-287-4071
Chrysanthemums

The Terra Ceia Farms
C. van Staalduinen and Sons
Rt. 2, Box 167
Pantego, NC 27860
800-858-2852
B, *Roots*

Thompson & Morgan, Inc.
P.O. Box 1308
Jackson, NJ 08527-0308
908-363-2225
B, P, S

Tranquil Lake Nursery
45 River Street
Rehoboth, MA 02769
508-252-4002
P

Twilley Seeds
P.O. Box 65
Trevose, PA 19053
215-639-8800
S

Van Bourgondien Bros.
P.O. Box 1000
Babylon, NY 11702-0598
800-622-9997
B

Van Dyck's Flower Farms, Inc.
P.O. Box 430
Brightwaters, NY 11718-0430
800-248-2852
B

Mary Mattison Van Schaik
Cavendish, VT 01542
802-226-7653
B

The Vermont Wildflower Farm
P.O. Box 5, Route 7
Charlotte, VT 05445-0005
802-425-3931
W

Vesey's Seeds Ltd.
York, PEI COA 1PO
Canada
902-368-7333
S

S = Seeds   P = Live Plants   B = Bulbs   W = Wildflower seeds and/or plants   H = Herb seeds and/or plants

Andre Viette Farm and Nursery
Rt. 1, Box 16
Fishersville, VA 22939
703-943-2315
P

Wayside Gardens
1 Garden Lane
Hodges, SC 29695
800-845-1124
B, P, Roses

We-Du Nurseries
Rt. 5, Box 724
Marion, NC 28752
704-738-8300
(Catalog: $2)
P, W

Well-Sweep Herb Farm
317 Mt. Bethel Road
Port Murray, NJ 07865
908-852-5390
(Catalog: $2)
P, S

White Flower Farm
P.O. Box 50
Litchfield, CT 06759-0050
203-496-9600
B, P

Gilbert H. Wild & Son
P.O. Box 338
Sarcoxie, MO 64862
417-548-3514
(Catalog: $3)
Daylilies, Iris, Peonies

The Wildflower Source
The Propagator's Private Source
8805 Kenman Road
Hebron, IL 60034
P, W

Wildginger Woodlands
P.O. Box 1091
Webster, NY 14580
P, W

Wildseed Farms, Inc.
1101 Campo Rosa Road
P.O. Box 308
Eagle Lake, TX 77434
800-848-0078
W

Wildwood Farm
10300 Hwy. 12
Kenwood, CA 95452
707-833-1161
(Catalog: $1)
P, California natives

Woodlanders, Inc.
1128 Colleton Avenue
Aiken, SC 29801
803-648-7522
(Catalog: $2)
P, Southern natives

Wrenwood
Rt. 4, Box 361
Berkeley Springs, WV 25411
304-258-3071
(Catalog: $2.50)
H, P

S = Seeds   P = Live Plants   B = Bulbs   W = Wildflower seeds and/or plants   H = Herb seeds and/or plants

GLOSSARY

Acid Having a pH level below 7.0.

Alkaline Having a pH level above 7.0.

Annual A plant that grows from seed, flowers, and dies, all in one year.

Axil The angle between a leaf and the stalk from which it is growing.

Basal cutting A cutting taken from the base of a plant.

Biennial A plant with a two-year life span, germinating and producing leaves in the first year, flowering and dying in the second.

Bract A leaflike part, most often located at the base of a flower or inflorescence.

Bulb A bud containing food stores that grows underground, producing leaves and flowers that appear above ground.

Bulbil A miniature bulb that forms in the leaf axil of some bulbous plants.

Bulblet A miniature bulb that forms below ground on the parent bulb.

Calyx A group of small, petallike parts surrounding the true petals of a flower.

Compost Organic matter that has broken down over time to form a crumbly substance with which soil is enriched and plants are fed.

Corm A fleshy underground stem, similar to a bulb.

Cormel A miniature corm that is produced from the base of a parent corm.

Cormlet Another name for a cormel.

Cotyledon The first leaves to appear on a seedling, containing enough nutrients to feed the seed for a short period.

Damping-off A potentially lethal fungal disease most often affecting seedlings.

Deadhead The removal of flower heads after blooming.

Eye A bud from which new growth will sprout.

Heaving The process of a plant being pushed out of the soil that occurs when the ground alternately freezes and thaws in winter.

Humus Decayed organic matter.

In situ This Latin term is usually used to mean sowing a seed outdoors where the plant will flower.

Limy Having a pH level above 7.0.

Mulch Organic or inorganic material that is laid over the soil in order to reduce moisture evaporation, to keep the soil cool in summer or to warm it in early spring, to restrict growth of weeds, protect delicate roots — the uses and benefits of mulch are almost limitless.

Neutral Having a pH level of 7.0.

Overwinter The process of bringing frost-tender plants through the winter by moving them indoors — the horticultural equivalent of Canadians spending the winter in Florida.

Panicle A loose flower cluster that begins blooming at the bottom, with uppermost flowers blooming later. The cluster does not end in a terminal flower.

Perennial A plant that lives for more than two years.

pH The scale used for measuring the degree of acidity or alkalinity of soil.

Pinching out The removal of growth at the tips of a plant.

Pricking out Transplanting seedlings, usually from a communal growing situation, such as flats, to individual pots.

Raceme A long flower cluster with one main stem to which individual flowers are attached by short stalks. There is no terminal flower.

Rhizome An underground stem that stores food, produces roots below ground and leaves and flowers above.

Rosette A radiating formation of leaves, often grown at the end of a short stem.

Self-seed The process of a plant releasing its seed, which will readily germinate and produce new plants.

Side-dressing See Top-dressing.

Spadix A dense, upright flowering spike resembling an exclamation mark, usually surrounded by a spathe.

Spathe One or more large bracts partially surrounding the flower, which is usually in the form of a spadix.

Spike A long flower cluster whose individual blooms are attached to the main stem without a stalk.

Stake Support by the means of upright props to which stems can be tied.

Top-dressing The application of fertilizer or organic matter around a plant, the material being left on the soil surface rather than being dug in. Also known as side-dressing.

Tuber An underground stem or root in which food is stored and from which roots and leaves grow.

Umbel A usually flat-topped cluster of flowers whose individual stems grow from a central point, as the spokes of an umbrella.

COMMON NAME/LATIN GENUS INDEX

Blue June grass	*Koeleria*	Calliopsis	*Coreopsis*	Chinese houses	*Collinsia*
Blue lace flower	*Trachymene*	Camass	*Camassia*	Chinese kidney bean	*Wisteria*
Bluelips	*Collinsia*	Campion	*Lychnis, Silene*	Chinese-lantern lily	*Sandersonia*
Blue marguerite	*Felicia*	Canary creeper	*Tropaeolum* (A)	Chinese lanterns	*Physalis*
Blue meadow grass	*Koeleria*	Canary grass	*Phalaris*	Chinese parsley	*Coriandrum*
Blue poppy	*Meconopsis*	Canary-bird flower	*Tropaeolum* (A)	Chinese trumpet flower	*Incarvillea*
Blue squill	*Scilla*	Canchalagua	*Centaurium*	Chinese yam	*Dioscorea*
Blue star	*Amsonia*	Candytuft	*Iberis* (P)	Christmas bells	*Sandersonia*
Blue succory	*Catananche*	Canterbury bells	*Campanula*	Christmas rose	*Helleborus*
Blue throatwort	*Trachelium*	Cape daisy	*Venidium*	Chufa	*Cyperus*
Bluets	*Hedyotis*	Cape forget-me-not	*Anchusa*	Cigar plant	*Cuphea*
Bluewings	*Torenia*	Cape fuchsia	*Phygelius*	Cilantro	*Coriandrum*
Bog bean	*Menyanthes*	Cape gooseberry	*Physalis*	Cineraria	*Senecio*
Bona nox	*Calonyction*	Cape lily	*Crinum*	Cinnamon vine	*Dioscorea*
Bonavist	*Dolichos*	Cape marigold	*Dimorphotheca*	Cinquefoil	*Potentilla*
Boneset	*Eupatorium*	Cape stock	*Heliophilia*	Climbing fumitory	*Adlumia*
Bonnet bellflower	*Codonopsis*	Caraway	*Carum*	Climbing lily	*Gloriosa*
Bouncing bet	*Saponaria* (P)	Cardinal climber	*Ipomoea,*	Climbing nasturtium	*Tropaeolum* (P)
Bower actinidia	*Actinidia*		*Quamoclit*	Clock vine	*Thunbergia*
Bower arguta	*Actinidia*	Cardinal flower	*Lobelia*	Cloud grass	*Agrostis*
Bowles' golden grass	*Milium*	Cardoon	*Cynara*	Coastal wallflower	*Erysimum*
Bowman's root	*Gillenia*	Carolina lupine	*Thermopsis*	Coat flower	*Tunica*
Brass buttons	*Cotula*	Cartwheel flower	*Heracleum*	Cobbler's bench	*Lamium*
Bridal wreath	*Francoa*	Castor bean plant	*Ricinus*	Cobra lily	*Darlingtonia*
Bride's bonnet	*Clintonia*	Castor oil plant	*Ricinus*	Cockscomb	*Celosia*
Brompton stock	*Matthiola*	Cat's ear	*Calochortus*	Colewort	*Crambe*
Broom corn millet	*Panicum*	Cat's-ears	*Antennaria*	Coliseum ivy	*Cymbalaria*
Buck bean	*Menyanthes*	Catchfly	*Lychnis, Silene*	Columbine	*Aquilegia*
Bugbane	*Cimicifuga*	Cathedral bells	*Cobaea*	Comfrey	*Symphytum*
Bugle lily	*Watsonia*	Catmint	*Nepeta*	Common stock	*Matthiola*
Bugleweed	*Ajuga*	Catnip	*Nepeta*	Compass plant	*Silphium*
Bugloss	*Anchusa*	Celandine	*Chelidonium*	Coneflower	*Echinacea,*
Bulbil lily	*Lilium*	Celandine poppy	*Chelidonium*		*Rudbeckia*
Bulrush	*Cyperus*	Centaury	*Centaurium*	Copihue	*Lapageria*
Burnet	*Sanguisorba*	Chamise lily	*Erythronium*	Copper tip	*Crocosmia*
Burning bush	*Dictamnus,*	Chamomile	*Anthemis*	Coral bells	*Heuchera*
	Kochia	Checkerbloom	*Sidalcea*	Coral pea	*Hardenbergia*
Bush violet	*Browallia*	Checkered lily	*Fritillaria*	Coriander	*Coriandrum*
Busy lizzie	*Impatiens*	Cheddar pink	*Dianthus* (P)	Corkscrew vine	*Phaseolus*
Butter and eggs	*Linaria*	Cherry pie	*Heliotropium*	Corn-cockle	*Agrostemma*
Buttercup	*Ranunculus*	Chervil	*Anthriscus,*	Corn flag	*Gladiolus*
Butterfly flower	*Schizanthus*		*Myrrhis*	Cornflower	*Centaurea*
Butterfly iris	*Moraea*	Chickabiddy	*Asarina*	Corn lily	*Clintonia,*
Butterfly lily	*Hedychium*	Chilean bell flower	*Lapageria*		*Gladiolus, Ixia*
Butterfly tulip	*Calochortus*	Chilean bellflower	*Nolana*	Corn marigold	*Chrysanthemum*
Butterfly weed	*Asclepias*	Chilean crocus	*Tecophilaea*		(A)
Butterwort	*Pinguicula*	Chilean glory flower	*Eccremocarpus*	Corn poppy	*Papaver* (A)
Button snake root	*Liatris*	Chiming bells	*Mertensia*	Cosmea	*Cosmos*
California bluebell	*Phacelia*	China aster	*Callistephus*	Cottage pink	*Dianthus* (P)
California fuchsia	*Zauschneria*	China fleece vine	*Polygonum*	Cotton grass	*Eriophorum*
California pitcher		China pink	*Dianthus* (A)	Cow herb	*Saponaria* (A)
plant	*Darlingtonia*	Chincherinchee	*Ornithogalum*	Cow parsnip	*Heracleum*
California poppy	*Eschscholzia*	Chinese forget-me-not	*Cynoglossum*	Cowbells	*Uvularia*
California tree poppy	*Romneya*	Chinese foxglove	*Rehmannia*	Cowslip	*Caltha, Primula*
Calla lily	*Zantedeschia*	Chinese gooseberry	*Actinidia*	Cranesbill	*Geranium*

Crape myrtle	*Lagerstroemia*	Dutchman's breeches	*Dicentra*	Feverfew	*Chrysanthemum* (P), *Matricaria*, *Pyrethrum*
Crape myrtlette	*Lagerstroemia*	Dwarf marigold	*Tagetes*		
Creamcups	*Platystemon*	Dwarf morning-glory	*Convolvulus*		
Creeping buttercup	*Ranunculus*			Fig marigold	*Mesembryanthe mum*
Creeping Charlie	*Lysimachia*	Dwarf snowbell	*Soldanella*		
Creeping forget-me-not	*Omphalodes*	Dyer's wood	*Isatis*	Filaree	*Erodium*
		Edelweiss	*Leontopodium*	Fire on the mountain	*Euphorbia* (A)
Creeping Jenny	*Lysimachia*	Edging lobelia	*Lobelia*	Fire pink	*Silene*
Creeping zinnia	*Sanvitalia*	Elecampane	*Inula*	Fire-cracker flower	*Brodiaea*
Crimson flag	*Schizostylis*	Elephant's-ear	*Caladium*	Firebush	*Kochia*
Crinum lily	*Crinum*	English daisy	*Bellis*	Firecracker plant	*Cuphea*
Crosswort	*Phuopsis*	English marigold	*Calendula*	Fireweed	*Epilobium*
Crown imperial	*Fritillaria*	English primrose	*Primula*	Five-spot	*Nemophila*
Crown of thorns	*Euphorbia* (A)	Eryngo	*Eryngium*	Flame flower	*Tropaeolum* (P)
Crown vetch	*Coronilla*	Estragon	*Artemisia*	Flame nettle	*Coleus*
Cuban lily	*Scilla*	Eulalia	*Miscanthus*	Flaming fountain	*Amaranthus*
Cuckoopint	*Arum*	Evening primrose	*Oenothera*	Flanders poppy	*Papaver* (A)
Culver's root	*Veronica*	Evening stock	*Matthiola*	Flax	*Linum*
Cumin	*Cuminum*	Everlasting	*Helipterum*	Flax lily	*Phormium*
Cup plant	*Silphium*	Everlasting pea	*Lathyrus* (P)	Fleabane	*Erigeron*
Cup-and-saucer vine	*Cobaea*	Fairy foxglove	*Erinus*	Flora's paintbrush	*Emilia*
Cupflower	*Nierembergia*	Fairy lantern	*Calochortus*	Floripondio	*Datura*
Cupid's dart	*Catananche*	Fairy primrose	*Primula*	Flossflower	*Ageratum*
Cupidone	*Catananche*	Fairy wallflower	*Erysimum*	Flower-of-an-hour	*Hibiscus*
Curled mallow	*Malva*	False alumroot	*Tellima*	Flower-of-Jove	*Lychnis*
Curry plant	*Helichrysum*	False chamomile	*Boltonia*, *Matricaria*	Flowering spurge	*Euphorbia* (P)
Cypress vine	*Ipomoea*, *Quamoclit*			Flowering tobacco	*Nicotiana*
		False coleus	*Perilla*	Flowers of the Western wind	*Zephyranthes*
Daffodil	*Narcissus*	False dittany	*Dictamnus*		
Daisy	*Bellis*	False dragonhead	*Physostegia*	Foam flower	*Tiarella*
Dame's rocket	*Hesperis*	False goatsbeard	*Astilbe*	Forget-me-not	*Anchusa*, *Brunnera*, *Myosotis*
Dames violet	*Hesperis*	False hellebore	*Veratrum*		
Dandelion	*Crepis*	False indigo	*Baptisia*		
Daylily	*Hemerocallis*	False lupine	*Thermopsis*	Fortnight lily	*Moraea*
Dead nettle	*Lamium*	False mallow	*Sidalcea*	Fountain grass	*Pennisetum*
Desert candle	*Eremurus*	False rock cress	*Aubrieta*	Fountain plant	*Amaranthus*
Desert evening primrose	*Oenothera*	False saffron	*Carthamus*	Four-o'clock	*Mirabilis*
		False Solomon's seal	*Smilacina*	Fox's brush	*Centranthus*
Desert hollyhock	*Sphaeralcea*	False spikenard	*Smilacina*	Fox-tail barley	*Hordeum*
Desert mallow	*Sphaeralcea*	False spiraea	*Astilbe*	Foxglove	*Digitalis*
Devil's paintbrush	*Emilia*	False starwort	*Boltonia*	Foxtail grass	*Setaria*
Devil's-paintbrush	*Hieracium*	False sunflower	*Helenium*	Foxtail lily	*Eremurus*
Devil-in-a-bush	*Nigella*	False sunflower	*Heliopsis*	Foxtail millet	*Setaria*
Diamond flower	*Ionopsidium*	Farewell-to-spring	*Clarkia*	Fraxinella	*Dictamnus*
Dill	*Anethum*	Fawn lily	*Erythronium*	French honeysuckle	*Hedysarum*
Dog fennel	*Anthemis*	Feather grass	*Stipa*	French marigold	*Tagetes*
Dogs-tooth violet	*Erythronium*	Featherbells	*Stenanthium*	French parsley	*Anthriscus*
Donkey's ears	*Stachys*	Feathered bronze leaf	*Rodgersia*	French spinach	*Atriplex*
Dragon arum	*Dracunculus*	Feathered columbine	*Thalictrum*	French willow	*Epilobium*
Dragon plant	*Dracunculus*	Featherfleece	*Stenanthium*	Fried eggs	*Limnanthes*
Dragonroot	*Arisaema*	Feathertop	*Pennisetum*	Fringe cups	*Tellima*
Dropwort	*Filipendula*	Fennel	*Foeniculum*	Fringe flower	*Schizanthus*
Drummond phlox	*Phlox* (A)	Fennel flower	*Nigella*	Fringe-bell	*Shortia*
Dusty-miller	*Centaurea*, *Senecio*	Fenugreek	*Trigonella*	Fringed galax	*Shortia*
		Fescue	*Festuca*	Fritillary	*Fritillaria*

Frostweed	Helianthemum	Golden-rayed		Horn of plenty	Datura
Fumewort	Corydalis	lily of Japan	Lilium	Horned poppy	Glaucium
Fumitory	Corydalis	Goldenray	Ligularia	Horned violet	Viola
Funkia	Hosta	Goldenstar	Chrysogonum	Horseheal	Inula
Galingale	Cyperus	Goodnight-at-noon	Hibiscus	Horsemint	Monarda
Gandergoose	Orchis	Gourd	Cucurbita	Hottentot fig	Mesembryanthe-
Garden heliotrope	Valeriana	Goutweed	Aegopodium		mum
Garden rocket	Hesperis	Granadilla	Passiflora	Hound's tongue	Cynoglossum
Garden spiraea	Astilbe	Grape hyacinth	Muscari	Houseleek	Sempervivum
Gardener's garters	Phalaris	Grass flower	Claytonia	Husk tomato	Physalis
Garland lily	Hedychium	Grass of Parnassus	Parnassia	Hyacinth	Hyacinthus
Gas plant	Dictamnus	Grassnut	Brodiaea	Hyacinth bean	Dolichos
Gay feather	Liatris	Greater celandine	Chelidonium	Hyacinth-flowered	
Gentian	Gentiana	Greater spearwort	Ranunculus	candytuft	Iberis (A)
Geranium	Pelargonium	Grecian stock	Matthiola	Hyacinth-of-Peru	Scilla
German primrose	Primula	Greek hay	Trigonella	Hyssop	Agastache,
Germander	Teucrium	Green-and-gold	Chrysogonum		Hyssopus
Ghost weed	Euphorbia (A)	Green-veined orchid	Orchis	Ice plant	Mesembryanthe-
Ghostplant	Artemisia	Gromwell	Lithodora		mum, Sedum
Giant Himalayan lily	Cardiocrinum	Ground laurel	Epigaea	Icelandic poppy	Papaver (P)
Giant hogweed	Heracleum	Groundsel	Senecio	Immortelle	Helichrysum,
Giant lily	Cardiocrinum	Guernsey lily	Nerine		Helipterum,
Giant summer		Guinea-hen flower	Fritillaria		Xeranthemum
hyacinth	Galtonia	Gymea lily	Doryanthes	Indian blanket	Gaillardia (A, P)
Gillyflower	Cheiranthus,	Hardy ageratum	Eupatorium	Indian cress	Tropaeolum (A)
	Matthiola	Hardy amaryllis	Lycoris	Indian cup	Silphium
Ginger lily	Hedychium	Hardy geranium	Geranium	Indian pink	Dianthus (A)
Globe amaranth	Gomphrena	Hardy gloxinia	Incarvillea	Indian plant	Sanguinaria
Globe candytuft	Iberis (A)	Hare's tail	Lagurus	Indian poke	Veratrum
Globe daisy	Globularia	Harebell	Campanula	Indian shot	Canna
Globe flower	Trollius	Harebell poppy	Meconopsis	Indian turnip	Arisaema
Globe mallow	Sphaeralcea	Harlequin flower	Sparaxis	Indian-cup	Sarracenia
Globe thistle	Echinops	Hawk's beard	Crepis	Innocence	Collinsia,
Globe tulip	Calochortus	Hawkweed	Hieracium		Hedyotis
Gloriosa daisy	Rudbeckia	Heart pea	Cardiospermum	Irish bells	Moluccella
Gloriosa lily	Gloriosa	Heart seed	Cardiospermum	Irish moss	Arenaria, Sagina
Glory flower	Eccremocarpus	Heart's ease	Viola tricolor	Ithuriel's spear	Brodiaea
Glory lily	Gloriosa	Hedgehog coneflower	Echinacea	Ivy-leaved toadflax	Cymbalaria
Glory of the snow	Chionodoxa	Heliotrope	Heliotropium	Jaburan	Ophiopogon
Goat's beard	Aruncus	Hellebore	Helleborus	Jack-in-the-pulpit	Arisaema
Goat's rue	Galega	Helmet flower	Scutellaria	Jacob's ladder	Polemonium
Godetia	Clarkia	Hen-and-chickens	Sempervivum	Jacob's rod	Asphodeline
Gold moss	Sedum	Heron's bill	Erodium	Jacobean lily	Sprekelia
Gold-dust	Alyssum (P)	Himalayan fleece		Japanese anemone	Anemone
Golden ageratum	Lonas	flower	Polygonum	Japanese hop	Humulus
Golden cup	Hunnemannia	Himalayan mayapple	Podophyllum	Japanese iris	Iris (Kaempferi)
Golden drop	Onosma	Himalayan poppy	Meconopsis	Japanese lily	Lilium
Golden flower		Hog cranberry	Arctostaphylos	Japanese silver grass	Miscanthus
of the Incas	Tithonia	Hollyhock	Althaea	Jerusalem cross	Lychnis
Golden garlic	Allium	Hollyhock mallow	Malva	Jerusalem sage	Phlomis
Golden knee	Chrysogonum	Holy flax	Santolina	Job's tears	Coix
Golden marguerite	Anthemis	Holy thistle	Silybum	Joe pye weed	Eupatorium
Golden rod	Solidago	Honesty	Lunaria	Johnny jump up	Viola tricolor
Golden stars	Sanvitalia	Hoop petticoat	Narcissus	Jonquil	Narcissus
Golden-glow	Rudbeckia	Hop	Humulus	Joseph's coat	Amaranthus

Jupiter's beard	Anthyllis, Centranthus	Live-forever	Sempervivum	Meadow rue	Thalictrum
Kaffir lily	Schizostylis	Liverleaf	Hepatica	Meadow saffron	Colchicum
Kenilworth ivy	Cymbalaria	Liverwort	Hepatica	Meadowsweet	Filipendula
Keys of heaven	Centranthus	Livingstone daisy	Mesembryanthe- mum	Mealberry	Arctostaphylos
Kidney vetch	Anthyllis			Melic	Melica
King's spear	Asphodeline, Eremurus	Loddon lily	Leucojum	Merry-bells	Uvularia
		London pride	Saxifraga	Mexican cigar flower	Cuphea
Kingfisher daisy	Felicia	Loosestrife	Lysimachia	Mexican fire plant	Euphorbia (A)
Kinnikinick	Arctostaphylos	Loosestrife	Lythrum	Mexican fire lily	Sprekelia
Kiss-me-over- the-garden-gate	Polygonum	Lord Anson's blue pea	Lathyrus (P)	Mexican firebush	Kochia
		Lords-and-ladies	Arum	Mexican ivy	Cobaea
Kiwi vine	Actinidia	Lotus	Nelumbo	Mexican marigold	Tagetes
Knapweed	Centaurea	Lovage	Levisticum	Mexican poppy	Argemone
Knit-bone	Symphytum	Love grass	Eragrostis	Mexican sunflower	Tithonia
Knotweed	Polygonum	Love-in-a-mist	Nigella	Mexican tulip poppy	Hunnemannia
Kolomikta vine	Actinidia	Love-in-a-puff	Cardiospermum	Michaelmas daisy	Aster (P)
Lablab	Dolichos	Love-lies-bleeding	Amaranthus	Mignonette	Reseda
Lace grass	Eragrostis	Luffa	Cucurbita	Mignonette vine	Boussingaultia
Laceflower	Trachymene	Lungwort	Pulmonaria	Milk thistle	Silybum
Ladies-tobacco	Antennaria	Lupin or Lupine	Lupinus	Milk-and-wine lily	Crinum
Lady's finger	Anthyllis	Madagascar periwinkle	Catharanthus	Milkweed	Asclepias
Lady's mantle	Alchemilla	Madeira vine	Boussingaultia	Millet grass	Milium
Lady's slipper orchid	Cypripedium	Madonna lily	Lilium	Miniature hollyhock	Sidalcea
Lady's slipper	Impatiens	Madwort	Alyssum (P)	Mint	Mentha
Lady's thistle	Silybum	Magic lily	Lycoris	Missouri evening primrose	Oenothera
Lady-in-the-bath	Dicentra	Maiden grass	Miscanthus		
Ladybells	Adenophora	Maiden pink	Dianthus (P)	Missouri hyacinth	Camassia
Lamb's ears	Stachys	Maiden's wreath	Francoa	Mist flower	Eupatorium
Lamb's tongue	Stachys	Maiden's-tears	Silene	Miterwort	Mitella
Languid ladies	Mertensia	Mallow	Lavatera	Moccasin flower	Cypripedium
Larkspur	Consolida	Mallow-wort	Malope	Mole plant	Euphorbia (A)
Lavender	Lavandula	Maltese cross	Lychnis	Molten fire	Amaranthus
Lavender cotton	Santolina	Manchuria	Jeffersonia	Molucca balm	Moluccella
Lcadwort	Ceratostigma	Mandrake	Podophyllum	Monarch of the veldt	Venidium
Lemon balm	Melissa	Mangles everlasting	Helipterum	Mondo grass	Ophiopogon
Lemon lily	Lilium	Manzanita	Arctostaphylos	Money plant	Lunaria
Lent lily	Narcissus	Marigold	Tagetes	Moneywort	Lysimachia
Lenten rose	Helleborus	Mariposa lily	Calochortus	Monk's-hood	Aconitum
Leopard flower	Belamcanda	Marjoram	Origanum	Monkey flower	Mimulus
Leopard lily	Lilium	Marsh flower	Limnanthes	Monkey musk	Mimulus
Leopard plant	Ligularia	Marsh marigold	Caltha	Montbretia	Crocosmia, Tritonia
Leopard's bane	Doronicum	Martagon lily	Lilium		
Lesser celandine	Ranunculus	Marvel of Peru	Mirabilis	Moonflower	Calonyction, Ipomoea
Licorice plant	Helichrysum	Mask flower	Alonsoa		
Lily	Lilium	Masterwort	Astrantia, Heracleum	Moonwort	Lunaria
Lily leek	Allium			Morning glory	Ipomoea
Lily of Peru	Alstroemeria	Matilija poppy	Romneya	Moss campion	Silene
Lily of the valley	Convallaria	Mayapple	Podophyllum	Moss pink	Phlox (P)
Lily of the Nile	Zantedeschia	Mayflower	Claytonia, Epigaea	Mother-in-law plant	Caladium, Calandrinia
Lily turf	Liriope				
Lily-of-the-Altai	Ixiolirion	Maypop	Passiflora	Mother-of-thyme	Thymus
Lily-of-the-Incas	Alstroemeria	Meadow clary	Salvia	Mount Atlas daisy	Anacyclus
Lily-of-the-Nile	Agapanthus	Meadow daisy	Bellis	Mountain asphodel	Xerophyllum
Lilyturf	Ophiopogon	Meadow foam	Limnanthes	Mountain avens	Dryas
		Meadow lily	Lilium	Mountain bluebell	Mertensia

Mountain bluet	Centaurea	Painted daisy	Chrysanthemum (P), Pyrethrum	Pot marigold	Calendula
Mountain box	Arctostaphylos			Pot marjoram	Origanum
Mountain daisy	Celmisia	Painted leaf	Euphorbia (A)	Prairie gentian	Eustoma
Mountain flax	Phormium	Painted nettle	Coleus	Prairie mallow	Sidalcea,
Mountain fringe	Adlumia	Painted tongue	Salpiglossis		Sphaeralcea
Mountain pink	Centaurium	Palm Springs daisy	Cladanthus	Prairie pine	Liatris
Mountain snuff	Arnica	Palma christi	Ricinus	Prairie pointer	Dodecatheon
Mountain spinach	Atriplex	Pampas grass	Cortaderia	Prairie snakeroot	Liatris
Mountain tassel	Soldanella	Panic grass	Panicum	Pretty Betsy	Centranthus
Mountain tobacco	Arnica	Pansy	Viola, Viola tricolor	Prickly poppy	Argemone
Mourning widow	Geranium			Prickly rhubarb	Gunnera
Mourning-bride	Scabiosa	Paper plant	Cyperus	Prickly thrift	Acantholimon
Mugwort	Artemisia	Papoose root	Caulophyllum	Pride of Madeira	Echium
Mullein	Verbascum	Papyrus	Cyperus	Primrose	Primula
Mullein pink	Lychnis	Paradise lily	Paradisea	Prince's feather	Amaranthus, Polygonum
Musk	Mimulus	Parsley	Petroselinum		
Musk mallow	Malva	Partridge pea	Cassia	Puccoon	Lithodora
Musk rose	Malva	Partridgeberry	Mitchella	Pudding grass	Mentha
Myrrh	Myrrhis	Pasque flower	Anemone, Pulsatilla	Purple bell vine	Rhodochiton
Naked boys	Colchicum			Purple loosetrife	Lythrum
Naked ladies	Amaryllis, Colchicum	Passion flower	Passiflora	Purple rock cress	Aubrieta
		Patience plant	Impatiens	Purple willow-herb	Lythrum
Namaqualand daisy	Venidium	Patient Lucy	Impatiens	Purslane	Portulaca
Nasturtium	Tropaeolum (A,P)	Peach bells	Campanula	Pussley	Portulaca
		Pearl grass	Melica	Pussy-toes	Antennaria
Natal grass	Tricholaena	Pearlwort	Sagina	Pyrethrum	Chrysanthemum (P)
Natal lily	Moraea	Pearly everlasting	Anaphalis		
Navelwort	Omphalodes	Pennyroyal	Mentha	Quaker bonnets	Hedyotis
Needlegrass	Stipa	Peony	Paeonia	Quaker-ladies	Hedyotis
Nepal silver grass	Miscanthus	Perennial carnation	Dianthus (P)	Quaking grass	Briza
New Zealand bur	Acaena	Perennial pea	Lathyrus (P)	Quamash	Camassia
New Zealand flax	Phormium	Perennial phlox	Phlox (P)	Queen Anne's lace	Ammi
Night-scented stock	Matthiola	Peruvian lily	Alstroemeria	Queen Anne's thimble	Gilia
Nippon bells	Shortia	Pheasant's eye	Adonis	Queen cup	Clintonia
None-so-pretty	Silene	Pig squeak	Bergenia	Queen of the prairie	Filipendula
Northern shorewort	Mertensia	Pilotweed	Silphium	Queen of the meadows	Filipendula
Obedient plant	Physostegia	Pimpernel	Anagallis	Rabbit-foot grass	Polypogon
Oconee bells	Shortia	Pin clover	Erodium	Rabbit-tail grass	Lagurus
October daphne	Sedum	Pincushion flower	Scabiosa	Ragged robin	Centaurea, Lychnis
Orach	Atriplex	Pincushion plant	Cotula		
Orange African daisy	Ursinia	Pineapple flower	Eucomis	Ragged sailor	Centaurea
Orange clock vine	Thunbergia	Pineapple lily	Eucomis	Ragwort	Senecio
Orange milkweed	Asclepias	Pitcher plant	Sarracenia	Rain lily	Zephyranthes
Orange sunflower	Heliopsis	Plains bristle grass	Setaria	Rampion	Phyteuma
Orchid	Bletilla	Plantain lily	Hosta	Rattleweed	Baptisia
Oriental iris	Iris (Kaempferi)	Pleurisy root	Asclepias	Red Morocco	Adonis
Oriental poppy	Papaver (P)	Plumbago	Ceratostigma	Red sage	Lantana
Orpine	Sedum	Plume poppy	Macleaya	Red Sally	Lythrum
Oswego tea	Monarda	Plume thistle	Cirsium	Red-hot-poker	Kniphofia
Our Lady's milk thistle	Silybum	Polyanthus	Primula	Redmaids	Calandrinia
		Pompoms	Cephalipterum	Regal lily	Lilium
Ox-eye	Buphthalmum	Poor man's weatherglass	Anagallis	Rheumatism root	Jeffersonia
Ox-eye daisy	Buphthalmum			Rhubarb	Rheum
Oysterleaf	Mertensia	Poor man's orchid	Schizanthus	Ribbon grass	Phalaris
Paint Indian	Lithodora	Poppy	Papaver (A,P)	Rock jasmine	Androsace

Common Name	Latin Genus
Rock purslane	Calandrinia
Rock rose	Helianthemum
Rock soapwort	Saponaria (P)
Rockcress	Arabis
Rocket candytuft	Iberis (A)
Rockfoil	Saxifraga
Rocky Mountain garland	Clarkia
Rodgersflower	Rodgersia
Rose campion	Lychnis
Rose mallow	Hibiscus
Rose moss	Portulaca
Rose of Sharon	Hypericum
Rose-of-heaven	Lychnis, Silene
Rosebay	Epilobium
Rosemary	Rosmarinus
Rosinweed	Silphium
Royal lily	Lilium
Royal sweet-sultan	Centaurea
Ruby grass	Tricholaena
Rue-anemone	Anemonella
Running box	Mitchella
Rupture-wort	Herniaria
Russian sage	Perovskia
Russian vine	Polygonum
Safflower	Carthamus
Saffron	Crocus
Saffron thistle	Carthamus
Sage	Salvia
Salt bush	Atriplex
Sand pink	Dianthus (P)
Sand verbena	Abronia
Sandberry	Arctostaphylos
Sandwort	Arenaria
Sarawak bean	Dolichos
Satin flower	Clarkia, Lunaria
Satin pod	Lunaria
Saxifrage	Saxifraga
Saxifrage pink	Tunica
Scabious	Cephalaria, Scabiosa
Scarlet lightning	Lychnis
Scarlet plume	Euphorbia (P)
Scarlet runner bean	Phaseolus
Scarlet star-glory	Quamoclit
Scorpion senna	Coronilla
Scotch moss	Arenaria
Scotch thistle	Cirsium
Scottish flame flower	Tropaeolum (A)
Sea fig	Mesembryanthe-mum
Sea holly	Eryngium
Sea hollyhock	Hibiscus
Sea lavender	Limonium
Sea marigold	Mesembryanthe-mum
Sea pink	Armeria, Limonium
Sea poppy	Glaucium
Sea purslane	Atriplex
Seakale	Crambe
Sego lily	Calochortus
Self heal	Prunella
Serbian queen	Ramonda
Serpent cucumber	Trichosanthes
Serpent gourd	Trichosanthes
Sesame	Sesamum
Shamrock	Oxalis
Shamrock pea	Parochetus
Shasta daisy	Chrysanthemum (P)
Sheep's bit	Jasione
Sheep's scabious	Jasione
Shellflower	Moluccella
Shepherd's clock	Anagallis
Shepherd's scabious	Jasione
Shirley poppy	Papaver (A)
Shoo-fly plant	Nicandra
Shooting star	Dodecatheon
Siberian bugloss	Brunnera
Siberian forget-me-not	Brunnera
Siberian lily	Ixiolirion
Siberian tea	Bergenia
Siberian wallflower	Erysimum
Side-saddle flower	Sarracenia
Signet marigold	Tagetes
Silver banner grass	Miscanthus
Silver crown	Chiastophyllum
Silver lace vine	Polygonum
Silver vine	Actinidia
Silverbush	Convolvulus
Skullcap	Scutellaria
Skunk cabbage	Lysichiton
Sky vine	Thunbergia
Skyflower	Thunbergia
Sleepy daisy	Xanthisma
Smartweed	Polygonum
Snail flower	Phaseolus
Snake gourd	Trichosanthes
Snake head	Chelone
Snake's head fritillary	Fritillaria
Snake's head lily	Fritillaria
Snakeroot	Cimicifuga
Snakesbeard	Ophiopogon
Snakeweed	Polygonum
Snapdragon	Antirrhinum
Sneezeweed	Helenium
Sneezewort	Achillea
Snow on the mountain	Euphorbia (A)
Snow-in-summer	Cerastium
Snowdrift	Lobularia
Snowdrop	Galanthus
Snowdrop windflower	Anemone
Snowflake	Leucojum
Soap plant	Chlorogalum
Soapweed	Yucca
Soapwort	Saponaria (A)
Solomon's seal	Polygonatum
Sorrel	Oxalis, Rumex
Sorrel rhubarb	Rheum
Southern star	Oxypetalum
Southernwood	Artemisia
Sow bread	Cyclamen
Spanish bayonet	Yucca
Spanish bluebell	Scilla
Spanish dagger	Yucca
Spanish flag	Quamoclit
Spear grass	Stipa
Speedwell	Veronica
Spider flower	Cleome
Spider lily	Crinum, Lycoris
Spider plant	Anthericum
Spiderwort	Tradescantia
Spiraea	Aruncus, Filipendula
Spring anemone	Pulsatilla
Spring beauty	Claytonia
Spring crocus	Crocus
Spring meadow saffron	Bulbocodium
Spring vetch	Lathyrus (P)
Spurge	Euphorbia (A,P)
Spurred snapdragon	Linaria
Squaw grass	Xerophyllum
Squaw root	Caulophyllum
Squawberry	Mitchella
Squill	Scilla
Squirreltail barley	Hordeum
Squirreltail grass	Hordeum
St. Bernard's lily	Anthericum
St. Bruno's lily	Paradisea
St. James' lily	Sprekelia
St. Patrick's cabbage	Saxifraga, Sempervivum
St.-John's-wort	Hypericum
Standing cypress	Gilia
Star ipomoea	Quamoclit
Star of the Veldt	Dimorphotheca
Star of Bethlehem	Ornithogalum
Star of the Argentine	Oxypetalum
Star of Texas	Xanthisma
Star tulip	Calochortus
Statice	Limonium
Stock	Matthiola
Stokes' aster	Stokesia

Common name	Genus	Common name	Genus	Common name	Genus
Stone cress	Aethionema	Texas bluebonnet	Lupinus	Wandering Jew	Tradescantia
Stonecrop	Sedum	Texas pride	Phlox (A)	Wandflower	Sparaxis
Storksbill	Erodium	Texas star	Xanthisma	Waterlily	Nelumbo
Strawberry geranium	Saxifraga	Thimble flower	Gilia	Wax pink	Portulaca
Strawflower	Helichrysum, Helipterum	Thoroughwort	Eupatorium	Welsh poppy	Meconopsis
Striped squill	Puschkinia	Three-birds-flying	Linaria	White Dutch runner bean	Phaseolus
Sulla clover	Hedysarum	Thrift	Armeria	White hellebore	Veratrum
Sultana	Impatiens	Throatwort	Trachelium	White lace flower	Ammi
Summer cypress	Kochia	Thyme	Thymus	White snakeroot	Eupatorium
Summer fir	Artemisia	Tickseed	Coreopsis	Whitecup	Nierembergia
Summer forget-me-not	Anchusa	Tidy tips	Layia	Whitlow grass	Draba
Summer hyacinth	Galtonia	Toad lily	Fritillaria, Tricyrtis	Wild artichoke	Cynara
Summer poinsettia	Amaranthus	Toadflax	Linaria	Wild ginger	Asarum
Summer savory	Satureja (A)	Tobacco	Nicotiana	Wild heliotrope	Phacelia
Summer snowflake	Leucojum	Toper's plant	Sanguisorba	Wild hyacinth	Camassia
Sun lovers	Heliophila	Torch lily	Kniphofia	Wild indigo	Baptisia
Sun moss	Portulaca	Touch-me-not	Impatiens	Wild lantana	Abronia
Sun plant	Portulaca	Trailing arbutus	Epigaea	Wild oat	Avena
Sun rose	Helianthemum	Transvaal daisy	Gerbera	Wild onion	Allium
Sundrops	Oenothera	Treasure flower	Gazania	Wild pansy	Viola tricolor
Sunflower	Helianthus	Tree mallow	Lavatera	Wild petunia	Ruellia
Swamp lily	Crinum	Trinity flower	Tradescantia	Wild pink	Silene
Swamp mallow	Hibiscus	Trout lily	Erythronium	Wild senna	Cassia
Swan river daisy	Brachycome	Trumpet flower	Datura, Incarvillea	Willow herb	Epilobium
Swan River everlasting	Helipterum	Trumpetleaf	Sarracenia	Windflower	Anemone
Sweet alyssum	Alyssum (A), Lobularia	Tuberose	Polianthes	Winged everlasting	Ammobium
Sweet balm	Melissa	Tufted pansy	Viola	Winter aconite	Eranthis
Sweet chamomile	Matricaria	Tufted violet	Viola	Winter cherry	Cardiospermum, Physalis
Sweet chervil	Myrrhis	Tulip	Tulipa	Winter daffodil	Sternbergia
Sweet cicely	Myrrhis	Tulip poppy	Papaver (A)	Winter savory	Satureja (P)
Sweet marjoram	Origanum	Tunic flower	Tunica	Wishbone flower	Torenia
Sweet rocket	Hesperis	Turk's-cap lily	Lilium	Woad	Isatis
Sweet scabious	Scabiosa	Turkeybeard	Xerophyllum	Wolfsbane	Aconitum
Sweet violet	Viola odorata	Turtle head	Chelone	Wood daffodil	Uvularia
Sweet William	Dianthus (Bien.)	Twin-flower	Linnaea	Wood spurge	Euphorbia (P)
Sweet William catchfly	Silene	Twinleaf	Jeffersonia	Woodruff	Asperula
Sweet woodruff	Asperula	Twinspur	Diascia	Woods poppy	Sanguinaria
Sweet-sultan	Centaurea	Umbrella grass	Cyperus	Worm grass	Sedum
Sweetpea	Lathyrus (A,P)	Unicorn plant	Martynia	Wormwood	Artemisia
Switch grass	Panicum	Valerian	Centranthus, Valeriana	Woundwort	Stachys
Sword lily	Gladiolus	Vervain	Verbena	Yang-tao	Actinidia
Tahoka daisy	Machaeranthera	Vine lilac	Hardenbergia	Yarrow	Achillea
Tampala	Amaranthus	Violet cress	Ionopsidium	Yellow ageratum	Lonas
Tara vine	Actinidia	Viper's bugloss	Echium	Yellow archangel	Lamium
Tarragon	Artemisia	Virginia bluebells	Mertensia	Yellow autumn crocus	Sternbergia
Tartar lily	Ixiolirion	Virginia cowslip	Mertensia	Yellow bristle grass	Setaria
Tassel flower	Amaranthus, Emilia	Virginia stock	Malcomia	Yellow rock jasmine	Douglasia
Tassel hyacinth	Muscari	Wake-robin	Trillium	Yellow sage	Lantana
Taterwort	Sanguinaria	Wall cress	Arabis	Yellow star	Helenium
Teasel	Dipsacus	Wall pepper	Sedum	Yellow waxbells	Kirengeshoma
Ten-weeks stock	Matthiola	Wallflower	Cheiranthus	Youth-and-old-age	Zinnia
		Wand flower	Dierama	Zebra grass	Miscanthus
				Zephyr lily	Zephyranthes

GENERAL INDEX

(For specific plants: See alphabetical listing in text, by botanical name.
See "Common Name/Latin Name" index on pages 303–310 for cross-reference to botanical name.)